PRENTICE HALL

HISTORY OF MUSIC SERIES

H. WILEY HITCHCOCK, editor

third edition

NINETEENTH-CENTURY ROMANTICISM IN MUSIC

REY M. LONGYEAR

School of Music
University of Kentucky

PRENTICE HALL   ENGLEWOOD CLIFFS, NEW JERSEY 07632

Library of Congress Cataloging-in-Publication Data

LONGYEAR, REY M. (REY MORGAN)
 Nineteenth-century romanticism in music.

 (Prentice Hall history of music)
 Bibliography.
 Includes index.
 1. Music—19th century—History and criticism.
 2. Romanticism in music. I. Title. II. Title: 19th-
century romanticism in music. III. Series.
 ML196.L65 1988   780'.903'4   87-18719
 ISBN 0-13-622697-3

Editorial/production supervision: Ben Greensfelder and Lisa A. Domínguez
Manufacturing buyer: Ray Keating

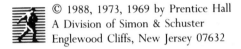 © 1988, 1973, 1969 by Prentice Hall
A Division of Simon & Schuster
Englewood Cliffs, New Jersey 07632

Cover photograph of a painting of Chopin by Delacroix
reprinted courtesy of the Bettmann Archive

Printed in the United States of America
10   9   8   7   6   5   4   3   2

ISBN 0-13-622697-3

PRENTICE-HALL INTERNATIONAL (UK) LIMITED, *London*
PRENTICE-HALL OF AUSTRALIA PTY. LIMITED, *Sydney*
PRENTICE-HALL CANADA INC., *Toronto*
PRENTICE-HALL HISPANOAMERICANA, S.A., *Mexico*
PRENTICE-HALL OF INDIA PRIVATE LIMITED, *New Delhi*
PRENTICE-HALL OF JAPAN, INC., *Tokyo*
SIMON & SCHUSTER ASIA PTE. LTD., *Singapore*
EDITORA PRENTICE-HALL DO BRASIL, LTDA., *Rio de Janeiro*

DEDICATION

To my colleagues, present and departed,
of the old University of Kentucky Faculty Club
"History table"
1964–1987

Music is the most Romantic of all the arts, as its subject is only the Infinite, the secret Sanskrit of Nature expressed in tones which fill the human heart with endless longing, and only in music does one understand the songs of the trees, flowers, animals, stones, floods!

E. T. A. Hoffman, Kreisleriana

[A Romantic work is] that kind of composition in which the artist freely gives himself up to the dominion of the imagination, considering all means as good, provided they produce effect. The grand requisite, therefore, in the romantic, is virtually to declare that the writer is not deficient in this quality, and that he has produced something piquant and new. It is to be doubted that many composers would venture to employ so dangerous a term, if they knew its true value.

The Harmonicon, 1830

What is Classic? What is Romantic? Two categories which, perhaps, are estranged only through exaggeration.

J. A. Delaire, "Des Innovations en musique,"
Revue musicale, 1830

It is difficult for the artist to live without Romanticism. If he does not introduce it into his works, he introduces it into his life; if he does not introduce it into his life, he preserves it in his dreams. . . . When one has gotten rid of Romanticism, one has generally lapsed into a distressing dullness.

Pierre Reverdy, Gant de crin, 1926

"I think it is charming," said Gwendolen, quickly. "A romantic place; anything delightful may happen in it; it would be a good background for any thing."

George Eliot (Mary Ann Evans),
Daniel Deronda, 1876

FOREWORD

Students and others interested in the history of music have always needed books of moderate length that are nevertheless comprehensive, authoritative, and engagingly written. The Prentice Hall History of Music Series was planned to fill these needs. It seems to have succeeded: revised and enlarged second editions of books in the series have been necessary, and now a new cycle of further revisions exists.

Six books in the series present a panoramic view of the history of music of Western civilization, divided among the major historical periods—Medieval, Renaissance, Baroque, Classic, Romantic, and Twentieth-Century. The musical culture of the United States, viewed historically as an independent development within the larger Western tradition, is treated in another book; two others deal with music in Latin America and the classical-music tradition of India. In yet another pair of books, the rich folk and traditional musics of both hemispheres are considered. Taken together, these eleven volumes are a distinctive and, we hope, distinguished contribution to the history of the music of the world's peoples. Each volume, moreover, may of course be read singly as a substantial account of the music of its period or area.

The authors of the books in the Prentice Hall History of Music Series are scholars of international repute—musicologists, critics, and teachers of exceptional stature in their respective fields of specialization. Their goal in contributing to the series has been to present works of solid, up-to-date scholarship that are eminently readable, with significant insights into music as a part of the general intellectual and cultural life of man.

H. WILEY HITCHCOCK, *Series Editor*

PREFACE

The spectrum of nineteenth-century music can be characterized by a large number of familiar and even overly familiar compositions, a larger number of worthy works that have fallen into neglect, and a shrinking mass of music still awaiting study, classification, and evaluation. To the general observer, the history of music of the nineteenth century resembles a panorama of mountains, some in shadow, separated by mist-shrouded valleys; in the limited space of this volume, I have sought to direct the reader's attention to various aspects of the peaks, describe salient aspects of their shadowy portions, and point out the intriguing features of the valleys.

In the nearly two decades since the publication of the first edition of this volume, there has been a great upsurge of interest in the music of the nineteenth century. Festivals of Romantic music have given listeners an opportunity to hear works in live performance that had been mentioned in histories of music but had lain on library shelves unperformed for decades. Unfamiliar operas have been revived in concert performance, in recordings, and on the stage, and much music that remained in manuscript or rare prints has been reprinted or published in such series as A–R Editions' *Recent Researches in the Music of the Nineteenth and Early Twentieth Centuries* and Garland's *The Symphony 1720–1840*. Enterprising performers have discovered the extensive amount of worthwhile repertory from this period awaiting imaginative re-creation, and recording companies have shown interest in the lesser-known works of a musically prolific and vital century. There has been much more music from this century made available for study, and more opportunities to hear it in live or recorded performance, often with the original instruments and performed in the style of the composers' original intentions.

Several important new landmarks of musical scholarship with particular pertinence to the nineteenth century have appeared, thus justifying a new edition of this book; among them are the journal *Nineteenth-Century Music*, *The New Grove Dictionary of Music and Musicians*, and Carl Dahlhaus's *Die Musik des 19. Jahrhunderts*, the sixth volume in the series (written under his supervision) *Neues Handbuch der Musikwissenschaft*. Numerous other articles, monographs, biographies, theses and dissertations, congress and symposium reports, and other studies have provoked re-examinations of this delightfully complex century.

Some of the procedures I have followed and some of the priorities I have assigned require explanation. The pronounced individuality of nineteenth-century composers virtually demands that my chapters be organized around composers rather than around genres or locales; for those who believe that the meaningful histories of music deal primarily with genres or styles, I respond that symphonies or operas do not write themselves, composers write them; and one of the hallmarks of Romantic composers was their preoccupation with individuality by creating the unique work of art. Yet since the most important contribution made by these composers was their music, attempts to relate their works to their psychological makeup must be left to others, and placing these composers in their cultural context has had to be done in the very broadest of terms.

A purely chronological approach, on the other hand, is not readily feasible. One can discern why from the following groups of composers: though the members of each group were nearly exact contemporaries, their musical developments reveal some similarities—but even more striking differences:

> Boieldieu, Spontini, and Hummel;
> Donizetti and Schubert;
> Franck, Bruckner, and Smetana;
> Borodin, Brahms, Ponchielli, and Saint-Saëns;
> Grieg, Rimsky-Korsakov, and Fauré;
> Puccini, Chausson, Elgar, and Janàček;
> Hugo Wolf, Mahler, MacDowell, and Debussy.

One can conduct a similar undertaking involving both musical and cultural history by juxtaposing operas from a given decade; those from the 1870's in the standard repertoire such as *Aïda, Boris Godunov, Die Götterdämmer-*

ung, Carmen, La Gioconda, Samson and Delilah, and *H.M.S. Pinafore* are offered as possibilities.

Though this volume has been substantially expanded from its original form, it is still a survey rather than a comprehensive history of nineteenth-century music; approximately 150 composers are discussed in this study as contrasted with the 629 in William S. Newman's magisterial *The Sonata Since Beethoven*. I have found it particularly necessary to exclude those composers whose influence did not significantly extend beyond the single medium in which they were active; I thus apologize to cellists, violinists, and organists for omitting Sebastian Lee and Grützmacher, Vieuxtemps and Wieniawski, Boëly and Karg-Elert. I also apologize to some specialists whose favorite composers I have had to delete: Verstovsky, Paine, Dudley Buck, Svendsen, Henselt, Goetz, Macfarren, Augusta Holmès, Sgambati, and Thuille are a few of those who were considered, but discussion of them and their music had to be omitted because of limitations of space. Chapter 8 presented a special problem since by 1900 virtually every European people had its own "national" art music, and my approach was limited to those national schools and their composers with an international significance. The volumes in the Prentice Hall series dealing with Latin America and the United States should more than compensate for the limited treatment I have given the music of these countries. Chapter 9 posed another problem because of the number of post-Romantic composers whose careers began with many important works written during the nineteenth century yet whose active musical lives continued well into the twentieth; for those who may consider my discussions of d'Indy, Puccini, Elgar, Mahler, and Richard Strauss to be too brief, I must point out that in this volume I have considered only their nineteenth-century careers and refer the reader to the volume in the Prentice Hall series on twentieth-century music for coverage of their later works.

Still another problem was posed by those post-Romantic composers who seem to have been suspended in a sphere between the nineteenth and twentieth centuries: Busoni, Skryabin, Reger, Pfitzner, Amy Beach, Rakhmaninov, Delius, Schreker, Metner, Cyril Scott, and Dukas—composers who represent the aural equivalent of the artistic movements Jugendstil and Art nouveau. As Dahlhaus once suggested, perhaps we need a separate period for the composers who bridge the two centuries without really being a part of either. Finally, there are several important subsidiary aspects of nineteenth-century music—aesthetics, musical journalism, musical historiography, reception history (how a composer's music was received during his time and after his death)—that I have had to mention only in passing or omit altogether.

Since this volume was intended primarily as a survey of nineteenth-century music, it has been designed to be usable for both compact and extensive overviews. The examples discussed are intended to serve as paradigms, and I have not included an anthology, printed or recorded, since most of the illustrations cited are easily available in a variety of formats. Wherever feasible, I have used the English titles of compositions if they have common currency, even at the risk of such incongruities as "Siegfried's Rhine Journey" from *Die Götterdämmerung*, or have translated generally unfamiliar titles into English, such as *Wallenstein's Camp* for *Valdštynuv Tábor*. I have endeavored to follow current practices in transliterating Russian proper names rather than perpetuate the antiquated French or German versions that still clutter concert programs; and to use, as far as current practice permits, the original rather than the German spellings of the names of Czech composers.

The bibliographical notes at the end of each chapter are highly selective and emphasize works in English published since 1978; those who desire further information should begin by consulting the bibliographies for the pertinent articles in *The New Grove*, and, for studies since 1967, *RILM Abstracts* (Répertoire internationale de la littérature musicale) which is now retrievable on database.

Space does not permit my extending personal acknowledgments or thanks to all of those whose comments and suggestions over the years have been so valuable in preparing the various editions of this book. Special thanks is due to my students at the University of Kentucky, whose reactions to various approaches and compositions have been very helpful, and to my many colleagues at the University who have volunteered suggestions and, in turn, have served as sounding boards for various analogies. I am particularly grateful to Allan Ho, Carl Cone, Dmitry Feofanov, Joanne Filkins, Cathy Hunt, Mina Miller, Jane Peters, and Kate Covington. Participation in various international colloquia enabled me to encounter the most recent ideas on the century from an international coterie of scholars, often in an informal setting, and I am particularly grateful for being able to share ideas with Frits Noske, Theophil Antonicek, Gudrun Busch, Andrew McCredie, Pierluigi Petrobelli, Gian-Carlo Paperi, and György Króo, among others. Lina Barrett and Carol Quin persuasively made me more cognizant of the contributions of women composers. Sabbatical leaves from the University of Kentucky and awards, especially by the John Simon Guggenheim Memorial Foundation and University of Kentucky Research Foundation, enabled me to engage in foreign travel and living, to hear many of the works discussed in live performance before native audiences, to see many of the works of art described in the first chapter, and to have the experience of working in European music libraries. As in previous editions, I am grateful to H. Wiley Hitchcock for his editorial encouragements and criticisms. Finally, I owe the greatest debts of all to my wife Katherine for her assistance and support in so many ways for so many years.

R.M.L.

Lexington, Kentucky

CONTENTS

ONE

ROMANTICISM AND MUSIC

To best understand a period in the history of music, one must place it within its historical and cultural context. The nineteenth century in particular is one in which musical trends are closely associated with historical and cultural developments; these we should examine, at least briefly, in order to provide a background for the music of the time.

THE HISTORICAL CONTEXT

A century as a point of reference is but an approximation. Historians speak of a "long nineteenth century" that ranged from 1789 (the outbreak of the French Revolution) to 1914 (the beginning of the First World War) or a "short nineteenth century" from 1815 (the final defeat of Napoleon) to the unification of Germany and Italy in 1871. As we shall see, there are similar differences of opinion as to the beginnings and endings of the Romantic period, or even of a musical "nineteenth century." We can best examine the historical context of musical Romanticism through an overview of the nineteenth century, organized around certain critical themes and topics.

War, Peace, and Revolution. Between 1792 and 1815 Europe was engulfed in, or at least strongly affected by, general war. Attempts by the monarchist powers to suppress the French Revolution led to French invasion and occupation of Belgium, Holland, the German Rhineland, and Italy, the last of these led by the 27-year-old Napoleon Bonaparte, who seized power in France in 1799 and subsequently extended his rule over most of Europe. A succession of defeats and reverses in Spain, Russia, and Germany led to his surrender in 1814 and, after a brief resumption of power in the following year, to his exile in the South Atlantic. Order was restored in Europe at the Congress of Vienna by a five-power coalition consisting of Britain, Austria, Russia, Prussia, and a royalist France under Louis XVIII.

Following Napoleon's final defeat came ninety-nine years of general peace. The European wars that were fought during this time were short and had limited objectives, and the subsequent peace treaties were sanctioned by an informal "Concert of Europe" which sought to preserve a balance of power.

The revolutions of 1830, 1848, and 1871 provide the "semicolons" in the narrative history of nineteenth-century Europe. Though the revolutions in Spain and Italy were put down by the great powers acting as a "Holy Alliance," those of 1830 in France, Belgium, and some German states could not be suppressed. The goal of these revolutions was the establishment of a constitutional secular state with limitations on the power of the king and nobility and guarantees of civil liberties and property rights—a political philosophy known then as Liberalism, with capitalism (the private ownership of property and the means of production) as its economic counterpart.

The revolutions of 1848, called "the revolution of the intellectuals" or "a typically Romantic revolution," were less successful, though more widespread, than the revolts of 1830. Yet the basic issues that provoked these revolts were eventually resolved; the gains of the revolutions of 1830 were extended, constitutional governments and the middle classes became ascendant, and voting rights were gradually extended to nearly all adult males by 1914.

The campaigns for the unification of Italy and Germany were revolutionary between 1815 and 1850, but their eventual effectiveness depended on abandoning the idealism of 1848 for a cooler realism exemplified by Cavour in Piedmont and Bismarck in Prussia. By 1871 both countries were united, under Piedmontese and Prussian leadership respectively, after the military defeats of Austria in 1859 and 1866 and France in 1870. The goal of freedom from foreign domination was not achieved in eastern Europe, however, until the end of the First World War, when the Austro-Hungarian Empire was dissolved and the western provinces of Russia were granted independence.

Demography and Urbanization. The first striking statistic of the nineteenth century concerns the growth of population: from around 200 million in Europe in 1800 to 505 million in 1914, with a sizable surplus that emigrated overseas. The second such statistic concerns the growth of cities: it is estimated that out of every seven persons born in rural Europe one remained on the land, one emigrated abroad, and five moved into cities. In 1800 London was the only European city with a population of a million, but by 1900 there were at least a dozen, mostly such major capital cities as Paris, Vienna, Berlin, and St. Petersburg (now Leningrad).

In the older cities, the pattern of expansion consisted of a central core surrounded by walls which were torn down and replaced by polygonal boulevards which became the sites for parades, urban festivities, and sometimes demonstrations. Industry and workers' housing were located in the suburbs. The newer factory towns had industry and housing for workers in the central city with the desirable residential quarters in the suburbs. With the invention of reinforced concrete and the elevator, cities grew upward; they grew outward as well with improved public transportation such as the streetcar and commuter railroad.

During the eighteenth century, except for a few large (by the standards of the time) capital cities like London, Paris, Vienna, or Naples, the locus of musical life was at a court, like Eszterháza or Oettingen-Wallerstein. During the nineteenth century, however, the large city was the center of musical activity with its public opera houses, large concert halls, conservatories, choral and concert-giving societies, and music festivals. Musicians settled in cities because of the educational and employment opportunities, whereas at the same time only in cities could enough competent musicians be found to form an orchestra or other performing group. The cities also contained an important musical infrastructure of music publishers, music stores, booking agents, instrument salesmen and repairmen, music critics, and others who were connected with music but who did not actually perform, compose, or teach it. The concentration of a musical audience in one place provided the economic base for these activities. In the course of the century increasing urbanization provided a decentralization of musical activity, with such subordinate cities as Manchester, Brussels, Milan, Prague, Budapest, and Moscow the sites of many premieres. Musical life in the nineteenth century was expanded and made accessible to more and more people.

Technological Developments. In the past, when historians wrote about the Industrial Revolution, beginning in England at the end of the eighteenth century and spreading throughout Europe, the United States, and Japan at the close of the nineteenth, they defined it as the making of goods, not by hand in small workshops as before, but by steam-powered machines in factories. Yet during the nineteenth century improved technologies, mutually reinforcing and affecting each other, also brought revolutions to agriculture, transportation, and communications; it was as if a kind of spiral had been set in motion, throwing off new innovations that in turn produced further improvements. At the close of the century a second industrial revolution arose, based not on iron, coal, and steam as was the first, but on steel, chemicals, and electricity.

Technological revolutions in agriculture fed the growing cities while fewer people were needed on the land to do the work of raising crops. Innovations in transportation produced the steamship, railway, and, at the end of the century, the internal combustion engine that powered automobiles and tractors. Inventions in communications included the telegraph, telephone, typewriter, and mechanized printing press. The world became increasingly interdependent through these mutually reinforcing innovations, and thousands of new occupations, most of which required a basic literacy and even advanced education, were created. And even though Europe's population had undergone an unprecedented increase, these new people were fed and employed.

Nationalism.   Perhaps the most complex and disruptive issue of the nineteenth century, the impact on Romanticism of nationalism will be discussed elsewhere in this chapter and its influence on music in chapter 8. The principal paradox of the century is this: whereas the improvements in transportation and communication, more widespread education, and economic interdependence brought peoples together (the eighteenth-century ideal of the "republic of letters" coming to fruition in the nineteenth-century scientific or scholarly international congress), one effect of nationalism was to drive peoples further and further apart.

Because of its many contradictory elements nationalism, like Romanticism, is difficult if not impossible to define, and one must seek to isolate and identify its most common characteristics. Foremost among them is language, allied with such cultural elements as literature, customs, religion, music (usually folk music), and a common history. Attachment to or desire for certain geographical territory (a "fatherland" or "motherland"), hopes for an independent or autonomous government if one does not already exist, and a feeling of some kind of separation from other linguistic or ethnic groups are part of the nationalist package. Each nationalism is different, but all carry strong emotional overtones which often make objective discussion impossible.

National conflicts principally affected the multi-national empires of Germany, Austria, and Russia. Attempts to inculcate a dominant national feeling in these states were perceived as violating the rights of the smaller ethnic groups. The language of the dominant power (German or Russian) as the administrative language enabled the central government to function better and was the language of higher and most secondary education, but was perceived as oppression by the other linguistic groups. As an example, few if any German- or Russian-speaking bureaucrats were willing to learn the languages of the various ethnic groups they served. Attempts at "Russification" or "Germanization" provoked ethnic resentments which in turn aroused fiercer Russian or German nationalisms.

Since political and ethnic frontiers often did not coincide, the cause of irredentism—the feeling that one's ethnic brothers were oppressed by a hostile or unsympathetic power—created further trouble: Italians in the Austrian South Tyrol after 1866, Bosnians occupied by Austria after the Turkish defeats in 1878, French in Alsace and Lorraine, provinces annexed by Germany in 1871—all provided problems for the occupying powers and issues with which to inflame public opinion at home. Some very clearly defined ethnic groups had no independent homeland: depending on his birthplace, a person of Polish descent could owe allegiance to Germany, Austria, or Russia, but not to Poland, which had been partitioned among the three powers in the late eighteenth century. During the next century two world wars, with nationalism as a main issue, had to be fought, with the ethnic questions settled mainly through mass transfers of population after 1945.

Quality of Life. When an eighteenth-century gentleman planned his travels, he would seek out those places where he could be best entertained and amused, well fed, and docilely served. For his purposes, civilized Europe consisted of a quadrilateral bounded by Naples, Seville, London, and Vienna, outside of which existed a few "islands" of culture, usually courts like those of Dresden, Berlin, Stockholm, and St. Petersburg. His nineteenth-century counterpart, on the other hand, would bound civilized Europe with a quadrilateral anchored by Stockholm, Glasgow, Barcelona, and Vienna, and would use different indices for measuring civilization: educational institutions, hospitals, libraries, literacy rates, concert halls, railroads, clean hotels, paved and lighted streets, and other urban amenities. Both the quality of life and the instruments that measured it drastically changed during the nineteenth century.

Before 1800 the overwhelming mass of the world's people worked from dawn to dusk, from childhood to old age, and with the knowledge that their children could expect the same kind of existence. The relative few who lived in the cities dwelt in crowded and dirty circumstances since privacy was a luxury and cleanliness was practiced mainly for cosmetic reasons. Epidemics and famines persisted well into the eighteenth century, when it was estimated that the labor of fifty peasants was necessary to support one city dweller.

A dramatic change in these circumstances took place in the nineteenth century, chiefly in the cities. Public sanitation and cleanliness became matters of health, to eliminate such dangers as the cholera epidemics in Paris during the 1830's that carried off Reicha, Herold, and Bellini. Improved medical care, exemplified by such discoveries as vaccination (a late eighteenth-century contribution), anaesthetics, antiseptics, and more professional and widespread medical education, prolonged and enhanced life. Gas and later electric lighting transformed the cities and permitted new illusions on the stage. The cities, as focal points for networks of transportation and communications, were the first to profit from the myriad innovations, inventions, and conveniences that enhanced the lifestyles of their inhabitants and served as magnets to attract persons from the countryside and small towns which had yet to receive these improvements.

The nineteenth century was not a century of sweetness and light for everyone, but there was a widespread feeling that conditions could and would be improved; the main issue was not whether, but how fast, these ameliorations would be made. The abolition of slavery and the slave trade; legislation regulating hours of work for children, women, and even men; laws protecting the vulnerable (like children, animals, prisoners, or the insane); the establishment of hospitals, libraries, and schools by philanthropists or the state; the idea that elementary education should be open to all and even compulsory, with secondary, higher, and professional education available at minimum cost for those who were qualified—all resulted from the conviction that life for everyone had to have a certain irreducible minimum of safety and decency. These convictions were often conveyed by passionate writers like Dickens, Zola, or Harriet Beecher Stowe, whose works goaded public opinion to eliminate or change the injustices that remained.

In sum, the nineteenth century was a good century for most of its inhabitants, who lived in a period of prevalent peace, under governments that increasingly came to protect civil liberties, stress fiscal responsibilities, and respond to injustice; and with rapid changes tending toward an improvement in the quality of life. More and more people had the leisure, income, and education to enjoy, and even participate in, the artistic and cultural trends that can be subsumed under the very general heading of Romanticism.

WHAT IS ROMANTICISM?

The very term "Romanticism" has conjured up, as Arthur Lovejoy has remarked, "one of the most complicated, fascinating, and instructive of all problems in semantics." Some writers have called for the abolition of this overly elastic term, yet what word could replace it?

Any period term, like Baroque or Romantic, can be used pejoratively, neutrally, or as a term of praise; as a convenient substitute for citing dates; to indicate a cluster of ideas perceived as common to the art, literature, music, and even social and political history of the time; or simply to mean what its users intend it to mean. To many writers on music, Romanticism has meant music between 1828 and 1880 in its narrowest and 1789 to 1914 in its broadest sense; in musical writing, too, one finds an analogy with the concepts of the "short" and "long" nineteenth century. Some have considered Romanticism, in opposition to Classicism, a phenomenon which recurs throughout artistic and intellectual history: J. S. Bach, Monteverdi, the troubadours, St. Paul, and Plato have been called "Romantics" by various writers. Others wish to limit the term drastically to refer to the German writers of the 1790's and the French writers of the 1830's who called themselves Romantics.

Among recent writers, one procedure is to consider Classicism and Romanticism as opposite sides of the same coin current between 1740 and 1830 (at its most limited) and 1910 (at its broadest); this eliminates searches for precursors or survivals or a jumble of "pre-," "post-," and "neo-" prefixes, but on the other hand does not fully take into account the changing clusters of musical and other ideas during the 90 to 170 years included in this period. Another approach is the extension of Romanticism well into the twentieth century by identifying such writers as Conrad, Yeats, Camus, Céline, and Faulkner, such artists as Rodin and Vlaminck, such political leaders as Hitler and de Gaulle, and even the student rioters of the 1960's as Romantics. Doubts have even been expressed about the wisdom of using the century as a unit of study for the nineteenth century, because of the period's disunity and fragmentation.

It is fruitless to try to create a single definition of Romanticism, or any other period term, that will be valid for all arts, all countries, and for all times; neither can we use the term "Romantic" with taxonomic precision to label compositions (or, for that matter, poems, paintings, novels, and buildings) as if they were dried plants exhibited as specimens in a herbarium. We should rather regard period terms and their subdivisions as simply a convenient way of implying that certain norms exist which at least tenuously link the personages and ideas subsumed under this heading, that other persons and configurations of thought are excluded, and also that a certain chronology exists even though the terminal dates at each end cannot be fixed with much precision and considerable overlapping occurs with adjacent periods.

CAN ROMANTICISM BE DEFINED?

Romanticism is a difficult period term to define because its protagonists, as opposed to their rationalistic predecessors, were so wary of definitions. Victor Hugo's statement that Romanticism was "a certain vague and indefinable fantasy" is as close to the mark as any attempt at a concrete definition; examination of salient characteristics will serve us better.

First of all, this movement was an international manifestation, strongest in Germany, quite influential in England, France, and Russia, but also evident in Bohemia, Poland, Spain, and Italy. Secondly, the nineteenth century was a period of extreme contrasts, and any idea expressed was certain to elicit its exact opposite. In religious thought, for example, one may compare the diverse ideas of Joseph Smith, Pope Pius IX, Ernst Haeckel, and Mary Baker Eddy and recall that religious martyrdom occurred not only in Uganda and Indo-China during this period but also in Paris under the Commune of 1871. This diversity explains why we can subsume under the heading of Romanticism such contradictory composers as Bruckner and Offenbach, Donizetti and Brahms, Chopin and Sousa. Thirdly, Romanticism repudiated Classic emphases on harmonious adjustment, discipline, moderation, and adaptation whereas it valued striving rather than achieving, becoming rather than being, emotional and inspired rather than rational expression. Classic "uniformitarianism," on the other hand, considered differences in opinion and taste to be evidences of erroneous deviation from the "rationalist collectivism" which taught that the artist should try to communicate not the unique but the views and sentiments common to an idealized mankind. Finally, none of the past seven centuries has ended without a significant change in musical style during its last decade. In the 1790's a new musical language became evident, albeit well-prepared by significant forerunners, and it existed side by side with the old musical language (Haydn, Pleyel, Rossini) for a few decades; a similar co-existence took place during the period from 1890 to 1914 (Debussy, Stravinsky, and subsequently Schoenberg as opposed to d'Indy, Elgar, and Mahler), the new idiom becoming around 1910, what is loosely called "modern" music.

Are we justified in calling the musical language which became discernible as a new idiom around 1790 and declined during the first decade of the twentieth century Romantic? Ernst Theodor Amadeus Hoffmann (1776–1822), a writer with unimpeachable Romantic credentials, considered J. S. Bach, Haydn, Mozart, and especially Beethoven to be Romantics, and Théophile Gautier (1811–72), a charter member of the French Romantic movement, bestowed a similar accolade on Berlioz and Chopin. Hoffmann remarked on several occasions that music, particularly instrumental music, was the most Romantic of the arts, and instrumental music was at least intellectually dominant between 1790 and 1910; it may also be noted that during the nineteenth century both opera and art-song had increasingly active instrumental accompaniments. Parallels, some more tenuous than others, can be drawn between the new expressive melody, the rhythmic experimentation, the coloristic use of harmony and instrumental timbres, the relaxation of and uncertainty about formal canons, the veneration and occasional misuse of the legacy of the past mingled with a sense of writing for the future, and the new tendencies in poetry, the drama, the novel, the pictorial arts, and architecture which are customarily called Romantic. A few of the external themes common to Romanticism in general that are reflected in the music of the nineteenth century deserve closer examination.

Individualism. The intense individualism and subjectivity of the Romantic composer, paralleling that of the Romantic poet, artist, or even ruler, have dictated the very organization of this volume by composers rather than by musical genres. There is no "typical" Romantic symphony, art-song, piano piece, or composer, much as there is no typical Romantic novel, poem, painting, or artist. What musical period can show such intense individualists as Beethoven and Wagner, or such deeply subjective composers as Chopin, Schumann, Chaikovsky, and Mahler? This individuality is reflected in the number of popular biographies of Romantic composers (to say nothing of the fictional novels or films about them) in which information about their lives overwhelms facts about their work. And in studying the lives of these composers one is amazed at the number of highly complex personages, from Beethoven and Weber to Mahler and Skryabin, with such relatively uncomplicated figures as Spohr, Verdi, Dvořák, and Fauré in the minority. The lives, letters, and memoirs of most of the preceding and succeeding generations of composers seem almost prosaic in comparison.

Intensity of feeling, which is better sensed through hearing the music itself rather than reading a verbal description of it, separates Romantic music from its eighteenth- and twentieth-century counterparts much as this same intensity divides Classic and "Modern" from Romantic in the other arts.

One form of this Romantic intensity of feeling has been called *Weltschmerz,* a term best understood as a feeling of world-weariness with overtones of frustration and as a melancholy which at its extreme can lead to pathological states of nihilism, insanity, and suicide. Goethe's *Werther* (1774), in which the protagonist kills himself over unrequited love, is a prototype of this pathological despair in literature. In music such Romantic pathology transpires most often on the operatic stage, with the "mad scenes" of such works as Bellini's *I Puritani,* Donizetti's *Lucia di Lammermoor,* and Thomas' *Hamlet,* or the suicides in Donizetti's *Lucia di Lammermoor,* Verdi's *Luisa Miller* (based on Schiller's *Kabale und Liebe,* one of the most powerful "*Sturm und Drang*" dramas), Wagner's *Flying Dutchman* and *Die Götterdämmerung,* and Puccini's *Madame Butterfly.*

There is a sweetly gloomy tone (*morbidezza*) in much Romantic music. This had occasionally surfaced during the Classic period in such works as Mozart's A minor Rondo, K. 511, and G minor String Quintet, K. 516, but it appears more strongly in some piano works by Field, Chopin, Glinka, Balakirev, and Skryabin, or in the *Weltschmerz* of Schubert, Chaikovsky, and Mahler. A counterpart to the morbidness that parallels the irrationalism and demonism of E. T. A. Hoffmann, Lenau and Poe in literature or the *Caprichos* (1790–1800) of Francisco Goya (1746–1828) and the nightmare paintings of Henry Fuseli (1741–1825) in art is the macabre diabolism of Berlioz, Liszt, and Mahler.

In contrast, and also as an example of one of many illustrations of the diversities and contradictions in Romanticism, there is a determined optimism in much Romantic music, best seen in the finales of many of the symphonies from Beethoven through Dvořák or in the apotheoses of the Lisztian symphonic poem—an optimism comparable to that of Victor Hugo (1802–85) and Alfred Lord Tennyson (1809–92).

Changes in this intensity of feeling mark the transition from Romanticism to post-Romanticism. The muting of this intensity through understatement in many of the works of Saint-Saëns, Chabrier, Fauré, Puccini, and Debussy constitutes one of the principal reactions against Romanticism and should also serve as a warning against lumping too many late-nineteenth-century composers under the heading "neoclassic." On the other hand, an exaggeration of intensity can be seen in the negation of the optimistic finale, from Chopin's B♭ minor Sonata through the suicidal despair of the last movement of Chaikovsky's Sixth Symphony and the concluding song of Mahler's *Das Lied von der Erde*, the forced optimism of the finales of Glazunov's Fourth and Mahler's Seventh Symphonies, and the ending of Richard Strauss's *Also sprach Zarathustra*, at first nostalgic and then cryptic.

Romanticism: Rebellious or Conservative?   Many studies of Romanticism emphasize the rebellious and revolutionary nature of the movement. The French Revolution had a strong initial impact on the young German and English Romantics, and Napoleon's meteoric rise at an early age was a great inspiration to youth throughout the century. Yet there were contrary aspects which oriented many Romantics in a conservative direction: the French Revolution shattered the "cake of custom" and enabled those with talent to rise, but it also led to the Reign of Terror, and Napoleon's conquest of Europe was at the expense of its peoples and the humiliation of its sovereigns, and it resulted in the atrocities so vividly depicted by Goya in his *The Disasters of War*. After 1815 German Romanticism took a different course, becoming tradition-oriented in seeking continuity with the medieval past and quietist in the face of the repressive political climate. One writer has commented that German Romanticism began as gunpowder, continued as magic powder, and ended as sleeping powder.

Beethoven was perceived as the supreme revolutionary rebel in music, and he was a nearly exact contemporary of Napoleon and of the first generation of German Romantics such as the Schlegel brothers and Tieck. Prometheus, who defied the gods by bringing fire to man, was a hero not only to such writers as Goethe, Shelley, and Byron but also the subject of a ballet by Beethoven and symphonic poems by Liszt and Skryabin; Faust, the eternal striver, inspired a large number of composers from Spohr to Busoni. Beethoven's rebellious example inspired, to varying degrees, such subsequent rebels as Berlioz, Schumann, Liszt, and Wagner.

The careers of Liszt and Wagner show the change from youthful firebrands—Liszt's enthusiasm for the welfare-state socialism of Saint-Simon in France and Wagner's active participation in the revolt in Dresden in 1849—to their later status as upholders of the established order, with Liszt celebrating the Dual Monarchy in Austria-Hungary and Wagner championing Prussian expansionism. Their evolution from revolutionary to conservative can be seen among other long-lived Romantics such as Wordsworth, Schelling, Delacroix, Gogol, and Dostoyevski, or in the curious career of Napoleon III, who began as a member of an Italian revolutionary secret society and a stager of comic-opera *coups d'etat* which ended in failure, came to power as an upholder of law and order in 1848, became president for life and subsequently emperor, and left his throne in disgrace after his defeat by Germany in 1870. Romanticism, in short, contained both revolutionary and conservative elements, sometimes in opposition, sometimes at the same chronological time or even within the same person.

Romanticism as Escape. The two principal historical trends of the nineteenth century, industrialization and nationalism, both provoked Romantic reactions. The Industrial Revolution, prominent only in England by 1800, had by the close of the century spread all over Europe and even to Japan and the United States. Though the Romantics appreciated the economic growth that provided financial support for the arts, the urban public that could be more easily reached, the expansion of education (many Romantics, like Rousseau, Pestalozzi, Macaulay, and Froebel, provided impetus for educational reform), and creature comforts like steamship and rail travel or the electric light, most Romantics rebelled against the ugliness of the "dark Satanic mills," the dehumanization of factory life in which workers were regarded as things, the exaggeration of materialism into a cult of progress, and the glorification of a mechanistic science. A new view of art took shape: whereas in the eighteenth century art was often degraded to an entertainment and diversion (accounting for the pretty superficiality of much art and music of the time), now it was ennobled as an escape, even as a substitute for religion. The feeling of a private world into which the composer would lead his audience is discernible in Beethoven's late sonatas and quartets and reaches peaks in Wagner's *Ring*, *Tristan*, and *Parsifal*,

Mahler's idea of the symphony as an entire world, and the twentieth-century exaggeration by Skryabin of an orchestral work as an entire synaesthesic universe.

The love of an unspoiled pre-industrial nature that characterizes much pre- and early Romantic poetry and painting (from Goethe, Wordsworth, Thoreau, and Constable to Ruskin, Corot, and the Barbizon school of painters) had a strong and powerful counterpart in music. Although Haydn was the only "nature-lover" of the Classic period, the number of such Romantic composers is legion, headed by Beethoven, whose "Pastoral" Symphony, almost contemporaneous with Wordsworth's *The Prelude*, bore the warning "With more of an expression of feeling than painting" to contrast with the naive musical imitations of Handel and Haydn. Space permits the mention of only the most conspicuous portrayals of nature by Romantic composers: the forest paintings in Weber's *Der Freischütz* or Wagner's *Siegfried;* the landscapes and seascapes of Mendelssohn and Gade; the Alpine pictures in Schumann's or Chaikovsky's *Manfred;* the love of wandering that permeates the music of Schumann and Brahms; the moods of the sea as depicted in Wagner's *Flying Dutchman* or Rimsky-Korsakov's *Sadko, Scheherazade,* and *Tsar Saltan;* or the love of travel shown in Mendelssohn's *Italian* and *Scottish* symphonies, Liszt's *Album d'un voyageur* and *Anneés de pèlerinage,* and Chabrier's *España.* Among some composers at the end of the century (Rimsky-Korsakov, Mahler, Delius), the love of nature became almost a religious pantheism, such as one finds in many Romantic poets and painters (Shelley, Mallarmé, Cézanne, Monet). And just as the attempts to portray nature impressionistically rather than realistically by such painters as J. M. W. Turner (1775–1851), Claude Monet (1840–1926), and Paul Cézanne (1839–1906) gave birth to twentieth-century styles of painting, so did a similar musical aesthetic, with nature as the dominant theme of his program music, cause Debussy to strike out along a new musical path and Schoenberg to evolve an entirely new kind of orchestral writing in his coloristic portrayal of "Summer Morning by a Lake" in his *Five Orchestral Pieces,* Op. 16 (1909).

Whether Romanticism was an escape from the political systems of the nineteenth century is a moot, if not meaningless, question. The variety, contradictions, and simultaneities of Romanticism at any particular time are reflected in the divergent political systems of the period; one need but recall that the regimes of Andrew Jackson in America, Tsar Nikolai I in Russia, Prince Metternich in Austria, and Louis Philippe in France all overlapped. As a general rule, the Romantic musician tended to support political stability, since this was necessary for the support of the arts, though welcoming and supporting changes that led to a more open society and the mitigation of censorship, repression, and the suppression of ethnic minorities. If we view the political spectrum from "left" to "right," the two extremes are seen in France, with the Communist anti-establishment rebel Albéric Magnard at one pole and the monarchist anti-Dreyfusard Vincent d'Indy at the other. Yet as a typically Romantic set of paradoxes, Magnard was one of d'Indy's pupils, and both fought the German invaders of their country, d'Indy as an infantry corporal in 1870 and Magnard (executed in 1914) as a guerrilla.

From the overt or implied political sentiments of the composers of the century one can distinguish, apart from nationalist ideas, a majority sentiment for what we would call a moderate bourgeois urban liberalism by nineteenth-century standards that would have been repelled by extremes of either democracy or reaction.

Romanticism and Nationalism. Romanticism as a movement was international, yet it appeared at different times in different places and spoke with different voices and accents. When we speak of Classicism, in music or any other art, we refer to an all-embracing movement unified by its cultural uniformity and its practitioners who crossed national boundaries with ease: Hasse, Gluck, Haydn, and Mozart in music, Voltaire, Thorwaldsen, Casanova, and Benjamin Franklin in other spheres of eighteenth-century activity. Romanticism, on the other hand, is always given a nationally qualifying adjective (German, Russian, French) despite the "family likenesses," as Barzun has called them, among the manifestations of this movement in all lands. And as nineteenth-century nationalism is characterized by the spread of national consciousness, identities, and artistic achievements to formerly suppressed or ignored ethnic and linguistic groups, musical nationalism is exemplified by the emergence of major voices with their own national as well as personal identities: the lands that produced Pushkin, Mickiewicz, Palacký, and Ibsen also produced Glinka, Chopin, Smetana, and Grieg.

There are two kinds of cultural nationalisms, defending and aggressive. Defending nationalism is characterized by dedication to achieving a cultural identity and by a strong emphasis on the arts; aggressive nationalism seeks to impose a cultural identity on others. Defending nationalism has a strong streak of idealism in it and can be international as well as national (as witness the careers of Verdi and Dvořák in music or the comparable careers of Walter Scott, Mazzini, Aleksandr Herzen, and Theodor Herzl), whereas an aggressive nationalism is closely identified with *Realpolitik*, xenophobia, and the suppression of counter-national tendencies. One can best see defending nationalism in the plots of the eastern European "national" operas, for their settings deal with times of troubles rather than national aggrandizement: Glinka's *A Life for the Tsar*, Erkel's *Hunyádi László*, and Smetana's *The Brandenburgers in Bohemia* are representative illustrations.

In the course of the century nationalism became aggressive in many lands and thus lost its Romantic connotations. In music the change is not as much in content as it is in context and in its associations. Wagner's aggressive nationalism after 1860 is less evident in *Die Meistersinger* and the *Ring* than in his venomous literary attacks on the French and the Jews, and even the most rhapsodic admirer of Brahms passes in silence over his *Triumphlied*, written to celebrate the German victory over the French in the Franco-Prussian War of 1871, which can be considered a watershed date in western Europe for the change from defending to aggressive nationalism. A subtle shift from defending to aggressive nationalism can be seen in several works in various countries written after this date: Bizet's *Patrie* overture, d'Indy's *Symphonie cévenole*, Chaikovsky's *Marche slave* and *1812 Overture*, Elgar's "Pomp and Circumstance" marches (paralleling the imperialist poetry of Rudyard Kipling), Dudley Buck's overture on "The Star-Spangled Banner," and the marches of John Philip Sousa which accompanied America's aggressive entry as a world power in 1898. Yet no musical compositions contain the bitter chauvinist venom that bubbles to the surface in some of the writings on music, not only of Wagner, but also of Saint-Saëns, d'Indy, and Pfitzner, and these make a shabby contrast to the friendly and cosmopolitan openness of the composers of the first half of the century like Beethoven, Schumann, Berlioz, Glinka, and Liszt.

Minor Themes. Even in some of Romanticism's minor themes, and in the contradictions within them, one can discern close parallels between music and the other arts. Romantic hedonism, especially in amatory matters (Shelley, Byron, Victor Hugo) is paralleled not only in the lives of Glinka, Liszt, and Skryabin but also in the operas of Massenet and Puccini; yet in Wagner's operas the love interest has a happy outcome only in *Die Meistersinger*, and one may note the immense number of nineteenth-century composers who died unmarried: Beethoven, Schubert, Chopin, Liszt, Bruckner, Sullivan, Musorgsky, Hugo Wolf. An early death terminating a meteoric career of intense creativity is a hallmark of the Romanticism of the first half of the century (Wackenroder, Novalis, Shelley, Keats, Byron, Géricault, the painter Philipp Otto Runge, Leopardi, Pushkin, Lermontov, Poe); it is paralleled not only by the short lives of Schubert, Bellini, Weber, Mendelssohn, and Chopin but also by the Romanticized views of the brief careers of Pergolesi and Mozart. Significantly, the idolization of the Romantic prodigy-composer who died young belongs to the first half of the nineteenth century. This is indicative of another trend: during the first half of the century Romanticism is characterized by youth, as witness the amount and quality of music produced by Beethoven, Rossini, Mendelssohn, Chopin, and Schumann before their thirtieth birthdays, whereas after 1850 (with Richard Strauss as the solitary exception) virtually every composer had but barely embarked on his career by the time he was thirty.

ROMANTIC WRITERS AND MUSIC

The seeds for the interpenetration of the arts which was such a salient characteristic of the nineteenth century were sown by Jean-Jacques Rousseau (1712–78), known chiefly as a social and educational philosopher and novelist but also gifted in music, musical criticism, and sketching, and regarded by many as the founder of the Romantic movement. To him, and to a lesser extent the writers of the French *Encyclopédie* (28 vols., 1751–72), can be credited the virtual mania for writing about music that arose around 1770.

During most of the eighteenth century, writings about music were by musicians for musicians, and the musical interests of the non-professional authors of the time were directed to such practical topics as the use of incidental music in the drama. After 1770 a greater interest in music is a hallmark of German literature, as seen, for example, in the frequent use of music as a literary effect, such as the expressive clavichord playing by Lotte in Goethe's *Werther* or Lady Caroline in Klinger's drama *Sturm und Drang* (1776), which gave its name to an entire if brief literary epoch. "Romantic" musicians as literary figures begin to appear in the mid-1770's and culminate in the incarnation of the Romantic musician, Kreisler, in the stories and novels of E. T. A. Hoffmann.

The writers associated with the movement known as Weimar Classicism—Christoph Martin Wieland (1733–1813), Johann Wolfgang von Goethe (1749–1832), Johann Gottfried Herder (1744–1803), and Friedrich Schiller (1759–1805)—had a lively and often Romantic interest in music. Herder collaborated with J. C. F. Bach, one of J. S. Bach's sons, translated the texts of Handel's *Messiah* and *Alexander's Feast,* and collected folk songs. Schiller distrusted the effect of music because of its appeal to sensuous natures, yet precisely because of its power he used incidental music extensively in most of his dramas, musical metaphors and characterizations in many of his literary works, and musical ideas as an ancillary but not insignificant part of his aesthetic system. Among Goethe's many other activities in Weimar, he wrote texts for *Singspiele* for amateur court productions and later served as director of the court theatre, where most of the significant operas of the 1780's and 1790's were performed. Yet the musical tastes of these writers were inherently conservative: Schiller ranked Gluck above Haydn and Mozart, Herder considered vocal music superior to "empty" instrumental music and disliked the dominance of music over text in Mozart's operas, and Goethe, though a champion of Mozart's music, rejected the settings of his songs by Beethoven and especially Schubert, preferring the simple tunes of Carl Friedrich Zelter (1758–1832).

Other interesting personages of the time with intense musical activities were C. D. F. Schubart (1739–91), an organist and composer as well as a poet, aesthetician, and journalist who was imprisoned for his libertarian ideas, and Johann Friedrich Reichardt (1752–1814), a composer and journalist whose activities on behalf of the French Revolution involved him in a celebrated literary feud with Goethe and Schiller.

The role of music in the thought of the German Romantics who came to maturity in the 1790's remains fully to be investigated. One can credit the increasing interest in music partially to the novels of J. J. W. Heinse (1746–1803), but the most influential of the early Romantic writers on music seems to have been Wilhelm Heinrich Wackenroder (1773–98), who influenced both Hoffmann and Ludwig Tieck (1773–1853). With both Wackenroder and Jean Paul (J. P. Friedrich Richter, 1763–1825), one senses the idea of music as a drug or balm; Wackenroder could listen to music attentively for only an hour, but found that music, apart from the particular mood created by a given composition, would stimulate his thought and imagination (Schiller similarly liked to have music played in an adjoining room while he wrote). "In the mirror of tones the human heart learns to know itself; it is how we learn to feel feelings," Wackenroder wrote, and his fictional musician Josef Berglinger heard "sounds that seem to be words" in music. Jean Paul's ideas on music were Romantic in their contradictions: he once compared music's effect to a lion's tongue licking at the heart "which tickles and scratches until the blood flows," yet later called music, rather than poetry, the "happy art." He preferred the "simple souls" of Haydn and Mozart to composers with great self-possession like Reichardt, and his description of Walt's hearing a Haydn symphony is so rhapsodic, colorful, and impassioned that one would suspect that Beethoven or Schumann had been the composer.

Though Tieck was a musical amateur, Hoffmann spent five years as Kapellmeister (musical director) in Bamberg and directed an opera troupe for a year; composed sonatas, chamber music, and several operas of which *Undine* (1816) is considered a landmark in German Romantic opera; wrote reviews for the *Allgemeine musikalische Zeitung*, the leading musical journal of the time; and created in Kreisler one of the greatest fictional musicians.

Tieck and Hoffmann both agreed that instrumental music was superior to vocal music. In his essay "Symphonien," published in 1814, Tieck regarded the "symphony," as he understood it, as the highest form of art and considered sonatas and chamber music merely as preliminary studies for it, yet he seems to be discussing Reichardt's music for *Macbeth* and Beethoven's music to *Egmont*. Despite his activity as an opera composer and conductor, Hoffmann gave instrumental, and particularly orchestral, music the palm. His statement "Music is the most Romantic of all the arts" recurs constantly throughout his writings, but in his essay "Beethovens Instrumental-Musik" he qualified it to refer to instrumental music alone. Other Romantic writers placed a primary emphasis on music; among them, Jean Paul stated that "no color is as Romantic as a tone," and Heinrich von Kleist (1777–1811) considered music the root of all the other arts.

Hoffmann tended to view all his musical heroes—Beethoven, Mozart, Haydn, even J. S. Bach and Palestrina—as Romantics. Though he esteemed Haydn for perceiving "the human in human life Romantically," he was among the first to appreciate the daemonic element in Mozart's music and compared Bach's eight-part motets to the "daring, wonderful, Romantic" construction of the Strasbourg cathedral. Hoffmann mocked the shallow appeal of virtuosos and repeatedly portrayed the dualism between the Romantic artist and the pseudo-cultured "Philistine," a favorite topic of later Romantic writers on music like Berlioz and Schumann.

Bettina Brentano von Arnim (1785–1859), who had studied music during her girlhood and had corresponded with Beethoven, was the most musically inclined, except for E. T. A. Hoffmann, among the German Romantic writers. To her, music was almost a divine art, both a sensuous experience through one's feelings and a sublime experience through one's soul, and could best be perceived as a subjective experience of one's intuition rather than through theoretical knowledge or analysis. One may contrast her exalted views on music with the distrust expressed by the more "moralistic" writers from Schiller to Tolstoy of the sensual feelings which music, even the best, could arouse.

All of the German Romantic writers, as well as such later poets as Baudelaire (1821–67) and Verlaine (1844–96), musicians like Skryabin and Ciurlionis, and even the historian Oswald Spengler (1880–1936), perceived music as part of a glorious synaesthesia, *audition colorée*, in which words were tones and tones colors. Heinse called music a "speech without consonants." Tieck asked, "Isn't it permitted and possible to think in tones and to make music in words and thoughts?" and Hoffmann described how, after hearing much music, he experienced a delirium preceding sleep in which he felt a synaesthesia of colors, tones, and odors. From a more practical standpoint, Runge wrote that "a painter must also be a musician and an orator," and throughout the century many artists wanted their paintings to be shown with musical accompaniment.

One of the problems concerning the study of the German Romantic writers and music, especially among those who wrote about music poetically, is to discover exactly what music they were describing. Wackenroder, for example, never mentions any specific composers or compositions, and with both him and Jean Paul one has the feeling that they are often describing an ideal music yet to be written but which was eventually composed by Weber, Schumann, and finally Wagner. In the same sense

Debussy, Skryabin, and Cyril Scott were to write the music poetically imagined by such later Romantics as Swinburne and Mallarmé.

Music played a less significant role in the writings of the French Romantics; it was not a major force until the 1880's, with the symbolist poets and the *Reúue Wagnerienne*. French Romanticism was later than its German counterpart and, except for Rousseau and Chateaubriand (1768–1848), did not fully develop until 1830. Henri Beyle (1783–1842), writing under the pen name of Stendhal, was the French writer most interested in music; although his biographies of Mozart and Haydn were at least partially plagiarized, his *Life of Rossini* (1824) is still a valuable document. Yet Stendhal disliked Weber's music. Although Honoré de Balzac (1799–1850) gave lip service to Beethoven and Alfred de Musset (1810–57) to Schubert, their chief delights were Italian opera and French Grand Opera; Balzac's two musical novellas, *Massimilla Doni* and *Gambara,* are rhapsodic analyses of, respectively, Rossini's *Mosè in Egitto* and Meyerbeer's *Robert le Diable*. The women writers of the French Romantic period found the musicians of the time most interesting as amatory partners. Théophile Gautier discussed only three composers in his *History of Romanticism* (1874): Berlioz, Chopin, and the insignificant Hippolyte Monpou (1804–41). Though he jokingly confessed to the Goncourt brothers that he preferred silence to music, he publicly supported Berlioz and was one of the first Frenchmen to come to Wagner's defense. The French Romantic novelists chiefly used music to portray social milieux, and their works are excellent sources for a sociological history of music.

In conclusion, the influence of Romantic writers on composers was greater than the influence of composers, even in Germany, on the writers. The Romantic writers contributed strongly toward including the composer and certain virtuoso performers (especially the singer Maria Malibran and the violinist Paganini) as participants in the cult of genius and as isolated and exalted personages. They also widened the audience for their music, especially for the composer or performer of instrumental music in Germany and England. Romantic literature is echoed through the music of the nineteenth century far more than Romantic music is discussed or even mentioned in the writings of the time. It is also important to recall that most nineteenth-century musicians had strong interests and capabilities in other fields, in contrast to the preceding century when such versatile figures as Rousseau, Schubart, and Reichardt were rarities. Berlioz and Wagner were significant literary figures apart from their music; Weber, Schumann, and d'Indy had more than a common competence as authors; and many composers wrote their memoirs or a series of essays on music. Spohr, Mendelssohn, and especially Mikolajus Ciurlionis (1875–1911) were gifted painters, and the latter's paintings with musical titles, e.g., "Serpent Sonata," represent a high point of Romantic synaesthesia. Many Romantic musicians were musical journalists, and such composers as Brahms, Chaikovsky, Saint-

Saëns, and d'Indy edited early music. Most Romantic composers were well-read and literarily sensitive to a degree unprecedented in the history of music, and only a few musical figures, like Bruckner and Dvořák, displayed the exclusive concentration on music characteristic of most eighteenth-century composers.

CONTINUATIONS OF ROMANTICISM: REALISM, NATURALISM, AND SYMBOLISM

Some literary historians date the end of Romanticism between 1843, when Victor Hugo's drama *Les Burgraves* failed, and 1849, when the last of the unsuccessful revolutions which had convulsed continental Europe was suppressed. Historians of the visual arts usually end Romanticism at about 1863, with the death of Delacroix and the revolt against French academic painting shown in the *Salon des Refusés*. The movements that followed—Realism, Naturalism, and Symbolism—represent the continuation of Romanticism, but along various lines, much as a river spreads out various arms to form a delta. It is possible to view Realism and Naturalism as the extension of the rebellious and revolutionary aspects of Romanticism, and Symbolism as its conservative antithesis.

The socially conscious aspects of Realism and Naturalism had little place in music, not even on the operatic stage where parallels between musical and literary trends are most obvious. There were no musical equivalents of Charles Dickens (1812–70), Gustave Courbet (1819–77), or Gerhard Hauptmann (1862–1946). The collaboration of late Romantic French composers like Alfred Bruneau (1857–1934) and Gustave Charpentier (1860–1956) with Naturalist authors like Émile Zola (1840–1902) had little effect on musical Romanticism. The operatic movement known as *verismo* in Italy at the end of the century was a degradation of Naturalism, employing its shock techniques for melodramatic purposes rather than for rousing an audience to seeking social reform and ending injustice. Musorgsky is the only nineteenth-century composer of major stature to be thoroughly influenced by Realism and Naturalism.

Realism takes a different turn in the music of Verdi, Wagner, and Liszt. Verdi's realism can be best seen in his portraits of Ernani, Odabella (in *Attila*), and especially Lady Macbeth in his operas of the 1840's and throughout his career, in his depictions of strong emotions at the expense of euphony or beautiful singing. Though Wagner had created his private operatic worlds as a retreat from real life, he depicted their internal details with great literalness through his meticulous stage directions and liberal reiteration of leitmotives, especially in the *Ring*. The eroticism of Wagner's *Tristan* and Liszt's "Vallée d'Obermann" from Book I (Suisse) of his *Années de Pèlerinage* is almost tangibly palpable (which can account for the swooning in the audience that often occurred during performances of *Tristan*), in contrast to the sublimated eroticism of Brahms, the perfumed eroticism of Skryabin's later works, or the theatrical sensuality of the heroines of Massenet and Puccini.

Symbolism is Romanticism at its least tangible and palpable and essentially consists of the use of often familiar ideas and symbols in new, unfamiliar, and even disorienting contexts. The early stages of Symbolism in music are best seen in Wagner's frequent association of leitmotives and tangible objects in the *Ring* and *Parsifal*, in which he thereby endowed spears, swords, gold, and other material objects with a considerably enhanced significance. Wagner's ideas on the union of the arts inspired many Symbolist poets like Baudelaire and Mallarmé.

Though several studies have explored Symbolism in literature and the visual arts, only beginnings have been made of the study of Symbolism and music. In general, we can say that Symbolism, with its slogan "art for art's sake," is a continuation of the quietism of Romanticism and that it is as international as Romanticism, Realism, or Naturalism.

Symbolism can best be identified as (1) the use of a symbol (pictorial, literary, or musical) that suggests rather than describes and often produces associations other than the idea it represents; (2) an elitist-religious (though not strictly orthodox) atmosphere; and (3) sometimes a deliberate effort to cross the boundaries of the arts in an attempt to integrate them, as shown by many Symbolist poems or pictures with musical titles.

Nineteenth-century Symbolism is evident not only in Wagner's operas but also in the cyclic forms of Franck and his disciples, especially d'Indy and Chausson, and in the often vague and ambiguous accompaniments to Fauré's settings of Symbolist poems as songs. Symbolism so intensely permeates the symphonies of Mahler, as with the paintings of his contemporary Gustav Klimt (1862–1918), that the techniques of semiology (the study of nonverbal symbols, a discipline not formally named until 1974) should be used to analyze his symphonies, often so free in form and unamenable to conventional structural analyses. Musical symbolism can be explicit and definite, as in Skryabin's later piano sonatas, or implicit and indefinite, as in the programmatic piano works of his countryman Nikolai Metner (1880–1951). However, not until Debussy's new pianistic and orchestral timbres, melodies, and non-functional harmonic progressions can we speak of a musical language of Symbolism. This is best seen in his setting of one of the leading Symbolist dramas, *Pelléas et Mélisande* by Maurice Maeterlinck (1862–1949), which had also inspired such diverse composers as Fauré, Sibelius, and Schoenberg. Musical Symbolism is another dividing line between the nineteenth and twentieth centuries, whether practiced by the Frenchman Debussy, the German Franz Schreker (1878–

1934), the Russian Skryabin, or the Englishman Cyril Scott (1879–1970), a Theosophist like Skryabin.

Neoclassicism, parallel to Romanticism especially in music and painting, can be best viewed as a kind of constant existing from 1800 to the near-present. In literature, Neoclassicism is best seen in the works of the French "Parnassian" poets. In painting, the best illustrations during the first half of the century are those by J. A. D. Ingres (1780–1867) in France and Pelagio Palagi (1775–1860) in northern Italy, and in architecture the "Greek Revival" which occurred even as far away as Russia and the United States; during the second half one often finds Neoclassicism associated with a kind of academic eclecticism, as with the paintings of William-Adolphe Bouguereau (1825-1905) in France and Hans Makart (1840–84) in Vienna, or the progressive Neoclassicism of Puvis de Chavannes (1824–98) which so greatly influenced many Symbolist painters.

In Chapters 7 and 11 the musical criteria of Neoclassicism will be discussed; for now it is sufficient to say that the Romantic composers inherited virtually all their forms from their Classic predecessors, and that the clarity and logically balanced structures which the Romantics considered the hallmarks of Classic music fascinated nearly every composer from Beethoven through Richard Strauss. Only in part was Neoclassicism an escape to a Romantically perceived eighteenth century with its order, stability, clarity, and balance, and a corresponding rejection of the irregularity and grandiloquence of Romanticism, the literalness of Realism, the gritty seaminess of Naturalism, and the vagueness of Symbolism. It is preferable, in describing the art and music of either the nineteenth or the twentieth centuries, to speak of Neoclassicisms in the plural, indicating that Neoclassicism was no more uniform than Romanticism. The constants of these artistic Neoclassicisms include simplicity, renewed emphases on form (which, however, take some surprisingly innovative turns), and selective retention and modification of all devices from the past: Neoclassicism did not eschew elements from the Baroque or Renaissance. Fauré, Ravel, and Max Reger represent the same kind of division between the nineteenth and twentieth centuries in music, from the standpoint of a revival of Classicism that looks forward to modern times, that Georges Seurat (1859–91) and the post-Impressionistic works of Paul Cézanne (1839–1906) do in painting, although this movement occasioned changes in painting far earlier than the comparable shifts in music.

THE END OF THE CENTURY

Because of the tremendous diversity of the nineteenth century, writers on Romanticism have despaired of trying to impose on it the kind of linear succession that is appropriate for earlier cultural epochs. There is no such agreement, for example, on those who should be included under the heading "late Romanticism" as there is for earlier internal calibrations of cultural periods like the early Renaissance or late Baroque. It is possible, though, to identify an early Romanticism around 1800; a full-blown Romanticism that begins around 1815, reaches a climax between 1830 and 1840, and wanes after that date; a late Romanticism with a number of divergent and even contradictory elements between 1850 and 1890; and a complex, tangled period of exaggeration of Romanticism (called by some "hyper-Romanticism," autumnal Romanticism, or post-Romanticism), repudiations and trivializations of Romanticism, all of which have been summed up by the expression "*fin de siècle*" (end of the century), with chronological boundaries from around 1885 to 1914, and embracing music as well as the visual arts and literature.

After around 1885 many of the continuations of Romanticism became exaggerated. Symbolism either withdrew into a world of virtual incomprehensibility to the general public or entered a realm of hothouse decadence with sophisticated perversions and malaises: the genesis of this "decadence" lies in the works of Baudelaire, Verlaine, Arthur Rimbaud (1854–91), and Algernon Swinburne (1837–1909), and its peaks are represented in the writings of Joris-Karl Huysmans (1848–1907), Marcel Proust (1871–1922), and Oscar Wilde (1854–1900), the drawings of Aubrey Beardsley (1872–98), and the macabre paintings of such "black Symbolists" as Odilon Redon (1840–1916), Félicien Rops (1933–98), Paul Delville (1867–1953), and James Ensor (1860–1949). Naturalism became grittier and more shocking, best illustrated by the scatological expletive with which Alfred Jarry's play *Ubu Roi* (1908) opens. Two cities, Vienna and Paris, were the locales of *fin de siècle* decadence, played against a backdrop of impending violence that was to culminate in World War I.

Cultural primitivism, in the later years of the nineteenth century, assumed a large number of forms and a wide variety of manifestations, mostly as a reaction against the "over-civilized" culture among the *fin-de-siècle* aesthetes. One aspect of cultural primitivism is a simplification that exceeds the bounds of Neoclassicism by focusing on the deliberately trivial. A second aspect is the impact of music and art from outside the Romantic cultural heartland. The International Exposition of 1889 was a high point of Western colonialism, and the "primitive" arts and music of Africa and Southeast Asia were introduced for the first time to the general public, creating an impact felt well into the twentieth century. Exotic and folk arts and music provided new stimuli to jaded tastes.

Cultural primitivism is the one constant in the art historians' catchall term "post-Impressionism," which includes the Tahitian figures of Paul Gauguin (1848–1903), the sunflowers of Vincent van Gogh (1853–1900), the jungle scenes of Henri Rousseau (1844–1910), and such artistic schools as Futurism, Cubism, Vorticism, and Expressionism.

Earlier in this chapter an analogy of Romanticism's branching out around 1850 with a river's spreading out arms to form a delta was presented. A delta is formed at the mouth of some rivers, e.g., the Mississippi; it is made up of swamps, marshes, occasional hummocks covered with jungle or scrub vegetation, intermixtures of fresh and salt water among isolated brackish pools, and offshore islands formed by silt deposits, with the central channel of the river lost among meanders, bayous, tributaries, and cut-off oxbow lakes. This was post-Romanticism between 1885 and 1914. There was no "center" in music or any of the other arts, none of the culmination and summary that we associate with the names of Michelangelo, Shakespeare, Pope, J. S. Bach, Mozart, or Haydn.

Even before World War I new changes were to terminate the intellectual outlook of the nineteenth century, not in the arts but in the sciences. Science was to change from applied technology, invention, and engineering into a pure science that was to become increasingly incomprehensible to the layman, who could understand Darwin but not the work of Albert Einstein (1879–1955) and Lord Rutherford (1871–1937) in atomic physics or Max Planck (1858–1947) in quantum physics, except that their theories shattered the orderly cosmology of the Newtonian universe much as Darwin's hypotheses shattered Protestant theology and Schoenberg's innovations undermined the system of tonality. Studies in psychological aberration and pathology culminated in the theories of the unconscious as elaborated in Vienna by Sigmund Freud (1856–1939); these had a strong impact on literature and art, for the unconscious became a new aspect of cultural primitivism. World War I simply swept away all remaining illusions: the year 1914 is a far more critical watershed date in history than even 1789, yet its terminal character was anticipated in the arts some years before Gavrilo Princip's first pistol shots at Sarajevo set World War I in motion.

BIBLIOGRAPHICAL NOTES

The Century in General. The best short general surveys of the history of the century, within a larger context, are in R. R. Palmer and Joel Colton, *A History of the Modern World* (5th ed., New York, 1983); Crane Brinton, J. B. Christopher, and R. L. Wolff, *A History of Civilization* (3d ed., Prentice-Hall, 1967); and Hugh Thomas, *A History of the World* (New York, 1979), which is organized around themes and topics rather than chronologically. For more detailed investigations of the century, separate volumes in individual historical series should be consulted. The leading American series, *The Rise of Modern Europe*, contains only one recent volume dealing with the nine-teenth century, William L. Langer's *Political and Social Upheaval 1832–1852* (New York, 1969). Other valuable studies of segments of the century include Franklin L. Ford, *Europe 1780–1830* (London, 1970), and two volumes by E. J. Hobsbawm, *The Age of Revolution 1789–1848* (New York, 1962) and *The Age of Capital 1848–1875* (New York, 1975).

The intellectual history of the nineteenth century is strikingly and synopti-cally presented in Crane Brinton's *The Shaping of Modern Thought* (Pren-tice-Hall, 1963) and, more recent, Franklin L. Baumer, *Modern European Thought* (New York, 1977); the economic history is given a readable and stim-ulating overview in Walt W. Rostow, *The Stages of Economic Growth* (Cam-bridge, Mass., 1960). Asa Briggs's *The Nineteenth Century* (London, 1970) is sumptuously illustrated with contemporaneous pictures and essays on various topics by different writers, and makes the century visually come to life. An adverse side of the period can be seen in Thomas Annan, *Photographs of the Old Closes and Streets of Glasgow 1868–1877* (reprint, New York, 1977), with pictures of one of industrial Europe's worst slums. Other surveys of the century that I have found helpful are Lewis Namier's *Vanished Supremacies* (reprint, New York, 1963) and a synoptic social history by a French historian (though its musical information should be used with caution), Charles Mor-azé's *The Triumph of the Middle Classes* (English translation, New York, 1968). A. F. Weber's *The Growth of Cities in the Nineteenth Century* (1899; reprint New York, 1969) is a statistical study.

Nineteenth-Century Art. The visual arts of the century receive a broad cover-age in John Canaday, *Mainstreams of Modern Art* (New York, 1959); more detailed studies with lavish illustrations include Kenneth Clark, *The Roman-tic Rebellion* (New York, 1973), William Vaughan, *German Romantic Painting* (New Haven, 1980), Robert Rosenblum and H. W. Janson, *Nineteenth-Cen-tury Art* (New York, 1984), Edward Lucie-Smith, *Symbolist Art* (New York, 1972), and Philippe Jullien, *The Symbolists* (English trans., New York, 1973). The Penguin Books *Style and Civilization* series provides inexpensive ac-counts of the architecture and art of the century, with well-written commen-tary.

Romanticism in General. The literature on Romanticism is copious, with at least 300 titles on the subject, with about fifty added each decade; I empha-size in this list recent titles in English. Among the classic studies of Romanti-cism are two seminal essays, Arthur O. Lovejoy's "On the Discrimination of Romanticisms" in *Essays in the History of Ideas* (Baltimore, 1948) and René Wellek's articles in *Concepts of Criticism* (New Haven, 1962), as well as Ir-ving Babbitt's wide-sweeping *Rousseau and Romanticism* (New York, 1919). Several of the major studies of Romanticism have little to do with music; among these are Mario Praz, *The Romantic Agony* (1931; English translation, New York, 1956), M. H. Abrams, *The Mirror and the Lamp* (New York, 1953), and W. T. Jones, *The Romantic Syndrome* (The Hague, 1961). The rebellious-revolutionary aspects of the movement are emphasized in Howard

Mumford Jones, *Revolution and Romanticism* (Cambridge, Mass., 1974), and Henri Peyre, *What is Romanticism?* (1974; English translation, University, Ala., 1977), which also describes the continuity of Romanticism into the twentieth century. Lilian Furst has given a good overview in *The Contours of European Romanticism* (London, 1979), though she neglects music and the visual arts. David Morse has given new interpretations in *Romanticism: A Structural Analysis* (Totowa, N.J., 1982), representing Romanticism as "a series of characteristic intellectual structures rather than as a climate of opinion," but gives more emphasis to music in *Romanticism: A Transformational Analysis* (Totowa, N.J., 1981). A current example of a literary theory of Romanticism is Tilottama Rajan, "Displacing Post-Structuralism," *Studies in Romanticism*, XXIV (1985), 451–74, though its methodologies do not seem readily applicable to music. His *Dark Interpreter: The Discourse of Romanticism* (Ithaca, N.Y., 1986) is based on German Romantic philosophy.

Collections of writings in English translation by major Romantic figures are contained in Howard E. Hugo (ed.), *The Viking Portable Romantic Reader* (New York, 1957), John C. Cairns, *The Nineteenth Century 1815–1914* (New York, 1965), and John B. Halsted, *Romanticism* (London, 1969). Morse Peckham has edited a short collection of illustrations of Romantic poetry, prose, and art, with an essay on four stages of Romantic style, in *Romanticism: The Culture of the Nineteenth Century* (New York, 1965).

Romanticism and Music. Since an extensive list of musical studies of the nineteenth century is presented in the bibliographical notes to chapters 10 and 11, I cite here only discussions of music in connection with Romantic thought wherein Romanticism in general is emphasized. Of these studies, I have found Morse Peckham's incorporations of music in his discussions of Romanticism to be quite thought-provoking, relying as they do not only on literature but also on philosophy, linguistics, semiology, and behavioral psychology; especially recommended are several of his essays in the collections *The Triumph of Romanticism* (Columbia, S.C., 1970) and *Romanticism and Ideology* (Greenwood, Fla., 1985). Among other studies, one of the best is H. G. Schenk, *The Mind of the European Romantics* (Garden City, 1969), with Jacques Barzun's *Classic, Romantic, and Modern* (New York, 1961) more speculative and controversial in his treatment of music. Friedrich Blume's *Classic and Romantic Music* (New York, 1970), based on his articles "Klassik" and "Romantik" in *Die Musik in Geschichte und Gegenwart*, relates musical Romanticism chiefly to its German literary counterparts.

Excerpts of Romantic writings on music are contained in Oliver Strunk, *Source Readings in Music History* (New York, 1950); Peter le Huray and James Day, *Music and Aesthetics in the Eighteenth and Early Nineteenth Centuries* (Cambridge, Eng., 1981); and Piero Weiss and Richard Taruskin, *Music in the Western World: A History in Documents* (New York, 1984).

Special studies of individual writers and music include Wilhelm Bode, *Die Tonkunst in Goethes Leben* (Berlin, 1912); R. M. Longyear, *Schiller and Mu-*

sic (Chapel Hill, 1966); Willi Reich, *Musik in romantischer Schau* (2 vols., Basel, 1946); Ronald Taylor, *Hoffmann* (New York, 1963); R. Murray Schafer, *E. T. A. Hoffmann and Music* (Toronto, 1975), in which the translations should be used with caution; Nora Haimberger, *Vom Musiker zum Dichter* (Bonn, 1976), also on Hoffmann; and Roman Nahrebecky, *Wackenroder, Tieck, E. T. A. Hoffmann, Bettina von Arnim; Ihre Beziehungen zur Musik und zum musikalischen Erlebnis* (Bonn, 1979). Linda Siegel has assembled a good selection in her *Music in German Romantic Literature* (Palo Alto, 1984); similar collections would be helpful for Romantic writings on music in other countries.

TWO

BEETHOVEN AND HIS PREDECESSORS

Whereas the *style galant* of the eighteenth century arose first in Paris and Naples, the ultimate source of musical Romanticism was the Venice of the seventeenth and early eighteenth centuries. Personal expression and subjective feeling make a work like Monteverdi's *L'Incoronazione di Poppea* (1642) sound surprisingly "modern," and the subsequent Venetian operas, with their expressive arias and highly organized ritornelli, led directly to the Venetian concertos of Tomaso Albinoni (1671–1750), Alessandro (ca. 1684–ca. 1750) and Benedetto (1686–1739) Marcello, and especially Antonio Vivaldi (ca. 1669–1741). In Vivaldi's music the future is discernible in such passages as the long melodic lines of his slow movements (Concerto for Three Violins, F major), the dotted unison ritornelli in other slow movements (C minor Violin Concerto, Fanna No. 92), and the dramatic syncopations, drumming basses, slow harmonic rhythm, and emotional turbulence of the Concerto for the Dresden Orchestra. The Vivaldian style was brought to Germany (especially Saxony-Thuringia) by his pupil J. G.

Pisendel (1687–1755), J. S. Bach, and finally, G. B. Platti (1690–1763), one of the major keyboard composers of the early Classic period.

PRECURSORS OF ROMANTICISM

There are two basic styles in Classic music, the light, airy *style galant* and the emotional, subjective *empfindsamer Stil*, the latter best seen in the music of two of J. S. Bach's sons, Wilhelm Friedemann (1710–84) and Carl Philipp Emanuel (1714–88). Wilhelm Friedemann was an extremely expressive composer whose output was small, more from laziness than from a supposed fondness for the bottle, and his subsequent influence was slight. On the other hand, C. P. E. Bach can be justly called the most original and one of the most influential composers of the Classic period. Geiringer has admirably described his musical style as

> a daring harmonic language with incisive dissonances and stunning chord-combinations; dramatic pauses, unexpected rests, alterations in tempo, and sudden changes in major and minor modes, an effect often increased by varying dynamics and the use of different registers.[1]

C. P. E. Bach sincerely believed that music should touch the heart, which, as he said, could not be done through "running, rattling, drumming, or arpeggios." His music is surpassed during the eighteenth century only by the major works of Gluck, Haydn, and Mozart, and his yearning appoggiaturas and strange, distant modulations were only tentatively approached by his more timid successors. His Sinfonia in E minor (1756)[2] contains virtually all the effects of the so-called *Sturm und Drang* symphonies of the 1770's, and his use of instrumental recitative (first "Prussian" sonata, 1742) looks ahead to Beethoven, Spohr, and Weber. Some of the appoggiaturas and modulations of his later fantasias anticipate the harmonic practice of Liszt and Wagner (Example 2–1).

Although C. P. E. Bach may be called the first "Romantic" composer, his influence is most immediately important in its effect on Mozart and Haydn. As a young man, Haydn diligently studied Bach's "Prussian" and "Württemberg" sonatas, and their strong influence is the chief difference between Haydn's best sonatas and the more brilliant and fluent keyboard works of Mozart. Mozart knew Bach's sonatas and their imitations written by German composers residing in France, but was most affected by

---

[1]Karl Geiringer, *The Bach Family* (New York, 1954), p. 335.
[2]Published in Karl Geiringer (ed.), *Music of the Bach Family* (Cambridge, Mass., 1955), pp. 141–55.

EXAMPLE 2–1. C. P. E. Bach, Fantasia II from *Die sechs Sammlungen von Sonaten, freien Fantasien und Rondos für Kenner und Liebhaber, Fünfte Sammlung* (published 1785).

Bach's symphonies, which he heard at Baron van Swieten's academies in Vienna in the early 1780's and which brought about the increased depth and richness of his last five symphonies.

The terms *Sturm und Drang* (storm and stress, taken from Maximilian Klinger's drama of 1776) or *crise romantique* have been loosely used to designate a tense, terse, excited musical style, incorporating surprises in dynamic changes and modulations and an extensive use of the minor mode, that was employed by some composers around 1770, especially in Haydn's symphonies and sonatas. Yet most of these effects are found in operas around 1730 and in much of C. P. E. Bach's keyboard music of the 1740's, and the period of the 1770's contains fewer instrumental compositions in the minor mode than do the preceding or the following decades.[3]

Haydn seldom composed in the *Sturm und Drang* idiom after 1773, not because his patron Prince Esterházy disliked it, but because his inter-

[3]See my study "The Prevalence of the Minor Mode in the Classic Era," *Music Review*, XXXII (1971), 27–35.

ests had turned to other musical ideas, chiefly opera, and his later attempts
to recapture the spirit of *Sturm und Drang* (e.g., symphonies nos. 78, 80,
83, 95) were not wholly successful.

The spirit of dawning Romanticism is most pronounced in Haydn's
symphonic introductions, the slow movements of his later symphonies (especially that of No. 102) and string quartets (the "Fantasia" of his Op. 76,
No. 6 quartet), and the "Representation of Chaos" in *The Creation* (1798).
Mozart, on the other hand, more successfully sublimated and assimilated
Sturm und Drang; even during what his biographers Wyzewa and Saint-
Foix call his *crise romantique* of the early 1770's, Mozart balanced tragic
works like his early G minor Symphony (K. 183) with sunny, *galant* works
like the motet *Exsultate, Jubilate,* and in later years paired his intensely
personal and tragic or daemonic works in the keys of C minor, G minor,
and D minor with contrasting gayer compositions, often for the same or
similar media. These contrasts are best seen in the opposition of D minor
and D major in his opera *Don Giovanni* or in the second and closing
theme-groups of his sonata-form movements in the minor mode, stated in
mediant major in the exposition but given an air of poignancy and even
high tragedy through their recapitulation in tonic minor. The sublimation
and assimilation of the *Sturm und Drang* style by Mozart, Clementi, Koželuch, and Dussek was to have greater influence on the future than Haydn's
use of this idiom.

Mozart's influence on Beethoven was immense: one need only compare two of their C minor piano sonatas, Mozart's K. 457 and Beethoven's
Op. 13, or "Pathétique," or their two piano concertos in C minor. The expansiveness of Mozart's later works in C major such as the String Quintet,
K. 515, the piano concerto, K. 503, or the "Jupiter" Symphony, K. 551,
foreshadows Beethoven's amplification and expansion of the instrumental
cycle in his middle-period works.

Mozart's ventures into chromatic harmony, most evident in his E♭
String Quartet, K. 428, and his *Requiem,* influenced Beethoven's contemporaries like Hummel and Spohr, who regarded themselves as Mozart's legitimate heirs.

LUDWIG VAN BEETHOVEN (1770–1827): HIS APPRENTICESHIP

Beethoven is the most important composer of the nineteenth century, for all his successors were influenced or even intimidated by his
works, which became the touchstone for Romantic critics from E. T. A.
Hoffmann onward. Beethoven's music is viewed as the culmination of the
"Viennese Classic" tradition or as the synthesis of all the varied streams of

the Classic style, yet it also furnished the impetus for virtually all instrumental and much vocal composition of the nineteenth century; not a single major composer of this period could wholly escape his influence.

Many writers have attempted to organize Beethoven's compositions according to "periods": from two to as many as five have been postulated, with three the most commonly agreed upon number. Beethoven's compositions written before the publication of his Opus 1 in 1795, however, constitute a separate period of apprenticeship, and groups of transitional works came between the first and second, and second and third, periods. Demarcations between periods can only be approximate, and there also is some chronological overlapping between periods, since Beethoven frequently had several compositions in progress at the same time.

Beethoven lived in Bonn until 1792 and during his stay there wrote works which reveal in embryo many of the salient traits of his style. The two most important of these early pieces, the twenty four variations on the arietta "Vieni, amore" by Vincenzo Righini (1756–1812), WoO[4] (without opus number) 65, and the Cantata on the Death of the Emperor Joseph II (Example 2–2), were written in 1790, although the variations were revised in 1802, probably not very extensively.

EXAMPLE 2–2. Beethoven, Cantata on the Death of Joseph II, WoO 87.

---

[4]*Werke ohne Opuszahl.*

The cantata is an excellent anticipation of Beethoven's "noble" style, seen at its best in his later hymn-like slow movements; it not only anticipates his *Missa Solemnis* but also Brahms' works for chorus and orchestra. The influence of the Mannheim symphonist and opera composer Ignaz Holzbauer (1711–83) has been found in this work; equally important influences are the styles of Gluck and his most important successor, Luigi Cherubini. This cantata may have induced Haydn to accept Beethoven as a pupil.

The Righini variations display several characteristics of Beethoven's style: aggressive contrary motion (Var. I), sharp and unexpected dynamic contrasts (Var. II), trills (Var. IV), tempo contrasts which anticipate the first movement of the Piano Sonata, Op. 109 (Var. XIV), hymn-like writing (Var. XVII), and the long coda (final variation); variation XXIII closely resembles the opening of the slow movement of his Piano Sonata, Op. 2, No. 2. The frequent inversions of chords, especially of the dominant seventh, provide both an interesting bass line and a harmonic drive. Mozart's piano variations are an obvious model, as are those by Beethoven's teacher in Bonn, Christoph Gottlob Neefe (1748–98).

INFLUENCES ON BEETHOVEN'S FIRST PERIOD

Beethoven studied with Haydn for two years after arriving in Vienna in 1792 and subsequently took lessons from the contrapuntist J. G. Albrechtsberger (1736–1809) and Gluck's disciple Antonio Salieri (1750–1825). Their influence, as well as those of Mozart and the French Revolutionary composers, has been extensively discussed in the Beethoven literature, but three other composers also substantially affected his first-period works: Muzio Clementi (1752–1832), Leopold Koželuch (1747–1818), and Emanuel Aloys Förster (1748–1823).

A Roman by birth, Clementi was taken to England at the age of fourteen and spent most his life there, except for concert tours and business trips. In the early 1780's he concertized on the continent, competed against Mozart (arousing his enmity) before the Emperor Joseph II, and entered into a tragic love affair which drove him from France in 1784 after he wrote some of his finest sonatas. After his return to London he wrote symphonies (now forgotten and mostly lost) in competition with Haydn, and during his long lifetime served as composer, teacher, publisher, and piano manufacturer. The sonatas, his most important compositions, extend from 1765 to 1821.

Clementi was a direct musical descendant of Domenico Scarlatti (1685–1757) and one of the great innovators in writing for the piano. He was the first important composer who really thought in terms of the modern piano, and his conception of the instrument is evident as early as the sonatas of Op. 2, written around 1770. Such characteristic forward-looking devices as powerful octaves, fast repeated notes, rapid chains of parallel thirds and sixths, fast scales and arpeggios, and thick, full, quasi-orchestral chords are often blended with legacies of the past like murky (broken octave) basses, two-voiced textures, or Scarlattian turns and ornaments. The sonatas of 1782 and 1783 (Opp. 7, 9, and 10) had a particularly strong impact on Beethoven. The singing, ornamental melodies over a slow harmonic rhythm or the sonority and spacing of the slow movement of Op. 9, No. 3, could easily be mistaken for a first-period Beethoven work, as can the Trio of the second movement of Op. 10, No. 1 (Example 2–3) which so admirably exploits the singing tenor register of the piano.

After the Op. 14 sonatas, Clementi's compositions show less freshness of inspiration despite such magnificent exceptions as the sonatas in F♯ minor (Op. 26, No. 2) and G minor (Op. 34, No. 2), since most of his sonatas between 1784 and 1804 were written for concert tours or other commercial purposes. His best late works, four sonatas and the *Gradus ad Parnas-*

EXAMPLE 2–3. Clementi, Sonata, Op. 10, No. 1, trio of second movement.

sum, were written between 1817 and 1826 and had a considerable influence on the second generation of Romantic piano composers.

Beethoven knew and esteemed Clementi's sonatas even though he did not meet him personally until 1807. Among Clementi's more discernible influences on the younger composer are the design of the first movement of the G minor Sonata (Op. 34, No. 2), in which the slow introduction is used in the development, a procedure which probably was a model for Beethoven's "Pathétique" sonata; furthermore, the use of the rhythmic pattern $\frac{2}{4}$ ♩ ♪♪♪ | ♩ in various guises throughout this movement anticipates the way that Beethoven unified the first movement of his Fifth Symphony. Similarities between Clementi's and Beethoven's themes often occur; one of the most striking is between the theme in the development of the first movement of Clementi's earlier G minor sonata, Op. 7, No. 3, and the contredanse theme in the variations in the last movement of the "Eroica" Symphony. Other harbingers of Beethoven's style in Clementi's piano works are his use of rhythmic motives from expositions in development sections and his explosive developments and finales, whose influence culminated in Beethoven's Sonata ("Appassionata"), Op. 57.

Many reasons have been advanced for the gross neglect of Clementi's compositions, among them Mozart's sarcastic personal comments ("a charlatan like all Italians") and incompetent editions of his music designed for pedagogical use rather than for musical merit; perhaps the chief reason is that aspiring pianists learn Clementi's sonatinas as youngsters and later regard them as representative of his *oeuvre,* which is like considering the "Minuet in G" and the *Album for the Young* typical specimens of Beethoven's or Schumann's music. Clementi at his best is a major composer of more than historical significance.

Leopold Anton Koželuch was one of the first Czech composers to migrate to Vienna toward the close of the eighteenth century. He was a prolific composer, and many of his works display Romantic traits, best seen in the slow introductions to his sonatas, which he sometimes repeats or echoes at the end of the first movement (a further influence on Beethoven's "Pathétique" Sonata), and in the slow movements of his works for piano and orchestra. There are also striking similarities between Koželuch's and Beethoven's rondo-type sonata finales, sequences, and thematic contrasts in sonata expositions. The sonata from which Example 2–4 is taken was most probably written in 1785.

The chamber music of Emanuel Aloys Förster, whom Beethoven regarded highly and to whom he sent pupils who wanted to study composition, bears the same relationship to Beethoven's early string quartets as Clementi's and Koželuch's piano works do to his first-period sonatas. Mozart's "Haydn" quartets and late quintets are obviously Förster's points of

EXAMPLE 2–4. Koželuch, Sonata, Op. 15, No. 1, first movement: (a) introduction; (b) opening of first theme-group; (c) portion of second theme-group.

departure. His style is quite contrapuntal (as could be expected of a composer who as a student arranged all the fugues from J. S. Bach's *Well-Tempered Clavier* for string quartet), and every member of the chamber ensemble has an important part to play. As Förster's String Quintet, Op. 19 (1802), shows, C minor meant to him what it did to Mozart and Beethoven. Such Beethovenian devices as a finale in minor with a fading-out coda ending in major; contrary motion in thirds even at the risk of dissonance; short, terse, businesslike closing themes in sonata-form expositions or rondo episodes; and "bonus" recapitulations with more music than in the exposition can be encountered in Förster's works. He is not merely a forerunner and early contemporary of Beethoven but also a significant if underestimated member of the Viennese Classic school of instrumental composition (Example 2–5).

  The direct influence that the music of the French Revolution and the Napoleonic Empire had on Beethoven's music is difficult to ascertain precisely. The dynamic and dramatic range of the heroic Gluckian opera had been greatly enlarged by Salieri and by the composer Beethoven most highly esteemed among his contemporaries, the Italian-born but Paris-resident Luigi Cherubini (1760–1842), whose even greater and more skilled enhancement of the dramatic rhetoric of opera began with his *Demofoönte* of 1788. Yet a number of tendencies evident in Beethoven's music developed simultaneously in France along parallel but not intersecting lines: these are best seen in the symphonies and operatic overtures of Etienne-Nicolas Méhul (1763–1817). Though the expanded orchestral sonorities and dynamic levels of the French "rescue opera" are strongly evident in Beethoven's "Eroica" and Fifth Symphonies as well as in his "rescue opera" *Fidelio*, the most important influence on Beethoven from France was the extreme simplicity of so much of the Revolution's ceremonial music, in-

EXAMPLE 2–5. Förster, String Quartet, Op. 16, No. 5, first movement (published 1798)[5]

[5]Published in *Denkmäler der Tonkunst in Oesterreich*, LXVII.

tended for massed bands and choruses in open-air performance (Example 2–6). Beethoven's use of diatonic, triadic simplicity to depict an atmosphere of heroism is one of the most striking features of his music, and his reliance on unclouded diatonic harmony throughout his career is one of the principal style-traits that separates his music from that of his contemporaries (Dussek, Spohr, Weber) who were experimenting with chromaticism and the effects possible from non-harmonic tones.

BEETHOVEN'S FIRST PERIOD

This period of composition extends from approximately 1794 to 1800, with the "Spring" Sonata for violin and piano, Op. 24, the First Symphony, and the B♭ major Piano Sonata, Op. 22, as the major terminal works. The piano, either in a solo capacity or in a chamber ensemble, is the dominant instrument.

Formal experimentation, deriving from Haydn's examples, is typical of Beethoven's early piano sonatas, with their structures ranging from the quite free forms of Op. 2, No. 2 and Op. 10, No. 2 to the clarity of form of Op. 22. The moods of the sonatas range from the tempestuousness of the two C minor sonatas to the expansiveness of Op. 7 and the playfulness of Op. 10, No. 2. Many of these sonatas are technically easy, but only an accomplished pianist can do justice to Op. 10, No. 3, the finest sonata of this period. Many of these sonatas have four movements, with the third generally called "scherzo." Perhaps because of Clementi's influence, Beethoven's piano sonatas are the most original of his first-period compositions.

Beethoven's chamber music for or with winds need not detain us long save to mention that his classicism is strongest in these works and that he abandoned this medium after his Septet, Op. 20 (which he came to detest) and the Serenade, Op. 25. His chamber music for strings consists of several duet sonatas of which the Op. 24 violin sonata is the most popular, a group of string trios of which Op. 3 is really a divertimento, and the six string quartets, Op. 18, in which Beethoven seems to be challenging Haydn's Op. 76 and Op. 77 string quartets. Quite noteworthy in the Op. 18 quartets are the lengthy slow movement in a tragic vein in Op. 18, No. 1, the dramatic C minor quartet (No. 4), and the last two of the group, in which the concise first movements seem to be preparing weightier subsequent movements; the variations in Op. 18, No. 5; and, in Op. 18, No. 6, the unusual finale, in which an adagio opening section with audacious harmonies, entitled "La Malinconia" (melancholy), precedes a joyous allegretto which contains short reminiscences of the adagio.

The orchestral works from Beethoven's first period include two

EXAMPLE 2–6. Gossec, "Aux Mânes de la Gironde" (1795)[6]

[6]Published in Constant Pierre (ed.), *Musique des fêtes et cérémonies de la révolution française* (Paris, 1899), pp. 322–27.

rather conventional piano concertos based evidently on Mozartean models: the C Major Concerto, Op. 15, a "military concerto" like Mozart's C major concertos K. 467 and K. 503, and the more intimate B♭ major concerto, Op. 19, which Beethoven began in Bonn and revised extensively. The First Symphony, Op. 20, is a rather conservative work, although its introduction was thought to be radical, since Beethoven omitted stating the customary unison tonic at the opening and began by going to the subdominant, establishing his tonic by circumscribing it. The second movement (as in the Op. 18, No. 4 Quartet) contains contrapuntal *tours de force*, a legacy of his study with Albrechtsberger; the third movement is a full-blown scherzo though entitled "menuetto," and the finale has the playfulness of Haydn's last movements.

The ballet *The Creatures of Prometheus*, first performed in 1801 and Beethoven's first major work for the stage, concludes his first period of composition.

Beethoven's style, though showing debts to his precursors, is unmistakably his own in these early Viennese works. The extremes in dynamics, tempos, and textures which supposedly upset Haydn are the most obvious breaches of Classic decorum, but one also notices Beethoven's predilections for wider-ranging tonal structures and the variety of conceptions which he brought to each type of instrumental movement.

The transitional works leading to Beethoven's second period were written during his progressive loss of hearing; in his own words he described the history of this catastrophe:

> I have been feeling, I may say, stronger and better, but my ears continue to hum and buzz day and night. I must confess that I lead a miserable life. For almost two years I have ceased to attend any social functions, just because I find it impossible to say to people: I am deaf. If I had any other profession I might be able to cope with my infirmity. . . . In order to give you some idea of this strange deafness, let me tell you that in the theatre I have to place myself quite close to the orchestra in order to understand what the actor is saying, and that at a distance I cannot hear the high notes of instruments or voices. . . . Already I have often cursed my Creator and my existence. Plutarch has shown me the path of *resignation*. If it is at all possible, I will bid defiance to my fate, though I feel that as long as I live there will be moments when I shall be God's most unhappy creature. . . . Resignation, what a wretched resource! Yet it is all that is left to me. . . .[7]

Of the principal works of this transitional period of 1801 and 1802, the piano sonatas between Op. 26 and Op. 31 show most clearly the disso-

---

[7]Emily Anderson (ed. and trans.), *The Letters of Beethoven* (London, 1961, 3 vols.), I, pp. 59–60.

lution of the composer's earlier style and his groping for new means of expression. An irregular order of movements, with a slow movement first and the "sonata-allegro" movement at the end, characterizes the Op. 26 and Op. 27 sonatas, the second of which is the popular "Moonlight"; novel, too, are the storminess of the "Tempest" Sonata, whose slow movement was partially influenced by the French funeral marches of the 1790's (but less so than the third movement of Op. 26), and the fine Op. 31, No. 3 sonata with its non-tonic opening, rich harmonies, and scherzo-like slow movement with sforzandi in unexpected places. Of the violin sonatas of Op. 30, the best is the second, a typical C minor work; also in this key is the powerful Op. 37 piano concerto, with a deeply expressive slow movement in the remote key of E major and an unusual finale. Here Beethoven seems to be challenging the D minor and C minor concertos of Mozart, works that he greatly admired.

The most novel elements of the Second Symphony are the lengthy slow introduction to the first movement and the finale, whose capriciousness and playfulness exceed Haydn's. The brilliant "Kreutzer" Sonata for violin and piano (Op. 47), originally written for the black violinist George Bridgetower (1780–1860) and completed in May 1803, is the terminal work of the first transitional period.

BEETHOVEN'S SECOND PERIOD

Most of Beethoven's popular works come from this period, which begins with the Third ("Eroica") Symphony and can be said to end with Beethoven's benefit concert at the Theater an der Wien in December 1808, which included the premieres of the Fifth and Sixth symphonies and the hastily written Choral Fantasy and the first public performance of the Fourth Piano Concerto and portions of the Mass in C.

The "Eroica" Symphony is the grandest and most grandiose specimen of the instrumental music of this time. Though the sonata had been gaining in length, the symphony had not, and Mozart's "Jupiter" Symphony (K. 551) and Haydn's last three symphonies (Nos. 102, 103, and 104) were the most monumental of the preceding works in this medium. Attempts have been made to trace the influence of the French Revolution in the "Eroica" Symphony, chiefly its prominent triadic themes; further investigation may show that the overtures to the "rescue operas" may have contributed to Beethoven's symphonic "breakthrough."

Those who have studied this symphony have frequently commented on Beethoven's introducing a new "theme" in the lengthy development section of the first movement; this was not a startling innovation, for J. C.

Bach and Mozart had done this, but what is novel is the new theme's reappearance in the immense coda. The second movement is a funeral march on an unprecedented scale, though Beethoven had made preliminary essays in his Op. 26 and Op. 31, No. 2 sonatas. The scherzo begins the vein of "cosmic humor" that culminates in the scherzo of the Ninth Symphony; its prevalent stepwise motion is balanced by the difficult horn fanfares in the trio. The finale is a set of variations on a bass line with an accompanying melody which Beethoven had previously used as a contradanse and as a ballet movement in *The Creatures of Prometheus,* Op. 43; the Op. 35, or "Eroica" Variations, a piano work based on the bass line more than the theme, is complementary to, rather than a study for, the Third Symphony's finale. Beethoven is said to have preferred this symphony above all his others.

The Fourth Symphony is a contrasting and delightful interlude (if unjustly neglected, like virtually all the works in B♭ major) before the Fifth Symphony, in which Beethoven was trying to achieve a certain cyclic relationship, rhythmic as well as thematic, between some of the movements and within the first movement, which is noteworthy for its intense concentration and the rhythmic motive which unites all its sections; however, such interesting elements are absent from the repetitious second movement, a "double variation" in the style of Haydn. The third movement, with its mysterious scherzo and rambunctious trio, was considered the most "Romantic" of all the movements by contemporaneous critics and is bound to the noisy finale by a ghostly transition over a steady drumbeat. The triumphant finale in C major is an excellent specimen of the "optimistic" solution of the conflict inherent in the symphony in a minor mode (in the recapitulation of the first movement the second and closing theme-groups are stated in tonic major but are overwhelmed by the coda in minor); the return of a portion of the scherzo at the end of the development section is an inspired idea; but the coda is unequaled in sheer noise until the patriotic finales of the Russian nationalist composers later in the century. The exquisite Sixth, or "Pastoral," Symphony achieves its contemplative effects through light orchestration and slow harmonic rhythm.

These symphonies show Beethoven's increasing impatience with the limitations of the instrumental technique of his time. A virtuoso performer himself who had heard and composed music for the best living instrumentalists, he demanded a comparable facility from his orchestral musicians. One need but cite the demands on the horn players in the "Eroica" Symphony or *Fidelio,* or on the technique of the string bass players in the trio of the third movement of the Fifth Symphony; Beethoven had previously heard a string bass virtuoso playing his cello sonatas on this instrument. Beethoven even emancipated the trumpets and timpani from their previously noisemaking and rhythm-emphasizing functions, yet he was no "orchestrator" in the modern meaning of the word, and several conductors, notably Felix Weingartner (1863–1942), have tried to revise his scoring.

Among the concertos, the G major Piano Concerto (No. 4) is one of Beethoven's most serene and contemplative works. The Violin Concerto (Beethoven also wrote an alternative version as a piano concerto) and the later Fifth ("Emperor") Piano Concerto show the influence of the "military" concertos of G. B. Viotti (1755–1824) and Pierre Rode (1774–1830), the most renowned violinists of the period. The "triple concerto," Op. 56, for piano, violin, and cello, is a lesser work.

Before discussing the sonatas of the period, a digression is necessary to examine briefly the form that Beethoven had inherited. From Mozart he obtained clean craftsmanship and the idea that the violin in the duet sonata was an equal partner rather than an accompanying instrument; from Haydn the piquant surprises that could arise through experimenting with the formal structure; and from Clementi the conception of the rhetorical drama and conflict inherent in the form, which Beethoven further intensified by transferring the dramatic elements of French "rescue opera" to instrumental music.

In the first movement, the center of gravity of the sonata of the time, the highly organized structure consisted of an exposition of thematic material heightened by a conflict of tonal centers as well as themes; a development, generally of previously presented material, whose conflicts arose through thematic fragmentation and motivic development, often contrapuntally treated, underlaid by fluctuating and unstable tonalities; and a recapitulation restating the exposition with certain changes to insure that the second and closing theme-groups would appear in the tonic, thus resolving the conflicts and ambiguities of the exposition. Haydn, more than Mozart, contributed a slow introduction to the first movement, which Beethoven either spun out at great length (Second and Seventh symphonies) or reduced to a mere gesture (Op. 31, No. 2, Op. 78 sonatas). Although there were a few grand codas in the Classic period, like the finale of Vanhal's Symphony in A minor, the outer movements of Haydn's Symphony No. 44, and the first or last movements of Mozart's large instrumental works in C major or C minor, Beethoven raised the coda to the status of a second development section.

The formal structure and time-scale of the first movement of Beethoven's Piano Sonata in C major, Op. 53, called "Waldstein" after one of the composer's first patrons, lies midway between the highly concentrated sonata-form movements of the Fifth Symphony or the Op. 95 string quartet and the immensely expanded first movements of the "Eroica" and the Ninth symphonies. The first theme-group is based on motives rather than themes, and the transition is long, with a chord of the augmented sixth as the pivot chord, in order to prepare the rather remote tonality of E major for the hymn-like second theme. A second transition, though in a stable E major, leads to a closing group whose key is ambiguous: is it E minor, E major, or the dominant of A minor? The E major chords have sevenths attached, making the dominant of A minor the most plausible key; attempts to cadence in E minor are prepared but constantly thwarted. A deceptive cadence prepares C major for the repeat of the exposition; the sequential pattern continues to F major for the opening of the development, which is based on motives from the first theme-group and a figuration pattern from the second theme-group (measure 49 of the exposition), treated in sequence. The retransition to the tonic begins imperceptibly, sinks to a low point (measure 142) and then rises to a peak of climactic fury, all on the dominant of C major, then subsides through scales in contrary motion to the recapitulation, in which a "bonus" of seven measures (167–73) intensifies the feeling of the home tonic through deviations from it in delaying the inevitable.

Beethoven effectively reconciles the demands that the second and closing theme-groups be recapitulated in the tonic by beginning the former group in A major but (through A minor) closing in C major and, after a slightly compressed transition, beginning his closing group in subdominant minor, and then resolving the ambiguities he had set up in the exposition by restating his theme in subdominant major. This emphasis on the subdominant leads the tonic and then the coda, which starts in the remote key of D♭ major and, on motives from the first theme-group that had previously been worked over in the first development, rises to a climax; but the intensity decreases with a final statement of the second theme, a slowing in the speed, and fermatas on the leading tone. A final rush, based on the first theme in the tonic, concludes the movement. One should note throughout the movement the transitional open spaces, the "lungs" which permit the music to breathe. Many similarities in principles of formal structure, emotional intensities, and scope are found between the "Waldstein" Sonata and the comparable work in minor, the popular "Appassionata" Sonata, Op. 57, in F minor like the storm movement of the "Pastoral" Symphony.

Fidelio, Beethoven's only opera, is a middle-period work although it underwent later revisions. The libretto was based on *Léonore, or Conjugal Love* by the French playwright Jean-Nicolas Bouilly (1763–1842), which had previously been set to music by two minor composers, Pierre Gaveaux (1761–1825) and Ferdinando Paër (1771–1839). *Fidelio* is virtually the last of the rescue operas and the only one which has survived in the repertoire. Though the lesser conventions of opera, especially those deriving from the *Singspiel*, were beneath Beethoven, as the opening and Rocco's "Gold" aria in Act I will testify, the composer's freedom-loving spirit and moral integrity rises to its height in Act II during the scene of Florestan in his dungeon cell, the climactic quartet of Act II when Leonore saves Florestan from his mortal enemy Pizarro, and the finale, in C major like the finale of the Fifth Symphony, with its triumphant echoes of the spirit of French revolutionary music. Of the four overtures which Beethoven wrote for the opera (contrast this with Rossini's using the same overture for at least three different operas!), the "Fidelio" overture written in 1814 is generally used to open the opera whereas "Leonore No. 3," a virtual symphonic poem recapitulating the high points of the drama, is performed during the change of scene for the finale of the second act.

The most experimental works of this period are the three string quartets of Op. 59 which Beethoven wrote for Count Rasumovsky, the Russian ambassador to Vienna who maintained a private string quartet. In homage to his patron, Beethoven incorporated Russian themes in the first two quartets; the theme of the trio of the third movement of the E minor quartet was also used by Musorgsky in the Coronation Scene in *Boris Godunov* (see Examples 8–3a and 8–5c). The F major Quartet has a first movement on a grandly expansive scale with many motives in each theme-group; its second movement is one of Beethoven's most unusual compositions because of the irregular resolutions of what seem to be dominant harmonies and the highly unusual and irregular sonata form. The E minor Quartet has a moving slow movement and a Hungarian-type finale which oscillates between C major and E minor, whereas the C major Quartet closes with a fugue which too many performers play at breakneck speed.

Beethoven's overtures, written chiefly for dramas but transcending their original function as curtain-raisers, are among the principal forerunners of the symphonic poem. Among the best are the previously cited "Leonore No. 3"; the overture to *Coriolan* (by Collin, not Shakespeare), a characteristic C minor work; and the overture to *Egmont*, for which Beethoven also wrote the incidental music frequently called for in Goethe's drama. Beethoven's songs, a good many of which date from his middle period, are the most neglected of his compositions. Their air of nobility is most successful in the settings of devotional texts (Op. 48) by the German poet C. F. Gellert (1715–69), those songs are from the first transitional period. The songs stem from and are the culmination of the heritage of J. F. Reichardt and other north German composers, rather than being precursors of the Lieder of Schubert.

Beethoven's second transitional period, which some consider the second part of his middle period, has been called by Newman the "period of invasion" because of the French conquest of Austria and occupation of Vienna in 1809. This period for Beethoven was one of experimentation and also one when his popularity in Vienna was at its zenith. Among the major works of this period are compositions which are stylistically linked to the heroic elements of the middle period, like the "Emperor" Concerto and the incidental music to Goethe's drama *Egmont*, the Seventh and Eighth

Symphonies, the "Archduke"piano trio, the piano sonatas from Op. 78 to Op. 90, and the string quartets Op. 74 and Op. 95, as well as some lesser-known works like the Piano Fantasia, Op. 77, and *Wellington's Victory*, or "Battle Symphony," Op. 91.

During this period Beethoven wrote genuinely Neoclassic works, the F♯ and G major Piano Sonatas, Opp. 78 and 79, the unjustly maligned incidental music to Kotzebue's drama *The Ruins of Athens* (an example of the "official" music of the nineteenth century), and the Eighth Symphony—homages to the past with an eye to the future. His other major works of this time are more experimental: the Seventh Symphony with its monothematic first movement and its preoccupation with rhythm; the virtually athematic first movement of the Op. 74, or "Harp," quartet; and the Op. 95 quartet with its astronomically high specific gravity unequaled until Sibelius' Fourth Symphony, unusual excursions into remote keys through enharmonic modulations, intensely concentrated first movement, and almost Rossinian conclusion. Whereas the first movement of the Op. 90 piano sonata is nearly as terse as that of the Op. 95 quartet, the second and final movement, almost Schubertian in its lyricism, is as spacious and expansive as the "Archduke" Trio, Op. 97, in which, in 1814, Beethoven made his last appearance as a pianist.

An insight into Beethoven's creative processes can be gained from his sketches for the finale of his Eighth Symphony. Composition was not easy for Beethoven; thematic ideas, of which only the germ of the final form is evident in their initial stages, had to be laboriously revised and polished. His jottings and revisions were set down in sketchbooks, many of which have been preserved though scattered among many libraries. As a reviser of his sketches, he may be compared with the mother bear of mediaeval legend whose cubs were born formless and then literally licked into shape. Example 2–7 shows this process.

In the initial sketch for the finale (a), the basic ideas of the opening are evident: the major third in triplet rhythm at the opening, the consequent idea with a descending melodic contour (measure 5), and the flat submediant as a harmonic interval (measure 9). Sketch (b) seems to be a regression, although the descending melodic line is improved and continued, the meter receives its final designations as ₵, and the contrast of triplets with duplets is not entirely abandoned. Sketch (c) Beethoven designated as "better": he restored the contrast of triplets and duplets but stopped the propulsive effect of the consequent idea. In the final form, the second measure of the earlier sketches is expanded through clever repetition, the opening has more rhythmic variety, the chromatic alteration in measure 8 gives more harmonic interest, the change of pitch location in measure 6 continues the effect of a descending melodic line, and the phrase is extended. The D♭ of the first sketch is saved until measure 17 and

EXAMPLE 2–7. Beethoven's sketches for finale of Symphony No. 8, Op. 93: (a) first sketch; (b) second sketch; (c) third sketch; (d) final version.[8]

Final form
(d) Allegro vivace

[8]After Gustav Nottebohm, "Neue Beethoveniana: Skizzen sur 7. und 8. Symphonie," *Musikalisches Wochenblatt*, VI:21 (21 May 1875), 260. I am indebted to Prof. Lewis Lockwood for this reference to the original source.

changed to a C♯, the reason for which is apparent only in the coda where it becomes the dominant of F♯ minor.

BEETHOVEN'S FINAL PERIOD

During this period, which began in 1815 and 1816 with the Op. 102 cello sonatas and Op. 101 piano sonata, Beethoven became almost totally deaf, led an eremitic and eccentric existence, and tried to gain custody of his nephew Karl, resulting in strife with the boy's mother and constant struggles between uncle and ward that culminated with Karl's running away and subsequently attempting suicide. Beethoven had increasing difficulty in conceiving, organizing, and shaping his musical ideas, which resulted in a lessened output of work, but among the compositions of this period are some of the most abstract and sublime ever written. Yet these works estranged Beethoven from his audience and alienated most of his colleagues, who could or would not follow him into the empyrean. From this period come his last five piano sonatas, his best bagatelles, his last five string quartets, the "Diabelli" Variations, the *Missa Solemnis,* and the Ninth Symphony.

This period can be called Beethoven's "contrapuntal" period. Fugues occur in the finales of the Op. 101, Op. 102, No. 2, Op. 106 ("Hammerklavier"), and Op. 110 sonatas, and contrapuntal devices characterize the variations of Op. 109 and the first movements of Op. 106 and Op. 111. The first movement of the C♯ minor Quartet (Op. 131) is a fugue, and portions of this fugue and the third of the variations from the slow movement of this quartet resemble the "paired imitation" of Josquin des Prez and his successors. The *Grosse Fuge,* Op. 133, originally intended to be the finale of the Op. 130 quartet, is the apogee of Beethoven's abstract counterpoint. That Handel was his principal mentor is especially apparent in the "Consecration of the House" Overture, Op. 124, and the fugal portions of the *Missa Solemnis.*

Beethoven overwhelmed the limits of Classical form in his sonata movements by blurring the demarcations between sections and theme-groups (the Romantically lyrical first movement of the Op. 101 piano sonata is an excellent illustration) and in creating such gigantic structures as the first movements of the "Hammerklavier" Sonata and Ninth Symphony. Frequent changes of key and tempo characterize many of these movements; in the first movement of the Op. 130 quartet, of average length for this period, there are sixteen tempo changes and six changes of key signature, ranging from six flats to two sharps. These two signatures, represent-

ing the flat submediant and major mediant relationships of the tonic key of
B♭ major, give further evidence of the composer's predilection, already apparent in his second period, for modulations by thirds in his sonata-form
expositions.

The slow movements of Beethoven's instrumental cycles in this period often become the musical centers of gravity, and sometimes (Opp.
109, 111) are final movements. Occasionally these slow movements have
programmatic titles, like "Cavatina" in the Op. 130 quartet or "Song of a
Convalescent's Thanksgiving to God, in the Lydian mode" from the Op.
132 quartet. Theme and variation form, often with a final variation or coda
containing chains of trills which add to the mood of sublimity, is common
in these movements. As early as 1806 Beethoven had become interested in
variations on a ground bass (the C minor variations, WoO 80), and the variations of his last period emphasize as constants the structure and basic harmonic scheme of the theme, with melody, meter, rhythm, pitch-locations,
and other musical elements all as variables.

The variations in the fourth movement of Beethoven's quartet in C♯
minor, Op. 131, excellently illustrate the variation technique of his late period, which has been called by many writers "character variation" since
each variation substantially alters the nature of the theme and assumes a
"character" of its own.

As Example 2–8, the "basic theme" with the main harmonic events
of the variations, shows, the theme is binary, consisting of two eight-mea-
sure phrases which are varied somewhat in their repetition; it is very simple, plastic, and almost neutral in its melodic content and in its harmony,
which does not go beyond secondary dominants or an occasional diatonic

EXAMPLE 2–8. Basic theme and main harmonic events of Beethoven, String Quartet
in C♯ minor, Op. 131, variation section.

supertonic chord. The main harmonic events are the stepped-up harmonic rhythm, involving a chain of secondary dominants, just before the cadence of the first half of the theme, and the emphasis on the subdominant in the second half of the theme. The most unusual feature of the theme is its subtle rhythm as its agogic accents come between the first and second beats of the measure.

Variation one (mm. 32–64) explores the stepwise aspect of the theme, with a countermelody in the first violin and then the cello for the written-out repeat (mm. 41–48); the second half of the variation explores the rhythmic principle but in diminution, and with the stepwise idea inverted. Variation two (mm. 65–98), slightly faster in tempo and 4/4 meter, is a stylized march, more restrained than the martial second movement of the Op. 101 piano sonata; in the first part the theme, with a triadic emphasis, alternates between the first or second violin and the cello. In the second half of the variation Beethoven emphasizes the idea of first a very linear contrary motion and then the unison.

Variation three (mm. 98–129) opens with paired imitation in the style of Josquin (a reminiscence of the canonic episode in the fugue which opens the quartet), with the major seconds of the theme expanded to minor or major thirds in the first half (mm. 98–113) and to a fourth in the prickly second half (mm. 114–29). Variation four (mm. 130–61), cited in Example 2–9a as a specimen of Beethoven's "romantic irony," changes to adagio tempo and 6/8 meter and the theme is almost unrecognizable, but its strongest notes are those of its triads; the second half of the variation, without the aggressive contrary motion of the first half, is more lyrical yet contains some formidable double counterpoint.

The phrase structure and harmonic foundations of the theme have been preserved nearly intact throughout the first four variations. Variation five (mm. 162–86), the only one that contains repeat signs, is a dissolution of the theme to its basic harmonic structure with an ethereal effect provided by double-stop sonorities, and with syncopations obscuring the return to 2/4 meter. Variation six (mm. 187–219), adagio and in 9/4 meter, plays to some extent the role of the adagio penultimate variation in several of Mozart's variation sets: the first part is a prolongation of the basic harmony, with critical notes emphasized by accents and chromatic coloring; but when repeated (mm. 195–202) the sublimity is undermined by mutterings in the cello which soon dominate the second half of the variation (mm. 203–19) in which Beethoven explores the possibilities of the dissonant intervals (augmented fifths, augmented and diminished fourths) which were concealed in the opening theme and its harmony.

Instead of a final concluding variation, there is a transition (mm. 220–30), with trills being first introduced, to a large coda (mm. 231ff) in which Beethoven finally abandons A major for simple but frantic statements of the opening of the theme in C major, A major, F major, and a fragmentary, rhythmically interrupted conclusion in A major with a minor plagal cadence. One is left with the feeling that this coda, despite the difficulty which it caused Beethoven (as shown in his sketches), may be an ironic self-parody. To reinforce this idea, the ensuing presto (a portion of which is cited as Example 2–9b) may well be the greatest piece of comic relief in the history of music.

In these variations, as in all of Beethoven's major late works, one feels that the composer sought to return to exploring the basic principles of music itself. A detail of the theme, whether it be melodic or harmonic, became for him the opportunity to explore all of its ramifications, in a different way from the development of themes in a sonata-form movement, yet with many of the same principles involved, especially those of the theme's fundamental notes and harmonic structures.

The C♯ minor quartet as a whole is one of Beethoven's most highly integrated works, as well as his last large-scale composition. Its seven movements are to be played without pauses except for specifically marked fermatas. Two of the movements are basically transitions: the third is in the style of an operatic recitative, and the sixth is a slow introduction to the finale, as in Mozart's G minor string quintet. The essence of the subject of the opening fugue recurs in the second part of the first theme-group in the finale, as an organic part of the composition and not as a nostalgic "flash-back" as in the Op. 101 and Op. 110 piano sonatas or the Ninth Symphony. As part of the underlying tonal structure, Beethoven explored Neapolitan tonal relations (the ♭II of the key, D major), most strikingly in the C♯ minor-D major keys of the first and second movements, as he had earlier done in the Appassionata Sonata and Op. 59, No. 2 String Quartet.

Of Beethoven's independent piano works of this period, the main set is called the "Diabelli" Variations because the composer-publisher Anton Diabelli (1781–1858) circulated one of his waltzes among a large number of composers, including Schubert, the aged Förster, and the eleven-year-old Liszt, with the request that each write a variation on it. Beethoven complied, and in fact wrote thirty-three variations on the theme; these not only explore all its harmonic, motivic, and musical possibilities but also, as Geiringer has shown, fit into an architectonic scheme in which the number of variations conforms to the structure of the theme; eight groups of four variations each following the theme's eight four-measure phrases, with Variation 33 as an epilogue.[9] In contrast to the grand scope of the "Dia-

---

[9]Karl Geiringer, "The Structure of Beethoven's Diabelli Variations," *Musical Quarterly*, L (1964), 496–503. A five-part structure is postulated in David H. Porter, "The Structure of Beethoven's Diabelli Variations, Op. 120," *Music Review*, XXXI (1970), 295–301, and a compositional history is given in William Kinderman, "The Evolution and Structure of Beethoven's 'Diabelli' Variations," *Journal of the American Musicological Society*, XXXV (1982), 306–28.

belli" Variations are the *Bagatelles* of Op. 126, conceived as an integrated musical whole, and the last four of the *Bagatelles*, Op. 119 (the others of this set having been composed earlier); they are enigmatically terse works which had a strong influence on Schumann and Brahms.

Just as the giant "Hammerklavier" Sonata stretches the capacities of performer and listener to the utmost, so does the Ninth Symphony. All its movements are immense specimens of their type—the first of sonata form, with a massive triple fugue in the development section, the second of the scherzo, and the third of the "double variation." The finale is a setting of Schiller's "Ode to Joy" for soloists, chorus, and orchestra, a project which had been in the back of the composer's mind for over thirty years. Its structure is essentially that of theme and variations, a form unusual in choral music, and a few of its notable moments may be cited; the recapitulation of snatches of themes from earlier movements, each rejected by an instrumental recitative in the cellos and basses; the simplicity of the theme, which led Spohr to reject it as a "Gassenhauer" (alley) tune; the sudden modulation at the end of the fifth variation from A major (dominant of the tonic) to F major (dominant of the new key of B♭), one of the best illustrations of Beethoven's sudden shifting of tonal planes; the military march variation for tenor soloist and male chorus, with the ensuing triple fugue followed by the statement of the theme in its entirety for the last time; the introduction of new material (G major, 3/2) after which this new material is combined with the theme in a simultaneous double fugue; the sublime and almost impossible vocal cadenzas for the soloists; and the breathtaking coda.

Whereas Beethoven in the late sonatas and quartets appears to be writing for a small, intimate, highly educated and musically sophisticated audience, in the Ninth Symphony he seems to be seeking to communicate his ideals (and Schiller's) to as large an audience, and in as colossal and heroic a manner, as possible. On the other hand, the *Missa Solemnis*, which caused Beethoven the greatest difficulty in its creation of all his compositions, is his most problematical work. The Austrian symphonic Mass had already been expanded to its limits, both musical and liturgical, by Haydn, and this medium was not as amendable to enlargement as were the sonata form and the variation cycle. Despite Beethoven's intense personal sincerity in this work and the sublimity of its outer movements (Kyrie and Agnus Dei), it is difficult to avoid considering the *Missa Solemnis* as one of the greatest failures in the history of music. For the work is uneven, even patchy in places, and the overlong conclusions of the Gloria and Credo, influenced by the choral writing of Handel, tend to stupefy rather than edify. The influences not only of Handel (whom Beethoven had come to consider the greatest of his predecessors) and Haydn, but also of Cherubini, Albrechtsberger, and the entire tradition of the heroic orchestral Mass from the middle Baroque onward are brought together in this work, for which

Beethoven had even studied Gregorian chant and sixteenth-century counterpoint. Beethoven's own deep feeling is most clearly evident in the personal prayers which he attached to the Kyrie and Agnus Dei, his setting of the words "et homo factus est" of the Credo in bold relief, and his transformation, in the Agnus Dei, of the fanfares and drumbeats which Haydn had earlier used in his *Mass in Time of War* (1796).

What perplexed Beethoven's contemporaries most and led them to believe that he had either taken leave of his senses or, because of his deafness, had no idea of the sounds he was writing, was actually a typical device of the period, "Romantic irony." Romantic irony in literature has been equated variously with parody, overstatement, exaggeration, misplaced emphasis, or destruction and recreation of the object or mood to indicate mastery of the material. Often in his late work Beethoven creates a sublime mood only to destroy it, as in the fourth variation of the slow movement in the C♯ minor Quartet (Example 2–9a), or in this same quartet to contrive a musical practical joke (Example 2–9b); note the portrayal of musicians who seem to have lost their place in the music, their attempts to restore order, and their finally fiddling away *sul ponticello* (on the strings near the bridge) like an orchestra of infuriated dwarfs. Beethoven's supreme example of Romantic irony is the enigmatic conclusion of his F major Quartet (Op. 135), in which he finally provides an answer for the deep philosophical statement "Must it be? It must be!" with which he opens the final movement.

BEETHOVEN'S LEGACY

No composer of the nineteenth century could wholly escape Beethoven's influence, for his musical activity was so universal that he must be regarded as the trunk of the tree of nineteenth-century music from which so many branches sprang.

Beethoven gave the strongest impetus, at least for music, to the idea that art with a strong ethical content was a substitute for, or at least as noble as, religion. A cluster of attitudes arose from this idea. The world, meaning publishers, music lovers, the middle-class audience, and the nobility (later the state), owed the composer a living. He, in his turn, deliberately aimed at creating the musical masterpiece, chiefly an instrumental cycle with at least one movement in sonata form, since such a work was the noblest, most serious, and most intellectually respectable sort of musical composition. The gestation period for such works was longer, as befits such higher-grade organisms; such works were individual entities to be published as separate opus numbers rather than in sets; and the greatest of these compositions were intended for posterity rather than for the demands

EXAMPLE 2–9. Romantic irony in Beethoven's Quartet in C♯ minor, Op. 131: (a) variation 4 in "fourth" movement; (b) coda of scherzo, "fifth" movement.

of the musical market. Performers, instrumental or vocal, should raise their technical skill or vocal ranges to the composer's demands, and the producer should meet the composer's stipulation for an increased number of performers; this widened the resources on which the future composer could call, but began to open a gulf between the composer, who became a specialist rather than a performer who wrote his own repertoire, and the journeyman musician or singer. The sociological features of nineteenth-century music, to be further discussed in Chapter 12, became apparent in Beethoven's time, and he gave these trends a powerful push, partly through his own forceful personality, which encouraged later composers along the same lines.

In his large instrumental cycles Beethoven displayed two contradictory attitudes: the first, implying tight condensation, fairly strict construction, and even some degree of connection between movements or their constituent sections, best shown in his Fifth Symphony, Op. 95 Quartet, and Op. 101 Piano Sonata, continued through Schumann and Brahms, and culminated in the later symphonies of Sibelius; whereas the second, characterized by an expanded and loose construction, a flexible order and number of movements, some programmatic elements, and even the implication that the symphony or sonata was what one chose to make it (most evident in the Sixth and Ninth Symphonies, "Hammerklavier" Sonata, and Op.131 Quartet), can be found in Schubert, Berlioz, Chopin, Bruckner, and Mahler. Beethoven widened the resources of tonality (macro-harmony), though micro-harmonic innovations (coloristic chords) were the property of his lesser contemporaries; he also strove to elevate counterpoint to the peak of nobility reached by J. S. Bach and Handel.

Beethoven's influence on instrumental music or the large choral work was stifling, or at least terrifying to subsequent generations of composers. Many of his younger contemporaries and successors focused their attention on forms which Beethoven had somewhat neglected, such as the song, song cycle, or small character piece, yet Beethoven had anticipated even these efforts in such works as his song cycle *An die ferne Geliebte*, Op. 98, and the *Bagatelles* of Op. 119 and Op.126.

BIBLIOGRAPHICAL NOTES

The literature about Beethoven is so extensive that only a brief selection of the best studies can be cited, with emphasis on those more recent than the bibliography of the article "Beethoven" in *The New Grove*.

Beethoven's Predecessors. There is an excellent biography of Clementi by Leon Plantinga (London, 1976), with a thematic catalogue of his works by

Alan Tyson (Tutzing, 1967) and a reprint of the first complete edition of his piano music (1803–19) by Da Capo Press (New York, 1973). For Koželuch, Milan Poštolka's biography in Czech (Prague, 1964) has a thematic catalogue and chapter summaries in German, but very little of the music, especially for piano, is available in modern editions. Few studies and even less music are available for Förster, whose late unpublished works I describe in "Klassik und Romantik in E. A. Försters Nachlass," *Musicologia Austriaca*, II (1979), 108–16.

Beethoven: Music. Georg Kinsky and Hans Helm, *Das Werk Beethovens* (Munich, 1955), is the standard thematic catalogue, with copious annotations and bibliographical listings. A new and more complete edition of Beethoven's music, replacing the old *Gesamtausgabe* (Leipzig, 1862–65), is being published by G. Henle Verlag in Munich, with several authoritative performing editions of the music as practical supplements.

Beethoven: Biography. Alexander Wheelock Thayer's *Life of Beethoven*, with excellent and extensive annotations by Elliott Forbes (Princeton, 1964, 2 vols.) is the classic account of Beethoven's life but without discussion of his music. Donald Tovey's unfinished *Beethoven* (London, 1944), though seemingly very disorganized, provides valuable insights into the music itself. Maynard Solomon's *Beethoven* (New York, 1977) includes more recent biographical information and discusses the composer's music also. New information concerning the relationship between Haydn and Beethoven is provided by James Webster's "The Falling-Out Between Haydn and Beethoven" in Lewis Lockwood and Phyllis Benjamin, eds., *Beethoven Essays: Studies in Honor of Elliott Forbes* (Cambridge, Mass., 1984), which also includes studies of some of the composer's works. Emily Anderson's translation of the *Letters of Beethoven* (London, 1961, 3 vols.), O. G. Sonneck's *Beethoven: Impressions of Contemporaries* (1926; reprint, New York, 1967), and Anton Schindler's not always reliable *Beethoven as I Knew Him*, translated and extensively annotated by Donald MacArdle (Chapel Hill, 1966) give excellent portraits of Beethoven the man. Robbins Landon's *Beethoven* (New York, 1970), is a documentary biography with many splendid pictorial illustrations. Martin Cooper's *Beethoven: The Last Decade* (London, 1970), an excellent study of Beethoven's life and music from 1817 until his death, includes a medical history. Transcriptions of the *Conversation Books* (questions and comments written out in notebooks for Beethoven) from 1818 onwards are being published in Leipzig.

Beethoven: Special Studies. Special issues of musicological journals for 1970, Beethoven's bicentennial year, contain detailed studies of individual aspects of Beethoven's life, works, and creative processes; my study of Beethoven and Romantic irony is included in Paul Henry Lang (ed.), *The Creative World of Beethoven* (New York, 1971). Many other essays on various aspects of Beethoven's music are contained in Nigel Fortune and Denis Arnold, *The Beethoven Companion* (London, 1970), Joseph Schmidt-Görg and Hans Schmidt, *Ludwig van Beethoven* (English trans. New York, 1970), and the reports of the international Beethoven congresses of 1970 (Bonn) and 1977 (East Berlin). The series *Beethoven Studies* (1973–   ) and the *Beethoven-Jahrbuch* (1953–   ) contain the most recent specialized studies of his music.

Beethoven: Genres. Among the full-length studies of Beethoven's individual genres are George Grove's *Beethoven and His Nine Symphonies* (1896; reprint, New York, 1962); Donald Tovey's masterly *A Companion to Beethoven's Pianoforte Sonatas* (London, 1951); William S. Newman's *The Sonata in the Classic Era* (3d ed., Chapel Hill, 1983), with particularly pertinent discussions of Clementi's and Beethoven's sonatas; and the various studies of Beethoven's string quartets by Daniel Gregory Mason (New York, 1947), Philip Radcliffe (2d ed., London, 1978), Ivan Mahaim (Paris, 1964, 2 vols., limited to the last quartets), and Joseph Kerman (New York, 1967), the last one controversial but often cited.

Beethoven: Sketches and Style. Several of Beethoven's autographs and sketchbooks have been published in facsimile; the latter, with transcriptions and commentaries, are making Gustav Nottebohm's *Beethoveniana* (Leipzig, 1927, 2 vols.) obsolete. An excellent introduction to the sketches and manuscripts of Beethoven are Alan Tyson's "Sketches and Autographs" and "Steps to Publication—And Beyond" in Arnold and Fortune, *The Beethoven Companion* (London, 1971). A detailed inventory and examination of the surviving Beethoven sketchbooks, with bibliographies of sketch studies of the works presented therein, is contained in Douglas Johnson (ed.), *The Beethoven Sketchbooks* (Berkeley, 1985). Excellent examples of sketch and editorial studies deserving special mention are Lewis Lockwood's "Beethoven's Earliest Sketches for the *Eroica* Symphony," *Musical Quarterly*, LXVII (1981), 457–78, and Bathia Churgin's "A New Edition of Beethoven's Fourth Symphony," *Israel Studies in Musicology*, I (1978), 11–53.

William S. Newman's *Performance Practices in Beethoven's Piano Sonatas* (New York, 1971) has evoked many discussions, especially on how to perform the composer's trills. A model study of a special aspect of Beethoven's style is Wolfram Steinbeck's "Ein wahres Spiel mit musikalischen Formen," *Archiv für Musikwissenschaft*, XXXVIII (1981), on Beethoven's scherzos and similar movements. Newman has traced Beethoven's legacy in "The Beethoven Mystique in Romantic Art, Literature, and Music," *Musical Quarterly*, LXIX (1983).

THREE

BEETHOVEN'S CONTEMPORARIES

The first three decades of the nineteenth century have frequently been called the "Age of Beethoven." This term is somewhat erroneous, for although Beethoven was the greatest composer of this period and virtually all his contemporaries came at some time into his orbit, it must be recalled that a large number of significant composers were active between 1800 and 1830. All of them had their roots deeply sunk into the eighteenth century, and some considered themselves Mozart's legitimate heirs; most of them accepted Beethoven's earlier compositions while rejecting the works of his final period. Yet in a sense the composers to be discussed in this chapter were more progressive than Beethoven and, perhaps because they refused to compete with him and sought different means of musical expression, had a more immediate influence on most of the younger composers who reached musical maturity between 1830 and 1850.

The pivotal internal date for this epoch is 1815, not only because in that year Napoleon was defeated and exiled to St. Helena while the Congress of Vienna completed its work in restoring the various parts of Europe to their legitimate sovereigns (hence the term "Restoration" often used to describe the period 1815–30), but also because around 1815 several musical changes occurred. Beethoven was withdrawing from the fashionable Viennese world into the abstractness of his late period while Hummel was at the height of his fame, Weber and Spohr were attaining full musical maturity, and younger composers like Rossini and Schubert were celebrating their first musical successes.

The Restoration period has been described as one of political reaction, but this conservatism did not extend to music. The creative energies that had been channeled into war (or would have been directed toward politics) now went toward innovations in all of the arts which came to their full flowering after 1830. Not only did such new musical forms as the Lied (German art-song) and the lyrical piano piece arise, but opera in Germany and Italy was rejuvenated through Weber and Rossini, and Dussek and Hummel set new paths for the sonata and concerto. New musical institutions, such as the middle-class (rather than aristocratic) salon, concert-giving organizations (often named "Philharmonic") and amateur choral societies, and music festivals arose to meet the demands for music from an expanded, if not always enlightened, middle-class audience.

JAN LADISLAS DUSSEK (1760–1812)

The change from Classic to Romantic is most strikingly seen in the works of Jan Ladislas Dussek (Dušek, Duschek, Dusík), ten years older than Beethoven and only four years younger than Mozart. An extremely peripatetic composer even by nineteenth-century standards, Dussek's career took him from his native Bohemia to Belgium, Russia, Germany, London, and Paris. He is said to have been a pupil of C. P. E. Bach; whether so or not, one can discern Bach's influence on Dussek's style.

Even in his early sonatas of the late 1780's and early 1790's, Dussek's works show a disintegration of the equilibrium characteristic of the High Classic period. Key-relationships between first and second theme-groups are sometimes quite remote (A♭-E in the Op. 5, No. 3 sonata) or sudden shifts of tonal planes to unexpected areas anticipate Beethoven (the abrupt shifts between theme-groups in the recapitulation in the first movement of Dussek's sonata Op. 35, No. 2). Phrase-dominated writing is the rule, and Dussek's harmonic Romanticism is evident in his frequent borrowings from minor to major, especially chords of the diminished seventh or minor subdominant, often reinforced with non-harmonic tones or chromatically moving inner parts. Within an individual sonata movement, Classic and Romantic melodic and harmonic patterns are often juxtaposed. Heavy and full sonorities, influenced by the English pianos, are quite frequent in Dussek's sonatas before 1800. Quite uncanny resemblances can be seen between Dussek's themes, devices, patternings, and tonal freedoms and Beethoven's slightly later sonatas.

Beginning with his Op. 44 sonata of 1800, Dussek's style became increasingly more Romantic. His sonorous piano writing remains full but is less chordal; it relies heavily on elaborate figurations and a more technically complex kind of writing, yet it retains a "singing" style for the piano. Many of these sonatas have programmatic titles.

Most surprising of all are Dussek's anticipations of a large number of subsequent Romantic composers, some of whom were not even born when Dussek composed these harbingers of their musical style. One can easily single out, for example, the anticipation of Mendelssohn in the second movement of the Op. 10, No. 3 sonata (ca. 1789); of Weber, Hummel, and many others in the "perpetual motion" kind of finales, some of which dangerously skirt the trivial; or even of such far-removed composers as Schumann and Brahms in, respectively, the "maggiore" section of the rondo and the trio of the minuet in the "L'Invocation" sonata of 1812. Rossini, Chopin, Smetana, and Dvořák are other composers whose styles seem to have been anticipated by Dussek. Yet little direct influence by Dussek on these composers can be definitely proven, since his works went out of fashion shortly after his death.

The most famous of Dussek's sonatas in his "Elégie harmonique," Op. 61, in the "Romantic" key of F♯ minor, written as an elegy for his talented pupil Prince Louis Ferdinand of Prussia (1772–1806), an original if undisciplined composer, praised by Beethoven and Spohr, who was killed at the battle of Saalfeld. The dramatic rhetoric of the sonata, the frequent key-changes within movements, and the disintegration of the second theme-group amid harmonic complexities anticipate Chopin and especially Liszt, as shown in Example 3–1.

JOHANN NEPOMUK HUMMEL (1778–1837)

Possibly of Czech ancestry, Hummel at an early age studied with Mozart and even lived in his home, and later he considered himself to be the chief heir of Mozart's tradition. A brilliant piano virtuoso and prolific composer of piano, church, and chamber music, he succeeded Haydn as Prince Esterházy's music director and later held important posts in Stuttgart and Weimar.

EXAMPLE 3–1. Dussek, Sonata in F♯ minor, Op. 61, first movement, opening of second theme-group.[1]

Hummel's early works show harmonic crudities and even direct quotations from Mozart just short of plagiarism (the piano entrance of the first movement of the D minor Piano Concerto and the finale of the "Jupiter" symphony, respectively, in the outer movements of the Op. 20 piano sonata), but his style later became more individual. Most noteworthy are the slow movements of his piano sonatas, with luxuriant fioritura figuration (even with 128th and 256th notes) well suited to the light action of the Viennese piano, as well as explorations of atmospheric devices and interesting sonorities and harmonic colors. Hummel's piano concertos, along with Spohr's violin concertos, were the chief models for the soloist-dominated

[1] Published in *Musica Antiqua Bohemica*, LXIII, 1–20.

nineteenth-century concerto, with frequent use of the minor mode, soulfully lyrical second themes in the first movements, and brilliant pianistic fireworks in the codas.

Hummel's chamber music is represented at its peak by his septets for piano, strings, and winds. The Op. 103 septet is called the "Military" because of its trumpet part. The suavity and elegance of the Op. 74 septet for piano, low strings, and winds, especially in the mysterious scherzo and genial variations, is comparable only to Schubert's "Trout" Quintet. The variations of Hummel's Notturno, Op. 99 (originally for piano duet and subsequently scored for wind ensemble), show that Schubert did not have an exclusive monopoly on Viennese charm and grace.

Hummel's Masses, along with Schubert's, are the last major essays in the Viennese classical style of church music; the E♭ and D major Masses are his best despite their stiff counterpoint, whereas the Mass in B♭ major is waltzlike in the Osanna and full of the tunefully sentimental effects which were to characterize much subsequent church music.

His most significant work, the F♯ minor Sonata, Op. 81 (1819), shows the new problems of the Romantic piano sonata. Though the opening theme clearly defines the key of F♯ minor, its continuation modulates to the dominant of A major and then to the remote key of C major. Hummel either found new paths for tonality as a structural device or severely weakened its role therein; opinions differ as to whether the C major section is a transitional theme, the start of an extensive second theme-group that eventually ends in A major, or a chromatically blurred delaying digression. The themes of the closing group and the codetta stay in A major. After a short development the recapitulation contains a varied treatment of the first theme, the C major theme in the exposition is now in A major, and the second and closing theme-groups are in the expected F♯ major. The other two movements are more conventional: the slow movement is replete with the figuration which so strongly influenced Chopin; and the finale is dualistic, with much transitional material needed to reconcile the "Hungarian" gypsy opening with the "severe" fugal second theme—which shows that J. S. Bach's *Well-Tempered Clavier* was more widely disseminated than welldigested at this time. (Example 3–2.) This sonata had a particularly strong influence on Schumann (especially his own sonata in F♯ minor, Op. 11) and Chopin.

Hummel's music at its best—the Op. 13 and piano duet sonatas; the polonaise for piano "La bella capricciosa," Op. 55; the B minor piano concerto, Op. 89; as well as the other works cited here—is suave, elegant, and gracious rather than profound or proclamatory and is also one of the main reasons why the instrumental, and especially piano, music of the 1830's is not a direct continuation of that of Beethoven or Schubert. If the term "Classic Romanticist" is again permitted in musical discourse, it would fit

EXAMPLE 3–2. Hummel, Sonata in F♯ minor, Op. 81, third movement, opening of (a) first and (b) second theme-group.

Hummel far better than Schubert, the composer to whom this expression has most frequently been applied.

LOUIS (LUDWIG) SPOHR (1784–1859)

Haydn was still composing when Spohr published his first work, and Wagner finished *Tristan und Isolde* in the year of Spohr's death. Though Spohr rejected most of Beethoven's music from the Fifth Symphony onward, he welcomed the early operas of Wagner. Though as a violin virtuoso he wrote most of his compositions for this instrument, wind players are his staunchest champions today, and he is best known now not for his music but for his reminiscences, which give a vivid picture of European musical life during the first three decades of the nineteenth century. Spohr was a universal composer, for he wrote even harp music (for his first wife) and works for piano as well as much chamber music, ten symphonies, choral music (including a Mass), operas, and concertos.

Spohr's chamber music ranges from duos for two violins to elaborately scored works like the Nonet, Op. 31, for strings and winds. Quite typical are the solo quartets, which the composer described as being "for violin, with second violin, viola, and cello"; the first violin parts have twice as many pages as any other part and are really violin concertos with string trio accompaniments. His most interesting chamber works are his double string quartets, Opp. 65, 77, 87, 136, not for string octet but two opposed string quartets, and his chamber music with wind instruments like the Nonet (its slow movement is probably Spohr's finest composition), the Octet, Op. 32, and the Quintet for piano and winds, Op. 52.

Spohr's brilliant violin concertos have passed into virtual oblivion except for the Eighth Concerto in A minor, called "Gesangscene" because it was modeled after the Italian *scena ed aria.* His clarinet concertos, though not particularly grateful for the instrument, are sometimes played.

Spohr's ten symphonies range from 1811 to 1857; some have programmatic titles. The best is the Fourth, *Die Weihe der Töne* (Op. 86, 1832), which includes a romanza-type slow movement in which a lullaby, dance, and serenade are stated by themselves and then combined (with 2/8 or 3/8 meters against an ostinato in 9/16) in the manner of the three dance orchestras in the finale to Act I of Mozart's *Don Giovanni;* a dotted march in the style of Spontini; an "Ambrosian Song of Praise" in counterpoint to a fugato; and an extended chorale prelude in Bach's style. The curious "Historical Symphony" (No. 6, Op. 120) is "in the style and taste of four different periods": that of Bach and Handel (1720), Haydn and Mozart (1780), Beethoven (1810), and the "modern" period of 1840. The first movement is like a Baroque-era French overture; the second utilizes the chromaticism of Mozart's slow movements; the third is more like a fast minuet by Schubert than a "cosmic" Beethoven scherzo; and the finale, opening with a crashing diminished-seventh chord, is less "modern" than the later works of Beethoven or Schubert, and may be a satirical treatment of the "modern" music of the time. The Seventh Symphony, titled "Earthly and Divine in Human Life" (Op. 121, 1841) and scored for two orchestras, anticipates the Liszt of *Les Préludes* in the second movement and the pseudo-religious Wagner of *Lohengrin* in the "Divine" finale. The program of the symphony would have appealed to both Liszt and Wagner, and Spohr's symphonies must be considered important antecedents of the symphonic poem, much as the monothematicism of many of his first movements may have influenced Liszt's "thematic transformation."

Spohr's most important operas are *Faust* (1816), the first major opera based on Goethe's drama, and his masterpiece, *Jessonda* (1823). Spohr was intentionally trying to create the great German opera and selected as his models not only those by his idol Mozart but also the French rescue opera. The grand arias and finales are the most interesting portions, but his operas are not as attractive as Weber's because Spohr lacked dramatic instinct and musical economy; he envied Weber's ability to write tuneful popular operas.

Among Spohr's once-popular oratorios, the most representative are *The Last Judgment* (1826), *Calvary* (1835), and (his best work in this genre) *The Fall of Babylon* (1840). He also wrote a Mass for Ten Voices (1820) in which he tried to combine sixteenth-century contrapuntal techniques with the harmonies of Mozart's *Requiem*. Spohr's oratorios are out of fashion because they contain almost unbearably cloying movements characterized by such effects as over-use of 9/8 meter and slow tempos, a lavish use of chords of the diminished seventh and augmented sixth, cadences consisting of a dominant thirteenth chord (major or minor) resolving on a weak beat to the tonic, and a melodic chromaticism often intensified by doubling the dissonant tones at the third or sixth below. Spohr's chromaticism stems from Mozart's, especially from such of his slow movements as those of the E♭ Quartet, K. 428, and the "Prague" Symphony, K. 504. Such passages as that shown in Example 3–3, with its wandering tonality finally settling into a cadence, influenced Spohr's successors.

Spohr's best works are his wistful, elegiac minor-mode first movements, hailed by many of his contemporaries as quintessentially Romantic and inherited by Mendelssohn; his deft scherzos whose influence was felt as late as Brahms; his expressive slow movements with their chromatic alterations which, on occasion, become cloyingly sentimental; and his light-hearted finales which are able to avoid the trap of trivial thematic material. As Example 6–5b will show, his chromaticism eventually led to Wagner's.

EXAMPLE 3–3. Louis Spohr, *The Last Judgment*.

Example 3–3. (Continued)

Spohr's concertos had a strong influence on those of Mendelssohn and Chopin, and echoes of his violin concertos, chamber music, and choral works can be heard throughout the nineteenth century.

CARL MARIA VON WEBER (1786–1826)

Weber has been hailed as the first genuinely "Romantic" composer, the first "modern" composer, and the first orchestrator. Although he was chiefly a composer of piano music and operas, he also wrote two symphonies, a few Masses and other choral works, songs, chamber music, and display pieces for clarinet and other wind instruments; he even began an autobiographical novel.

Weber's piano music is written in an extremely personal and individual style. With his large hands and long thumbs he could easily play the full chords spanning a tenth and the wide leaps in a rapid tempo which make his music so difficult for most pianists. A striking characteristic of his style is his poetically coloristic piano writing, almost as if "orchestrated"— not just a virtually orchestral range of sonority, as in Clementi and Beethoven, but an actual imitation of orchestral sounds, like the timpani strokes in the second movement of the Op. 24 piano sonata, the timpani rolls and horn-like arpeggios opening the Op. 39 sonata, or the string tremolos in the solo piano part of the Op. 32 concerto. Weber is the first composer whose piano works have been successfully transcribed for orchestra, as witness Berlioz's and Weingartner's transcriptions of *Invitation to the Dance* or Hindemith's *Symphonic Metamorphoses*, three movements of which are based on Weber's four-hand piano pieces. Other Weberian traits are a facile homophonic writing and a brilliance deriving from Mozart's sonata-rondo finales.

Weber's sonatas clearly show the weaknesses of early Romantic extended instrumental forms. To the person accustomed to Beethoven's sonatas, Weber's first movements have magnificent openings, but the lyrical themes are not suitable for development, the transitions sag, the second themes are not as strong as the first themes, and the developments are filled with sequences and passage-work, often over diminished-seventh chords. The slow movements and scherzos are fine, but the finales, although containing breathtaking virtuoso passages, lack the quality of "summing up" the instrumental cycle. The sonatas and other works reflect what might be called a "narrative" approach to musical form, most apparent where actual programs were conceived by the composer, as in the Fourth Sonata in E Minor or the Konzertstück in F minor for piano and orchestra.

As a composer of four-hand duets for one piano, Weber deserves to rank with Mozart and Schubert, especially in the pieces of Op. 60. His variations are chiefly ornamental; the most interesting individual ones are those in "national" styles—mazurkas, Spanish dances, and especially polaccas, which are among his favorite vehicles for virtuosity.

The concertos, chiefly for piano or clarinet, have strong links with the eighteenth century through their quasi-martial openings. Noteworthy are the abbreviated concertos, especially the Konzertstück in F minor for piano, with its exuberantly joyous finale, and the Concertino for clarinet and orchestra. The two symphonies, both in C major and both dating from 1807, are remarkably surprising and fresh works, apparently modeled on Mozart's "Paris" Symphony, K. 297, and Beethoven's First Symphony; Weber's First, with its cyclic use of the raised fourth degree of the major scale, anticipates the "Turkish" elements of *Abu Hassan* and *Oberon*.

Weber's four best operas are his masterpieces. *Abu Hassan* (1812), with only three characters and one act, is a delightful Turkish *Singspiel*, a worthy successor to works on similar topics by Gluck, Grétry, and Mozart. The other three operas share certain characteristics: the supernatural "marvelous" element is important, and all incorporate "grand arias" for the protagonists with contrasting romances for the lesser characters, a legacy of the rescue opera. *Der Freischütz* (1821) and *Oberon* (1826) contain much nature-painting, with the real hero of the former the German forest in its benign (the huntsmen's chorus in Act III) or malignant aspects (the "Wolf's Glen" in the finale of Act II). *Euryanthe* (1823), a chivalric drama with an impossibly absurd libretto, is less successful than Weber's other operas, probably because in it he was striving to write the "great German opera." *Euryanthe* is considered "connected" and "through-composed" because the numbers are linked by accompanied recitatives and ariosos rather than by *secco* recitative or spoken dialogue, but set-numbers are easily distinguishable. Weber made some use of recurrent "reminiscence motives" associated with characters (especially the villainess Eglantine) or states of mind, a technique to be developed more fully by Wagner in his leitmotives.

Weber's operatic overtures are sonata-form movements skillfully constructed from the opera's main themes. The overture to *Oberon* is a good illustration: the introduction contains Oberon's horn call, the ritornello from the fairies' chorus in Act I, and the march for Charlemagne's court in Act III; the first theme-group is the conclusion of the Act II quartet; the second theme-group contains the middle section of Hüon's aria in Act I; and the closing theme, also developed in the coda, is the conclusion of Rezia's grand aria "Ocean, Thou Mighty Monster." Weber's technique of creating operatic overtures later degenerated into the thematic potpourris that were to become commonplace as preludes to operettas and musical comedies.

Weber's musical style contains elements common to both his vocal and instrumental music. His melody is highly individual, with much of its sweetness coming from an assimilation, rather than direct quotation, of the style of German folk and popular music. His themes are conceived in terms of regular phrases, whereas the bravura vocal themes seem instrumental. His use of non-harmonic tones on the beat produces a romantically yearning quality and in rapid tempos gives an effect of brilliance, yet the harmonic background is diatonic in contrast to Spohr's modulatory-chromatic atmosphere. Weber's rhythm is very elastic, with much reliance on the ambiguity of hemiola, as when in 6/8 meter he produces the effect of 3/4. His love for dotted rhythms gives a martial tone to the first movements of his concertos and to his cantata *Kampf und Sieg*, written to celebrate Napoleon's overthrow, and provides a chivalric tone to his characterization of his knightly heroes (Example 3–4). Weber tends to overuse diminished-seventh chords in creating a daemonic atmosphere, as in *Der Freischütz* or the storm in *Oberon*. The chord of the major ninth as a dominant harmony is a hallmark of his style.

It was as an orchestrator that Weber's influence was most pronounced. His orchestra is that of Beethoven, with the trombones as permanent members rather than occasional visitors, but he differs from his contemporaries by making imaginative and atmospheric use of the winds as solo instruments or choirs, especially the clarinet and French horn. The celebrated finale of Act II of *Der Freischütz* has been called an "arsenal of Romanticism" with its string tremolos, mysterious and spectral harmonies in the trombones or low woodwind instruments, and the special effects that accompany the casting of the magic bullets. Weber's unique keyboard style had some influence on Chopin and Mendelssohn, and his last three operas, especially their orchestral colors, had a strong effect on Berlioz and Wagner; the popularity of his music in France influenced the *opéra lyrique* of Gounod and Thomas. Weber's best works are his finest operas, the inner movements of his sonatas, and the four-hand pieces of Op. 60; and the clarinetist is grateful to Weber for having written some of the finest staples of his repertoire.

EXAMPLE 3–4. Weber, Adolar's aria, Act I of *Euryanthe*.

FRANZ SCHUBERT (1797–1828)

Schubert was the youngest, most prolific, and musically most important of the composers discussed in this chapter, although he was initially the least appreciated by most of his contemporaries, probably because he was not able to appear in the salons or before the public as a virtuoso performer. His personal shyness, especially in getting his larger works performed, and his arduous attempts to earn a living through his compositions, contributed to his precarious existence. An astonishingly prolific composer, his musical fecundity can be shown by one striking illustration: during the year 1816 he wrote 179 compositions, ranging from dances for piano and songs to two symphonies, an opera, and the Mass in C major. Within each of the genres of his works, e.g., song, sonata, etc., one finds compositions ranging from triviality to inspired genius. Though he wrote for every available medium, he was least successful in composing operas or works for solo instrument and orchestra, further evidence of his distance from the prevalent virtuoso temperament.

Schubert's *oeuvre* may be divided into three chronological periods. The first extends from 1811 to 1819, the year of the "Trout" Quintet for piano and strings and the A major Piano Sonata, D. 664.[2] The second period ranges from 1820 to 1827 and includes such tantalizingly incomplete works as the Quartetsatz in C minor (D. 703), the "Unfinished" Symphony, and the C major Piano Sonata (D. 840), as well as his three great string quartets. The two piano trios and the song-cycle *Die Winterreise* are transitions to his third and final period, which embraced scarcely more than a year but contained his greatest compositions. It is most convenient to consider Schubert's works by genres rather than by periods, since his songs developed along a path different from his instrumental music and his dance music resists attempts at chronological ordering.

Piano Music. Schubert composed at least twenty-three piano sonatas, some incomplete. Isolated early piano pieces may be sonata movements. The Sonata, D. 617, for piano duet and the Grand Duo in C, D. 812, which has been orchestrated in the mistaken belief that it was the sketch of a "lost" symphony, complete the list.

The sonatas display a considerable variety. Those from the A minor (D. 845, Op. 42) onward generally have four movements. They vary in total length from the exquisitely concise A major (D. 664, Op. 120) to the expansive last Sonata in B♭ (D. 960). Although a few begin with attention-getting

---

[2]Schubert's works are known by their numbering in *Franz Schubert: Thematisches Verzeichniss* (Kassel, 1978), a revision of O.E. Deutsch's *Schubert: Thematic Catalogue* (New York, 1951), rather than by their opus numbers, which are chronologically inaccurate owing to the amount of music published with opus numbers after the composer's death.

boldness, most open with the quiet statement of a lyrical theme, often in question-and-answer form. The titles of the third movements oscillate between "menuetto" and "scherzo"; their trios contain some of Schubert's loveliest music. The slow movements are song-like, sometimes a theme and variations; characteristic of those in three-part, rondo, or modified sonata form is a more active and interesting accompaniment at the reprise of the opening theme. The finales, the weakest movements, tend to sprawl and are generally inferior to the closing movements of the composer's best symphonies or chamber music. The sonatas lack the technical difficulties of those by Beethoven, Weber, or Hummel yet are scorned by many pianists, probably because of their general lack of brilliance and some passages which sound even more orchestral than Weber's piano music, e.g., the second theme-group of the A minor Sonata, D. 784, especially in the recapitulation.

Schubert's short character pieces derive not from the epigrammatic bagatelles of Beethoven, but from the eclogues, dithyrambs, rhapsodies, and impromptus by two Czech composers residing in Vienna, Jan Vaclav Tomašek (Tomaschek, 1774–1850) and Jan Hugo Vořišek (Worzischek, 1791–1825). The forms of these pieces are generally ternary or rondo with coda. The best known of Schubert's essays in the smaller forms are the *Moments musicaux*, D. 780 (ca. 1823), and two groups of Impromptus; the finest are the *Drei Klavierstücke*, D. 946, of 1828.

Schubert also wrote copious quantities of dance music—waltzes, Ländler, ecossaises, and "German dances," chiefly in waltz tempo. The waltzes are not individual compositions but chains of dances like those of his contemporary Josef Lanner (1801–43) or the later waltzes of the Johann Strausses (Sr., 1804–49; Jr., 1825–99), with each individual waltz containing six or more separate dances. The most interesting of the dance pieces are the polonaises and marches for piano duet. The spirit of Viennese popular music permeates not only the marches and dances but many of Schubert's larger works, for example the zither effect of the scherzo of the D major Sonata (D. 850, Op. 53) or the trio of the scherzo of the A major Sonata (D. 959).

Among Schubert's miscellaneous piano works are several sets of variations, for which he preferred a theme opening with a dactylic rhythm; short pieces which may be sonata movements; a magnificent Allegro in A minor for piano duet (D. 947); some rondos for piano duet which are allegretto, lyrical, and contemplative as opposed to the fast, flashy, and brilliant virtuoso rondos of his contemporaries; and a few divertimentos, all of considerable length, of which the most enjoyable is the *Divertissement à l'hongroise*, D. 818, one of the many souvenirs of Schubert's visits to Zselis as music master to the Esterházy family. The greatest of these miscellaneous compositions is the four-hand Fantaisie in F minor, D. 940 (1828), in which Schubert seemed to be aiming toward a one-movement instrumental cycle midway between Mozart's fantasies for mechanical organ (K. 594, 608) and a one-movement sonata. The work contains delightful and effective illustrations of the composer's love for contrasting minor and major forms of his themes (Example 3–5).

Orchestral Music. Of Schubert's nine symphonies, the first six are early works, the Seventh is but a sketch (although at least three attempts have been made to complete it), the Eighth is unfinished, and the Ninth (erroneously called the Seventh by some) was rejected by most orchestras during the nineteenth century. The early symphonies were written for the ensemble of the Imperial and Royal Stadt-Konvikt, of which Schubert was concertmaster during his student days; they call for an orchestra like that of late Haydn or early Beethoven but with solo flute and solo oboe assigned a more prominent role. It would seem that Schubert did not dare to compete with any of Beethoven's orchestral works written after *Prometheus*. Schubert's C minor Symphony (No. 4, D. 417) emulates the Beethoven of the C minor Quartet (Op. 18, No. 4) rather than the C minor sonatas or symphony; it has an unusually bumptious scherzo and some wonderful-major-minor contrasts in the finale. The Second Symphony (B♭, D. 125) is only superficially Classic, for the extensive use of winds with high tessituras in their parts, the frequent borrowed harmonies from minor, the minuet-type movement in minor (like that of the Fifth Symphony, D. 485, also in B♭ major), and the unusual yet logical tonal relationships in the sonata-form movements are all Romantic traits. The Fifth Symphony, written for the orchestra directed by Otto Hatwig in which Schubert played viola and which performed several of his other symphonies, has the light instrumentation of early Haydn or Mozart and in many ways is closely modelled on Mozart's G minor Symphony, K. 550; it is the most popular of these early symphonies. The Sixth Symphony, D. 589, seems strongly influenced by Rossini's overtures.

With the Eighth Symphony (D. 759) of 1822, Schubert began a new style of symphonic composition. The formal structure of the two completed movements show Schubert at his most adventurous, for in the first movement the introductory material dominates both the recapitulation and the coda (the recapitulation begins directly with the oboe-clarinet theme) and the idea of the second theme appears in the closing group. The unusual development section in the second movement has confused more than one analyst, and its second theme contains one of Schubert's most magical contrasts between minor and major (C♯ minor–D♭ major). Schubert did begin to sketch a scherzo, and even orchestrated the first two pages, but abandoned the movement in the middle of the trio. Various hypotheses have been advanced for Schubert's failure to complete the symphony; it is most logical to assume that compositional problems, rather than any incident in Schu-

EXAMPLE 3–5. Schubert, Fantaisie in F minor, D. 940: (a) opening theme; (b) opening theme stated in major mode; (c) closing theme of first section; (d) fugal treatment (see bass line) of (c) in minor.

(a)   Allegro molto moderato

Example 3–5. (Continued)

Example 3–5. (Continued)

(d)

bert's life, compelled him to cease work on this symphony and proceed to compositions for other media. In 1825 (not 1828, as stated in pre-1978 accounts) Schubert began his most ambitious and largest orchestral work, the so-called "Great C Major" symphony (D.944) which he may have completed as early as 1826; its "heavenly length" (Schumann's term), its imaginative writing for brass instruments, its insistent dotted rhythms, and its driving finale influenced Schubert's logical successor, Anton Bruckner.

Almost all the overtures, especially those "in the Italian style," show the influence of Rossini's domination of Viennese musical life during the 1820's. The so-called *Rosamunde* Overture was actually written for a drama called *Die Zauberharfe;* in this overture Schubert seems intoxicated by his first chance to write for an orchestra of professionals and in the tutti passages tends to overwhelm the listener with sheer volume of sound. The incidental music, D. 797 (1823) to the drama *Rosamunde, Princess of Cyprus* is an example of the series of misfortunes that adversely affected Schubert throughout his career: the play was so bad that it was withdrawn after its second performance. The music itself was highly praised; small wonder, for it is the finest dramatic incidental music between Beethoven's *Egmont* and Mendelssohn's *A Midsummer Night's Dream,* and it has been conjectured that the entr'acte to Act II is the "missing" finale to the "Unfinished" symphony, largely because of the common key of B minor and the similar instrumentation, Schubert later used the last entr'acte for the slow movement of his A minor quartet (D. 804, Op. 29) and as one of his most popular impromptus for piano (D. 935 #3).

Chamber Music. From his early youth Schubert was an avid violist in the family string quartet.[3] Thirty-six chamber works (excluding duet sonatas), some only fragmentary, can be counted; of these, the last three

---

[3]The number of composers of magnificent chamber music who were also violists is amazing; besides Schubert, one need only mention Mozart, Beethoven, Dvořák, Hindemith, and Quincy Porter.

string quartets, the String Quintet with two cellos, the "Trout" Quintet, the piano trios, and the Octet are outstanding.

The chamber music with piano is represented chiefly by the two trios (D. 898, Op. 99, and D. 929, Op. 100) and the "Trout" Quintet, D. 667, so called because the fourth of its five movements is a set of variations on Schubert's own song "Die Forelle." Noteworthy is Schubert's use of the singing tone of the piano, often in the high register, to the accompaniment of the strings. The Octet (D. 803) for clarinet, bassoon, horn, and strings, with its six movements a late example of the Classic-era divertimento, is among Schubert's most delightfully expansive works. Both the first and last movements have slow introductions, that of the finale quite ominous in contrast to the lighthearted main body of the movement; the slow movements include variations as well as one of Schubert's finest and most lyrical song-like forms.

Of the string quartets, the ones in A minor (D. 804, Op. 29) and D minor (D. 810) are the most popular; the G major (D. 887) is seldom performed because of its length and its fatiguing effect on performers. The A minor Quartet is noteworthy because of its major-minor contrasts in the first movement and its somber third movement with a contrasting trio in major; the D minor for its daemonic energy, unusual for Schubert, in the outer movements and its slow movement, variations on his song "Death and the Maiden." The most sublime of the instrumental works is the Quintet in C major (D. 956) for string quartet with an additional cello, which provides a warmer sonority than does the second viola of the customary string quintet. In the first movement the opening theme contains some of Schubert's finest harmonic coloring (see Example 10–7a; the second theme-group, opening in E♭ major rather than the expected G major, is one of his loveliest ideas; the closing group, a quietly mysterious Hungarian march, seems to be in B major at first but then suddenly shifts to the proper key of G major, the key of the codetta which contains a reminiscence of the second theme. Unusual features in this quintet include the somber trio of the lighthearted scherzo and the strange cadence, including the lowered second degree, in the Hungarian-style finale.

Vocal Music. During his lifetime Schubert was principally known as a composer of vocal music. He was unsuccessful in opera but wrote much fine choral music, and he can be regarded as the establisher of one of the few new musical forms of the nineteenth century, the Lied or art-song.

Most of Schubert's larger choral works stem from his attempt to secure a position as a church composer that would provide him with both support and time for composing. His first four Latin Masses are early works and strongly influenced by Michael Haydn (1737–1806), but his A♭ (D. 678, 1822) and E♭ (D. 950, 1828) Masses are the last significant examples of the large-scale Viennese Classic Mass. The garbled texts of several portions of these Masses are most probably due to Schubert's careless attempts to write down the text from memory rather than from any unorthodox beliefs. Schubert also wrote two major oratorios (*Miriam's Song of Triumph*, D. 942, and the incomplete *Lazarus*, D. 689) and delightful secular part-songs, many for male voices; their warm sonority contains some of Schubert's boldest harmonic experiments.

Schubert's Lieder must be understood in terms of the limitations of their predecessors. During the eighteenth century the atmosphere for solo song was restrictive: despite the efflorescence of German lyric poetry, the poets desired their works to be independent artistic productions, not merely librettos for song, and the composer was subject to the dictum "Sing your songs while composing them without using an instrument or adding a bass," which deprived the composer of the two areas in which he could operate most freely and independently: interesting accompaniment and refined harmonic expression. Poets preferred a simple strophic song that would support their verses; Schiller denounced the "constant strumming on the piano" as song accompaniment; and many songs were printed on only two staves, with the upper one being the voice part, an indication that the pianist was to sing the melody while playing.

Music assumed a more important role in the songs of the later eighteenth century. Reichardt's songs are generally strophic, often hymn-like, with sometimes elaborate melodies with wide ranges and accompaniments generally limited to doubling the voice part or to broken arpeggiated chords in the right hand. Zelter's songs were more esteemed by poets than musicians and their influence on Schubert's songs was minimal. More important influences were the songs and ballads of Johann Rudolf Zumsteeg (1760–1802), Schiller's classmate; several of his ballads resemble the operatic scena with its ritornelli, accompanied recitatives, independent piano preludes and postludes, arias in differing tempos, and even passages in the style of melodrama with the text declaimed over the music. Less well known influences on Schubert's songs are the works of the Viennese song composers, especially Nikolaus Freiherr von Krufft (1779-1818), whose songs contain quasi-folk song melodies, independent piano accompaniments, and ventures toward the through-composed song. Operas, whether Mozart's *Magic Flute* and other *Singspiele* or the French "rescue operas" then popular in Vienna, may have been an unconscious influence on Schubert's song writing.

Schubert's songs span his entire creative career, from 1811 to 1828, and number more than six hundred, some of them different settings of the same poem. His choice of poets was quite catholic, including not only Goethe and Schiller but also lesser eighteenth-century figures like Klopstock, Hölty, and Matthisson; Romantic poets like the Schlegel brothers and the early Heine and Rückert; his versifying friends like Schober and

Mayrhofer; and German translators of Shakespeare and Sir Walter Scott. Hölderlin and Eichendorff are the only significant German poets of the time whose words Schubert did not set to music.

Schubert's songs display a great variety but can be fitted into certain broad classifications. The strophic songs, with the same melody for each verse, include many of the fine songs in the cycle *Die schöne Müllerin;* they often have delightful piano preludes or postludes. Common are modified strophic songs, in which Schubert's work changes in melody, accompaniment, or harmony (such as shifting from major to minor or the reverse), in order to have the music follow more closely the mood established by the text. Songs in the character of the operatic scena are usually early works and influenced by Zumsteeg; they tend to be lengthy and sectional, with extraneous material (like the sixty-measure piano interlude in "Der Taucher," D. 111) and, as in Zumsteeg's comparable works, sometimes an "interlocking" tonality with an ending in a key other than the original tonic. Condensations of the scena type led to Schubert's through-composed songs, sometimes in ballad style like "Der Erlkönig" (D. 328) and generally unified through recurring themes, tonal schemas, or accompaniment patterns. One need only compare Schubert's "Der Erlkönig" with the near-contemporaneous setting of this poem in 1818 by Carl Loewe (1796–1869), Schubert's leading north German counterpart as a songwriter, to see the difference between inspired genius and highly capable talent. Only in the setting of humorous texts, such as the amusing Goethe ballads "Hochzeitslied" and "Der Zauberlehrling" (the "Sorcerer's Apprentice" poem that was to inspire Paul Dukas) did Loewe surpass Schubert.

In many of the strophic songs a frequent device is the placing of the melody exclusively in the vocal part with the accompaniment merely sustaining the harmony and creating rhythmic motion, as in Reichardt's or Krufft's songs; but Schubert's melody demands an accompaniment that will bring out its latent harmony. More frequent are songs in which the accompaniment holds the song together; who can forget the repeated triplets of "Der Erlkönig" or the varied patterns of "Ganymed" (D. 544)? The piano preludes and postludes, as well as many accompaniments, contain much descriptive tone-painting. The songs containing an alternation of declamation and arioso, with recurring themes or tonalities unifying the work, are less frequent but include some of his greatest compositions, ranging chronologically from "Gruppe aus dem Tartarus" (D. 583, 1817) to the Heine songs in the so-called *Schwanengesang* (D. 957). In "Memmon" (D. 541) the melodic line contains wide leaps, and in "Der Doppelgänger" (D. 957, No. 13) the declamation, reinforced by a dramatic chaconne-like accompaniment, borders on expressionism; such songs are among the ancestors of the vocal styles of Wagner, Hugo Wolf, and even Schoenberg and Webern.

Among Schubert's favorite song types are the hymn-like, often on a topic dealing with Greek antiquity ("Lied eines Schiffers an die Dio-skuren," D. 360) or the elegiac (the settings from Goethe's *Wilhelm Meister*). Some of the most popular are those dealing with nature, especially water or night, and those which approach (and have virtually become) folk songs, like "Der Lindenbaum" from *Die Winterreise*, D. 911. Space does not permit even a list of the great Schubert songs, for over a hundred can be considered such.

According to the reminiscences of his friends, after Schubert found a poem he thought suitable for setting he would read it aloud, derive his musical inspiration from this reading, and then write down the song, after which he would revise his setting. Schubert did not add expression marks to the voice parts of his songs, since he felt that the text was direction enough. Leopold von Sonnleithner, one of his contemporaries, described how Schubert wanted his songs performed:

> [More than a hundred times] I heard him accompany and rehearse his songs. Above all, he always kept the most strict and even time, except in the few cases where he had expressly indicated in writing a ritardando, morendo, accelerando, etc. Furthermore, he never allowed violent expression in performance. The Lieder singer, as a rule, only relates experiences and feelings of others; he does not himself impersonate the characters whose feelings he describes. . . . With Schubert especially, the true expression, the deepest feeling is already inherent in the melody as such, and is admirably enhanced by the accompaniment. Everything that hinders the flow of the melody and disturbs the evenly flowing accompaniment is, therefore, exactly contrary to the composer's intention and destroys the musical effect.[4]

Musical Style. Schubert's most beloved melodies are generally found in his strophic or folklike songs, the second themes of his sonata-form movements, his slow movements, and the trios of his scherzos. His rhythmic innovations are few but interesting; noteworthy among them are the displaced accents in the scherzo of his C minor Symphony; the hemiolas in the scherzo of his D major Sonata (Op. 53, D. 850) in which the macro-rhythm consists of four measures of 3/2 followed by six measures of 3/4; or the cross-rhythms in the Allegro in A minor (D. 947).

Two striking aspects of Schubert's harmony may be considered: color harmony and modulation. By the former is implied the non-functional use of such sonorities as diminished-seventh and augmented-sixth chords, for atmospheric and coloristic reasons rather than for modulation. Such color harmony may be a rhetorically amplifying device, as in the opening of the C major String Quintet, or one for establishing a mood in the piano

[4]Cited in O. E. Deutsch (ed.), *Schubert: Memoirs by His Friends* (London, 1958), p. 116.

prelude of a song, as in "Am Meer" (D. 957, No. 12). Schubert's most notable modulations are generally abrupt, often sudden shifts to a mediant or submediant. Example 3–6 is one of his most magical modulations; although it seems like an extreme shift (C♯ minor to C major), it can be best explained enharmonically as a shift from the dominant to its mediant (G♯ major to B♯ major). Another surprising effect is an abrupt change to a different tonality in the course of a leisurely transition to what one would expect to be the dominant, as in the *Grand Rondeau* in A major, D. 951. In the course of a minor theme Schubert often ventures into the flat supertonic (Neapolitan), as in Example 3–5a.

EXAMPLE 3–6. Schubert, Sonata in B♭ major, D. 960, second movement.

Schubert's expanding the tonal content of his sonata-form movements has been unfairly criticized as "discursiveness." The enlarged tonal spectrum takes place not in the transitions, as with Hummel, but in the theme-groups themselves. The first theme-group of the first movement of the D major sonata, D. 850 (Op. 53), passes through a number of third-related keys, as shown in Example 3–7, before returning to the home tonic at the start of the transition.

Second theme-groups frequently begin not in the dominant where one would expect but often in a flat mediant or submediant key in major-mode works, such as the ♭VI of the C major string quintet, or even the flat submediant minor (F♯ minor) in the last B♭ major sonata, D. 960, thus giving rise to the expression "three-key exposition" to describe many of the ma-

EXAMPLE 3–7. Tonal plan of Schubert, Piano Sonata in D Major, D. 850 (Op. 53), first theme-group, first movement. Based, with my additions, on Hellmut Federhofer, "Terzverwandte Akkorde und ihre Funktion in der Harmonik Franz Schuberts," in Otto Brusatti (ed.), *Schubert-Kongress Wien 1978*, p. 65.

ture expositions. Such a descriptive term is accurate only if we remember that Schubert often returns to the expected dominant of the original key, even in some minor-mode works such as the outer movements of the "Death and the Maiden" quartet, D. 810, wherein the first themes open in D minor, the second theme-groups open in F major, and the closing groups end in A minor. Schubert's recapitulations are often tonally less predictable than Beethoven's, and his codas sometimes include some of his most daring harmony. Even the tonal plans of some sonata-form movements can be highly surprising, as in the "abridged sonata form" (sonata form without development) of the second movement of the "Trout" quintet, D. 667:

	FIRST THEME	SECOND THEME	CLOSING THEME
Exposition	F major	F$\sharp$ minor G as leading tone to A$\flat$ major	D major–G major
Recapitulation	A$\flat$ major	A minor	F major

    The oft-told story of Schubert's starting to take lessons in counterpoint from Simon Sechter (1788–1867), the theorist later to be Bruckner's teacher, has created the legend that Schubert was not skilled in counterpoint, but his fugal writing is not easy to find fault with, and few composers could find more appropriate countermelodies for songlike themes. Schubert's formal weaknesses can be traced chiefly to his luxuriant melodic inventiveness and his leisurely attitude toward unfolding his musical ideas, but even his lengthiest transitions are far above the level of padding, and when he wanted to be concise, as in "Gruppe aus dem Tartarus" or the A major Sonata, D. 664, he was admirably successful. The legend that Schubert was a spontaneous composer who neither sketched nor revised is false, for his drafts for the B minor Symphony and Fantaisie in F minor show that he was as rigorous a self-critic as Beethoven or Brahms, and such a spontaneous-sounding song as "Der Erlkönig," supposedly composed as fast as the young Schubert could write it down, went through four revisions

within a six-year period before he felt it ready for publication. Like all prolific composers, Schubert's work was uneven, but his best works are masterpieces and his weakest compositions possess touches of charm. Perhaps
it is a belated testimony to his genius that his impact on the history of music was not fully felt until thirty years or more after his premature death,
and that today he is one of the most difficult composers to categorize, for
he has been called a Classicist, a post-Classic composer, a Romantic, a Romantic Classicist, or a mixture of all of these.

LESSER COMPOSERS, MOSTLY PIANISTS

Space permits discussion of only a few of the numerous other composers active during the first three decades of the nineteenth century.

John Field (1782–1837), Irish by birth and a pupil of Clementi, lived
in Russia during most of his career, and strongly influenced not only
Chopin but the entire course of Russian piano music from Glinka to Kaba-
levsky. Although he also wrote sonatas, concertos, and chamber music for
piano and strings, he is best known for his nocturnes and was the first to
use the term for piano music. Typical of Field's nocturnes are arpeggiated
left-hand accompaniments given sonority through the sustaining pedal,
over which the right hand plays, often in the high register, a dreamily singing melody elaborated with fioritura and occasional harmonic clashes with
the left hand (Example 3–8); these devices had a strong influence on

EXAMPLE 3–8. Field, Nocturne in C minor.

Chopin. A less frequently encountered kind of nocturne, often originally for another medium (usually piano and strings), consists of a suavely elegant melody with a simple accompaniment. One might say of Field's urbane and lyrical piano concertos (as of many of his time) that the orchestral tuttis in the first movements are quite Classic whereas the piano solo portions are Romantic. The slow and final movements of these concertos often correspond, respectively, with the two kinds of nocturnes just described. Field's polished piano concertos, despite the lack of bravura fireworks, deserve to be ranked at least with those by Hummel.

Paris was the locale of a number of transplanted virtuosos who developed techniques of performance and composition to astound the new middle-class audience whose musical background and taste were limited. The most noteworthy were Friedrich Kalkbrenner (1785–1849), Henri Herz (1803–88), Franz Hünten (1793–1878), and the best of this group, Sigismond Thalberg (1812–71). The salon pieces of the American Louis Moreau Gottschalk (1829–69) stem from this tradition. The most respected of these virtuosos was the violinist Nicolo Paganini (1782–1840), whose satanic appearance and brilliant concertos and caprices captured the imaginations of Berlioz, Schumann, and Liszt, although Spohr detested his rival. Virtuosity, display, and showmanship are the primary constituents of this music, with the typical vehicles paraphrases and reminiscences of popular operas, or variations, decorating the melody with silvery arabesques or blazing fireworks, on popular tunes or operatic airs. Though the musical value of these works is often deprecated or scorned, Thalberg's larger works are respectable and Paganini's caprices often show piquant and imaginative touches, especially the A minor Caprice which inspired variations by such later composers as Brahms and Rakhmaninov. At least a cursory examination of the virtuoso literature of this time is necessary in order to understand the reaction against it by Schumann, Mendelssohn, and Chopin, or the desire of Alkan and Liszt to surpass it. Above all, these composers conquered most of the problems of piano technique, raised the general level of piano playing, and gave the modern piano and its performers a primary place in the public imagination that was to endure for over a century.

Another group of pianists, who operated within the virtuoso tradition but wrote more substantial music, was of Germanic origin; they were associates of Beethoven and transmitted his musical ideas and works, especially to England. These pianist-composers are best known today for their piano etudes, which incorporated the techniques needed to perform Beethoven's music into the fingers of subsequent generations of pianists; their other piano music is a little-explored link between Beethoven's pianistic style and that of Mendelssohn and Schumann. The most important of these composers were Ferdinand Ries (1784–1838); Carl Czerny (1791–1857), one of Beethoven's few pupils, who in turn gave piano lessons to Beethoven's nephew Karl and also to Liszt; and Johann Baptist Cramer (1771–1858), whose piano etudes, with Beethoven's annotations, Czerny used in teaching Karl. Mention should also be made of a non-pianist composer, Franz Danzi (1763–1826), whose wife Margarethe (1768–1800) was also a composer; his suavely elegant chamber music and concertos, many for wind instruments, are a link between the Classicism of Mozart and the Romanticism of Weber, with whom he was briefly associated.

The most imaginative and musically influential composer of this group was Ignaz Moscheles (1794–1870), whose biography (by his wife) is second only to Spohr's and Berlioz' *Memoirs* as a vivid firsthand account of musical life in the first half of the nineteenth century. Moscheles' influence ranged far into the century, affecting nearly every pianist-composer who came to maturity between 1830 and 1860. His G minor Piano Concerto, Op. 58 (published 1820) is the most significant link between Beethoven's piano concertos and those by Mendelssohn, Liszt, Brahms, and especially Saint-Saëns. Moscheles' etudes, especially those of Op. 70 (1825–26) and Op. 95 (1836), are surpassed only by Chopin's. One need only hear the fifth and twelfth of the Op. 70 etudes or the fourth ("Juno") of the Op. 95 set to see Moscheles' strong influence on Brahms' piano writing (Example 3–9). Also deserving mention are Moscheles's large chamber ensembles for winds, strings and piano (the sextet, Op. 35 of 1815 and the septet, Op. 88, of 1832) and the large-scale *Grande sonate symphonique*, Op. 112

EXAMPLE 3–9. Moscheles, Etude, Op. 70, No. 5.

Example 3–9. (Continued)

(1845), for piano duet. As a young man Moscheles inhabited the world of Beethoven, Hummel, and Schubert but in his later years influenced, taught, and even outlived many of the succeeding generation of composers, who represent the efflorescence of musical Romanticism.

BIBLIOGRAPHICAL NOTES

Dissertations, especially that of H. A. Craw (University of Southern California, 1964), are the chief recent source of studies of Dussek's music. Benyovsky's *J. N. Hummel, Mensch und Künstler* (Bratislava, 1934) needs to be replaced by a comprehensive biography, for which Dieter Zimmerschied's *Die Kammermusik J. N. Hummels* (Mainz, 1966) and Joel Sachs's *Kapellmeister Hummel in England and France* (Detroit, 1977) and their catalogues of Hummel's works will be among the main foundations. Dussek's sonatas comprise six volumes of the series *Musica Antiqua Bohemica;* good modern editions of Hummel's sonatas and piano pieces are urgently needed.

Clive Brown's *Louis Spohr: A Critical Biography* (Cambridge, England, 1984) is an excellent study; Folker Göthel's thematic catalogue, *Thematisch-bibliographisches Verzeichniss der Werke von Louis Spohr* (Tutzing, 1981) is a starting-point for further studies of Spohr's music. Göthel has presented a corrected and copiously annotated version of Spohr's reminiscences as *Louis Spohr: Lebenserinnerungen* (Tutzing, 1968), which should be used in preference to the bungled translation *(Louis Spohr's Autobiography*, 1865; reprint New York, 1969) or the abridged translation by Henry Pleasants, *The Travels of Louis Spohr* (Norman, 1962). The three symphonies of Spohr discussed in this chapter (Nos. 4, 6, and 7) are reprinted in Series C, volume IX, of *The Symphony 1720–1840* with a preface by Joshua Berrett. More of Spohr's music, especially the imaginative piano trios, needs to be made available in modern practical editions or even reprints.

The standard biography of Weber in English is by John Warrack (2d ed., London, 1976), who has also edited a collection of Weber's writings on music

(Cambridge, England, 1981). William S. Newman's magisterial *The Sonata Since Beethoven*, 3d ed. (Chapel Hill, 1983) contains an excellent discussion of the sonatas by the composers in this chapter, especially Dussek and Hummel.

The best studies in English of Schubert's music are those by Maurice J. E. Brown, including his *Schubert: A Critical Biography* (London, 1958), *Schubert's Variations* (London, 1954), and *Essays on Schubert* (London and New York, 1966, rev. 1977). Alfred Einstein's *Schubert: A Musical Portrait* (New York, 1951) is a fine appreciation rather than a detailed investigation. Richard Capell's *Schubert Songs* (2d ed., London, 1957) has been the standard study of these works. Otto Erich Deutsch's *Schubert: Memoirs by His Friends* (London, 1958) has been enlarged in a German edition (1964), forming the first volume of a new series of Schubert's complete works.

The 150th anniversary of Schubert's death in 1978 brought forth special issues of *The Musical Times*, *Nineteenth-Century Music* (also in 1979), and a congress in Vienna, its papers published in Otto Brusatti (ed.), *Schubert-Kongress Wien 1978* (Graz, 1979). Eva Badura-Skoda and Peter Branscome have edited *Schubert Studies: Problems of Style and Chronology* (Cambridge, England, 1982) with especially good essays on the songs and on the chronology, based on paper studies, of Schubert's later works. Reinhard van Hoorickx's "Schubert: Discoveries Since 1970," *Music Review*, XLV (1984), 220–50, describes the most recent finds among manuscripts and sketches.

Arthur Loesser's *Men, Women and Pianos* (New York, 1954) and the chapter "A Riot of Pianists" in Alan Walker's *Franz Liszt: The Virtuoso Years* (New York, 1983) brilliantly capture the milieu of the Paris-based piano virtuosos; Walker's book also contains a chapter on Paganini, of whom the standard studies are Geraldine de Courcy's *Paganini the Genoese* (2 vols., Norman, Okla., 1957) and a more recent study (Neptune, N.J. 1979) by Leslie Sheppard and Herbert Axelrod. Patrick Piggott's *The Life and Music of John Field* (Berkeley and Los Angeles, 1973) is a model study of this neglected composer's music. Three of Field's piano concertos are in volume XVII of *Musica Britannica* and his solo piano music is being reprinted by Garland. The old series of Schubert's works is gradually being replaced by a new edition begun by Bärenreiter-Verlag in 1968.

The pre-history of the Lied and ballad is easier to trace now, thanks to facsimile reprints of song collections by Reichardt and Zumsteeg, examples of the pre-Schubert Viennese song in *Denkmäler der Tonkunst in Oesterreich*, LXXIX, and several settings of Gottfried August Bürger's ballads published in *Das Erbe deutscher Musik*, XLV–XLVI (1970).

Selected piano works by Tomašek and Voříšek have been edited by Dana Zahn for G. Henle Verlag, with Voříšek's fine D major symphony in Volume 34 of *Musica Antiqua Bohemica*. Garland Press is reprinting many important works by Moscheles and others in their series *The London Pianoforte School* (1984–).

FOUR

THE GERMAN ROMANTIC
EFFLORESCENCE

A large group of composers born between 1803 and 1813 dominated the music of most of the nineteenth century. The vacuum created by the deaths of Weber, Beethoven, and Schubert between 1826 and 1828 enabled some younger composers to rise meteorically to prominence while still in their early twenties; those that did not die at an early age substantially changed their musical styles around 1850. With these composers this and the following chapter are principally concerned. Liszt and Wagner, on the other hand, took longer to mature as composers but compensated through long lives and continuing musical influence; their impact on the music of the century will be discussed in Chapter 6.

The years between 1830 and 1850 were particularly yeasty for music. The young composers, fictionally represented by Schumann's "League of David," were joined against the "Philistines," with Paris and the German cities the principal arenas of the combat and with their battles fought in the press as well as in the concert hall or opera house. The young composers revered Beethoven, though his influence tended to paralyze their imaginations in writing in the larger forms; they highly esteemed Weber; and a few of them came to appreciate Schubert. They were more closely associated with the other arts, especially literature, than any preceding group of composers.

FELIX MENDELSSOHN-BARTHOLDY (1809–1847)

Of all these composers, Mendelssohn was closest in spirit to the eighteenth century, chiefly through his impeccable craftsmanship and sense of proportion. A highly facile and prolific composer, he left a large amount of music that still remains unpublished, and his *oeuvre* still awaits the critical scholarship and cataloging that, for example, Maurice J. E. Brown and Otto Erich Deutsch have given to Schubert's music.

Mendelssohn was second only to Mozart as a prodigy in composition. When we reflect that Mozart's first genuinely individual and independently meritorious works, like the G minor Symphony, K. 183, and the motet *Exsultate, Jubilate,* are the products of his sixteenth year, Mendelssohn's comparable precocity is apparent in such works from his sixteenth and seventeenth years as the Op. 20 Octet, the Concerto in A♭ for two pianos, and the Overture to *A Midsummer Night's Dream.* Our admiration for these first major works can only be heightened when we recall that they were written after a period of intense study of figured bass and counterpoint in the tradition of J. S. Bach and the Berlin theorists under Carl Friedrich Zelter (1758–1832). Though it is fashionable to regard Mendelssohn's later works as representing a decline in his creative powers, such a verdict is as unjust as that which has been passed on Schumann's later compositions.

Mendelssohn's music must be evaluated by genres, not chronologically (only his first seventy-two opus numbers were published during his lifetime) and also in terms of the various facets of his creative personality: elfin and fey, soulfully expressive and sentimental, fussy-tempered, or elegiac. In various compositions Mendelssohn is the landscape or seascape painter, the Bach enthusiast, or the representative of Victorian and Biedermeier Protestantism. Many of these personalities exist isolated in individual pieces, single movements of an instrumental cycle, or even in theme-groups of a sonata-form movement constructed with impeccable craftsmanship.

Instrumental Works. Mendelssohn revived the organ as a medium of composition. Although Beethoven, Moscheles, and other pianists played the organ, they regarded it as a medium for improvisation rather than composition, and the near-century between J. S. Bach's last works and

Mendelssohn's organ compositions are virtually a desert for the organist. Mendelssohn's organ sonatas are more like Baroque than nineteenth-century sonatas, for sonata-form movements are few, with the first movements preludes or even variations in the style of a chorale-partita. The Sixth Sonata (D minor), with its chorale variations, fugue, and concluding andante, is considered the best of these works.

Mendelssohn's piano music is underrated, partly owing to the popularity of the *Songs Without Words* as teaching pieces or the tendency to regard his two published concertos for piano as "student" concertos. An occasional performance of the *Variations sérieuses*, Op. 54, brings to light one of the finest sets of piano variations between Beethoven and Brahms, with each variation exploring a different facet of piano technique and sonority. Though Mendelssohn's piano sonatas are very early works, his Fantasy in F minor, Op. 28 (1833), which he had originally planned to call "Scottish sonata," is a one-movement sonata that in its general form seems based on Beethoven's "Moonlight" sonata, with an evocative slow movement, a lyrical intermezzo in major, and a tempestuous finale in minor; the finale seems influenced by Beethoven's "Appassionata" sonata.

The *Songs Without Words* (not Mendelssohn's original title, for the first set, Op. 19B, was published in London in 1832 as "Original Melodies" and in his letters he called them "Romances for Piano" and "Piano Pieces") are Mendelssohn's best-known piano works; they were published in sets throughout his musical maturity. More than just piano miniatures, most of them are instrumentalized songs that take advantage of the singing quality of the piano. Some, however, are character pieces and subsequently acquired descriptive titles (not Mendelssohn's) such as the "Funeral March" in E minor (Op. 62, No. 3) or the "Spinning Song" (Op. 67, No. 4) with its revoiced augmented-sixth chords creating almost Bartók-like dissonances. Such smaller works as the three fantasies of Op. 16 (especially the exquisitely elfin second one), the *Album Leaf*, Op. 117, and the *Capriccio*, Op. 18, are equal in musical value to the Schubert impromptus. The Beethoven of the sonatas between Op. 27 and Op. 90, Weber, Moscheles, and to a lesser extent Field were the chief influences on Mendelssohn's keyboard style.

Mendelssohn's chamber music has been unjustifiably neglected. One must admire the freshness of the Octet, Op. 20, especially the exuberant first movement and fey scherzo, and the craftsmanship of its sixteen-year-old composer. As in some of his other early works, Mendelssohn experimented with cyclic recapitulation in its highly contrapuntal finale. Among his string quartets are two masterpieces, the effervescent D major Quartet, Op. 44, No. 1, with its wistful "song without words" type of slow movement, and the powerful F minor Quartet, Op. 80, written shortly before his death in 1847 as a requiem for his beloved sister Fanny. Perhaps the best of the chamber works is the D minor Trio, Op. 49, with its elegiac first movement and fine scherzo; highly appreciated also are his two cello sonatas, especially the D major, Op. 58, with its exuberant first movement in typically Mendelssohnian 6/8 meter, flowing but not driving (Example 4–1); its second movement is wryly wistful, with an ironic ending comparable to that of many of Heine's poems.

Mendelssohn's orchestral music is the best known part of his *oeuvre*, with his programmatic concert overtures containing the best examples of his skillful orchestral writing. The overture to *A Midsummer Night's Dream* was followed seventeen years later by additional incidental music to the drama, but the tendency to perform this music apart from the play has resulted in the unfortunate elimination of many fine individual pieces. The best overtures are seascapes, like *Hebrides* and *Melusine;* the dramatic portrayals (*Ruy Blas*) are weaker. Excellent examples of sonata form, these overtures stand midway between those of Beethoven and the symphonic poems of Liszt and had an important influence on succeeding generations. Although Mendelssohn's piano concertos have fallen out of favor, probably because of their overuse as student concertos in the past, his Violin Concerto in E minor is one of the few works in the history of music that has an equally great appeal to performer, listener, scholar, and audience, because of its pervasive melodiousness, skillful solution of the problems of balance between soloist and orchestra, exquisite scoring, and deft finale in Mendelssohn's best elfin vein.

Of the fourteen early symphonies written between 1821 and 1824, only the last was published (as Op. 11) during Mendelssohn's lifetime; most of the other symphonies are for string orchestra. The *Hymn of Praise*, often called his Second Symphony, is really a choral cantata. The "Reformation" Symphony in D minor, written to commemorate the three-hundreth anniversary of this religious movement, and containing the "Dresden Amen" in the introduction and Luther's hymn "A Mighty Fortress Is Our God" in the finale, has a deft scherzo, a rather fussy first movement, and a finale with many skillful contrapuntal touches in its treatment of Luther's hymn but also some bombastic moments; it is interesting to compare this movement with the prelude to Meyerbeer's *Les Huguenots*, which also utilizes Luther's hymn. Mendelssohn's most popular symphony, the "Italian," is beloved because of the deftness of its outer movements and the tenderness of its contemplative inner movements; this symphony was not published during Mendelssohn's lifetime because he hoped eventually to revise the finale, with which he was dissatisfied. Mendelssohn's finest symphony is his last, the "Scottish" in A minor (1842), with its magnificently elegiac first movement, exquisite scherzo, wistful slow movement, and driving finale which is marred, however, by a bombastic coda; all four movements are skillfully linked through "motto" themes that appear in various guises. The

EXAMPLE 4–1. Mendelssohn, Sonata in D major, Op. 58, first movement.

basic form of the principal motive (motive X in the analysis in Example 4–2) is an ascending scale outlining a plagal octave (e-E in A minor or major) which contains two interlocking segments, labelled *a* and *b*. Most of the thematic material of the symphony is derived from motive X, whether in minor (the introduction, Example 4–2c, or the first theme of the first movement) or major (the first theme of the scherzo, Example 4–2e, or the coda of the fourth movement, Example 4–2g). Motive Y, with its leap of a fourth followed by a descending half-step, is associated chiefly with second theme-groups, as in Example 4–2d, and permutations of this motive often occur in transitional passages. Reversing motive X provides a descending scale outlining a plagal octave; in minor, it is the source for the first theme of the fourth movement (Example 4–2f) and, in major, for the second theme of the second movement. Both basic motives are combined in the opening of the second theme of the first movement (Example 4–2d). The themes accompanying Example 4–2 are but a few of those that are derived from Motives X and Y.[1]

Vocal works. During the nineteenth century Mendelssohn's choral works were ranked above his instrumental compositions. Among his large oratorios, *St. Paul* (1836) derives from Handelian dramatic oratorio, with some movements drawing on Bach's four-part chorale style; *Elijah* (1846) is a more felicitous fusion of these elements with the oratorio style of Spohr and the English anthem, its influence evident in the motet-like choruses like "Be not Afraid" and "He Watching Over Israel." The contemplative choruses and arias are the best moments in *Elijah*, and the confrontation of Elijah with the priests of Baal is a fine dramatic moment with effective touches of satire, but the dramatic choruses (e.g., "The Fire Descends") are inferior to their Handelian models, and in the conclusion of the first part too much reliance is placed on a jog-trot rhythm. Despite its shortcomings, *Elijah* is one of the finest large choral works of the nineteenth century and for a long time was considered inferior only to Handel's *Messiah*. Among the other large choral works are several chorale cantatas which Mendelssohn left unpublished, choral pieces for the Anglican liturgy written for England, and several Psalms, set either as cantatas for soloists, chorus, and orchestra (such as Psalms 42, 95, 98, 115, and especially Psalm 114 for double chorus) or in motet style, such as those for unaccompanied double chorus that comprise Op. 78 (Psalms 2, 43, and 22), written for the Berlin cathedral. Throughout these works one encounters Mendelssohn's smooth and singable vocal counterpoint, dramatic use of homophony for crucial textual depictions, and unobtrusive but effective orchestral accompaniments.

---

[1]For a more detailed analysis, see my "Cyclic Form and Tonal Relationships in Mendelssohn's "Scottish" Symphony," *In Theory Only*, IV (1979), 38–48.

EXAMPLE 4–2. Mendelssohn, Symphony in A minor, "Scottish," Op. 56: (a) Motive X; (b) Motive Y; (c)–(g), themes derived from these motives.

Among the secular choral works, the outstanding composition is the cantata *The First Walpurgis Night*, a setting of Goethe's ballad and a masterpiece, with some of Mendelssohn's best dramatic writing in the chorus where the druids propose to imitate ghosts and goblins, and loveliest nature painting in the overture and opening chorus wherein winter gives way to spring. The models for this work were the dramatic cantatas by Andreas Romberg (1767–1821). Despite attempts at imitation by Schumann, Gade, Brahms, and Dvořák, Mendelssohn's composition never had a true successor and remains unique in the musical literature.

Mendelssohn's songs are the most neglected of all his works, perhaps because they follow the tradition of the strophic songs of the Berlin school, especially those of his teacher C. F. Zelter, rather than the ideas of Schubert. As examples, "Neue Liebe" is in Mendelssohn's best elfin vein and "Die Liebende schreibt" has the intimacy that one associates with Schumann. Several songs published under Mendelssohn's name among his

Opus 8 and Opus 9 are really by his sister Fanny, including Queen Victoria's favorite, a setting of Grillparzer's "Italien." A plea should also be made for Mendelssohn's part-songs, whether the duets for women's voices or the mixed or male quartets; these were intended for social gatherings and musical recreation, not for the concert hall.

It is difficult to make a capsule description of Mendelssohn's general style in a limited space because of the many facets of his creative personality. The elfin and landscape-painting Mendelssohn is most familiar and popular today; such indications as "presto agitato" over a composition in the minor mode will show the fussy-tempered Mendelssohn; and Example 4–1 shows the opening of one of his best exuberant works in 6/8 meter, with a prevailing diatonic style, impeccable craftsmanship, and singing melodies. Example 4–3 shows Mendelssohn in a soulfully elegiac mood: note the regularity of the phrases, the expressive but restrained harmony, the frequent internal cadences within a measure (the so-called "feminine endings"), and the wistful touches imparted by minor triads, mostly well prepared with secondary dominants, in an essentially major key. The four-part writing is in an almost vocal style, and one could imagine words, especially with religious import, set to the melody. Mendelssohn is least successful in writing music with a message or in portraying emotions of conflict or stress.

Mendelssohn frequently returned to completed compositions (*Hebrides* Overture, D minor Trio, *The First Walpurgis Night*) to make thorough revisions which are superior to the original models. He was not only a composer but a leading pianist, organist, and conductor of his time; his repertoire as conductor ranged from Palestrina and Lassus through Schumann, and that as organist included the intimate chorale preludes as well as the virtuoso preludes and fugues of Bach.

The administrative chores resulting from his efforts to make Germany the musical center of Europe hastened Mendelssohn's early death. The Leipzig Conservatory which he founded set the model for professional music education in Germany as well as the Anglo-Saxon countries, and his endeavors to reform church music, though the most visible results were the anthems of the English Victorians, markedly contributed to the revived interest in the Protestant musical heritage of J. S. Bach and his predecessors. His efforts on behalf of the music of the past were a practical reinforcement and encouragement to the infant discipline of musicology.

ROBERT SCHUMANN (1810–1856)

German Romanticism, literary as well as musical, culminates in the works of Robert Schumann. His highly individual style, which derived from

EXAMPLE 4–3 Mendelssohn, Variations, Op. 83, theme.

many sources, chiefly Beethoven, Schubert, Hummel, and Dussek, had a strong influence on the music of the later nineteenth century; he was also a musical journalist who battled for new music.

Schumann's music may be divided into five chronological periods, each demarcated by a major crisis in his life. The first period, ending in 1833 with his contemplated suicide, was the epoch of the Abegg Variations, Op. 1, and the Papillons, Op. 2, and terminated with the Intermezzi, Op. 5, on a theme by his future bride, Clara Wieck. The second period began in 1834 with his recovery of mental equilibrium and ended with his marriage to Clara in 1840 despite the continued opposition of her father. During these six years Schumann assumed the editorship of the *Neue Zeitschrift für Musik* and wrote his greatest piano compositions, beginning with *Carnaval*, Op. 9, and ending with *Faschingsschwank aus Wien*, Op. 26.

Schumann's marriage to his beloved Clara in 1840 inspired a "year of song" in which 127 songs, many of them his finest works in this genre, were written (some, published several years later, carry opus numbers as high as 142); 1841 was the year of orchestral music, 1842 the year of chamber music. Opinions vary as to the termination of this creative period: Einstein (in *Greatness in Music*), seeking more for a round number than an accurate date, cites Op. 50, the secular oratorio *Paradise and the Peri;* Knepler (*Musikgeschichte des XIX. Jahrhunderts*) the year 1844; E. A. Lippman (article "Schumann" in *MGG*) 1847, the year of the D minor Piano Trio. The middle years of the 1840's were fallow for Schumann and saw his abandonment of musical journalism in 1844 and a breakdown in 1845, followed by a "cure by counterpoint" which resulted in the canonic studies and sketches for pedal-clavier (a piano with a pedal keyboard like that of the organ) and the fugues on B-A-C-H (B♭-A-C-B♮), replete with intricate contrapuntal devices.

It is fashionable today to deprecate the music of Schumann's last period, but the years between 1849 and 1851 were among his most productive and include his best neglected music. Yet his increasing mental deterioration, despite his continuing to compose important works until the end of 1853, resulted in his forced resignation as conductor in Düsseldorf in 1853, his attempted suicide in 1854, and his subsequent confinement in a mental institution until his death.

Piano Music. Not only did the piano dominate Schumann's creative activity between 1828 and 1839, but most of his successful later works, particularly songs and chamber music, relied heavily on this instrument, and most of his essential musical characteristics are revealed in his piano music.

His split personality was incorporated in his early years in the imaginary characters Florestan and Eusebius, whom Schumann depicted in *Carnaval* and had "sign" individual articles in his journal and in the Davidsbündler Dances; a few of these dances and the F♯ minor Piano Sonata, Op. 11, were written under "joint authorship." Florestan is the capricious, tempestuous, impulsive figure who, in the dance beginning as in Example 4–4 "stopped, and his lips trembled sorrowfully"; Eusebius, on the other hand, is the contemplative, introspective dreamer (Example 4–5). In many of the compositions with epilogues (Davidsbündler Dances, *Arabeske*, *Dichterliebe*) Eusebius has the last word. Schumann's third personality, the judicious and arbitrating Master Raro, is first evident in Schumann's articles

EXAMPLE 4–4. Schumann, Davidsbündler Dances, Op. 6, No. 9, "Florestan."

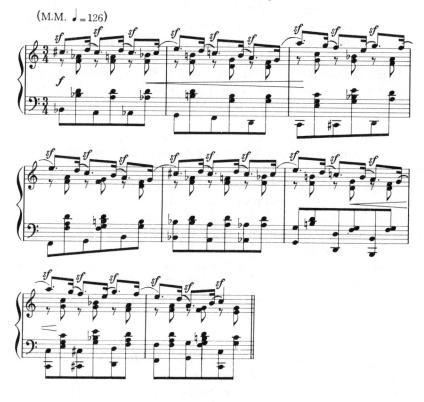

EXAMPLE 4–5. Schumann, *Carnaval*, Op. 9, "Eusebius."

and becomes prominent in his music after 1844, especially in sonata-form movements and contrapuntal studies.[2]

In Schumann's earlier piano works the dominant idea is that of the masked ball, wherein various characters, portrayed in short epigrammatic character pieces, flit back and forth; the earliest example is *Papillons*, based on the masked ball toward the end of Jean Paul Richter's novel *Flegeljahre*, which also contains the characters Walt and Vult, models for Florestan and Eusebius. *Carnaval* is another masked ball in which Clara Wieck (Chiarina), Schumann's temporary fiancée Ernestine von Fricken (Estrella), Chopin, Paganini, and the figures of the Italian *commedia dell'arte* appear in waltzes (influenced by Schubert's) and promenades; at the end Schumann's "League of David," his musical colleagues and their ancestors like J. S. Bach, Beethoven, and Weber, sally forth against the "Philistines," the purveyors of empty virtuoso piano music and the Classic epigonoi who, in Schumann's words, "wrote music by the yard." The Davidsbündler Dances, later works despite an earlier opus number than *Carnaval*, are the culmination of the masked ball idea.

This gave way to series of character pieces, either indefinite atmospheric portraits (*Fantasiestücke*, Op. 12) or the delightful pictures in the *Scenes from Childhood*, Op. 15; in later years Schumann returned to works of this type in the *Waldscenen*, Op. 82, *Bunte Blätter*, Op. 99 (incorporating movements withdrawn from *Carnaval*), and the *Songs of the Dawn*, Op. 133. His greatest piano works are the sets of large pieces, especially the *Symphonic Etudes*, *Kreisleriana*, the *Novelletten*, the *Faschingsschwank aus Wien*, and the *Fantasie* in C major.

Except for the later piano collections, the sets of piano pieces are not helter-skelter assemblages of individual pieces gathered into an arbitrary collection; they are often, if not always, unified by subtle means. Schumann's delight in musical acrostics is evident as early as his Abegg Variations (in German notation, the name is spelled out as A–B$\flat$–E–G–G); *Carnaval* is based on permutations of the letters in the name of the Sudeten town of Asch near which Ernestine von Fricken lived; "Asch" (A$\flat$–C–B$\flat$) is even permutated to S C H – u – m – A – n – n by using the notes E$\flat$–C–B–A. Other unifying devices include the bass line of the theme of the

---

[2]Schumann's ailments have led to a considerable amount of ill-informed speculation. His mental illness, according to the late Erwin Strauss, M.D., was not schizophrenia but a manic-depressive psychosis. Florestan and Eusebius may therefore be viewed as the manic and depressive aspects of the composer's psyche, with Master Raro as a superego attempting to control the deviant facets through contrapuntal and formal structures. Schumann's illness was exacerbated by the stresses of his conducting position in Düsseldorf with which he was unable to cope. The crippling of the ring finger of his right hand which forced him to abandon piano playing in 1832 was presumably, according to the orthopedist Robert Leffert, M.D., in the *Harvard Medical School Health Letter* of June 1986, from a motor-control disorder, still a difficult diagnosis to establish.

Impromptus, a technique derived from Beethoven's "Eroica" Variations; harmonic structures in most of the *Symphonic Etudes;* and motivic connections between movements in his larger instrumental cycles, most evident in the G minor Piano Sonata, the Piano Quintet, and the Fourth Symphony. Schumann was not consistent in his use of cyclic forms, however, and the analyst must not expect to find cyclic relationships in all of this composer's works.[3] To achieve tonal coherence, Schumann often relied on a kind of "macrotonal architecture" that incorporated a framework of relationships among primary and subsidiary tonal centers.

Schumann's organization of his cycles of larger piano pieces may best be seen in his *Kreisleriana,* Op. 16, one of his finest sets of piano pieces (Figure 4–1). Although there is no motivic connection between the individual numbers as in *Carnaval* or *Scenes from Childhood,* the unity of the cycle is established through subtle means, like the use of the key of B♭ for the slow numbers which serve as points of rest, the surprise cadence of Number 4 which leads directly to the following number, and the balanced contrasts in moods, even within individual numbers wherein the sections are marked by tempo as well as key changes. That Schumann did *not* intend this work to have a conventional finale is shown by his treatment of the last two numbers: the coda of the seventh piece, quiet and chordal in contrast to the agitation of the main number, leads to an epilogue in E♭ major, after which the final number, in G minor, is dominated by a ghostly riding rhythm with bizarre syncopations in the bass (relating to the syncopated harmonic rhythm of the opening number) and a mysterious ending. Writers have sought to find a direct connection between individual numbers of this work and episodes in the career of E. T. A. Hoffman's fictional character Kreisler, the eccentric, wild *Kapellmeister,* but any relationships are at best metaphorical, and none of the numbers is a programmatic painting of any of Kreisler's adventures. Schumann's middle-sized piano works, including single compositions like the *Arabeske* or *Blumenstück* as well as individual *Novelletten* or *Nachtstücke,* are modified rondo forms, often with codas.

The three sonatas for piano (Op. 11 in F♯ minor, Op. 14 in F minor, and Op. 22 in G minor) represent, along with Chopin's three mature sonatas, the culmination of the early Romantic sonata. The F♯ minor sonata, like the early fragment in B minor that Schumann later published as Op. 8, seems the one most influenced by Hummel's F♯ minor sonata, Op. 81 (which Schumann highly esteemed and sought to perform), but transcends it in originality, structural ingenuity, and demands on the performer's mu-

---

[3]One writer has gone so far as to conjecture that Schumann's themes were based on a numerological code. See Eric Sams, "Did Schumann Use Ciphers?" *Musical Times,* August 1965 (and the editorial comments); "The Schumann Ciphers," May 1966.

FIGURE 4–1. Organization of Schumann's *Kreisleriana*, Op. 16. Based, with my additions and revisions, on Karl H. Wörner, "Schumanns 'Kreisleriana,'" *Sammelbände der Robert-Schumann-Gesellschaft*, II (1966), 58–65.

NUMBER	KEY-CENTER	STRUCTURE	REMARKS
1 (most agitated)	d	ABA	Syncopated harmonic rhythm; influence of Bach's arpeggio preludes
2 (very expressive and not too fast)	B♭	ABACA + coda	"Eusebius in highest apotheosis"; two intermezzi in faster tempos; coda one of Schumann's most dissonant passages
3 (very excited)	g	ABA + coda	Insistent rhythms; coda the dynamic climax of the set
4 (very slow)	B♭	ABA	"Melodic improvisation"; prevailing avoidance of tonic in root position; ends with a surprise cadence to V of g
5 (very lively)	g	ABACDCBA	Scherzo; motive- and rhythm-dominated
6 (very slow)	B♭	ABA	Slow movement; songlike; delayed tonic
7 (very fast)	c–E♭	ABACBA + coda	Technique of first number; foreshadowing of scherzo of second symphony; coda with a surprise epilogue in E♭
8 (fast and playful)	g	ABACA	Persistent 6/8 "riding" figure; syncopated bass relates to number 1; avoids any resemblance to conventional finale

sicality and technique. The first movement, after an extensive character piece that serves as introduction and is brought back during the development, has an unusual three-key exposition (F♯ minor–E♭ minor–A major) with the parallel in the recapitulation (F♯ minor–C♯ minor–F♯ minor); at the end the common tone A leads to the intimate song-like second movement in A major. The scherzo is ambiguous in its key-center (F♯ minor or A major?), and this is paralleled in the main theme of the rondo finale (Example 4–6), sometimes cited as an illustration of Schumann's "backing" into his real key-center (apparently starting in F♯ minor but with the real goal A major). A parallel relationship to the tonal structure of the first movement can also be seen in the use of E♭, but now E♭ major, as a subsidiary tonality. The ambiguity of tonality in the finale is resolved only in the last statement of

EXAMPLE 4–6. Schumann, Sonata in F♯ minor, Op. 11, fourth movement.

the theme, apparently starting in D♯ minor and ending in F♯ major. The tonal architecture in this sonata is among Schumann's most original and effective.

As for the other two piano sonatas, that in F minor was originally published with five movements and called "Concerto Without Orchestra"; the similarity in the first movement to the so-called "double exposition" of a concerto and the improvisatory nature of the outer movements are more concerto- than sonata-like. The G minor sonata was the one begun earliest, with the slow movement deriving from a song Schumann wrote in 1828, but with its cyclic thematic structure and adherence to Beethovenian models it seems the most "conservative" in structure and style of the three sonatas.

Two other cycles have some kinship to the sonata. In the C major Fantaisie, Op. 17, Schumann was seeking a new kind of form between fantasy and sonata in three movements, with the first a very free sonata movement, the heroic second movement dominated by full-chordal harmonizations of a powerful melody, and a slow movement as an epilogue-like finale, perhaps influenced by the slow-movement endings of Beethoven's Op. 109

and Op. 111 piano sonatas. The *Faschingsschwank aus Wien*, Op. 26, the last of Schumann's great works for piano, is not a sonata (though he started it as such) but a five-movement cycle opening with an immense waltz containing a quotation from "La Marseillaise" (a "subversive" tune in Metternich's Vienna), three picturesque inner movements, and a finale in sonata form. After the *Fasschingschwank* Schumann devoted only limited attention to cycles of piano pieces, with the best of the subsequent ones the *Bilder aus Osten*, Op. 66, for piano duet, influenced by Rückert's Oriental poetry (1848); the *Forest Scenes*, Op. 82, of the same year; and the *Gesänge der Frühe*, Op. 133 (1853), based on Hölderlin's *Diotima* poems. The last set is one of Schumann's last works; its first piece is particularly noteworthy because of its bold pan-diatonic harmonic clashes.

Songs.   Schumann wrote 127 songs in 1840, the "year of song" during which he married Clara Wieck. These songs, furthermore, are the ones most frequently performed, whether individual songs like "Mit Myrthen und Rosen" and "The Two Grenadiers" or the song cycles *Myrthen, Liederkreis,* and *Frauenliebe und Leben.*

The most striking characteristic of Schumann's best songs is the close relationship between voice and piano. What Schumann had previously confided to the singing tone of the piano was now given to the voice but without relegating the piano to the background as a mere accompanying instrument. Preludes, postludes, and interludes play a major role; the preludes are generally short, even to the point of merely getting the singer started, whereas the interludes often unify the song (as in "Der Nussbaum"), and the postludes continue and intensify the mood of the song after the singer finishes. The finest postlude is the conclusion of *Dichterliebe,* for it leads from the ironic mood of the last song back to the contemplative "Eusebius" mood of the first song of the cycle. Another trait of Schumann's songs is a close relationship between poetry and music; not since the troubadours, trouvères, and Minnesänger had words and notes been so beautifully united. Heinrich Heine's gently ironic verses inspired Schumann's best songs, as did the full-blown romanticism of Rückert and the nature poetry of Eichendorff; Robert Burns's poems inspired the best folklike settings. In Schumann's later years, when his creative imagination sometimes flagged, such good poems as those by Lenau, set as Op. 90, or by Mary Queen of Scots, used in his last fine songs (Op. 135, 1852), roused his latent talents.

Schumann's strophic songs are generally simple and folklike; those of Op. 79 are vocal companions to his *Album for the Young.* The declamatory songs, like "Ich grolle nicht" from *Dichterliebe,* are more melodious than Schubert's; the chordal, hymnlike songs are generally late works. The song-cycles are unified in various ways: cyclic interrelationships in *Dichterliebe,* similarities between the outer songs in *Frauenliebe und Leben,* or

tonal relationships between songs in *Myrthen, Liederkreis,* or the Mary
Stuart songs.

Orchestral Music. Schumann's orchestral works include four symphonies and a quasi-symphony without a slow movement (the Overture,
Scherzo, and *Finale,* Op. 52); concertos for piano (Op. 54), violin (unpublished until 1937), and cello (Op. 129), as well as some miscellaneous concert pieces, the best of which are the vibrant Konzertstück for four horns,
Op. 86; the one-movement concerto for piano and orchestra, Introduction
and Allegro appassionato, Op. 92; and four overtures, the earliest written
in 1851. In recent years the symphonies have seldom been performed, and
the Cello Concerto is neglected because its contrasts are too subtle, its poetic atmosphere too unrelieved, and its virtuosity too unevident, though
cellists know how difficult it is.

The First Symphony is partially cyclic, with the epilogue to the slow
movement in the trombones becoming the main theme of the scherzo;
more cyclic are the Second and Fourth. In the Second Symphony the
"motto" theme, proclaimed by the brass in the introduction, recurs at climactic moments in the scherzo and the finale, and the main theme of the
slow movement (in minor) becomes the second theme (in major) in the finale. All the movements are related in the Fourth Symphony, a highly concise work based on germ-motives like Beethoven's Fifth Symphony which
set a pattern for symphonic writing that continued well into the twentieth
century with Sibelius's Seventh Symphony. In some of these orchestral
works Schumann attempted to dissolve the boundaries between movements, most successfully in the Cello Concerto.

In his book *Style and Idea* Arnold Schoenberg effectively contradicted the frequently encountered nonsense about Schumann's "poor" orchestration by stating that if the orchestration were changed, much of the
typically Schumannesque quality of these works would be lost. Schumann
wanted certain tone colors and especially wanted blends of tone, subject to
the natural limitations of the brass instruments (it is interesting to note the
virtual liberation of his horn parts in the later orchestral works), and we
should not blame the composer for not wanting his orchestral works to
sound like those of Mendelssohn or Berlioz.

Chamber Music. Most of Schumann's best chamber music was
written in 1842, the year of the three string quartets, the Piano Quintet,
and the Piano Quartet. After he recovered from his breakdown of the mid-
1840's Schumann's renewed interest in this medium resulted in three piano
trios, three violin sonatas, miscellaneous chamber music including winds,
and even piano accompaniments for Bach's solo violin and solo cello works
and for Paganini's caprices.

That Beethoven's later works were Schumann's models is most evident in the Piano Quartet; it is not mere coincidence that E♭ is the common

key of this work and Beethoven's Op. 127 string quartet. Schumann's string quartets are the finest between Schubert's and Brahms's, but the most exciting of his chamber works is the Piano Quintet. Cyclic relationships abound in his work, one of the most striking being the combination of the opening themes of the outer movements as a double fugue, a coda to the quintet as a whole rather than just to the finale. All of the chamber works show some kind of formal experimentation in attempting to create new paths for the sonata form and scherzo (A major Quartet) or finale, especially the Piano Quintet, the structure of which is shown in Figure 4–2. Note in this finale Schumann's combination of sonata-rondo principles with the expanded recapitulation and "second development" of Beethoven's larger works. The themes of this movement are all related: all but one begins on the second half of the *alla breve* measure, and that exception is a countermelody to theme (d) which is first stated in the development and recurs in the recapitulation, a section which boasts in turn a new theme which recurs after the double fugue.

The tonal structure of the finale, as shown in Figure 4–2, makes sense only when one considers the tonal architecture of the quintet as a whole. Though E♭ major is the basic tonality of the quintet, there are two subsidiary tonal centers, C minor-major and G♭ major. The C minor opening of the finale is not only a large-scale vi–I progression but has its inception in the C minor of the second movement. The appearances in the finale of such keys as B major (enharmonic C♭ major), E♭ minor as a "recapitulation" key, and C♯ minor and its tonal cousins, all keys within the tonal orbit of G♭ major, have as their precedents the G♭ and C♭ major openings of the transitions and the closing theme in the first movement, and the A♭ minor (also the minor subdominant of E♭) of the second u.:o in the scherzo.

Of the chamber music of Schumann's last period, the D minor Trio, Op 63 (1847), is the best example. A complex work that demands many hearings for its message to be revealed, it shows that late Schumann can be almost as difficult as late Beethoven for the listener. Although the lyricism in this trio is sometimes hectic, and portions of the second movement and finale give the listener the impression that Schumann is merely going through the motions, there are nevertheless many adventurous harmonies, and few passages in chamber music are as striking as the *sul ponticello* section of the first movement. Deserving special mention are the three violin sonatas, the first (A minor, Op. 105) dating from 1851 and the last not published in final form until a century after Schumann's death; these sonatas rank with Mendelssohn's cello sonatas as the finest duet sonatas between those of Beethoven and Brahms. The many chamber works including winds, such as the *Fantasiestücke*, Op. 73, for clarinet and piano and the *Märchenerzählungen* (Fairy Tales), Op. 132, for clarinet, viola, and piano (the third will demonstrate the strong influence Schumann had on French

FIGURE 4–2. Structural analysis of the finale of Schumann's Piano Quintet, Op. 44.

SECTION	THEME	MEASURES	TONAL CENTERS	CORRESPONDENCE TO RONDO-SONATA FORM
A	a	1–21	c–g	Exposition: theme
	b	21–29	E♭	
	a	29–37	g–d	
	b	37–43	B♭–V of g	Transition
B	c	43–51	G (III)	First episode, corresponding
	d	51–77	G with sequences	to second theme-group in sonata form
A	a	77–85	e–b	Theme, but in remote key
Transition		85–94	B (enharmonic ♭VI)	
C		95–164		Developmental second episode
	d	95–114	Tonal flux	
	e/d	114–136	V of E–c♯	e as counter-melody to d
	a	136–164	c♯–g♯–d♯ (enharmonic equivalent of tonic minor)	Retransition
A	a	164–172	e♭–b♭	Recapitulation: theme
	b	172–178	G♭–V of B♭	
B	c	178–186	B♭ (V)	First episode, dominant
	d	186–212	B♭–E♭	Tonic major established
A	a	212–223	c–g (vi–iii)	Theme in related key
D	f	224–248	E♭ (I)	Closing theme of sonata-form; also re-establishes tonic major
Fugato	a	248–274	c (vi)	"Second development"
E	e/d	274–299	E♭ (I)	Unifies development with recapitulation
Transition		300–318	E♭ (I)	Prepares double fugue
Double fugue		319–378	E♭ (I)	Combines major form of (a) with opening theme of first movement
D	f	378–401	E♭ (I)	Reprise of closing theme
Coda	a	401–427	E♭ (I)	Conclusion based on major form of (a)

music of the late nineteenth century) provided a welcome relief from the virtuoso display pieces and fantasies on airs from popular operas that were the wind player's usual solo repertoire.

Choral Music. Schumann came late to this genre. His first published choral work, *Paradise and the Peri*, a secular oratorio, contains fine movements but is hindered by Thomas Moore's saccharine text. The *Mass*, Op. 147, and *Requiem*, Op. 148, both written in 1852 for Düsseldorf, are not difficult works but are quite effective. *Manfred*, Op. 115 (1848–49), based on Byron's poem and scored for narrator, chorus, and orchestra, is a splendid work; its overture is the most frequently performed of Schumann's later compositions, and though the choral parts are subsidiary there is much fine music to accompany the narration, especially in nature-painting scenes like the invocation of the witch of the Alps; the appearances of the shade of Astarte contain some of Schumann's most expressive music. His one opera, *Genoveva* (1850), was beset with numerous problems, not the least of these the libretto. A continuation of the medieval-chivalric legend with virtually continuous set-numbers like *Euryanthe*, *Genoveva's* greatest misfortune was its having been composed after *Tannhäuser* and *Lohengrin*.

Schumann's greatest late work is his *Scenes from Faust*, composed between 1844 and 1853. Rather than select numbers which would make a continuous narrative, he selected individual scenes, mostly from the second part of the drama. Considerable cyclic unity joins the scenes; the solos are among the few instances where Schumann could transfer his mastery of song composition to the brief aria with orchestra; the declamation, especially that of Faust, must have been studied by Wagner; and the third part contains the most sublime music between Beethoven's death and Brahms's full maturity. A comparison of Schumann's original conclusion with his later version of the ending provides an excellent illustration of how his first thoughts were superior to his revisions.

Musical Style. Rhythm is Schumann's chief driving force. Following Beethoven's example in the first movements of the Fifth and Seventh Symphonies or the last movement of the C♯ minor Quartet, he wrote many pieces dominated by insistent rhythms, either monorhythmic like the eighth of the *Kreisleriana* pieces or sectional, with each portion dominated by a pronounced rhythm, as in the first number of the *Faschingsschwank*. Unfortunately, Schumann sometimes overworked the idea of insistent rhythm to the point of obsession; one can count the same pattern repeated thirty-two times in the finale of the Fourth Symphony, for example. Yet Schumann's masterly use of syncopation, hemiola, rhythmic displacement, polyrhythms, and syncopated harmonic rhythm makes him a master of rhythm comparable only to Beethoven, Berlioz, Brahms, and Stravinsky.

Schumann's harmony is seldom strikingly dissonant. More characteristic of his style is a lingering on non-harmonic tones in the melody with a gentle accompaniment aided by the sustaining pedal, especially in "Eusebius"-like numbers such as the coda of the *Arabeske*. Another typical device consists of powerful march-like passages with full chords in both hands and a fast harmonic rhythm. Schumann's bass lines are superb, and his harmonic imagination is best shown through a lavish use of inversions and secondary dominants. Schumann, as well as Chopin, was an innovator in writing around but avoiding the tonic, as in Example 4–4, and thus directly contributed to the "psychological tonality" of Liszt and Wagner.

That Schumann was a magnificent melodist is shown not only in his songs but also in his piano music; one can easily imagine words set to the seventeenth of the Davidsbündler Dances or the sixth of the *Kreisleriana*. Often Schumann will pluck, as it were, a melody from the notes of his accompaniment. Less frequent are compositions based on motives rather than melodies, as in the fifth of the *Kreisleriana*, in which the interplay of motives, rhythms, and harmonies provides the musical interest. In some of the later works, like the fourth of the Marches, Op. 76, written under the stimulus of the revolutionary events of 1848, or the third of the *Bilder aus Osten*, Op. 66, Schumann concentrates on insistent reiteration of square-cut melodies.

Several writers have assailed Schumann's formal structures as weak or even as contributing to the deterioration of tonality and sonata form. In his works of the 1830's and early 1840's he experimented with formal and tonal structures to a considerable extent: those of the F♯ minor piano sonata and E♭ major piano quintet that have been discussed in this chapter are two of his more unusual ventures. In his later works Schumann became seemingly more conservative in his treatment of form but compensated by seeking a kind of seamless form in which the conventional articulations between theme-groups or sections became blurred, a procedure practiced by the later Beethoven in many of his sonata-form movements; one can see Schumann's use of such a process in the first movements of the violin sonatas and cello concerto or the overture to the *Scenes from Goethe's Faust*.

THE GERMAN ROMANTIC LEGACY

Two women composers deserve inclusion in this section in their own right as composers, not because of their personal connections (which hindered as well as helped their musical development). Fanny Mendelssohn Hensel (1805–47) was denied the extensive musical education given her younger brother Felix ("Music can and must be only an ornament for you," her father wrote her when she was fourteen) but utilized her ability as pianist and composer effectively in organizing and directing the Mendelssohn family's Sunday musicales; of her 500-odd compositions, only 28 were published, including some songs published under her brother's name. Her most ambitious published work is an excellent piano trio in D minor, Op. 11, composed in the year of her death. Clara Wieck Schumann (1819–96) wrote most of her works before her marriage in 1840, including a piano concerto composed during her teens; such later works as her two scherzos for piano and variations, Op. 20, on a theme by her husband show a very original composer, though her Piano Trio, Op. 17 (published 1847), lacks the power and intensity of Fanny Hensel's trio.

Mendelssohn's music became the model for the "academic" composer in Protestant lands, especially in Germany, Scandinavia, and the Anglo-Saxon countries, in choral music as well as for the instrumental cycle. His portrayals of nature served as a model for future generations. During the second half of the nineteenth century Mendelssohn's music was revered in England to the point of adulation, and one may speculate whether the violent reaction against his music that took place during the early years of the twentieth century was part of the general reaction against the Victorian ethic and aesthetic.

Schumann's legacy, on the other hand, was more enduring and more widely disseminated. As a music critic, he played a major role in publicizing the music of Beethoven and Chopin and in building the posthumous reputations of J. S. Bach and especially Schubert; his essays on music are equalled as literary works only by those of Berlioz, Hanslick, and George Bernard Shaw.

Schumann's influence on subsequent generations worked in several different directions. His ideas of instrumental music and especially the instrumental cycle were a happy mean between those of Mendelssohn and Berlioz and thus strongly influenced the general revival of instrumental music after 1860, and not only in Germany. Brahms was his most obvious disciple (Schumann's D minor violin sonata and the Concert Allegro with Introduction, Op. 134, dedicated to Brahms, could easily be mistaken for compositions by Brahms), but one must include Lalo, Saint-Saëns, Fauré, Chaikovsky, Grieg, and even Borodin, Sibelius, and Rakhmaninov. Schumann's example undoubtedly liberated his close friend Liszt from being merely a purveyor of virtuosic galops and opera transcriptions, and Schumann's harmony led to the "psychological tonality" of Liszt and Wagner.

Schumann's influence moved downward as well as outward. His contemporary Robert Franz (1815–92) published about 350 songs between 1843 and the onset of his deafness in 1868; most of these are simplifications of the Schumannesque Lied, from the standpoints of the technical demands on pianists and singers as well as of the musical content itself, as can be discerned by comparing the setting of a given poem by Franz with that by Schumann. Schumann's enthusiastic and effusive emotional expressiveness and fine harmonic coloring were soon to be debased into a "hearts and flowers" sentimentality, so well exemplified by the songs and piano music of Adolf Jensen (1837–79) or the drawing room ballads and wedding songs of the American Oley Speaks (1874–1948). One need but compare two ballads, Schumann's "The Two Grenadiers" and Speaks' "On the Road to Mandalay," to see the downward direction that resulted from the popularization of Schumann's style.

BIBLIOGRAPHICAL NOTES

The best biography of Mendelssohn in English is Eric Werner's *Felix Mendelssohn, A New Image of the Composer and His Age* (New York, 1963; revised German ed. Zürich, 1980); unfortunately, the author overstates Mendelssohn's "modernism," and the book suffers from an awkward translation. Many of the letters have been translated into English (*Mendelssohn's Letters*, transl. Gisella Selden-Goth, New York, 1945). Percy M. Young's *Introduction to the Music of Mendelssohn* (London, 1949) is still quite serviceable, as is Karl-Heinz Köhler's *Felix Mendelssohn-Bartholdy* (rev. ed., Leipzig, 1972). Several collections of letters have been translated into English; however, many unpublished ones were destroyed by family members after Mendelssohn's death.

Among the various special studies, R. Larry Todd has admirably traced the composer's early career in *Mendelssohn's Musical Education* (Cambridge, England, 1983) which includes his figured bass and contrapuntal studies. Todd's "Of Sea Gulls and Counterpoint," *Nineteenth-Century Music*, II (1979), 197–213, shows the revisions of the *Hebrides* overture, and my "Cyclic Form and Tonal Relationships in Mendelssohn's 'Scottish' Symphony," *In Theory Only*, IV (1979), 38–48, is a more detailed analysis of this work than that cited on pp. 90–93.

Susanna Grossmann-Vendrey discusses Mendelssohn and earlier music in her *Felix Mendelssohn Bartholdy und die Musik der Vergangenheit* (Regensburg, 1969). The proceedings of a Mendelssohn symposium in 1972 were edited by Carl Dahlhaus as *Das Problem Mendelssohn* (Regensburg, 1974). Mendelssohn's carefully crafted orchestration is well explored in Thomas Ehrle's *Die Instrumentation in den Symphonien und Ouvertüren von Felix Mendelssohn Bartholdy* (Wiesbaden, 1983).

Mendelssohn's complete works (with many lacunae) were reprinted by Gregg and Kalmus; the original series is continued in the *Leipziger Ausgabe der Werke Felix Mendelssohn-Bartholdys*.

A good musical biography of Schumann is still lacking. None of the biographies has the immediacy of J. W. von Wasiliewski's (Dresden, 1858; English translation as *The Life and Letters of Robert Schumann*, Boston, 1871, reprint New York, 1975), by one of the composer's closest associates during his last years. Alan Walker's compilation of a group of uneven essays, *Robert Schumann, The Man and His Music* (2d ed., London, 1976) has a German counterpart in Julius Alf and Joseph Kruse, eds., *Robert Schumann, Universalgeist der Romantik* (Düsseldorf, 1981). Peter Ostwald's psycho-biographical *Schumann: The Inner Voices of a Musical Genius* (Boston, 1985) contains much information distilled from the composer's letters, diaries, and household journals but has little about the actual music, if also some sensational speculation about Schumann's private life. (The diaries and journals have been published in annotated editions, Leipzig 1971 for the *Tagebücher* and Leipzig, 1982–83 for the *Haushaltbücher*.)

Eric Sams's *The Songs of Robert Schumann* (New York, 1969) contains fine analyses and paraphrased translations of the texts of each individual song. Leon Plantinga's *Schumann as Critic* (New Haven, 1967) is a superb assessment of Schumann as a writer on music, reinforced by examination of the music that Schumann discussed; it supersedes all other studies of Schumann's musical aesthetics. Existing English translations of Schumann's writings are not wholly satisfactory because of Schumann's often convoluted and flowery German prose. Wolfgang Boetticher's work in progress, *Robert Schumanns Klavierwerke* (Wilhelmshaven, 1976–) is more solid than his Nazi-era biography of Schumann (Berlin, 1941). The twelve-year friendship of Schumann and Mendelssohn has been celebrated in a book of essays edited by Jon Finson and R. Larry Todd, *Mendelssohn and Schumann* (Durham, 1984), with a particularly penetrating study of Mendelssohn's last style by Friedhelm Krummacher.

Schumann's complete works, prepared under his widow's supervision, have been reprinted by Gregg and also Kalmus; works that Clara Schumann sought to suppress, like the Violin Concerto and the piano variations that immediately preceded Schumann's attempted suicide, have been published separately. G. Henle Verlag is publishing sumptuous new and authoritative editions of Schumann's piano music as well as piano works by Fanny Mendelssohn Hensel.

Nancy Reich's biography of Clara Schumann (Ithaca, 1985) is a thorough study. Marcia Citron has discussed Fanny Mendelssohn Hensel's songs in *Musical Quarterly*, LXIX (1983), 570–94, and Carol Quin is preparing a biography of this interesting composer.

FIVE

ITALIAN AND FRENCH ROMANTICISM

Musical Romanticism developed later in Italy and France than in Germany and Austria. The reasons are easy to explain: in Italy opera was the dominant medium and its audiences were conservative until the 1840's, the period of the drive for unification of Italy (the *Risorgimento*), whereas in France the rescue and revolutionary operas of the 1780's and 1790's gradually disappeared with the advent of the Directory and the subsequent rise to power of Napoleon. In both areas instrumental music occupied a secondary role, in Italy for the entire century.

ITALIAN INSTRUMENTAL MUSIC TO 1870

With opera the dominant medium in Italy, other genres enjoyed extremely fragile ecological niches. Instrumental music, whether from across the Alps or by native Italian composers, was too often regarded as "*musica filosofica*" and given only limited support, even in such musically sophisticated urban centers as Milan, Turin, and Florence.

In northern Italy, musical Neoclassicism (as well as pictorial and architectural) flourished, with the leading musical representatives violinist-composers like Alessandro Rolla (1757–1841), who also wrote grateful works for the viola, and Giovanni Battista Polledro (1781–1853)—both composers of violin concertos, one-movement symphonies, and chamber music. The most striking transitional figure was Bonifazio Asioli (1769–1832), an Italian contemporary of Beethoven. Asioli's F minor symphony of 1801 is a more "advanced" work than Beethoven's first symphony, but Beethoven soon left Asioli behind, as comparison of the nearly contemporaneous "Pastoral" symphonies by both men will show. The dignified and serious music of Francesco Basili (1767–1850), some of whose orchestral music is almost as rhythmically intricate as that of the late Schumann, still awaits investigation.

Farther to the south, Niccolò Zingarelli (1752–1837), who had made his reputation as an opera composer during the previous century, wrote fifty-five one-movement symphonies, many austerely contrapuntal, as well as prodigious quantities of church music for the cathedral in Naples, where he was musical director as well as director of the conservatory. His pupil and subsequent administrative successor Saverio Mercadante (1795–1870) wrote symphonies and concertos for wind instruments for classmates during his student days in Naples and later a number of "characteristic symphonies" on Neapolitan or Spanish folk tunes and programmatic orchestral fantasies with such grandiloquent titles as "The Arab's Lament," "Sacred and Profane," not to mention his most grandiose late work (dictated after he had gone blind), a four-movement descriptive fantasy commemorating the Polish insurrection of 1863.

ITALIAN OPERA TO 1853

Opera in nineteenth-century Italy was not an elitist entertainment for the aristocracy or bourgeois intelligentsia, but a popular art form like today's musical theater. There was a constant demand for new works, with composers and librettists working under intense pressures to produce effective works, within the parameters of familiar conventions, for money-conscious impresarios and for singers, aware of their popularity and "star" status, who seldom hesitated to change the music written for them or to demand something more effective. One may compare the opera composers of the early nineteenth century to the scriptwriters for popular television series who must turn out episodes within familiar frameworks and subject to immediate criticism from stars, producers, and the mass public. The musical products that resulted were in international demand, in Vienna, Paris, Madrid, or London as well as on the Italian peninsula.

Eighteenth-century Italian opera had been divided into two basic categories: the *opera seria*, serious opera, with plots based on Greek mythology or ancient history and with music characterized by vocal virtuosity (especially for the sopranos, male or female), sometimes extensive choruses, and often special orchestral effects; and *opera buffa*, comic opera, with lively tempos and diatonic harmonies, plots from real life but filled with intrigue and complications, and, in less skillful hands, much padding and repetition. Toward the end of the century the two genres were blended into the *opera semiseria*, influenced by the realism of English novels and French *opéra comique*. Serious elements entered the world of the comic opera, especially *opera seria*-like arias; one need but contrast the characters and music of Donna Anna and Leporello in Mozart's *Don Giovanni* (1787), the epitome of the *opera semiseria*.

An immense number of composers were active in producing these various types of opera in the early years of the century, whether outside of Italy (Dresden, then Paris) like Ferdinando Paër (1771–1839), whose solemn operatic marches sound much like Beethoven's heroic music, or on the Italian scene, like Simon Mayr (1763–1845), the chief transmitter of Mozart's style to Italy. Two composers in particular, Giuseppe Nicolini (1762–1842) in the serious genre and Stefano Pavesi (1779–1850) in the comic (and both also wrote symphonies and church music), may be cited among the many who prepared the way for Gioacchino Rossini, the composer who brought these operatic genres to their culmination.

Rossini (1792–1868) is an important pivotal figure in the history of nineteenth-century opera. He codified the conventions of the Italian opera inherited from his predecessors and brought them to a peak; on the other hand, he discarded many of the formulas of the previous century and established new conventions, especially in his serious operas. Through most of the twentieth century he was esteemed for a few of his comic operas and his sparkling and effervescent overtures, but a "Rossini revival" in the 1970's focussed new interest on his serious operas.

Rossini's first successes date from 1813 in both the serious (*Tancredi*) and comic (*L'Italiana in Algeri*) genres. In 1815 he was called to Naples, where he perfected his craft, being able to write for a permanent opera company with stellar singers, a good orchestra, and adequate rehearsals. So many operas streamed from his prolific pen (abetted, one must admit, by a good amount of self-borrowing) that he enjoyed an international reputation by the time he was thirty.

In 1824 he settled in Paris, where he produced French versions of his Italian works and wrote two of his masterpieces, the *opéra comique Le*

Comte Ory (1828) and *William Tell* (1829). With the latter, his career as a composer of operas ended, although he continued to compose short piano pieces, songs, and church music. Among the reasons advanced for his refusal to continue operatic composition, the most probable are his difficulties with the régime of Louis Philippe, which assumed power in France after the July Revolution of 1830 (the earlier government of Charles X had promised Rossini a pension), and an extended period of ill health which lasted until 1855.

Rossini's opera overtures are among the exciting and thrilling works in this genre. They generally consist of a slow introduction, a fast main section in abridged sonata form with the development section replaced by a transition back to the tonic, and a coda in an even faster tempo. Characteristic of them are piquant woodwind solos, driving rhythms, and crescendos consisting of a repeated motive to which instruments are added in succession.

The arias often follow a stereotyped form consisting of the following elements: (1) an orchestral *ritornello*, usually melodically related to the cavatina that will follow; (2) a florid accompanied recitative that establishes the dramatic situation; (3) the first main part, often called a *cavatina* (strictly speaking, this term was reserved for an "entrance aria"), *cantabile* or simply *primo tempo*, in a slow tempo with an expressively ornamented melody, of which Example 5–1a is a good example; (4) a short faster section (*tempo di mezzo*), sometimes with ensemble or choral passages, that often sets a change in dramatic action; (5) a *cabaletta*, in a fast tempo, with virtuoso fireworks for the singer which could often sound better-suited to a clarinet than to the voice, as in Example 5–1b; and (6) an optional *stretta* in an even faster tempo, guaranteed to elicit a shower of applause. Often one or more obbligato instruments would participate in the aria. Rossini was assailed for writing out his vocal ornaments, but it is necessary to remember (as Spohr testifies about his travels in Italy during this time) that both singers and instrumentalists inserted ornaments into anything they were performing, and Rossini merely codified an established tradition. The assertion has been made that Isabella Colbran, his principal singer, mistress, and later, wife, was losing her voice and that Rossini ornamented her parts in order to conceal her vocal deficiences, yet similar "coloratura" writing occurs in the principal male roles.

Rossini's ensembles sometimes have pseudo-canonic openings, with each singer entering in turn, but they bear only a surface relationship to the contrapuntal writing in Cherubini's operas or Beethoven's *Fidelio* and are really strophic with only very rudimentary counterpoint. Other ensembles follow the basic structure of the aria, with multiple participants in the opening recitative and with lyrical passages (*arioso*) expanding it into a scene or *scena*, and the *tempo di mezzo* greatly expanded to include con-

EXAMPLE 5–1. Rossini, cavatina "Bel raggio lusinghier:" *Semiramide*, Act I. (a) cantabile, (b) cabaletta.

versation-like declamation over a brilliant orchestral melody. Rossini's development consisted of minimizing the solo arias and replacing them with scene-complexes that would include one or more short arias and extend over several minutes or even an entire act, as in Act III of *Otello*. He also enriched his "chain finales" by skillful alteration of dynamic and static sections. The Italian operas are generally in two acts, but those written for France have as many as four, in keeping with the French love for dramatic spectacle; the choral writing in the French operas is therefore more elaborate, and seen at its best in the second act finale of *William Tell*.

Though in 1854 Rossini called himself "the last of the Classicists," his expressive Romanticism is evident at least as early as the third act of *Otello* (1816) and is more prominent in the serious operas, with their plots derived from literature (Scott, Shakespeare, Schiller) or history, than in the comic operas with their involved plots drawn from popular theater. The tinctures of chromaticism in the cantabiles (as in Example 5–1a), the atmospheric orchestral introductions to the overtures or the nature settings in operatic acts (as in *La donna del lago* of 1819, based on Scott's *The Lady of the Lake*), and the enriched harmonic and orchestral resources—especially in his final operatic masterpiece *William Tell*—show the extent of Rossini's Romanticism.

Rossini was the true composer of the counter-revolution which spread over Europe after 1815. In his novel *Le Rouge et le Noir* Stendhal describes an ultra-Royalist salon where the only fit topics of conversation were Rossini and the weather. The Paris of the Bourbon restoration, the London of George IV, and the Vienna of Metternich were most hospitable to Rossini's music; this hampered the careers of Beethoven and Schubert during the 1820's, and in France younger composers like Auber and Herold were driven to strong efforts to emancipate themselves from Rossini's influence.

Italian Romanticism during the 1830's is best seen in the music of the Sicilian-born Vincenzo Bellini (1801–35), who wrote almost exclusively for the operatic stage during his short career. Bellini is most praised for his long, arched vocal melodies, which require a superb singer, almost always a soprano, for their proper performance (Example 5–2); he may have ab-

EXAMPLE 5–2. Bellini, *La Sonnambula,* Act I.

sorbed this style through his teacher Zingarelli, whose generally undistinguished operas contain progressive moments like the aria "Ombra adorata aspetta" from *Giuletta e Romeo* (1796). A large number of Bellini's melodies consist of passages with a prevailing dotted rhythm that occasionally imparts a martial cast (see Example 5–3a). A trait typical of Bellini's ritornelli, later adopted by Verdi, is an interruption of the melody just before the final cadence, after which the prevailing accompaniment pattern is reestablished and the singer begins.

EXAMPLE 5–3. (a) Bellini, *Norma*, Act I; (b) Verdi, *Luisa Miller*, Act I.

Though Bellini's harmonic resources and orchestral palette are often limited, sometimes producing an effect of monotony, he excelled as a melodist (Verdi praised his "long, long, long melodies such as no one before him had written"), especially in his slow cantabiles, and as a setter of musical scenes, as in the opening of Act II of *Norma* where the heroine contemplates, then renounces, the murder of her sleeping children.

Gaetano Donizetti (1797–1848) represents the robust, vigorous side of post-Rossinian Italian opera. An extremely prolific composer who worked constantly under the pressure of meeting deadlines, he is best known for his operas, though he wrote several chamber and orchestral works during his student days, and much church music, now almost completely forgotten. His sixty-six operas range from one-act farces (the sparkling *Il campanello di notte*, 1836) through comic operas (*Don Pasquale*, 1843, the last successful Italian opera buffa until Verdi's *Falstaff* fifty years later) and tearjerking *semiseria* operas (*Il furioso all'isola di San Domingo*, 1833) to grand operas, some based on English history (*Anna Bolena*, 1830; *Maria Stuarda*, 1835). Often his serious operas are vehicles for sopranos with both dramatic and coloratura qualities, particularly his best-known opera *Lucia di Lammermoor* (1835). His later operas, many for Paris or Vienna, show increasing musical sophistication.

Though in Donizetti's operas one often discerns a writing-to-formula, he seems to have striven especially in the serious operas to achieve a kind of dramatic unity with continuous music. Within the cantabile-cabaletta arias or ensembles he often expanded the *tempo di mezzo* section from its transitional role between the two basic sections, often through an orchestral melody over which the singers declaim conversationally. Both he and Bellini used ariosos—lyrical and expressive accompanied recitatives—to expand the introductory recitatives into a *scena* with an orchestral introduction, often atmospheric.

Saverio Mercadante, whom we have previously encountered in this chapter as an orchestral composer, is the remaining link between the post-Rossinian *opera seria* and Verdi's early music dramas. A highly prolific composer with about sixty operas to his credit, Mercadante is best known for advances over his contemporaries in harmony and operatic orchestration (he was a violinist who had also studied cello, flute, and clarinet); his simplifying of vocal lines for musical and dramatic effect, though more so for male than female singers; and his striving to get away from the stereotyped closed cantabile-cabaletta structure to the scene-complex, in which several individual "numbers" are tonally and even thematically linked, in order to achieve a better musical and dramatic portrayal of the personages in the opera. *Il Giuramento* (1837) is Mercadante's best-known opera; in its attempt at dramatic realism, musical integration of the scene-complexes into a continuous structure, and finely-wrought instrumental obbligatos which interact with the voice, it is closer to Verdi than to Bellini or Donizetti.

Giuseppe Verdi (1813–1901) was the greatest Italian composer of the nineteenth century. Though the passage of time led many critics to deprecate his works, except for the last four operas, as "barrel-organ music," subsequent reappraisals have led to renewed esteem and heightened respect for Verdi as composer and musical dramatist.

Verdi's career as a composer spanned over sixty years, from occasional works written for concerts in Busseto in the mid-1830's to the completion of *Four Sacred Pieces* in 1897; his operas range from *Oberto* (composed in 1838) to *Falstaff* of 1893. Among major composers, only Schütz, Haydn, and Stravinsky have had such extensive creative careers. Because Verdi's was so long, we shall consider in this chapter only the operas through *La Traviata* of 1853, and will reserve discussion of the subsequent changes in Verdi's musical style and the works of his next forty years in Chapter 9.

With his third opera, *Nabucco* (1842, based on the Biblical account of king Nebuchadnezzar), Verdi achieved his first major success; this work and *I Lombardi* of the following year were written for Italy's premier opera house, La Scala of Milan, and are large-scale, opulent works. After quarreling with the administration of La Scala and deciding to write for other opera houses, Verdi embarked on an intensely productive period which he later called his "years as a galley slave" (*anni di galera*), in the course of which he enriched his musical style and the operatic legacy that he had inherited with a succession of works that emphasized psychological and dramatic portrayals of the major personages and attempts to escape the routine formulas and conventions of the "cavatina operas," as he scornfully termed them. During this period he was contending with political and religious censorship, singers and opera-house directors, and a public which soon became international. One can justly compare the Verdi of the 1840's with his contemporaries among novelists, Honoré de Balzac and Charles Dickens, who similarly turned out a series of successful and esteemed works under pressure. Verdi's main works of the 1840's, besides those mentioned, are *Ernani* (1844), *Macbeth* (1847), and *Luisa Miller* (1849), derived respectively from Victor Hugo's revolutionary drama of the same name, Shakespeare, and Schiller's *Kabale und Liebe.*

Verdi's important early operas, which span the eleven years from *Nabucco* to *La Traviata*, are a culmination of many earlier trends, among them the spectacular aspects of Rossini's *Mosè in Egitto* (also a Biblical opera) and *Guillaume Tell*, Bellini's efforts to dissolve the boundaries between recitative and aria, and Donizetti's expansion of the *scena* and search for continuous music drama as opposed to a string of set-numbers linked together by recitative. The influence of Mercadante's "reform operas" from *Il Giuramento* onwards is prominent in Verdi's works from *I Lombardi* well into the 1850's. To the operatic heritage he had received, Verdi added his own gifts, chiefly his ability to write memorable, singable, effective tunes, create dramatic scenes, employ overpoweringly propulsive and energetic rhythms, and treat the orchestra with increasing adeptness in getting away from (but not entirely avoiding) the "big guitar" effect for which Donizetti and Bellini had been reproached. To illustrate Verdi's advances over some of his predecessors, contrast Bellini's gentle soprano cantilena in Example 5—3a with Verdi's robust baritone cabaletta in Example 5—3b, or Donizetti's rather ordinary cabaletta in Example 5—4b with Verdi's more intense treatment of comparable material in Example 5—4c.

Verdi's musical forms at their simplest can be diagrammed as *aaba* or *aabc* for the cantabiles, with the qualifying statement that the second and successive *a* sections are varied and that *b* is in a related key, usually third-related to the tonic, and the cabalettas are often strophic with the first stanza ending on the dominant and the second on the tonic, with the chorus joining in the stretta. The kind of large-scale tonal organization characteristic of Mozart's finales or Wagner's operas was not for Verdi; his attitude toward tonality as a structural device was quite empirical. Most critical in Verdi's development during the 1840's was his establishment of a scene-complex which, following the model of Act III of Rossini's *Otello*, could extend over an entire act. Cantabile-cabaletta structures for arias or duets, if retained, could frame an act-length scene-complex as in Act II of *Rigoletto*, but with important musical and dramatic material in the *tempo di mezzo* sections. (For example, the "Miserere" in Act III of *Il Trovatore* is the

EXAMPLE 5–4. Donizetti, *Lucrezia Borgia,* Act I duet: (a) cantabile; (b) cabaletta; (c) Verdi, *La Traviata,* Act III duet, cabaletta.

tempo di mezzo section between a cantabile and cabaletta.) Some of the clichés that Verdi retained, such as the cadenzas at the end of cantabiles, the vocal fireworks of cabalettas and strettas, or the marches by a band on the stage, can be regarded as necessary concessions to the public for which Verdi was writing.

Recurrent musical themes, often called "reminiscence motives," provide dramatic continuity, especially in *Ernani, I due Foscari,* and *Rigoletto* (its curse motive, here a chord progression, is cited at the end of Example 5-5). The dramatic high points of the Verdian opera of this period are the ensembles or the *gran scena,* employing the techniques of the cantabile part of an aria without the ensuing cabaletta. The most striking example is the Lady's sleepwalking scene in Act IV of *Macbeth:* an earlier composer would have made this a "mad scene" as in the last act of *Lucia di Lammermoor,* whereas Verdi made this a truly dramatic scene, with hushed comments by the lady-in-waiting and the doctor on Lady Macbeth's cantabile, which is as long-breathed a melody as any by Bellini, underlaid by a gestic orchestral ritornello.

Often Verdi adopted striking scorings for individual numbers in his operas, such as the six cellos that accompany Zaccaria's recitative and prayer in *Nabucco,* the virtual violin concerto with vocal accompaniment that is the third act finale of *I Lombardi,* or the high divided violins that depict Violetta's illness in *La Traviata.* The main weight of the opera, how-

EXAMPLE 5–5. Verdi, *Rigoletto,* Act I.

ever, is carried not by the orchestra but by the voices, with often sharply-characterized vocal types, especially the high baritone, robust tenor, and sopranos who must often portray wide ranges of emotion.

An understanding of Verdi's early work is incomplete without a knowledge of the political drive for the unification of Italy known as the Risorgimento. Many of Verdi's early operas (*Nabucco, I Lombardi, La Battaglia di Legnano*) are thinly disguised political tracts into which the audiences could read appeals for liberation from foreign, especially Austrian, domination. Passages that seem like vulgar, bouncy brass band music are really intonations of the mass songs of the revolutionary Carbonari or "Young Italy" movements, and Verdi's early period finally ended with the suppression of and temporary setbacks to the unification movement after the Austrian victories over the Italian insurgents in 1849.

Verdi's operas of the early 1850's—*Rigoletto, Il Trovatore,* and *La Traviata*—can with equal correctness be considered the culmination of the works of his early period, as products of a self-contained period, or as harbingers of the future. The first two operas are concerned with the portrayal of such violent matters as murder, torture, kidnapping, seduction, dishonor, and hatred, with little concern for the subtleties of musical or dramatic character portrayal, whereas *La Traviata* is a psychological drama, a bourgeois tragedy in contemporaneous dress.

Many of the traits of Verdi's earlier operas survive in *Rigoletto* and *Il Trovatore* and can be seen in the soldiers' chorus from the latter opera, the bouncy chorus of courtiers in Act II of *Rigoletto*, or stereotyped set-numbers like "Di quella pira" in *Il Trovatore* or the duet at the end of Act II in *Rigoletto*. The duet concludes a scene-complex that embraces the entire act; it is preceded by a *cantabile* for the heroine Gilda, with no ensuing cabaletta, in the rather remote (albeit distantly third-related) key of E minor going to C major, with its tonic the pivot note to the A♭ major of the cantabile of the duet; the *tempo di mezzo* includes a section of heightened declamation for Rigoletto that parallels the portion cited in Example 5–5; and the cabaletta has a strong dramatic rationale (Rigoletto's declaration of vengeance) as well as a musical one. On the other hand, musical tendencies which were to flower in Verdi's later operas become apparent at this time; foremost is an impassioned musical declamation, neither recitative nor aria nor Wagnerian sung speech, but rather to be compared to the vocal parts in Monteverdi's Venetian operas of the 1640's. As a general rule, such declamation is given to the baritone (Example 5–5). The combination of subtle harmonic refinements, effective ritornelli which set the scene rather than merely announce a favorite aria for the audience, and restraint in the use of vocal fireworks or other musical stereotypes gives greater depth to the soprano arias, evident in the "Miserere" from *Il Trovatore*, Gilda's cantabile in Act II of *Rigoletto*, or the whole third act of *La Traviata*.

FRENCH OPERATIC GENRES

French opera throughout its history presents a process of thesis, antithesis, and synthesis. The thesis is the serious, stately, and sometimes pretentious *grande musique* of Lully, Rameau, Gluck, Meyerbeer, or d'Indy, whereas the antithesis is the *petite musique agréable* of *opéra comique*, operetta, or parodies of serious works. The synthesis occurs when the *petite musique* approaches its serious counterpart in style and topic, as in the rescue opera or *opéra lyrique*.

Gluck's legacy persisted in France longer than in any other nation. The nobility of his style, combined with the powerful expressive devices of the *Sturm und Drang* which were brought to Paris by German instrumental composers, the melodious tunes of the eighteenth-century *comédie mêlée d'ariettes*, and the ideals of the French Revolution; all contributed to the rescue opera which arose in the mid-1780's but lost its vitality after 1800. Gluck's ideas were also continued by Antonio Salieri (1750–1825), who spent most of his life in Vienna; Luigi Cherubini (1760–1842); and especially Gasparo Spontini (1774–1851), whose grand historical operas, like *La Vestale* and *Fernand Cortez*, display a heroically monumental simplicity, contain rich orchestration, and were to influence both Berlioz and Wagner. At the same time, *opéra comique* was reverting to its earlier form of a sentimental play interspersed with musical interludes, chiefly syllabic and strophic ariettes, romances, and couplets, with simple ensembles and finales. In 1800 the leading composer in this genre was Nicolas Dalayrac (1753–1809), who also wrote rescue operas and string quartets.

During the first two decades of the nineteenth century the rivalry of François-Adrien Boieldieu (1775–1834) with Niccolò Isouard (1775–1818) stimulated the growth of *opéra comique*. Boieldieu was the better composer, but Isouard could write more popular tunes and had the better librettos, many of which poke fun at the pretentions of bourgeois society. The rivalry exhausted both men: Isouard died in 1818 and Boieldieu's muse was fallow between that year and 1825.

The advent of Rossini in Paris threatened to extinguish a viable French school of composition. After the failure of his *Olympie* in 1819 Spontini left for Berlin, and the younger French composers shamelessly aped Rossini's musical mannerisms. Yet *opéra comique* as a native French genre was revived in 1825 with Boieldieu's *La Dame blanche* and *Le Maçon* by the prolific D. F. E. Auber (1782–1871). *Opéra comique* was to enjoy two decades of success with such works as Auber's *Fra Diavolo, La Part du diable,* and *La Sirène,* and *Zampa* and *Le Pré aux clercs* by L. J. F. Herold (1791–1833). Though Rossini's influence remained audible in the overtures and the vocal fireworks of the *première chanteuse de roulades*, the French style was prominent in the delightful ariettes, deft ensembles, and the prevailing dance-like rhythms (Example 5–6). Around 1845, with the later works of Auber and the early works of Ambroise Thomas (1811–1896), *opéra comique* assumed a depth of seriousness and expression which was to become the *opéra lyrique* of the 1860's.

EXAMPLE 5–6. Herold, *Le Pré aux clercs*, Act III.

Auber's *La Muette de Portici* (or *Masaniello*, 1828) was the first example of French Grand Opera, a genre characterized by a historical plot with elements of realism, influenced by the historical dramas of Friedrich Schiller and the historical novels of Sir Walter Scott (1771–1832), and by a mixture of various musical styles, from the symphony and the grand aria down to the trivial dance tunes of the ballet. It was designed to appeal to the tastes and political sympathies of the middle-class audience which patronized the Opéra after the July Revolution brought the high bourgeois class to power. Spontini's influence was strong on Auber's work and its immediate successor, Rossini's operatic swan song *William Tell*. Of the composers of Grand Opera, Giacomo Meyerbeer (1791–1864, *recte* Jakob Liebmann Meyer Beer) was the most important.

Meyerbeer, a virtuoso pianist in his boyhood, studied operatic composition in Italy and wrote six operas there, culminating in his first international success, *Il Crociato in Egitto* in 1824. The following year he moved to Paris, though he did not take up permanent residence there. In 1831 his *Robert le diable* established his reputation as a composer of Grand Opera. *Les Huguenots* followed in 1836, *Le Prophète* in 1849, but his masterpiece, *L'Africaine*, though begun in 1837, was not performed until after his death. The supreme musical eclectic of all times, Meyerbeer combined virtually every known device in his operas for the sake of creating telling effects. His style ranges from the crassest vulgarity, as in the "Shadow Song" from *Le Pardon de Ploërmel* (1859) or the quickstep in *Les Huguenots* derived from the Lutheran chorale "Ein' feste Burg," through melodies which had a telling effect on the listeners of the time but today seem bombastic, as in Example 5–7, to the expressive movements of the love duets in *Les Huguenots* and *L'Africaine* and Vasco da Gama's grand air "Ô Paradis" in Act III of the latter opera. Meyerbeer rivaled Berlioz in introducing new or-

EXAMPLE 5–7. Meyerbeer, *Les Huguenots*, Act IV.

chestral effects, especially for spectacular scenic tableaux. Much of his music has a veiled sonority because of his predilection for extreme flat or sharp keys, with the result that the sympathetic vibrations of open strings are not available as they are in such "brilliant" keys as G, D, or A major; his harmonic effects, chiefly enharmonic or third-related modulations, were widely plagiarized. Meyerbeer had an extremely important influence on the opera of the second half of the century, especially on Wagner's earlier operas, the nationalist historical operas of eastern Europe, and Verdi's operas between *La Traviata* and *Otello*. The exoticism of *L'Africaine* and the orientalia of Félicien David (1810–76) were models for such operas as Verdi's *Aïda* and Saint-Saëns' *Samson and Delilah*.

Opéra lyrique, which began around 1850, was a more intimate counterpoise to the grandiose operas of Meyerbeer, and the best works in this genre have a charm and delightfulness not present in any of the contemporaneous schools of operatic composition; Charles Gounod (1818–93), Ambroise Thomas (1811–96), and Jules Massenet (1842–1912) are its best composers. The plots deal almost exclusively with love and are often distortions of literary masterpieces; the classic example is Thomas' version of *A Midsummer Night's Dream* in which Queen Elizabeth, Shakespeare, and Falstaff are among the *dramatis personae*. The expressiveness of *opéra lyrique* derives chiefly from piquant chromatic seasonings, compound meters (especially 9/8 and 12/8), and long, lyrical melodies, frequently with "feminine" endings in internal cadences. Example 5–8, from the love duet in Massenet's masterpiece *Manon*, is an excellent illustration of *opéra lyrique* at its best; Gounod's *Faust* and *Romeo and Juliet* and Thomas' *Mignon* are the other major representative operas of this genre. The operas by Georges Bizet (1838–75) also belong to the tradition of *opéra lyrique*, including his masterpiece *Carmen*, notwithstanding the realism of its libretto or its Spanish local color. Massenet's *Werther* (1892), one of the last of the true *opéras lyriques*, exhibits a considerable tonal freedom (such as the unrelated tonal plateaux that lead to a climactic theme in the Act I love duet) and may be regarded as one of the most important precursors of the style of Debussy's *Pelléas et Mélisande*.

Operetta arose as a reaction to *opéra lyrique*, a genre scorned by Théophile Gautier as "Gluckism . . . broad, slow, slow . . . going back to plainchant." Adolphe Adam (1803–56), a pupil of Boieldieu and a prolific composer of *opéras comiques*, began a lighter style of composition which culminated in the vivacious operettas of Jacques Offenbach (1819–80), whose musical style is summed up in the title of one of his biographies, *Can-Can and Barcarolle*. Much of Offenbach's music faithfully depicts the vulgarity of Napoleon III's "Second Empire"; however, his posthumously performed *The Tales of Hoffmann* is free of the tawdry effects that characterize many of his operettas and should be considered one of the major *opéras lyriques*. The vogue of operetta continued in France well into the twentieth century and simultaneously spread to other nations, most significantly to Vienna where a special tradition of operetta arose, represented at its peak by *Die Fledermaus* and *The Gypsy Baron* by Johann Strauss, Jr., and *The Beggar Student* by Karl Millöcker (1842–99), perhaps the best work of this genre.

Contemporaneous with the new French opera was the development of the dramatic ballet in France. The ballet had been an integral part of Grand Opera, and many ballets were inserted into operas adapted for the Opéra in Paris, whether *opéras lyriques* like Gounod's *Faust*, foreign operas of the past like Mozart's *The Magic Flute* or Weber's *Der Freischütz* (for which Berlioz arranged the music), or even Wagner's *Tannhäuser*. The leading composer of French ballet music was Léo Délibes (1836–91), whose *Sylvia* and *Coppélia* are the scintillating acme of this genre; Délibes also wrote *opéras lyriques*, of which *Lakmé* is the most famous. Throughout the nineteenth century French ballet had an extremely strong influence on its Russian counterpart, whether in Glinka's operas or in Chaikovsky's ballets.

After 1870 opera lost its almost exclusive domination over French music and became only one of the forms of musical expression open to the rising generations of French composers who will be discussed in Chapters 7 and 9.

EXAMPLE 5–8. Massenet, *Manon*, Act I.

FRYDERYK (FRÉDÉRIC) CHOPIN (1810–1849)

Chopin permanently left his native Poland in November 1830 and settled in Paris in the following year. In *Lutetia* (1837), the poet Heine evaluated him as a composer and pianist of the first rank and the darling of the aristocratic public of Paris; assessing the national influences on Chopin's music, Heine remarked that Poland contributed chivalric sensitivity and historical sorrow; France, grace and easy charm; and Germany, Romantic melancholy. (One might add that Italy gave Chopin his melodic cantilena through Bellini's music and the traditions of operatic singing, including ornamentation.) Heine continued that Chopin "is therefore neither Pole, Frenchman, nor German; he betrays a much higher origin . . . from the land of Mozart, Raphael, Goethe; his true fatherland is the realm of poetry."

Chopin was essentially a composer for the piano; the songs and chamber music are peripheral in his *oeuvre*, though his Cello Sonata can be ranked with the duet sonatas of Mendelssohn and Schumann as the most significant in this genre between those of Beethoven and Brahms. Though Chopin has been regarded as a composer who could work effectively only in the smaller forms, only in the preludes is he a genuine miniaturist like Schumann, Grieg, or MacDowell. The small number of his instrumental cycles has often been cited as evidence that he could not successfully write large-scale compositions, yet in his larger free forms (polonaises, ballades, fantasias, etc.) he often displayed a considerable structural imagination, as shown in Figure 5–1.

FIGURE 5–1. Chopin, Third Ballade, Op. 47.

SECTION	SUBSECTION	MEASURES	KEY-CENTER	REMARKS
Exposition	(1–155)			
A (1–53)	a	1–8	A♭ (I)	
	b (with variants)	9–26	A♭ (I)	
	c	27–36	A♭–V of F	
	a	37–53	A♭ (I)	
B (54–115)	d	54–63	F (VI)	Modulates through C as common tone
	d′	64–104	f–V of C	
	d	105–115	C (III)	
C¹		116–135	A♭ (I)	
C²		136–144	A♭ (I)	Variant of d′
B	d	145–155	A♭ (I)	No modulation
Development	(156–211)			
	d′	156–183	c♯–B (♭III)	
	d	184–187	E (♭VI)	B pedal
	a	188–211	E–c–E♭ (V)	Retransition 204–211
Recapitulation	(211–240)			
A	a	212–229	A♭ (I)	Climax; only sustained *ff* section in the Ballade
C¹		230–238	A♭ (I)	
Final cadence: V₇ of vi; vi; V₇; I (238–240)				

Although the influences of Hummel, Field, and Weber are pronounced in the early works, written before his departure from Poland, many of Chopin's individual stylistic traits are also evident in these compositions. The best of them, like the Polonaise for cello and piano, the slow movements of the two concertos, several of the Etudes, Op. 10, and the Variations, Op. 2 (which elicited Schumann's remark, "Hats off, gentlemen, a genius!"), could not be mistaken for works by any other composer. Most of Chopin's popular compositions were written between 1831 and 1840, a period of composition which can be demarcated by the Nocturnes, Op. 9, and the B♭ minor Piano Sonata. A late period began with such major works as the F♯ minor Polonaise and the A♭ major Ballade and, except for a few short pieces written during his last series of illnesses, concluded in 1846 with the *Polonaise-Fantaisie*, Op. 61, and the Cello Sonata, Op. 65. The best of these late works have a spaciousness of conception (which was not always successful) in the larger pieces, and interesting refinements in the smaller works, like the cross-rhythms in the so-called "Minute" Waltz.

Almost all of Chopin's smaller compositions are based on dances, especially the Polish mazurka and the international waltz. The forms, basically ternary, are sometimes expanded into rondos. Though such dances as the Eᵇ (Op. 18) and Gᵇ (Op. 70, No. 1) waltzes and the D major Mazurka (Op. 33, No. 2) are suitable for dancing, as witness their orchestral transcriptions in the ballet *Les Sylphides*, most of the dances are as highly stylized as the movements of J. S. Bach's suites; representative specimens are the A minor Waltz (Op. 34, No. 2) or any of the mazurkas in C♯ minor. The mazurkas, spanning Chopin's entire creative career, show the greatest variety in mood and contain some of the most interesting melodic and harmonic ideas of any of his compositions. Chopin seems to have sought a musical compatibility between individual mazurkas or waltzes within an opus number.

Chopin's middle-sized works include relatively minor compositions like the variations and impromptus as well as such major works as the nocturnes, scherzos, polonaises, and ballades. The nocturnes, popular because of their relative technical ease, range in expression from salon pieces like the F♯ major (Op. 15, No. 2) to such major works as the C♯ minor (Op. 27, No. 1) and G major (Op. 37, No. 2); the C♯ minor (Example 5–10a) is one of the composer's most pessimistic compositions, relieved by a stirring middle section and a consolatory coda, whereas the G major has some of the composer's most adventurous modulations. Among Chopin's four scherzos, the one in Bᵇ minor is most frequently performed; the middle section of the one in B minor is the Polish Christmas carol "Lulajze Jezuniu."

Chopin's six mature polonaises are considered among his most important group of compositions. They display a wide variety of mood: delicacy in the C♯ minor, funereal lament in the Eᵇ minor, a stirring processional quality in the A major (the so-called "Military" polonaise), lament again in the C minor with its harmonically interesting trio, Sarmatian wildness in the F♯ minor, and powerful virtuosity in the Aᵇ major. Basic to Chopin's polonaises are the moderate tempo triple meter, the accompaniment rhythm ♪♫ ♪♪♪ ♪, the elongated or otherwise emphasized second beat in the melody, and the cadences on third beats. Within these frameworks Chopin achieves an amazing variety of expression and mood.

Of the fantasies, the relatively early but posthumously published *Fantaisie Impromptu*, though one of Chopin's most familiar compositions, is really an impromptu with the "Fantaisie" in the title not Chopin's. The *Polonaise-Fantaisie* (Op. 61), one of his last works, contains a magical introduction establishing the third-related harmonies that help subtly unify a seemingly discontinuous composition through the contrast of tonally stable and unstable passages. The Fantaisie in F minor, Op. 49, is one of the composer's most significant works; apart from the opening march, its structure, resembling a free sonata form, was one of the most important antecedents of the "double-function" form of Liszt's B minor Sonata. The G minor, A♭ major, and F minor Ballades are among Chopin's most important compositions (though the F major Ballade is less successful) and excellently illustrate his technique of creating a large work through juxtaposing and effectively repeating short sections which by themselves would have been admirable preludes or nocturnes.

Chopin's few large instrumental cycles have been dismissed by critics from Schumann and Liszt to the present because of their supposed imperfections in form. The two piano concertos, both early works, stem from the tradition of Dussek and Field, and Spohr's influence is strong in the F minor Concerto. Apart from the juvenile C minor Sonata, Chopin's three essays in this genre consist of the B♭ minor (Op. 35) and B minor (Op. 58) piano sonatas and the G minor Cello Sonata. Common to them all are recapitulations which begin directly with the second theme-group in the first movement, the first theme being either omitted because of its having been worked over so intensively in the development (B♭ minor Sonata) or presented later in a kind of "mirror" recapitulation (Cello Sonata); Brahms was somewhat influenced by these recapitulations. The finales range from the terse, enigmatic, toccata-like finale based on triplet figuration in the B♭ minor Sonata, a complete antithesis to the usual "optimistic" or "climatic" finales of the nineteenth-century instrumental cycle, to the well-developed and extensive finales of the other two sonatas.

Chopin's architectonic genius at its best is seen in the Third Ballade, Op. 47, where he skillfully creates a musical structure loosely based on sonata form yet ingeniously and freely treated, with a tonal structure akin to that of the sonata-rondo form. Figure 5–1, a structural analysis of this ballade, can only show this in outline, for space does not permit citation of the numerous examples of the melodic variation which further serves to unify this work.

Chopin's melody ranges from figuration and passage-work whose main interest is harmonic and pianistic to a languid cantilena with its ornamentation often derived from vocal music, particularly the vocal portamento; Chopin would often exquisitely vary his melody with ornamental figuration, as in the F minor Ballade. Many of Chopin's singing melodies, whether major (the Op. 9, No. 2 Nocturne or the middle section of the *Fantaisie Impromptu*) or even minor (Op. 63, No. 3 Mazurka), were carried over into twentieth-century popular music.

Chopin's "modal" effects do not derive solely from deliberate and consistent use of the lowered second and seventh or sharpened fourth degree of the scale, but rather from the ambiguity between the diatonic and altered forms of these scalar degrees. The early polonaises of Op. 71 best show the ambiguous leading tone, whereas the mazurkas contain the best illustrations of the conflict between the raised and natural fourth degrees of the scale (Example 5–9a, b) often found in Slavic folk music (Example 5–9c). The lowered second degree of the scale is the reverse of the leading tone's drive to the tonic; this gives the melody in Example 5–10a its despairing character and in another composition results in the kind of cadence typical of Bartók's music, where the leading tone and lowered second degree are sounded simultaneously (Example 5–10b).

EXAMPLE 5–9. Ambiguous use of raised and natural fourth degree of scale in (a) Chopin, Mazurka, Op. 56, No. 2; (b) Chopin, Mazurka, Op. 50, No. 3; (c) Slavic folk music (from Jan Seidel [ed.]), *Národ v Písni*, Prague, 1941, p. 247).

EXAMPLE 5–10. Lowered second degree of scale in (a) Chopin, Nocturne, Op. 27, No. 1 and (b) Chopin, Mazurka, Op. 56, No. 3.

Liszt perceptively remarked that Chopin's main harmonic contributions were the extension of chords, chromatic and enharmonic inner parts, and embellishing notes in melodic figuration which are found in Italian vocal ornamentation. Abraham has coined the term "harmonic parenthesis" to describe the extension of chords; it consists of a passage in fast harmonic rhythm containing mostly dominant-tonic relationships which starts in the home key and returns to it and thus cannot be considered a true modulation. One of the simplest illustrations of this device is shown in Example 5–11. In larger and later works like the sonatas, ballades, and fantasias such

EXAMPLE 5–11. Chopin, Nocturne, Op. 9, No. 2.

harmonic parentheses are longer and more extensive and often involve a lavish keyboard figuration. One of Chopin's favorite modulatory points of departure is an unresolved dominant-seventh chord in third inversion, fortissimo, followed by runs and scale passages. Non-tonic beginnings are among Chopin's favorite devices; among them are the opening of the G minor Ballade with a cadential formula beginning with the "Neapolitan" chord (its root the flatted supertonic) which continues into the opening theme of the Ballade, and the magnificent dominant preparation of the A♭ major Polonaise. The mazurkas Op. 17, No. 4, Op. 24, No. 2, and Op. 59, No. 1 are wonderful specimens of tonal ambiguity equaled only by the A minor Prelude. Chopin sometimes relied on an "interlocking" tonality in which a composition begins in one key and ends in another; for example, the F major Ballade ends in A minor (Chopin's deliberate intention, according to Schumann).

Ignaz Moscheles' comment about Chopin's "harsh modulations which strike me disagreeably when I am playing his compositions" has been quoted out of context so often that the remainder of his statement needs to be supplied; he further said that such modulations no longer shocked him, since when Chopin played them "he glides over them in a fairylike way with his delicate fingers." Moscheles evidently could not play Chopin's music with understanding, for almost all of Chopin's dissonances are passing, not to be intensified or emphasized, and are an integral part of his (as well as Schumann's) piano coloring. Chopin's harmony had some influence on that of Liszt and Wagner (compare the ending of the Op. 48, No. 2 Nocturne with the finale of the *Faust Symphony* and the "Magic Sleep" motive of Act III of *Die Walküre*), but had its strongest impact on early twentieth-century composers like Ciurlionis and Skryabin, who extended Chopin's ideas to perhaps the ultimate reaches of tonal harmony.[1]

Chopin's counterpoint is not the revival of Baroque fugal devices as with Hummel or Schumann but rather the use of independent part-writing, free canonic writing, and the contrapuntal treatment (best seen in the Op. 62 nocturnes) of harmonic and melodic dissonances. The source of the latter techniques can be seen in Bach's etude-like works like the C minor prelude from Book I of the *Well-Tempered Clavier*. An increased reliance on counterpoint and a correspondingly decreased emphasis on melodic ornamentation are striking characteristics of Chopin's late style.

Chopin's rhythm, though dominated by the dance, is highly flexible; one need but think of the cross-rhythms between 3/4 in one hand and 6/8 in the other in the A♭ Waltz, Op. 42, and the E major Scherzo. He has two kinds of rubato: one kind where, in his words, "the singing hand may deviate . . . but the accompanying hand must keep time," appropriate to some of his music in which a steady left-hand accompaniment supports the right hand's silvery washes of color, often in irregular groupings of notes, characteristics of the *Berceuse* and *Barcarolle;* another kind is an alteration of tempo, either slowing or quickening, necessary for his nocturnes or stylized dances.

Chopin carefully marked the proper preparation of his trills, and the performance of his compound appoggiaturas should be generally on the beat as in the eighteenth-century style. Since the pedals of Chopin's time gave the piano less sustaining power than today's, the composer's indications for pedaling should be approached with caution.

HECTOR BERLIOZ (1803–1869)

Occasionally a composer will appear whose music is so original and so apart from the musical mainstream of his time that he is misunderstood not only by his contemporaries but also by succeeding generations. Gesualdo, Wilhelm Friedemann Bach, Janáček, and Varèse are such composers, and Berlioz is the only nineteenth-century composer to be compared to them.

---

[1] In her study "Zur Genesis des 'Prometheischen Akkords' bei A. N. Skrjabin," *Musik des Ostens,* II (1963), 170–3, Zofia Lissa shows that the "Chopin chord," a major thirteenth spelled C–B♭–E–A, is the ancestor of Skryabin's "mystic" chord C–F♯–B♭–E–A.

In comparison with his contemporaries, Berlioz's *oeuvre* is relatively scanty, consisting of a dozen major works plus songs, concert overtures, occasional pieces for ceremonial occasions, and early works written for the Prix de Rome competition during his student days. Frequently several years elapsed between conception and completion, or completion and performance, of a major work; one of the most tragic passages in Berlioz's memoirs is an account of the deliberate suppression of a symphony lest its completion and performance beggar him and his family. Berlioz earned his living not through composition but through musical journalism, arrangements of Weber's and Gluck's operas for performance in Paris, and poorly paying sinecure positions. Few composers have had to persist in their creative work in the face of so much official discouragement, misunderstanding, and lack of support; comparable examples are more apparent in the annals of science or medicine.

Berlioz's works may be divided into three chronological periods. The first was one of apprenticeship, chiefly devoted to writing works in competition for the Prix de Rome, which provided a government stipend for study in Italy and Germany; these compositions served as sources of themes and ideas for later works, and Berlioz has been criticized for such borrowings—by critics who forget similar re-uses of ideas by a host of composers, including J. S. Bach and Handel. The second period, characterized by an expansion of musical resources, began with the *Symphonie Fantastique* and ended with the *Damnation of Faust* (1846, although some numbers were written in 1829). The final period, which a few writers have termed neo-classic, culminated in his greatest work, the opera *Les Troyens* (1856–58, performed in 1863).

Berlioz was the last heir of the grand, monumental, Classic tradition of Gluck, Lesueur, and Spontini, and took Beethoven's innovations, especially those of the Ninth Symphony, as points of departure. Weber's operas and the best ideas of the lyrical aspects of French *opéra comique* were lesser influences. One cannot state with certainty whether Berlioz or Chopin was the first to employ certain new structural and harmonic devices, or whether Berlioz or Meyerbeer initiated certain orchestral effects. Certain it is, however, that Berlioz's visits to England, Germany, and especially Russia had a most invigorating effect on the younger composers of these countries. His *Treatise on Instrumentation* founded the science of orchestration; he was among the first of the modern conductors, being driven to this profession by the indifference or incompetence of the conductors in Paris; and his writings on music are equaled only by those of Schumann, Eduard Hanslick (1825–1904), and George Bernard Shaw (1856–1950).

Berlioz is one of the most misunderstood composers. His tempestuous life and love affairs were well publicized, but much of his apparent eccentricity was a kind of "role playing" on his part to help call attention to his music. The occasional massive effects which he specified for actually a small fraction of his music were inviting to caricaturists (one Parisian portrayal had him riding in a giant, horse-drawn bass drum), and even today the general impression of Berlioz's music held by those not well acquainted with his works is that of noise, tempest, daemonic dissonance, and legions of brass and percussion players.

Berlioz's religious works show the contradictions of his style. The *Requiem* (1837) and what he called his "Babylonian" and "Ninevite" *Te Deum* (1849) are the two works which have been most responsible for the legend about his music's noisiness and the immense numbers of players necessary to perform it, yet *L'Enfance du Christ* (1855) is a delicate, gentle work which derives not only from the intimate oratorios of Lesueur but also from the socially conscious aspects of the French Catholic revival during the nineteenth century. In a class by itself is the song cycle *Nuits d'été* (1841), with its long melodic lines for the voice and its subtle orchestration; this work wholly contradicts the typical misconceptions of Berlioz's music.

Berlioz's operas have been unsuccessful not on musical or dramatic grounds or even because of their vocal problems (though a few singers gave Berlioz the excuse that his music would ruin their voices) but because they are not adaptable to the limitations of the conventional operatic stage. *Benvenuto Cellini* (1834–38) is known today chiefly through its overture and the "Roman Carnival" extracted from the finale of Act II. His masterpiece *Les Troyens* contains a wide variety of musical and dramatic effects and moods, from the multi-orchestral statement of the "Trojan March" in Act I to the intimacy of the love duet in Act IV; the weakest parts of this opera are the bows to operatic convention in Act III. *Les Troyens* is particularly impressive in its retrospective, summarizing, and "testamentary" character as the culmination of the tradition of idealized Humanism in opera that began at the very end of the sixteenth century and continued through Baroque opera, Gluck, and Spontini. In a way, one could call *Les Troyens* a neo-classic opera. A similarly retrospective opera, *Béatrice et Bénédict* (1860–62), the composer's last work, is a deft *opéra comique* in the best traditions of this genre and the one opera by Berlioz which can best be accommodated to the restrictions of the stage; as a musical farewell it ranks with Verdi's *Falstaff* or the last movement of Beethoven's Op. 135 quartet as a masterpiece of gentle, enigmatic humor.

Aside from the concert and operatic overtures, Berlioz's five remaining large works are orchestral compositions, with or without voices. Four of them have been called "symphonies" although only the first, the *Symphonie Fantastique*, really deserves this title. *Harold in Italy* (1834), with an obbligato solo viola, is neither symphony nor concerto but a bit of both. The "dramatic symphony" *Romeo and Juliet* (1839) contains extensive choral passages in its outer movements, but its central second movement is

purely orchestral, for Berlioz felt that such scenes as Romeo's solo medita-
tion, the ball, and the love scene between Romeo and Juliet would be best
expressed without the hindrance of words. The *Funeral and Triumphal
Symphony* (1840) is exclusively for winds, although strings and a chorus
were subsequently added to the finale; it consists of a grand funeral march,
an "oration" for solo trombone, then after a thrilling fanfare an "apotheosis"
in quick-march style. The change of instrumentation in French army
bands, wherein oboes and bassoons were supplanted by saxophones and
saxhorns, has made this work a rarity in performance. The symphonic idea
disappeared with *Lélio* (1832), an unsuccessful "sequel" to the *Symphonie
Fantastique* that adds narrator and chorus to the orchestra. *The Damnation
of Faust*, which Berlioz first called a "concert opera" and finally "dramatic
legend," is neither symphony, oratorio, opera, nor cantata but contains elements of all these genres.

Berlioz's musical style is misunderstood because it differs so greatly
from that of his contemporaries or even his immediate successors, and his
antecedents like Spontini, Reicha, and Lesueur are unfamiliar even to most
musical scholars. Berlioz was not a pianist and, unlike nearly all Romantic
composers, was not affected by the literature or the musical thinking for
the piano; however, the idea that his harmonic language derived from the
guitar (his principal instrument) has been overstated.

Berlioz is the true founder of the "modern" orchestra, as his stipulation for numbers of instruments, especially in the string section, shows.
Berlioz demanded his additional performers not for volume but for sonority, especially in his brass writing; he knew that it took many string players
to achieve a true pianissimo, and he wanted additional winds in order to
have unified tone colors on a chord. He requested additional timpani not
only to have a triad or four-part chord playable on those instruments but
also to provide additional sonority for orchestral chords on the mediant.
Occasions when volume for volume's sake is demanded are few in his music; more characteristic are passages with extremely delicate scoring (the
third movement of the *Symphonie Fantastique* or the inner movements of
Harold in Italy) or a festive brilliance of violins and winds in their high registers (the ball scene in *Romeo and Juliet*). Berlioz was the first composer
to utilize fully the improvements in instruments, particularly the French
woodwind and brass instruments, that had resulted from the technological
and metallurgical innovations of the Industrial Revolution. Yet in his use
and disposition of even his largest vocal and instrumental resources, Berlioz
at all times remained the practical musician. Many of his scores contain
elaborate directions for the placement of the performers, thus showing his
consciousness of the effects producible by a spatial distribution of sound
sources.

Largely because of the satirical "Amen" fugue in the *Damnation of*

Faust and Ferdinand Hiller's remark that Berlioz believed "neither in God nor in Bach," Berlioz has been erroneously viewed as a hater of counterpoint. His contrapuntal point of departure was the last movement of Beethoven's Ninth Symphony, and the number of fugal passages in his works, of which the finale of the *Symphonie Fantastique* or the introductions to *Harold in Italy* and *Romeo and Juliet* are representative, should lay to rest any statements that Berlioz was anti-contrapuntal; in fact, the opening chorus of the *Te Deum* is as good fugally as any of Mendelssohn's essays in this genre. Berlioz's most characteristic contrapuntal device is the combination of two themes, often for a programmatic purpose; this effect may have been derived from the double-fugue variation in the last movement of Beethoven's Ninth Symphony, if not from opera.

Berlioz's harmony is strikingly original, chiefly because of his free use of diminished-seventh chords as modulatory pivots, his love for "weak" or so-called "modal" progressions to the third or sixth degrees of the scale, his employment of orchestral timbres to reinforce harmonic change or to underline the part writing, and his use of seemingly arbitrary or even dissonant effects which on closer examination are surprisingly logical (e.g., the relationship between B♮ and C♮ in the second movement of *Harold in Italy*, which at first seems gratingly dissonant but highly reasonable after one hears the coda of this movement). Berlioz hated abuses of non-harmonic tones, especially appoggiaturas, and criticized even the tame use of them in Herold's *Zampa* (1831) as well as Wagner's more radical employment of them in *Tristan*. One of Berlioz's favorite dissonances consists of suspensions delayed well past the expected moment of resolution. He also delighted in the flat submediant, often in an inner part, as an expressive degree of the scale.

One of Berlioz's most striking harmonic effects is his use of successions or juxtapositions of seemingly unrelated chords rather than chord progressions with their implications of musical directionality. The following passages from the "Agnus Dei" of the *Requiem* (Example 5–12) illustrate in outline his effective use of (a) non-directional chords to prepare the eventual dominant-tonic cadence in G major (compare this passage with Example 4–6 from Schumann's F♯ minor Sonata); (b) the "modal" flavor of the final "Amen," which includes secondary triads preceded by and resolving to the tonic without the customary intervening chords, but note that the enharmonic submediant (with A♭ rather than G♯) and the Neapolitan chord are given similar treatment; and (c) the descending bass line, its notes alternating with the tonic, that provides the rational justification for the seemingly unrelated chords in (b).

The difficulty that most analysts have had with Berlioz's harmonic style is that his harmonic language is not that of his Germanic precursors and contemporaries, from J. S. Bach to Brahms, which consists of direc-

EXAMPLE 5–12. Berlioz, *Requiem*, Op. 5, Agnus Dei. Harmonic plans of (a) opening (measures 1–13); (b) final "Amen"; (c) descending bass line of (b).

tional chord progressions as part of long-range tonal goals. It is, however, upon these Germanic works that so many textbooks and treatises on harmonic analysis have been based, setting up criteria by which Berlioz's harmonic writing is judged as arbitrary, unskillful, or clumsy in comparison, say, to that of Mendelssohn. Example 5–13 is an illustration of Berlioz's short-range harmonic logic: though the internal cadences are on C major and the remote E major, the section begins and ends in F major.

Berlioz's melodic gifts escape many listeners because his melodies are often long, asymmetrical, and even seemingly arbitrary: recently the melody in Example 5–13 has been claimed as a quasi-serial melody, but note how the sparse accompaniment and harmony give it a tonal orientation. Berlioz often loved to reharmonize melodies on their recurrence, a technique best shown in the second movement of *Harold in Italy*. Berlioz's melody also has a wonderful rhythmic flexibility, seen not only in Example 5–13 but also in the opening allegro of the *Benvenuto Cellini* overture and the horn theme of the hunt and storm in *Les Troyens*.

Rhythm is the most exciting aspect of Berlioz's music. In his letters and memoirs he repeatedly complained about the inadequacies of many orchestral musicians in coping with his rhythmic writing. It is not so much the use of syncopation or rhythmic experiments like the 7/4 meter of the dance of the soothsayers in *L'Enfance du Christ* that makes his rhythm so original, but the subtle "sprung rhythms," the cross-rhythms, the entrances stipulated where the performers do not expect them, the differences be-

EXAMPLE 5–13. Berlioz, *Romeo and Juliet*, Op. 17, Part II (Romeo Alone).

tween macrorhythm (meter) and the microrhythm of individual lines or short groupings of notes, and even what Renaissance composers would have called "proportions" (the coda of the third movement of *Harold in Italy*).

Berlioz's form is loose but logical. His use of the recurrent *idée fixe* in the *Symphonie Fantastique* and his recapitulation of previously heard themes in *Harold in Italy* (deriving directly from the finale of Beethoven's Ninth Symphony) and the *Requiem* were supplanted by less obvious and systematic procedures in his later works. According to Barzun, rhythm and tempo have structural functions for Berlioz. Tonality does not play as important an organizing role in his music as it did in the works of his Germanic contemporaries, and Berlioz must share with Chopin the responsibility for weakening the effect of tonality as a major structural device. Rushton has coined the term "arcade form" to describe the musical structures of Berlioz that are built up from a series of relatively short and equal spans which can be defined by themes, tonalities, lengths, and even dynamic levels. Arcade form may coincide with elements of sonata form, as in the first movement of *Harold in Italy*, or not, as in the second movement of *Romeo and Juliet* where the musical structure, thematic and tonal, has baffled analysts who sought to find in it a conventional rondo or sonata form. Saint-Saëns remarked that Berlioz was more of a poet than a musician, probably because of the ways in which the narrative and illustrative elements of his music took precedence over traditional harmonic, rhythmic, or structural formulas.

For the listener, the impact of the rhythm and the orchestral sonority in Berlioz's music often obscures the unconventional and original treatment of other musical materials. So much is made from the idea of contrast: compare the sheer massiveness of the *Te Deum* with its meticulous attention to detail, especially in varying the accompanimental patterns of a repeated theme, or the variety and brilliance of Berlioz's allegros with his deliberate uses of monotony to create an expression either of humility (the offertory of the *Requiem*); of inexorable, relentless power (the "Judex crederis" of the *Te Deum*); or of a nocturnal amorous atmosphere (the love duet in Act IV of *Les Troyens*). Berlioz paints a better picture of Hell than any other composer (*Symphonie Fantastique, The Damnation of Faust*) but his contrasting heavens are rather bland. Berlioz's structural niceties are often obscured by the wealth of detail in his transitional passages.

Berlioz changed many elements of his style from work to work, probably from an intense desire to avoid repeating himself. As a result, his output was relatively small in comparison to nearly all other composers (his highest opus number is 28, for *Le temple universel* for two mixed choruses and organ of 1861). With the "apotheosis" of the *Funeral and Triumphal Symphony* or the *Reverie and Caprice* for violin and orchestra he showed that he could write in a popular vein, but his heart was in the monumental works which were accepted by only a limited segment of his audience. Each of his major works differs in several essential respects from its companions, and Barzun has pointed out the disagreement among students of Berlioz's music about which of his works is the greatest or most representative. Few composers, moreover, are less amenable to pigeonholing, categorizing, or the tracing of influences; Berlioz exists in a kind of splendid isolation, though his influence is greater than is generally supposed or was generally admitted.

BIBLIOGRAPHICAL NOTES

Italian music of the nineteenth century has been most recently surveyed in Vincenzo Terenzio's *La musica italiana nell'ottocento* (2 vols., Milan, 1976); Italian instrumental music is given an overview in Sergio Martinotti's *Ottocento strumentale italiano* (Bologna, 1972). I have edited three volumes of Italian symphonies, mostly from the nineteenth century, in the series *The Symphony 1720–1840*, ed. Barry Brook (New York and London, 1980–).

Since the late 1960's Rossini's music has undergone extensive reappraisal with several articles and dissertations, but as yet no biography has replaced the older studies by Giuseppe Radiciotti (3 vols., Tivoli, 1927–29), Francis Toye (London, 1934), and Herbert Weinstock (New York, 1968). William Ashbrook's *Donizetti and His Operas* (Cambridge, England, 1982) is the standard study with Barblan and Zanolini's *Gaetano Donizetti* (Bergamo, 1983) the main Italian biography; special investigations may be found in the *Journal of the Donizetti Society* (1974–). The starting point for research on Bellini's music, as for much Italian opera of the period, is Friedrich Lippman's scholarly and analytical *Vincenzo Bellini und die italienische Opera Seria seiner Zeit, Analecta musicologica,* VI (1969); English-language biographies include those by Leslie Orrey (London, 1969) and Herbert Weinstock (New York, 1971).

Extensive lists of recent studies of Verdi's music may be found in the newsletter of the American Institute for Verdi Studies, located at New York University. The standard study of the operas is Julian Budden's *The Operas of Verdi* (3 vols., London, 1978–81; see also the review article by Gary Tomlinson, "Verdi after Budden," *Nineteenth-Century Music,* V (1981), 170–82). William Weaver's *Verdi: A Documentary Study* (London, 1977) contains not only translated documents but also many sumptuous illustrations; Weaver's and Martin Chusid's *A Verdi Companion* (New York, 1979) consists of a group of specialized essays by various authors. David Kimbell's *Verdi in the Age of Italian Romanticism* (Cambridge, England, 1981) follows the composer's life through *La Traviata;* Frank Walker's *The Man Verdi* (New York, 1962) remains the best survey of the composer's career, though an extensive biography by Mary Jane Matz is in preparation, on the scale of Franco Abbiati's standard Italian biography (4 vols., Milan, 1959). The proceedings of the Istituto di studi verdiani in Parma, begun in 1960, and the special issues of *Studi verdiani* (Parma, 1982–) contain more specialized studies. Morse Peckman's essay "Romantic Historicism in Italy" in his *Romanticism and Ideology* (Greenwood, Fla., 1985) contains stimulating conjectures on "aggression" in opera from Rossini to Verdi.

W. L. Crosten's *French Grand Opera* (New York, 1948) is an unsurpassable study of the cultural milieu of this genre. Martin Cooper's *Opéra Comique* (New York, 1949) and my dissertation on D. F. E. Auber (University Microfilms, 1957) survey the lighter counterpart, but *opéra lyrique* has yet to receive a definitive investigation, since T. J. Walsh's *Second Empire Opera* (New York, 1981) is devoted more to the Théâtre Lyrique than to the music performed there. Karin Pendle's *Eugène Scribe and French Opera of the Nineteenth Century* (Ann Arbor, 1981) deals with music as well as the writings of French opera's leading librettist.

The memoirs of Gounod (English translation, New York, 1895) and Massenet (English translation, Boston, 1919) and the biographies of Bizet by Mina Curtiss (New York, 1958) and Winton Dean (London, 1962) and James Harding's biography of Massenet (London, 1970) give at present the best picture of *op-*

éra lyrique in English. Offenbach's work in its cultural milieu is marvelously studied in Sacheverell Sitwell's *La Vie parisienne* (London, 1937) and Moss and Marvin's *Can-Can and Barcarolle* (New York, 1954); the portion of his diary dealing with his American voyage has been translated by Lander Mac-Clintock as *Orpheus in America* (New York, 1957). Richard Traubner's *Operetta: A Theatrical History* (New York, 1984) is a useful reference work for this genre.

Chopin's life and works have produced chiefly rhapsodic, quasi-poetical appreciations, not only from critics (for example, J. G. Huneker, *Chopin: The Man and His Music,* New York, 1901) but even from scholars (Hugo Leichtentritt, *Chopin,* Berlin, 1905). Gerald Abraham's *Chopin's Musical Style* (4th ed. London, 1960) is a splendid study of his music, and Arthur Hedley's *Chopin* (3d ed. London, 1974) corrects many of the legends about this composer. Edward Waters' annotated translation of Liszt's *Life of Chopin* (New York, 1963) makes available a fine appreciation and memoir, even if this biography is probably Liszt's ideas as edited by the Princess Carolyne de Sayn-Wittgenstein. The main recent biography (which deserves an English translation with account taken of more recent research) is Gastone Belotti's *Chopin l'uomo* (3 vols., Milan, 1974), which examines the composer's human and artistic personality rather than analyzes his music. Krystyna Kobylańska's *Frédéric Chopin: Thematisch-bibliographisches Werkverzeichnis* (Munich, 1979) is the standard thematic catalogue. Other investigations include a collection of essays edited by Alan Walker (London, 1966), Jim Samson's highly praised *The Music of Chopin* (London, 1986) and several recent articles by Jeffrey Kallberg: "Chopin in the Marketplace," *Notes,* XXXIX (1983), exploring his relationship with his publishers; "Compatibility in Chopin's Multipartite Publications," *Journal of Musicology,* II (1983), on the relationship of individual pieces within given opus numbers; and "Chopin's Last Style," *Journal of the American Musicological Society,* XXXVIII (1985), on Chopin's ultimate compositions. The excellent performing editions of Chopin's music being prepared by G. Henle Verlag in Munich replace all earlier versions.

Jacques Barzun's classic biography, *Berlioz and the Romantic Century* (3d ed., New York, 1969), influenced in its musical portions by Tom Wotton's *Berlioz* (1935; reprint, London, 1969), should now be read in light of the more soberly factual biography by Hugh MacDonald (London, 1982). Special numbers of *La Revue musicale* (1956) and *Revue de musicologie* (1977) contain essays on the composer's musical style. Special studies of the music include Brian Primmer's *The Berlioz Style* (London, 1973) and, of special merit, Julian Rushton's *The Musical Language of Berlioz* (Cambridge, England, 1983). A new edition of Berlioz's literary works is in progress; those in English translation include David Cairns's translation of the *Memoirs* (London, 1970) and Jacques Barzun's of *Evenings with the Orchestra* (2d ed., New York, 1973). The *New Berlioz Edition,* begun in 1968, is a model of scholarship and editorial practice.

SIX

THE MUSIC OF THE FUTURE

The year 1848 is the dividing point in the musical as well as the narrative, social, and cultural history of the nineteenth century. The revolutions of 1848 and 1849 which convulsed continental Europe all ended in failure. During this time Berlioz and Chopin sought safety in England; Schumann and Johann Strauss paid tribute with marches, the former to commemorate the revolutionaries and the latter to celebrate the victors; Liszt wrote his heroic elegy *Funérailles* as a memorial to his friends who fell in the Hungarian uprising; and Wagner was so actively involved in revolutionary activities that he was driven into exile.

Although literary historians consider 1848 the terminal date of Romanticism, the changes in music that took place after that year gave nineteenth-century Romanticism in music a new lease on life which was to be valid for another forty-five years. It is true that the deaths of Mendelssohn, Chopin, and subsequently Schumann created a vacuum which was filled by Liszt and Wagner, though these two composers had written important works before 1848; that Berlioz and Verdi substantially changed their musical styles; and that as Meyerbeer's reputation was waning, *opéra comique* and Grand Opera coalesced into *opéra lyrique*. Yet all the new developments had important roots in the immediate past, and though 1848, like 1870, is an important "watershed date" in the general history of the nineteenth century, it is not a year marking stylistic convulsions like 1600, 1740, or 1910; 1848 is a date dividing a musical epoch like 1550, 1690, 1770, or 1945.

Terms like "music of the future" and "new German school" are often used to describe some of the musical developments that took place after 1848. The phrase "music of the future" has been attributed to a hanger-on in Liszt's circle (Liszt himself did use it, but in quotation marks), and became a pejorative term among conservative critics in Germany and France; the term "new German school" approximately describes only the compositions by Liszt and his circle during the 1850's and 1860's. This "new music" had several important antecedents: Beethoven's late works, Berlioz's and Chopin's compositions, and less "respectable" parents like Spohr, Spontini, and Meyerbeer.

Protagonists of the "new German school" felt that Beethoven had said all that was worth saying in the media of absolute music and that the symphonies, sonatas, and string quartets produced after his death were inferior to their models. Spohr and Berlioz had shown that the program symphony was a way to a new ideal of expression, and Berlioz had also revealed the new orchestral colors available to the composer. Paganini exhibited a new concept of virtuosity which Liszt transferred to the keyboard, and Weber, Spohr, and Berlioz had been the principal founders of the discipline of conducting. Beethoven's ideas for the enrichment of the large instrumental cycle led to large works intended to be played without pauses between its movements and with thematic links between them—Schubert's "Wanderer" and F Minor Fantaisies, Mendelssohn's Violin Concerto and "Scottish" Symphony, Schumann's Fourth Symphony and Cello Concerto, for example. The declamatory songs of Schubert were just becoming known. Although the Italianate "number opera" provided opportunities for the singer, it was coming to be viewed as dramatically false and musically sterile; Meyerbeer's Grand Operas were more theatrically effective but made too many concessions to the public. Harmonic and instrumental colors were to provide the main channels for musical expression in new forms, instrumental or vocal, and thus provide edification and emotional release for an audience that had to be specially trained through musical journalism.

FERENC (FRANZ) LISZT (1811–1886)

Liszt was born only thirty miles from Vienna, his mother was Austrian, and from childhood he resided chiefly in central or western Europe;

though bearing a Hungarian name and publicly identifying himself as Hungarian, he could not speak the language (he was most at home in French), and despite his Hungarian rhapsodies he was not a truly nationalist composer. He was, in fact, the most international musical figure between Gluck and Stravinsky.

Liszt's works fall into five chronological periods with the years 1839, 1848, 1861, and 1869 as the approximate points of demarcation. His work, however, has not been subjected to the searching examination or chronological-bibliographical study that the works of other major composers have received. He revised most of his early works during the 1850's, and his songs span his entire career without revealing the radical changes of his piano music.

First Period. Though Liszt wrote a number of boyhood compositions, his first mature works date from around 1834: the two "Apparitions" and the highly unusual *"Harmonies poétiques et religieuses"* after a poem by Lamartine (part of which was retained in the "Pensée des morts" in the later set of pieces with the same name) which may have been begun the year before and revised in 1835 before publication. The most important works of the first period are the *Transcendental Etudes;* the *Album d'un voyageur,* impressions of his idyllic stay in Switzerland with Marie d'Agoult between 1835 and 1836, which he revised in 1855 as the first volume (Switzerland) of the *Années de pèlerinage;* and the *Grand galop chromatique* of 1838 or shortly before, which Liszt did not revise. Most of Liszt's later changes were in structural cohesion and pianistic layout, though he drastically pruned some of the Swiss numbers for their later appearance.

Liszt also began the piano pieces depicting the impressions of his Italian stay with Marie in 1837–39, though they were not published until 1858 as the Italy volume of the *Années de pèlerinage;* here Liszt's interest in literature and the visual arts is strongly evident. The volume ends with a climactic work, the so-called "Dante Sonata," really based on Victor Hugo's poem "Après une lecture de Dante" as a "Fantasia quasi Sonata" rather than on incidents in *The Divine Comedy.* Liszt was not yet ready for full-scale sonata composition.

Most of the *Transcendental Etudes* are works of great virtuosity, although "Paysage" with its premonitions of Brahms's style, the delicate "Feux follets" with its use of a motive which Bartók later employed in his Fourth String Quartet, and "Harmonies du soir" provide poetic contrasts. The final version of 1852 was a simplification of the virtually insuperable pianistic difficulties of the 1826 and 1839 editions. The fourth of these etudes well illustrates the varied treatment of a melody which Liszt developed into the "transformation of themes," as Example 6–1 shows, as well as Liszt's piano technique; Example 6–1b is a specimen of the so-called "thumb melody" for which Liszt was famous.

In contrast, the individual pieces of the *Années de pèlerinage* range

EXAMPLE 6–1. Liszt, excerpts from "Mazeppa," *Transcendental Etudes.*

from the quietly lyrical piece ("Eclogue," "Sposalizio") to full-fledged symphonic poems for the piano like "Vallée d'Obermann," the most remarkable work in the two sets, or the dissonant "Il Penseroso," which anticipates the strange harmonies of his late works. Such harmonic devices as altered chords, third-related progressions, or unresolved dissonances are evident even in these early compositions. The *Grand galop chromatique,* a fine specimen of bravura display, anticipates not only Offenbach's can-cans but also the circus-like music with piquant dissonances later effectively employed by Prokofiev and Shostakovich. Many critics have difficulty in reconciling the advanced style of these works with their chronology, for they are contemporaneous with the most popular piano compositions of Schumann and Chopin; Liszt was later to write polonaises, ballades, and a berceuse with a pedal point on D♭ like Chopin's. Paganini's violin playing influenced not only Liszt's keyboard technique but also his sense of "showmanship," whereas Berlioz's influence was important chiefly in guiding Liszt's steps toward program music.

 Second Period. Liszt spent the years from 1839 to 1847 as a touring virtuoso, concertizing all over Europe, even in Ireland, Portugal, Russia, and Turkey; giving as many as four recitals (Liszt invented the term) a week, many of them from memory; travelling under primitive conditions, by stagecoach and often at night; and being the object of the kind of adulation bestowed today upon rock stars. He had little time for composition, though he began to write songs and was especially influenced by the gypsy musicians whose improvised playing he encountered during his return trips to Hungary after 1839; the famous *Hungarian Rhapsodies* were the result. He also began to sketch many of the works which were later to be completed in Weimar after he retired in 1847 from his hectic performing career. The most representative works from this period are the piano transcriptions, paraphrases, reminiscences, and other arrangements of works by other composers, to which he often brought his own contributions almost to the point of reinterpreting a previously existing work, as in the *Réminiscences de Don Juan* (1841), a fantasia on motives from Mozart's *Don Giovanni*, which is as striking a Romantic interpretation of Mozart's opera as E. T. A. Hoffmann's story "Don Juan." Though some of Liszt's transcriptions date from his Paris years, he continued to arrange works in other media for the piano throughout his life. The operatic paraphrases were meant to be appreciated by those who knew their operas well and were among the most popular works on Liszt's tours; in these works he developed many of the techniques of thematic manipulation and tonal organization that he was later to use in the orchestral compositions of his Weimar period. He also transcribed songs, chiefly Schubert's or his own (the Petrarch sonnets and the *Liebesträume* were originally songs); orchestral works by Beethoven and Berlioz; and even J. S. Bach's Weimar organ works. In a day when permanent symphony orchestras were rare, Liszt's transcriptions brought many unfamiliar works before the general public and undoubtedly aroused in many the desire to hear the original versions. During these virtuoso years Liszt showed himself altruistically willing to devote his talents to playing the major works of Schumann and Chopin, since they were physically incapable of doing so.

Third Period. From 1848 to 1861 Liszt was musical director and conductor in Weimar, producing concerts and conducting operas. During this period he wrote his most frequently performed large compositions, devoted his energies generously to helping Berlioz and Wagner, revised almost all of his earliest compositions into their final form, and assumed responsibility for the writings on music which appeared under his name.

The piano works of this period include the intimate Consolations and the *Harmonies poétiques et religieuses*, essentially a continuation of the *Années de pèlerinage*, which include reworkings of earlier compositions, transcriptions, and the grand heroic elegy *Funérailles* (its middle section, similar to the trio of Chopin's A♭ major Polonaise, has given rise to the erroneous legend that this piece is a "tombeau de Chopin"). The two polonaises, two ballades (the second fine if repetitious), and a few shorter works seem directly inspired by Chopin. The most significant of Liszt's piano compositions of this period, and the most influential piano composition for the second half of the nineteenth century, is the B minor Piano Sonata, completed in 1853 and dedicated to Schumann.

For this one-movement, cyclically connected structure which combines the salient elements of contrast and unity of both the sonata-form first movement and the multi-movement instrumental cycle, Liszt had several precedents: the later fantasies of C. P. E. Bach, Mozart, and Schubert; the first movement of Clementi's G minor Sonata, Op. 34, No. 2, in which the pervasive thematic transformations of a single motive in all sections of the movement, including the slow section between development and recapitulation, anticipates the structure of Liszt's B minor Sonata; a one-movement *Grande sonate mélancolique* (1814) by Moscheles which surprisingly anticipates Liszt's rhetorical devices; and the ballades, *Polonaise-Fantaisie*, and especially the F minor Fantasy of Chopin. Liszt pursued this one-movement form to its logical conclusion not only in the B minor Sonata but also in some of his symphonic poems and A major Piano Concerto.

Figure 6–1 shows in outline form the combination of structures in the Sonata in B minor, with significant motives and some of their transformations. Note the overlapping between "development" and "slow movement," although the "finale" corresponds with the recapitulation. The apparently capricious introduction, with its tonal center of G minor, is later seen as ingeniously logical: G is a pivot note for the diminished seventh that serves as the dominant of B minor. A tonic chord of B minor in root position (which earlier composers would have considered essential to establish the tonality) does not appear until the start of the transition to the second theme-group. Notice how the "closing group" is a lyrical transformation of the originally driving and hectic motive C.

The boundaries between exposition and development in this sonata are blurred, as in many of Beethoven's later sonata-form movements (Liszt had previously played in recital all of the late Beethoven sonatas), hence the seams of the fast part of the development section are difficult to find. The second part of the development section may be considered analogous to the slow movement of an instrumental cycle. New material (X), which is a contrast through its tonal stability in F# major and its homophonic texture, is introduced, is repeated in the same key after a tonally unstable contrasting section that treats previously heard motives, and returns in the coda. The restatement of motive A in the return of the introduction, with a tonal center of F#, leads one to expect a tonal as well as thematic recapitulation, but the enharmonic reading of F# as Gb and its use as a springboard for the diminished seventh as the dominant of Bb minor, the key of the fugue, is a surprise; the proper "recapitulation" occurs only with the appearance of the "second theme" (motive D) in the tonic B major. Despite transient modulations, the coda is in B major throughout.

Unity in other respects is only apparently broken down: although there are 15 changes of key signature, 12 major tempo changes, and 17 changes of time signature, these have mostly structural functions: the "second theme" is in 3/2 meter, the "X" theme is in 3/4 meter in contrast to

FIGURE 6–1. Liszt, Sonata in B minor, structural-tonal analysis.

"MOVEMENT"	SECTION	MOTIVE	KEY CENTER
"First Movement" (mm. 1–330)	Slow Introduction (1–7)	A	g
	Exposition (8–178) First theme-group (8–24 + 25–31)	B, C	b
	Transition (32–104)	B, C, A	b to V of D
	Second theme-group (105–119)	D	D
	Second transition (119–152)	B, C	around D
	Closing group (153–178)	C'	D
	Development (179–459)		
Part I (197–330)	Continuation of allegro (197–300)	B, C', D	Tonal flux
	Recitativo (301–310)	D	c♯, f
	Transition (311–330)	B, C, B/C	to B pedal
"Slow movement"	Andante sostenuto (331–346)	X	F♯
Part II, development	Quasi adagio (347–62)	C'	A
(331–459)	Contrast section (363–96)	D, B	F♯, G, V/F♯
	Reprise (397–452)	X, C'	F♯
	Retransition (453–59)	A	F♯
"Finale" (460–760) "Scherzando" (460–532)	Recapitulation (460–649) Fugue = first theme-group (460–522); subject inverted 509–15	B + C	b♭-E♭
	Correspondence to mm. 25–31 (523–32)	B, C	E♭-b
	Transition (533–565)	B, C, A	b-E♭-V/b
	Second theme-group (600–615)	D	B
	Second transition (119–152) omitted		
	Closing group (616–641)	C'	B
	Transitional close (642–649); (parallels 179–196)	B	to V/g♯
Coda (650–760)	Stretto quasi presto (650–672) (parallels incalzando, 255–276)	C'	g♯-V/B
	Presto (673–681)	A	b-B
	Prestissimo (682–699)	B	B
	Apotheosis (700–710)	D	B
	Peroration (andante sostenuto) (711–28)	X	B
	Epilogue (allegro moderato) (729–60)	C, B, A	B

Transformation of motive A in coda:

the prevalent quadruple or duple meters in the sonata, almost all of the key changes are in the development, and almost all of the tempo changes are in the coda. That Liszt intended this work to be one of high integrity rather than a virtuoso showpiece is shown by its ending, quiet and almost mystical rather than a shower of fireworks.

Among the other important works of the Weimar period are compositions for piano and orchestra, three of them major works. The earliest of these, the E♭ Piano Concerto, loosely adheres to a three-movement form (the second movement contains a slow movement, a scherzando in which the triangle is prominent, and a recapitulation of part of the first movement) with cyclic interrelations between movements, an omnipresent first theme, and interesting transformations, with the lyrical theme of the slow movement becoming the bumptious march of the finale. The A major Piano Concerto is a more successful work, in one movement with two contrasting themes, the first of these subject to the greatest variety of changes, though some critics have complained that the march-like transformation of the opening theme near the concerto's end is excessively bombastic. The *Totentanz* is a set of free variations on the "Dies Irae" chant of the Requiem Mass and the finest example of Liszt's "satanic" compositions, which had so much influence on Stravinsky and Prokofiev.

As a result of the urgings of his friend the Princess Carolyne de Sayn-Wittgenstein, Liszt directed his attention to purely orchestral compositions and while in Weimar wrote twelve of his thirteen symphonic poems and two programmatic symphonies. Though he needed help in orchestrating the *Mountain Symphony* (the weakest and most padded of his symphonic poems) and the first version of *Tasso*, with the final version of this work Liszt showed that he could handle the orchestra effectively if somewhat conventionally, his scoring being more like Spohr's than that of Berlioz or Wagner.

The symphonic poems derived on one hand from the concert overtures of Beethoven and Mendelssohn and on the other from the programmatic symphonies of Spohr and Berlioz; in scope and extent they occupy a position midway between overture and symphony. Programmatic works, their general structures are quite varied and their analysis is still a subject of controversy. Those symphonic poems which were originally conceived as overtures (*Tasso, Les Préludes, Orpheus, Prometheus*) most closely resemble sonata forms, whereas those based on philosophical poems (*Ce qu' on entend sur la montagne* by Victor Hugo—the so-called "Mountain Symphony"—and *Die Ideale* by Schiller) are attempts at the double-function form of the B Minor Sonata. *Les Préludes* is the most tightly organized work, with *Tasso, Mazeppa* (based on the fourth Transcendental Étude, with elaborate introduction and coda), *Orpheus* (a restrained work which many regard as Liszt's masterpiece in this genre), and *The Battle of the Huns* (based on Kaulbach's painting of the combat between the Huns and the Christian army and the most program-dominated symphonic poem) the other major works. These and Liszt's other symphonic poems influenced virtually every subsequent composer except such devotees of absolute music as Bruckner and Brahms: one can clearly see the influence of *Orpheus* on Franck, *Héroide funèbre* and *Mazeppa* on Mahler, and *Tasso* and *Die Ideale* on Richard Strauss; and the achievements of the eastern European nationalists or the French composers after 1870 would have been unthinkable without Liszt's orchestral works.

Of Liszt's symphonies, the *Faust Symphony*, composed in 1854 and first performed in 1857, is regarded by many as Liszt's greatest composition. Its introduction is very "modern," with much use of the augmented triad and diminished seventh as referential sonorities where no key is defined: Example 10–8a shows how Liszt used this triad to harmonize an aspect of the "Faust" theme that contains all twelve notes of the chromatic scale without any repetition and thus can be regarded as a "proto-tone-row." The first movement, "Faust," contains almost all of the themes of the symphony, whereas the second movement, "Gretchen," is chromatically lyrical and almost sensuous. The third movement, "Mephistopheles," is Liszt at his most interesting, for although he diabolically parodies the Faust themes to show that Mephistopheles cannot create, only destroy, when Gretchen's theme recurs toward the end of the movement it is undistorted, thus showing that she has escaped Mephistopheles' baleful control. The work concludes with a setting of the final chorus from Goethe's drama.

The rarely performed *Dante Symphony* is even less a symphony than the earlier "Dante Sonata" is a sonata. The first movement, "Inferno," is basically ternary in structure rather than a sonata design; the first part, in an ultra-chromatic D minor, contains Dante's text placed in the parts of the performers of the proclamation: "Abandon all hope, ye who enter," whereas the central part depicts the tragic story of Francesca da Rimini, in F♯ major and 7/4 meter. The transition back to the first part is not a fugue or "scherzando" but a grand crescendo indicated by Liszt as "to be interpreted as a blasphemous mocking laughter." The second movement, "Purgatorio," is basically ternary, with the opening in an ambiguous D major, the central fugue in a chromatic B minor, and the real key of B major evident only at the end, with the setting of the "Magnificat" for women's or boys' voices. Toward its end the chord successions outline a whole-tone scale, thus sounding like an anticipation of Vaughan Williams's choral style. Liszt did not set the "Paradiso" ending of Dante's original *Divine Comedy.* Originally the symphony was to have been part of a multi-media production that would incorporate painted dioramas, probably why it fails to follow standard symphonic procedures. Both of these symphonies are descendants of the program symphonies of Berlioz and lead to the large-scale, free-form symphonies of Mahler.

Liszt's songs are the least known of all his works. The Petrarch sonnets and *Liebesträume* are more successful in their piano versions, but "Es muss ein Wunderbares sein" has the intimacy of Schumann; "Tristesse," a late song, anticipates the chromaticism of Hugo Wolf; and the best song, "Ihr Glocken von Marling," anticipates the lyric song of the twentieth century. Many of Liszt's songs have overwritten piano accompaniments, and "Die drei Zigeuner" even sounds like a Hungarian rhapsody with vocal accompaniment; the French songs, of which "Oh! quand je dors" is the best, belong to the tradition of the romance rather than the German Lied.

Fourth period. After several disappointments in his efforts to make Weimar a major musical center, Liszt resigned his post as musical director in Weimar in 1858 and in 1861 followed Princess Carolyne to Rome. After deciding not to marry her, Liszt went into a period of semi-retirement and in 1865 took the preliminary holy orders toward entering the Catholic priesthood (he was called the Abbé Liszt but could not hear confessions nor celebrate the Mass); during this time he focussed most of his attention on religious works. Of the important piano compositions of the time, the Legends have religious topics, but in style they and the Mephisto Waltz (better in its piano than its orchestral version) hearken back to the Weimar period, during which years Liszt had become interested in choral music.

Liszt's first major Mass, the festive Mass for the dedication of the basilica in Esztergom (Gran), dates from 1855 and is orchestrally and stylistically related to the best symphonic poems, the Consolations, and the *Harmonies poétiques et religieuses;* along with the very subjective setting of Psalm 13, it exemplifies Liszt's ideas for à "humanitarian" church music which would be "devotional, strong, and drastic—uniting on a colossal scale the theatre and the Church, dramatic and sacred, superb and simple, fiery and free, stormy and calm, translucent and emotional." In this statement— and in these works—one is reminded not only of the social Catholicism of the Abbé Lamennais and his followers who remained in the Church but also of the "triumphalism" of Pius IX, Pope from 1846 to 1878 and a friend of Liszt. In contrast, the *Missa Choralis* (1865) is a very austere work for chorus with light organ accompaniment, without any of the fanfares, cymbal crashes, and rich harmonies of the Esztergom Mass or the Hungarian Coronation Mass of 1867.

Liszt's two oratorios, *St. Elizabeth* (1857–62) and *Christus* (1862– 67), are similarly contrasting, for the former is virtually an opera, akin to the historical works of Meyerbeer and early Wagner, whereas the restrained *Christus* resembles in spirit the *Missa Choralis*.

Most of Liszt's large-scale organ works date from this period, though the most massive of them, the fantasy and fugue for organ on the chorale from Meyerbeer's *Le Prophète*, "Ad nos, ad salutarem undam," dates from 1850 and combines formal and harmonic innovations with some of the techniques and effects of the operatic fantasia. Tours de force of virtuosity, not only in the demands on the performer's technique but also in motivic manipulation, treatments of chromaticism, and exploration of the farthest reaches of tonality, are the prelude and fugue on B-A-C-H (in German notation, B♭-A-C-B♮) and the variations on the bass line of the first chorus of Bach's Cantata No. 12, "Weinen, Klagen" (which Bach later used for the "Crucifixus" of his B minor Mass); Liszt's variations end with a setting of the chorale with which Bach ended the cantata.

Fifth period. Liszt's "twilight," as Szabolcsi has called it, began in 1869 and was marked by a sharp change in style, as astonishing as that in the music of the late Beethoven or Stravinsky. Although in public life Liszt was constantly shuttling between Rome, Budapest, and Weimar, the recipient of many honors and the teacher of an international coterie of piano students, in his creative life he was essentially cut off from the main currents of music, his late work refused by publishers and rejected by his former disciples.

These late works, almost entirely works for the piano or for the church, show harmonic experimentation and a breaking down of tonality. *Via Crucis* (Stations of the Cross), Liszt's major choral work of this period, contains contrasts between austere modal harmonies and adventurously altered chords, a free use of the augmented triad (found also in his late piano piece "Unstern," Example 10–8b), parallel empty and diminished fifths, the whole-tone scale, and clashing harmonies employed with the economy and even brutality of Musorgsky.

In contrast, the "Fountains of the Villa d'Este" from Book III of the *Années de pèlerinage* is Liszt's best-known late work; composed in 1877 when Debussy was fifteen and Ravel two, it anticipates most of the devices of so-called musical Impressionism: pan-diatonic planing[1] of superposed triads, themes that are more suggested than stated, whole-tone or other gapped scales, added-sixth chords, and iridescent keyboard sonorities. In keeping with Liszt's interests of his late years, there is a quotation (albeit with more "modern" quartal harmony) of the "Rheingold" motive from Wagner's *Ring* (Example 6–2b) and a footnote with a Scriptural quotation.

Example 6–2 illustrates some of these devices. Note the diatonically arpeggiated planed seventh chords after the sustained dominant harmony, followed by similarly planed seventh chords in first inversion treated in sequence (reduction in 6–2a), and the "Impressionistic" effect in 6–2c, where the leading tone (E♯) in the melody does not resolve, as expected, to F♯ but instead avoids this gravitational pull and at the opening is harmonized by an augmented dominant triad (mm. 49–52); the pentatonic melody under a static harmony in mm. 55–59, the lowered leading tone effect in measure 60, and the outlining of a tritone in mm. 61–62 which is then repeated without harmonization.

Musical Style. Liszt was psychologically an extremely complex and contradictory person, and the same can be said for his music, of which a capsule description of his style from his 1300-plus compositions is difficult to provide. Some elements, though, are strikingly prominent. Many of Liszt's advanced harmonic and melodic devices are occasionally encountered in his early piano works, such as altered chords, unresolved dissonances, tonic chords with added sixths, root movements by thirds or tritones, or even whole-tone scales. A favorite device is the planing of similar chordal sonorities: first- or second-inversion triads, parallel thirds (sometimes with another set in contrary motion), diminished sevenths to create stormy effects, or empty perfect fourths or fifths to create an effect of austerity or horror. Conversely, Liszt often uses chords of the augmented sixth as climactic harmonizations of "bel canto" melodies, whether drawn from operas he transcribed or his own cantabile themes.

Modal writing becomes more evident after 1850, deriving more from Gregorian chant (or attempts to imitate it) than from folk music as with Chopin, Brahms, d'Indy, or the Russian *kuchka*. Modal effects are often exaggerated by the use of unrelated chord successions, as Berlioz had done earlier from the *Requiem* onward, or by the use of a dominant chord with a lowered third, thus vitiating the leading-tone practice of the previous four centuries of music.

Liszt's use of counterpoint is chiefly marked by dramatic use of fugal

---

[1]Parallel successions of chords, also called "chord streams" or "gliding" chords.

EXAMPLE 6–2. Liszt, "The Fountains of the Villa d'Este" from *Années de Pèlerinage*, Book III (1877), excerpts.

techniques, but usually the fugal writing becomes homophonic after the entrance of the subject in all the voices. Occasionally there is fugal development, as in the inversion of the subject in the fugue of the B Minor Sonata.

From the standpoint of tonality, Liszt must share honors with the

Wagner of *Tristan* and the later *Ring* for breaking down the tonal pulls of nineteenth-century music. Modal writing, planing of intervals or chords, and emphasizing tritones helped, but several other devices need to be mentioned.

One is the virtual replacement of the traditional circle of fifths with a circle of thirds, as it were, whether diatonically related and thus close (the flat mediant or submediant in a minor key), chromatically altered but still relatively close by mid-century standards (after Beethoven, the tonal relation of sharped mediant to the tonic, E major to C major, resumed with Liszt), or chromatically altered and jarringly remote, as the sudden juxtaposition of E minor after C♯ major as early as the "Sonnet 104 of Petrarch" in the Italian *Années de pèlerinage*. The use of the sharped major mediant in a minor key (E major after C minor, for instance) is original with Liszt in the "Dante Sonata" (close and opening of the so-called "exposition") or even in such sonata-form expositions as *Tasso* or the outer movements of the *Faust Symphony*. Repetition, not only of themes but of sometimes sizable sections of music, is one of Liszt's ways of providing relative tonal stability, even when the repetitions are sequences or blocks of music repeated a step or half-step higher.

Atonality is a dangerous term to use in describing the music of any nineteenth-century composer. It has been unfortunately employed to describe the opening of the "Vallée d'Obermann" from the Swiss *Années* which is really a "floating tonality" going through a variety of keys in rapid succession; the opening section begins and ends in E minor and the piece's triumphant outcome is E major. The adjective "atonal" has also been applied to the highly chromatic prelude and fugue on B-A-C-H, chiefly because the notes of this motive promote tonal instability and the prevalence of diminished-seventh harmonies destroys any feeling of key. The fugue subject, in retrospect, is in B♭ major despite its chromaticism, and the work ends in B♭ major. The term "atonality" deserves to be used in terms of "diatonic atonality" in the very late works, especially with "Unstern" or the "Bagatelle Without Key."

Tonality and structure with Liszt, as with all other nineteenth-century composers, are inseparable. Liszt's music has often been the object of the reproach of "formlessness"—which his defenders, beginning with Wagner in his essay on Liszt's symphonic poems of 1857, did not really counter, saying merely that Liszt had his "own" form which was taken from the subject of the symphonic poem or program symphony. Liszt's themes are often obliquely defined in key (the first theme of the B minor sonata, for instance). In freer-form works the main subject, after an introduction which starts around a key and gets away from it, is generally stated in a key other than the tonic ("Sposalizio"); the recitative-like transitional passages between sections sometimes imply a key other than the actual outcome (exposition of the first movement of the *Faust Symphony*); and the lack of tonal closure between sections often makes it difficult to determine where given sections of a sonata form begin or end.

Yet Liszt, more often than not, amazes the listener with firm long-range tonal plans, even though their outcomes are perceivable only after the fact. *Funérailles* is one such piece: the dissonant introduction, with low piano sonorities reproducing the clangor of large bells and planed diminished-seventh chords creating some striking dissonances, contains a D♭ pedal which turns out to be the submediant of the tonic key, F minor. The later *Evocation of the Sistine Chapel* can be misunderstood as the musical equivalent of the picture postcards that had become popular around the 1860's—as maltreatments of Allegri's *Miserere* and Mozart's *Ave Verum Corpus*—but the B♭ augmented triad near the opening is also a dominant sonority of G minor in which the *Miserere*, often chromatically reharmonized, is set; and the G major ending is surprising after so much B major for the *Ave Verum Corpus*. Only with some of the piano works of the 1880's, to which I have assigned the term "diatonic atonality," is the expectation of tonality really absent.

Liszt's influence was felt throughout the entire second half of the nineteenth century and well into the twentieth. One of the greatest altruists in the history of music, Liszt aided nearly every composer who came into his orbit, from Chopin to MacDowell and Debussy, and trained an entire school of pianists. Echoes of Liszt's harmony and musical rhetoric can be found in the work of nearly every composer of the late nineteenth and early twentieth centuries; in fact Liszt, more so than Berlioz or Wagner, is the truly seminal figure for most twentieth-century music. The variegated facets of his musical personality were to find many echoes—the heroic in Mahler, the satanic diabolism in late Mahler, Stravinsky, and Prokofiev, the landscape painting (how different from Mendelssohn's) in Debussy and Ravel, the economy of means and use of striking dissonances in Schoenberg's Op. 11 piano pieces and in the works of Bartók, who considered Liszt more important than either Wagner or Richard Strauss in the development of music. Liszt was the dominant figure of the "progressive" trends in music, even to Webern and Messaien, although many today reject his aesthetic, his melodrama, his rhetoric, his optimism—which shows most clearly in the apotheoses of his symphonic poems—as well as his lapses of taste into bombast, roaring chromatic octaves, delicate chromatic filigrees at cadences, or overly rich harmony; those who dislike Liszt's music on these grounds should examine his more astringent late works.

RICHARD WAGNER (1813–1883)

Wagner is still the most controversial composer of the nineteenth century. Though his influence on the subsequent history of music was not as overwhelming as was once believed, no one can deny his important position in the second half of the century, the magnitude of his achievement, or the problems he posed for virtually every operatic composer who came after him. We should therefore look at the musical milieu from which his operatic ideas came (his other works are relatively unimportant in comparison), his chronological development as seen in his operas, and the salient aspects of his musical style.

After Weber's death in 1826 German opera became provincial again, for Germany, still a geographical abstraction, lacked the musical centralization and splendor of Paris or the many urban agglomerations of Italy which supported opera. Musical conditions outside Berlin and Vienna were rather primitive, and German opera had to compete with the French and Italian repertoire, which was better sung and easier to conduct or perform. The "great German opera," for these and other reasons, seemed an unattainable dream, though models existed in Beethoven's *Fidelio* and Weber's *Euryanthe;* Spohr labored in vain, Mendelssohn and Liszt evaded the challenge, and Schumann made the last unsuccessful attempt with *Genoveva* in 1850. Some of the younger German composers saw in *Der Freischütz,* Weber's most popular opera, a model: Albert Lortzing (1801–51) found his inspiration in the folklike *Gemütlichkeit* of Max's aria in Act I and the Huntsmen's chorus in Act III, while the horror story elements like the Act II finale inspired Heinrich Marschner (1795–61) in *Der Vampyr* (1828) and *Hans Heiling* (1833). French and Italian influences dominated the most successful German works like *Martha* (1847) by Friedrich von Flotow (1812–83) and *The Merry Wives of Windsor* (1849), its third act a minor masterpiece, by Otto Nicolai (1810–49).

Wagner's ideal was a German opera that would occupy an artistic position and status equal to that of the greatest symphonic music, with the theatre a locus for edification and ennoblement rather than mere entertainment (an idea that Schiller had pursued since the mid-1780's) and through his ambition, his will, and his egomania he succeeded, after numerous setbacks that would have broken ordinary spirits. The help he received from Spontini, Liszt, King Ludwig of Bavaria, and the members of the cult that grew up around his music were valuable, but his single-minded and egocentric determination was the principal factor in his eventual triumph; even some of his obstacles were of his own making.

Wagner's early works extend to 1848; his juvenilia need not detain us here, and we should concentrate on his four major operas of this period: *Rienzi* (1837–40, performed 1842 revised 1843), *The Flying Dutchman* (1841, performed 1843, revised 1846, 1852, and 1860), *Tannhäuser* (1843–45, revised 1860–61, 1867, 1875), and *Lohengrin* (1845–48, performed 1850 though the composer, then in exile, was not to hear it until much later). *Rienzi* is a grand historical opera written, it was thought, to outdo Meyerbeer, but its real parents are the grand operas of Spontini; only its overture is now generally known, but this work established Wagner as an operatic composer and obtained for him a post as conductor in Dresden. *The Flying Dutchman*, a work of greater significance, is the first of the "psychological dramas" in which Wagner was to excel, and the first practical demonstration of his theory of myth as the best source of plot for the music drama. *Tannhäuser* and *Lohengrin* are syntheses of Grand Opera devices, psychological music drama, and the medieval legends that excited many Romantics.

One who studies these works is struck by the various points at which Wagner either adheres to or departs from the operatic conventions established by Weber or Meyerbeer. Despite the continuous texture, arias and "set-numbers" are evident but are connected into scene-complexes; with Wagner the "scene-complex opera" replaces the "number opera" comprised of discrete set-numbers like arias, ensembles, or choruses with full cadences and pauses for applause between them. *The Flying Dutchman's* arias seem overwritten, especially Senta's ballad in Act II; it was the number of the opera written earliest and has the burden of explaining many of the incidents of the drama that went before or are to come. However, Elisabeth's "Dich, teure Halle" in *Tannhäuser* is a magnificent specimen of the traditional grand aria, and Wolfram's song to the evening star in this opera shows that Wagner could write a "hit tune" as well as any composer. Not until *Lohengrin* did Wagner display a thorough mastery of the duet. Wagner's large-scale ensembles are the most spectacular parts of these early operas and are most successful when they follow traditional conventions, like the march in Act II or the pilgrims' choruses in Acts I and III of *Tannhäuser*. The finales tend to follow the Spontini-Meyerbeer tradition, with the whole company on the stage; the longest finale is that of Act II of *Tannhäuser* with its prolix tournament of song and its hero's praising the charms of Venus in the chivalric accents of Weber's knightly heroes like Adolar or Hüon. *Lohengrin* contains the most interesting departure from the conventional spectacles, for they become muted, restrained, and subdued, and what seems to be a massive buildup to a climax in Elsa's procession in Act II is thwarted by Ortrud's denunciation. In all these operas Wagner shows a great love of contrast: Act III of *The Flying Dutchman*, in which Wagner effectively contrasts the merrymaking of the Norwegian sailors with the spectral atmosphere of the Dutchman's ship, is an excellent illustration.

In retrospect, Wagner did not make as much of a break with traditional operatic and musical conventions as either his enemies or his admirers claimed. Wagner's treatment of the voice in his early operas is quite noteworthy: though the voice dominates the orchestral accompaniment, much of what is to be sung is in a measured, quasi-melodious recitative akin to arioso (Wagner insisted that his singers perform from the standpoint of dramatic realism rather than for vocal effect), with the orchestra establishing an introductory atmosphere, interjecting comments, playing reminiscence motives, linking sections together, and even serving as a giant continuo. At its worst the effect is dull, compounded by a square-cut phrase syntax in the vocal parts with an overuse of a rhythm, but it can also rise to the heights of dramatic declamation, as in the hero's narrative in Act III of *Tannhäuser*, in which he describes his pilgrimage to Rome and its unsuccessful outcome.

Wagner's orchestra in these operas is not unusually large, and the additional resources he demands are chiefly for on-stage fanfares, but in *Lohengrin* he discovered the expressive effects of the English horn and bass clarinet. Wagner's use of the brass ranges from the "heavy artillery" noise of *Rienzi* to the great restraint of *Lohengrin*. Harmonically, Wagner was no more adventurous than Spohr, Liszt, or Chopin at this time; it is Spohr's chromaticism that pervades the Pilgrims' chorus and Elisabeth's prayer in *Tannhäuser*. Beginning with *Lohengrin*, Wagner associated keys with certain characters or incidents: A major (also the key of the prelude) for Lohengrin, F♯ minor for the conspiracy of Telramund and Ortrud, E♭ major and its related keys for Elsa, A♭ minor for accusations. In his recitatives Wagner is most tonally adventurous: in "Die Frist ist um" of Act I in *The Flying Dutchman* he uses one of his finest recitatives to get from B minor to C minor by way of floating diminished-seventh chords, although the ensuing aria has a conventional tonal scheme. The third act of *Tannhäuser* shows how Wagner was groping to achieve the dramatically and tonally unified structures characteristic of his later operas: the heightened declamation, accompanied by reminiscence motives, of the hero's pilgrimage (in A minor) is a harbinger of his later style, but set-pieces like the Pilgrims' chorus and Elizabeth's prayer are reminiscent of the Grand Opera tradition, and the tonality of E♭ major begins and closes the act.

With *Lohengrin* Wagner stopped composing, not only because his time was occupied with disputes with his superiors in Dresden, participation in the abortive revolution of 1849, proscription and exile to Switzerland, but because he felt that this opera marked a terminal point in his musical style. He had found it necessary not only to write the words as well as the music to his operas but also to train his performers and educate his audience; now he would have to begin all over again by developing a new kind of opera and explaining, in a series of essays (especially *The Art-Work of the Future* and *Opera and Drama*), his theories of what musical drama should be. After intensive study of both Nordic mythology and ancient Greek tragedy, in 1848 he made the first draft of a libretto, starting with what eventually became the last opera in the cycle, and in 1850 the first musical sketches for his cycle of music dramas *Der Ring des Nibelungen* (*The Ring of the Nibelung*), which he was not to complete until 1874.

The prologue, *Das Rheingold,* was finished in 1854 and *Die Walküre (The Valkyrie)* in 1856 (the works not performed, though, until 1869 and 1870 respectively), but he abandoned *Siegfried* at the end of the second act in 1857. Though in 1864 and 1865 he resumed work on what he had already done, he did not begin composing the third act until 1869, after his musical style had undergone substantial changes, and finished it two years later. The hiatus beween the second and third acts was filled by *Tristan und Isolde* (1857–59, first performed 1865), originally intended as a "practical" opera which would not require elaborate staging or scenery, and *Die Meistersinger* (1861–67, first performed 1868), Wagner's most beloved opera, praised even by those who dislike his other works. *Die Götterdämmerung (The Twilight of the Gods),* the last and greatest of the *Ring* cycle, was finished in 1874, and the entire cycle was given in Bayreuth in 1876 in a theater designed to Wagner's specifications. *Parsifal,* his final opera, which he called a "festival drama for consecration of a theater" *(Bühnenweihfestspiel),* was composed between 1877 and 1882.

Although Wagner often went counter to his theories in the actual composing of his operas, we should nevertheless examine the basic philosophy of his operatic ideals as stated in his essays.

Wagner first of all sought to restore the idea of drama as a thoroughly integrated art, in which plot, poetry, music, scenery, costume, and action would be combined (the *Gesamtkunstwerk*); in Wagner's own words, "The highest collective art work is the drama; it is present in its ultimate completeness only when each kind of art, in its own ultimate completeness, is present in it." Hence Wagner wrote not only the music but also the words and the stage directions for his music dramas.

From his survey of the history of dramatic music, Wagner felt that this art had grown corrupt and separated from its original purpose. The drama was no longer the ultimate object but merely a vehicle for music; music, which should be the means for the fullest realization of the drama, had become in itself the ultimate goal. In addition, music had become separated from poetry and dance and had developed its own autonomous laws, thereby becoming artificial. Song had degenerated into the operatic aria; the sacred dance had declined into the French ballet with its quadrille tunes; and music itself had become a concern not of the heart but of the mind through the use of musical artifices, particularly counterpoint. The orchestra, which Beethoven had raised to a peak as an expressive medium, was relegated by the Italians to service as a mere accompaniment for the singers or was utilized by the French (especially by Meyerbeer) as a means for producing stunning but superficial effects.

Wagner's two basic problems in creating music dramas were the unification of speech and song and the reconciliation of drama and music. In unifying speech with song, Wagner sought a middle ground between bald prose on one hand and rhymed poetry on the other. His solution, seen most clearly in *The Ring of the Nibelung* (its poetry composed before its music), was a reversion to the technique of ancient north European poetry in which common consonants in alliteration (the *Stabreim*) would not only provide coherence but would also permit contrast and antithesis which could be underlined by the music, especially through harmonic modulation. The *Stabreim* also eliminated the constraints on musical phrase-structure imposed by the rhymed verse and regular metric accents of traditional opera poetry (even that of Wagner's earlier operas), thus demanding more rhythmically flexible settings than the square-cut four-measure phrase so often used in the operatic set number. Speech, therefore, was intensified into tone language, with equal parity given to words and music. This tone language would be the principal vehicle for dramatic action, for soliloquy, and for dialogue.

The reconciliation between music and drama was to be provided by the orchestra, which would serve, in Wagner's words, as "the soil of infinite universal feeling . . . the perfect complement of scenic environment . . . [to dissolve] the solid motionless floor of the actual scene into a fluid, pliant, yielding, impressionable, ethereal surface whose unfathomed bottom is the sea of feeling itself." Instrumental music, as Beethoven had shown, could express everything that speech could not; it could arouse indeterminate emotions, comment on the action taking place on the stage, and, through the power of association, could recall past incidents, ideas, and feelings, and could actually produce more precise impressions than words alone could do. The orchestra would thereby complement the voice, bearing it along on the surface of harmony as a boat is borne on the surface of the ocean.

The form of the opera was to be a continuous unfolding of musical ideas as dictated by the plot. This was in contrast with the "number opera," in which self-contained arias, ensembles, and choruses were linked together by spoken dialogue, recitatives, or transitions. The plots were to be based on myth or legend; although Wagner wanted a "human" drama, the personages of myth or legend were larger than life and thus better able to serve as the incarnations of the basic questions of life itself: love, goodness and evil, heroism, faith, renunciation. In *The Flying Dutchman, Tannhäuser*, and *Lohengrin*, Wagner had already made use of medieval legend, which he was to continue in *Tristan and Isolde* and *Parsifal; The Ring of the Nibelung*, on the other hand, was based on pagan Nordic mythology.

Wagner did not consistently apply his theories of opera to his music dramas. To begin with, he was too good a musician and too experienced a man of the theatre to be completely fettered by theories, even his own. In a way, *Die Meistersinger* is a repudiation of his operatic theories, for it is written in rhymed verse, the characters are drawn from sixteenth-century

Nuremberg and seem like real persons rather than mythological beings or legendary personages, and there are numerous set-numbers of the kind encountered in traditional opera—choruses, arias (especially Walther's "Prize Song"), a ballet, even a quintet—embedded in the musical fabric. On the other hand, Wagner showed that his essential ideas of continuous musical flow, supported and reinforced by the orchestra, could be effectively applied to the "comic opera."

Revolutionary as Wagner's theories may have seemed at the middle of the nineteenth century, his music dramas nevertheless had many antecedents: the "symphonic style" of the operas by Mozart, Cherubini, and Beethoven; the continuous texture of Weber's *Euryanthe* and Meyerbeer's mature operas, in which the boundaries between the set-numbers were blurred; and the cyclic instrumental forms, with thematic linking, from Beethoven's Fifth Symphony onward. Wagner's concept of the *Gesamtkunstwerk*, where all operatic devices are united in a whole, stemmed not only from Gluck's operas but also from the dramas of Goethe, Schiller (whose *Die Braut von Messina* of 1803 would have been the first *Gesamtkunstwerk* had there been adequate musical and theatrical resources in Weimar), and Schubert's friend Franz Grillparzer (1791–1872). Even at his most innovative, Wagner preserved links with the musical past.

Only in *Das Rheingold* (effective because of its stage effects and fast action) and *Siegfried*, the least popular of Wagner's mature operas, did the composer's theories interfere with his instinctive musical and theatrical sense. Wagner's vocal melody, often just another strand in the orchestral texture and chiefly devoted to expressing the text, is sometimes perfunctory or is doubled by the orchestra, yet one sometimes finds full-fledged arias or dry but measured recitative, with the string section serving as the continuo. Wide leaps, generally fifths or minor sevenths, are one of Wagner's favorite expressive devices; the most extreme example may be found in Kundry's part in *Parsifal*, which established a precedent for the even wider leaps in the operas of Richard Strauss, Schoenberg, and Berg. Wagner's vocal melody is seldom "tuneful," for it is designed to carry the short textual lines and quick exchange of dialogue in the dramatic poem. Wagner's declamation demanded a new type of singer,[2] but there were several precedents for those roles which demanded endurance: Meyerbeer's heroic tenors or the heroines of Cherubini's *Medea*, Beethoven's *Fidelio*, and Weber's *Euryanthe* and *Oberon*.

Except for the on-stage brass instruments, Wagner used in his early operas a more conventional and less adventurous orchestration than Berlioz. The orchestra in the *Ring* is the largest because Wagner was creating

---

[2]It is interesting to note that throughout the history of his operas their heroines have been better cast than their heroes (Heldentenors), most of whom were originally baritones.

an entire dramatic world in which special effects were necessary. In Wagner's orchestra the increased number of wind instruments allows a homogeneous timbre on a chord; the English horn and bass clarinet (especially in *Tristan*) are as expressive for Wagner as the clarinet and horn were for Weber; the Wagner tubas for the *Ring* provide a solemn tone color to contrast with that of the horns or the heavy brass (best seen in the "Annunciation of Death" in Act II of *Die Walküre*); the bass trumpet, contrabass trombone, and tuba extend the compass of the brass section downward. Correspondingly, an increased number of string players is required to balance the additional wind instruments. Wagner's fortissimos are not constant, and he could orchestrate as delicately as any of his successors. His design for the sunken orchestra pit at Bayreuth, with the brass and percussion farthest under the stage, proves conclusively that he was interested more in sonority than in volume. Several features are typical of Wagner's orchestral sound: extended vertical structures with many doublings of chord-tones; upward extension of the ranges of the string instruments; frequent division of the string sections into many parts; string unisons on short turning figures accompanying a sonorous wind melody, evident as early as the overture to *Rienzi;* a great use of the cellos and even violas as melodic instruments; and a lavish employment of both fingered and bowed tremolos. Wagner often used the valved brass instruments, especially the horns, to strengthen the middle register of his orchestra, and such dramatic brass unisons as the trombone entrance in the *Tannhäuser* overture or the "treaty" motive in the *Ring* are still vividly exciting.

The leitmotive, which may be most simply defined as a musical identification of a character, an object, or a state of mind, is Wagner's most important external means of unifying his operas. In his early operas the leitmotive is melodic, sometimes even phrase-like (Example 6–3a), and should really be termed a "reminiscence" motive which reinforces the impression of a situation which occurred earlier (Verdi and Erkel were among the more conspicuous utilizers of this device). In his mature operas Wagner treats the leitmotives differently, owing much to the thematic transformations of Berlioz, Schumann, and especially Liszt; other precedents for such melodic, rhythmic, and harmonic alterations of still recognizable motives can be traced to Beethoven's development sections and even the development of subjects and countersubjects in J. S. Bach's fugues. Most of Wagner's leitmotives are melodic, but a striking chord progression (Example 6–3b) or even a rhythmic pattern (Example 6–3c) may suffice to recall earlier incidents.

The transformation of leitmotives occurs mainly through distortions of intervals or rhythmic patterns and reharmonizations. Significantly, the great majority of leitmotives in Wagner's mature operas are "open at both ends" in that they can be used in a sequence, preceded or followed by a

EXAMPLE 6–3. Wagner's leitmotives: (a) The Forbidden Question (*Lohengrin*, Act I); (b) Destiny (*The Ring of the Nibelung*); (c) Hunding (*Die Walküre*).

(a)

(b)   (c)

modulation, or the leitmotive itself can be modulatory, often enharmonically; Example 6–3b constantly fulfills this function in the last three operas of the *Ring*. Attempts have been made to reduce the basic number of leitmotives and to find relationships between apparently dissimilar ones; like all the sweeping theories that have been applied to Wagner's unconscious creative process, there are grains of truth in such attempts, but also a tendency to read too much into the existing musical evidence. There is some association between leitmotives and keys, evident in the earliest sketches for the *Ring*: the Valkyries ride in B minor; the Norns spin in E♭ minor; and just as Brünnhilde awakens, in *Siegfried*, to a harmonic progression from E minor to C major, so Siegfried, in Act III of *Die Götterdämmerung*, regains consciousness after his assassination by Hagen to the same progression, but from E♭ minor to C♭ major. Often there is much repetition of leitmotives since Wagner did not wish to leave too much to the audience's imagination; thus in Act I, Scene 3 of *Die Walküre*, where Siegmund discovers the sword in the ash tree, the "sword" motive is repeated some twenty-one times. One of the essential functions of the leitmotive is to substitute for the dramatic "aside," wherein the audience is informed of a situation not known to the actors on the stage; a good example occurs in *Siegfried*, when the orchestra tells the audience of Mime's plot against the hero.

The *Ring* contains the most extensive use of leitmotives because of the necessity for continuity in this long tetralogy which depicts a mythological universe divorced from mundane reality. Leitmotives are fewer in the other operas; because they depend so much on atmosphere (especially *Tris-*

tan and *Parsifal*), there is less need for recapitulatory reminiscence, and the few leitmotives used are even more striking and have more of an individual character than those of the *Ring*. Leitmotives are essential ingredients of Wagner's musical fabric, which has been called "endless melody" but is really a replacement of authentic cadences with deceptive cadences or other modulations. Although leitmotives sometimes occur in the voice part, they are usually embedded in the orchestra.

As the leitmotive is Wagner's most important external unifying device, harmony and tonality are his principal internal architectonic means. Although an extensive discussion of Wagner's harmony is not possible here, we should at least examine the principles of his harmonic practices and some of their applications.

Wagner has been called a "chromatic composer," but even in *Tristan*—his most notoriously chromatic work—he writes lengthy diatonic passages, as in the parts associated with Kurvenal. In the more chromatic sections Wagner achieves tonal stability by using "tonal cells" which often consist of a major or minor triad (the tonic), usually inverted, and containing a leitmotive; a diminished or half-diminished seventh chord; a dominant seventh, also containing a leitmotive; then a deceptive cadence, after which another character often sings or there occurs an orchestral interlude. The "open-ended" leitmotives permit several possible resolutions—sometimes to the tonic, more often to the dominant or a new tonic through a deceptive cadence, or to a diminished-seventh chord, which even in traditional practice has four possible resolutions. The longer leitmotives, like those signifying Valhalla or Siegfried's destiny, can be treated sequentially to give the effect of rising tonal plateaux. When Wagner concludes a musical section within a scene, the cadence is often to the dominant of the tonic. When he interrupts the effect of tonal stability, he uses deceptive cadences or coloristic harmony, chiefly the famous "Tristan chord" (Example 6–5c) or another chord of the half-diminished seventh or the augmented sixth, yet in the passage shown in Example 6–4 he uses the diatonic "Grail" leitmotive to create a contrast with the tonal ambiguity of augmented triads in sequence.

Parsifal, Wagner's last opera, has the sharpest contrasts in its harmonic vocabulary. In the second act Wagner seems to be reverting to the earlier style of *Lohengrin* in the scenes with the Flower Maidens, and the Parsifal-Kundry duet in this act utilizes the altered harmonies characteristic, not of *Tristan*, but of the erotic piano pieces of Adolf Jensen, e.g., the *Chants d'Ionie*, Op. 44. The motive of the "Dresden Amen," symbolizing the Grail, and the "Faith" motive are sternly diatonic yet "open-ended," as shown by the ending of the Grail motive on an augmented triad in the fifth measure of Example 6–4; both motives are treated sequentially as a series of tonal plateaux. The chromatic harmony of *Tristan* is raised exponentially

EXAMPLE 6–4. Wagner, *Parsifal*, Act II.

sein Stamm ver-fiel mir, un-er-lös't soll der Hei-li-gen Hü-ter mir schmachten,

"Grail" motive

und bald, so wähn' ich, hüt ich mir selbst den Gral.

Ha-ha!

in the prelude to the third act of *Parsifal* (a depiction of the hero's search
for the Holy Grail and by implication, God) in one of the most tonally free
and unstable passages in nineteenth-century music, achieved through the
interlocking of B♭ minor and G♭ major triads at the opening, followed by
planed diminished-seventh chords with a chromatic bass line in contrary
motion, a highly linear counterpoint, and the absence of any sense of tonal
closure. One can trace Wagner's harmonic and tonal development by comparing the preludes to the third acts of *Tannhäuser, Lohengrin, Die Meistersinger, Siegfried,* and *Parsifal.* In sharp contrast, the "Good Friday
Magic" scene of the third act is very clear-cut in its tonalities (from B major
to D major), with a transparent and basically diatonic harmonic vocabulary
similar to that of Brahms.

Certain operas get their "tone" from individual chords. The "Tristan
chord" in Example 6–5c and other uses of the half-diminished-seventh
chord in a non-functional role, especially in the love duet in Act II, are the
basic atmosphere ingredients of *Tristan.* The pitches of this chord remain
the same, but in the prelude they provide a supertonic chord to an A minor
tonality that is implied but never stated; in the second act the pitches are
stated enharmonically as F–C♭–E♭–A♭ and resolve within the harmonic orbit
of A♭ major. The diatonic "resolution" of the "Tristan chord" which eventually ensues is a 6–5 (G♯–F♯) melodic progression over a B major triad, the
climax of the "Love Death" motive in Act II, and both motives, with their
original pitches, are stated as the curtain falls at the end of the opera. The
major-minor sonority of *Die Meistersinger* is given variety by the use of the
half-diminished seventh in its functional role as a chord of the dominant
ninth with missing root, with the prevailing diatonicism invigorated by pan-
diatonic linear counterpoint and chromatic elaborations in the active inner
parts. The augmented triad supports the chromatic portions of *Parsifal* in
portraying pain and anguish (Wagner may have gotten this idea from Liszt)
but has no independent significance in Wagner's other operas; in *Die
Meistersinger* it accompanies Walther's rejection by the Mastersingers and
especially Beckmesser; in *Die Walküre* it is the harmonization of the "Ho-
jo-to-ho" motive of the Valkyries; and in *Die Götterdämmerung* it distorts
diatonic leitmotives.

In discussing Wagner's "microharmony" (individual chords and their
immediate contexts) one must remember that many of the most typical
"Wagnerian" effects were very much in the air during the first half of the
nineteenth century; Example 6–5 shows a few specimens thereof. Wagner
neither invented these harmonic ideas nor was he the last to use them, but
by employing them in striking dramatic and musical configurations, or with
unique voicings and chromatic alterations, he made them seem exclusively
his own. His followers misinterpreted his harmonic thought by trying to
write harmony for its own sake and by seeking, often in vain, completely

EXAMPLE 6–5. (a) Beethoven, Piano Sonata, Op. 31 No. 3, first movement (1802); (b) Spohr, Double String Quartet, Op. 65, first movement (1823); (c) Wagner, *Tristan and Isolde*, prelude (1859); (d) Chausson, *Le Roi Arthus*, Act I (1886–1895).

new and novel sonorities and effects. Examples 6–5d and 7–2a show how difficult it could be for Wagner's successors to escape his influence, and how the use of this chord (perhaps inadvertent on Chausson's part) could so easily lead to a charge of plagiarism, since Wagner had made this particular harmonic sonority so indisputably his own personal property.

Wagner's elaborate and extensive tonal structures serve to unify scenes, acts, and even entire operas. His macrotonality (the tonal plan of an act or even a long scene) extends over lengthy stretches of time-space through his use of a "psychological" tonality more evident to the ear than to the eye. This derived from the tonal plateaux in Beethoven's longer development sections; the "writing around the tonic," by emphasizing its dominant, so characteristic of Schumann, Chopin, and Liszt; and Chopin's "tonal parentheses" and lengthy dominant preparations. We should also remember that after 1850 it was no longer necessary to define the tonic of a key by stating it in root position on a strong beat; when this occurs it is usually a signal that a modulation is about to take place.

From *Das Rheingold* onward, only two of the operas (*Die Meistersinger* and *Parsifal*) end in the keys in which they began, and only Act II of *Parsifal* has a similarly closed tonal structure. Wagner achieves tonal unity through a network of interlocking tonalities, with the act as the largest structural unit. For dramatic reasons, governed usually by the number of persons on the stage, Wagner divided acts into scenes. These are not discrete and tonally closed but are connected, either abruptly through deceptive cadences in the early operas, or increasingly smoothly beginning with *Lohengrin;* as an example, the B♭ major of the "Bridal Chamber Scene" (with the famous wedding march) of Act III is followed by a smooth transition to the E major of the second scene of the act. Sometimes the scenes, or major subdivisions within them, are separated by orchestral interludes.

The scenes, in turn, are subdivided into sections of varying lengths and structures; it is at this level that Wagner scholars most frequently disagree as to the structural unit that is involved. Wagner postulated a "poetic-musical period" which would have a unity of feeling or dramatic action and a unity of key, yet contradicted himself later by writing of the extended expression possible through modulation into the most varied keys and back again, and subsequently by stating in a letter of 1859 that the secret of his musical form was in his "art of transition"; from his illustration, the second scene of the second act of *Tristan*, we cannot be sure whether he was referring to literary, dramatic, or musical transition. The principal question is whether Wagner conceived of his "periods" as broad dramatic divisions or as contiguous units made up of a few musical phrases. It is certain, though, that Wagner admitted that his "endless melody" could be interrupted with structural divisions that corresponded somewhat to the dramatic ones. Figure 6–2 shows the macro-structure of Act III of *Die Walküre*, in which the scenes are divided into sections of varying length and the main dramatic and tonal elements are identified. Note the massive dominant preparations that occur in individual acts: the "Ride of the Valkyries" of Scene 1 of Act III is in B minor and the scene and motive recur in the same key at the end of Scene 2, preparation for the E minor-major to-

FIGURE 6–2. Wagner, *Die Walküre*, Act III.

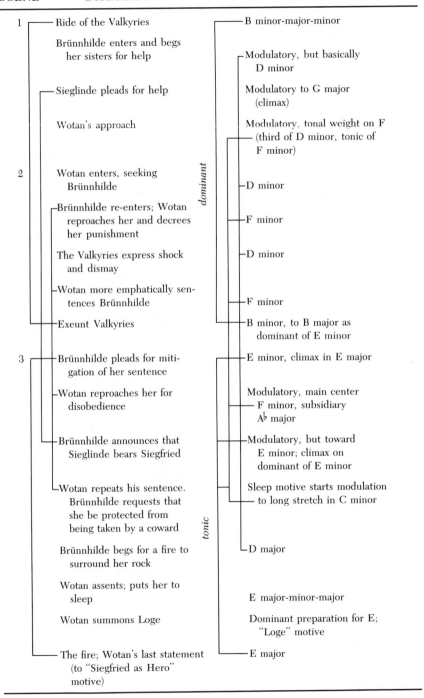

SCENE	DRAMATIC ACTION	TONAL CENTER
1	Ride of the Valkyries	B minor-major-minor
	Brünnhilde enters and begs her sisters for help	Modulatory, but basically D minor
	Sieglinde pleads for help	Modulatory to G major (climax)
	Wotan's approach	Modulatory, tonal weight on F (third of D minor, tonic of F minor)
2	Wotan enters, seeking Brünnhilde	D minor
	Brünnhilde re-enters; Wotan reproaches her and decrees her punishment	F minor
	The Valkyries express shock and dismay	D minor
	Wotan more emphatically sentences Brünnhilde	F minor
	Exeunt Valkyries	B minor, to B major as dominant of E minor
3	Brünnhilde pleads for mitigation of her sentence	E minor, climax in E major
	Wotan reproaches her for disobedience	Modulatory, main center F minor, subsidiary A♭ major
	Brünnhilde announces that Sieglinde bears Siegfried	Modulatory, but toward E minor; climax on dominant of E minor
	Wotan repeats his sentence. Brünnhilde requests that she be protected from being taken by a coward	Sleep motive starts modulation to long stretch in C minor
	Brünnhilde begs for a fire to surround her rock	D major
	Wotan assents; puts her to sleep	E major-minor-major
	Wotan summons Loge	Dominant preparation for E; "Loge" motive
	The fire; Wotan's last statement (to "Siegfried as Hero" motive)	E major

dominant

tonic

nality of Scene 3, with E major the basic key of Wotan's farewell, the immense "coda" of the third act.

Several attempts have been made to determine the form of the smaller structural units of which Wagner's scenes are composed. Older analytic attempts sought to find large groupings of about one hundred measures within a scene which, in turn, could be divided into shorter units that could be grouped into certain musical forms: the ternary or arch *(Bogen)* form A B A; the *Bar* form, an A A B structure most familiar and used in *Die Meistersinger* (Walther's prize song in Act III being the best example) but which often occurs in the *Ring* and is also the form of Tannhäuser's account of his pilgrimage to Rome; and two lesser-used forms, the strophic $(A^1 A^2 A^3 \ldots A^n)$ and the refrain (rondo) form A B A C A.

More recent studies have tried to identify periods as units consisting of ten to twenty measures which would represent an interlocking between text and music, defined by a division in the verbal text or by some change in the organization of the basic musical components (usually tonality, theme, and harmony) in a kind of "musical prose" dominated by irregular phrase- and poetic lengths, and which could be grouped within a scene to achieve a tonal, if not a formal, symmetry. Still another approach has been to view Wagner's musical prose as comprised of a hierarchy of sentences and paragraphs, with the concept of "poetic-musical periods" valid only through the first act of *Tristan,* and the paragraph rather than the sentence (in keeping with Wagner's placing a lesser emphasis on tonality) becoming dominant after *Die Meistersinger.* Major subdivisions within long scenes have been identified as "movements" in the symphonic sense, though the attempts to impose sonata form on them are forced and unconvincing. Writers are in agreement that the prevailing texture is that of a symphonic web containing leitmotives, with cadences constantly evaded, thus avoiding tonal closure, and that the modulatory texture of Wagner's music and the lack of exact coincidence between thematic, harmonic, and dramatic patterns make it difficult to find the boundaries between particular periods.[3]

Wagner's counterpoint is not traditional but is empirically derived from part-writing. Following Berlioz' example, he combined leitmotives for

---

[3]Only a few of the many analytic approaches to Wagner's music can be cited here. Many of the earlier ventures are ably summarized in David R. Murray, "Major Analytical Approaches to Wagner's Style: A Critique," *Music Review,* XXXIX (1978), 211–22. Among the subsequent ones I have included are the macrotonal approaches of Robert Bailey, "The Structure of the *Ring* and Its Evolution," *Nineteenth-Century Music,* I (1977), 48–61 and William Kinderman, "Das 'Geheimnis der Form' in Wagners 'Tristan und Isolde,' " *Archiv für Musikwissenschaft,* XL (1983), 174–88. The concept of "period" structure and its aftermath is described in Carl Dahlhaus, *Richard Wagner's Music Dramas* (English trans. Cambridge, Eng., 1979), and his earlier writings in German cited in Murray's study, with the ideas on "sentences" and "paragraphs" from Peter Dennison, "Musical Structuring and Its Evolution in Wagner's *Ring,*" *Miscellanea Musicologica,* XIV (1985), 29–56. Patrick McCreless, *Wagner's Siegfried* (Ann Arbor, 1982) follows an eclectic approach.

programmatic purposes, but such passages as the combination of three motives in the prelude to *Die Meistersinger* (Example 10–11) are *tours de
force* rather than normal practice. Wagner's bass lines, especially in the
Tristan prelude, repay study, and the active inner parts in the chromatic
passages of his later operas inspired Richard Strauss and the young
Schoenberg.

Wagner's music, especially his mature operas, did not become internationally known until the last quarter of the nineteenth century, after the
construction in 1876 of the *Festspielhaus* in Bayreuth, which became a
place of pilgrimage for aspiring musicians. The international Wagner cult
was more literary than musical, and Debussy's remark that Wagner had
been "a beautiful sunset mistaken for a dawn" was lost not only on composers but also on musical historians. Those who tried to follow directly in
Wagner's footsteps were generally unsuccessful: Engelbert Humperdinck
(1854–1921) had the best luck with his *Hansel and Gretel* (1893), in which
German folk songs and children's songs were blended with a fairy-tale libretto in a musical fabric similar to that of *Die Meistersinger*. Though
Wagner's chromaticism and empirical polyphony inspired Hugo Wolf,
Richard Strauss, and Schoenberg, the reaction against his heavy sonorities
and mythologizing led to the lightened textures and sonorities of much
French music, culminating in Debussy and Fauré. *Tristan* (particularly
such passages as the prelude, opening scene, and love duet in Act II) and
Parsifal had a stronger influence than the *Ring* on late-Romantic French
music. This is evident not only in Example 6–5d but also in the opening
of Chabrier's *Gwendoline* (whose librettist, Catulle Mendès, was a leading
French Wagnerite) or the ascending tonal plateaux in the love duet of the
first act of Massenet's *Werther*. Only deliberate acts of anti-Romantic "sac-
rilege," such as Chabrier's "Souvenirs de Munich," a set of quadrilles in
dance tempo based on motives from *Tristan*, could fully expunge Wagner's
influence from the minds of many French composers, many of whom (like
Chausson and d'Indy) had a curious love-hate relationship with Wagner's
music and sought to extricate themselves from its spell.

Wagner's influence was not limited to music alone but echoed in the
literature and even politics of succeeding generations and nations. His portrayals of women, especially Venus, Isolde, and Kundry, may have affected
the discipline of psychoanalysis in its formative years. Even in recent years
the memory of his music dramas resounds in such disparate works as
J. R. R. Tolkien's mythic fantasy *The Lord of the Rings* (1954–55) and William Gaddis's comic novel *JR* (1975) to the same extent that it did in the
works of the French and Russian symbolist writers and painters, the turn-
of-the-century decadents, and such founders of twentieth-century literature
as Thomas and Heinrich Mann, Proust, Joyce, Paul Claudel, E. M. For-
ster, and Willa Cather. Wagner's exegetes could find virtually everything

they desired in his librettos and prose writings to support their interpretations, with the result a bewildering variety of standpoints for explaining Wagner's work—Christian, Theosophical, occult, Transcendentalist, Symbolist, Marxist, Fascist, Socialist, and racist. On the negative side, Wagner's works and writings bear some responsibility for the development of fascism, not only through Hitler but also through the Italian poet-dramatist Gabriele d'Annunzio and several French writers. Of all the German figures of the nineteenth century, only Marx and Nietzsche had impacts equal to Wagner's on subsequent thought; like them, he could be attacked and parodied, but never ignored.

From the musical standpoint, Wagner created more problems for the future of opera than he solved. Despite Nietzsche's claim that Bizet's *Carmen* had "Mediterraneanized" music, the "number opera" was equally a dead end for the composer, and its future was that of entertainment music like Franco-Viennese operetta and American musical comedy or of deliberate archaism, as in Stravinsky's *The Rake's Progress* (1951). The composers who chose to follow Wagner's operatic path had to choose between two pitfalls: was the music to be subordinate to the text and accompany a vocally declaimed libretto, as in the *Ring*, or was opera to be a "symphonic poem with words" like *Tristan*? These questions still remain unanswered.

OTHER COMPOSERS

A few other composers were allied with the trends of the "music of the future" and thus deserve at least brief mention. Charles-Valentin Alkan (*recte* Morhange, 1813–88), an eccentric, eremitic composer of Jewish origin, wrote piano works of nearly impossible length and difficulty, of which his Symphony for Piano and his "Aesop's Banquet," the variations which conclude his *Etudes in all the Minor Keys*, are his best. Alkan paralleled rather than influenced Liszt, and Franck is the most important composer who came within his orbit. Many pianists concede the effectiveness of Alkan's music in performance but question whether it is worth the time that must be spent to master its intricate technical difficulties.

Of all the composers in Liszt's circle, Peter Cornelius (1824–74) was the best. Because so much of his time was spent in being Liszt's secretary and translator, his output was limited. *The Barber of Bagdad* (1858) is a masterpiece which is excelled only by *Die Meistersinger* and *Falstaff* among nineteenth-century comic operas; it contains exquisite Lisztian harmony without sentimental effusions, one of the finest love duets in the literature, and magnificent choral writing. Cornelius' expressive art-songs, of which the *Christmas Songs* of Op. 8 are good illustrations, undoubtedly influenced the sensitive religiosity of many of Wolf's songs. Those acquainted with Cornelius' works deplore the altruism which drove him to furthering the careers of Liszt and Wagner instead of writing more music.

Though associated with Liszt, the highly prolific Joachim Raff (1822–82) was an eclectic whose early works were influenced by Mendelssohn and whose late works presage the revival of Baroque instrumental forms (see Example 9–9a). He wrote in all the genres, but chiefly instrumental music; the Third (Im Walde) and Fifth (Lenore) are regarded as the best of his eleven symphonies, and his "geographical suites"—musical travelogues—provided models for Richard Strauss' Aus Italien and the Caucasian Sketches of M. M. Ippolitov-Ivanov (1859–1935). The music of Felix Draeseke (1835–1913), who considered Liszt's late works too radical, is very eclectic but is better constructed than Raff's.

BIBLIOGRAPHICAL NOTES

Liszt. Alan Walker's Franz Liszt: The Virtuoso Years (New York, 1983) takes the composer to 1847; it is the first of a projected three-volume study, and though it does not say much about the music, it corrects most of the errors of earlier biographies (see the extensive review article by Allan Keiler in Musical Quarterly, LXX (1984), 374–403.) The most recent complete biography is by Eleanor Perényi (New York, 1975). Of the surveys of the music, Humphrey Searle's The Music of Liszt (2d ed., New York, 1966) and the collection of essays edited by Alan Walker, Franz Liszt: the Man and His Music (2d ed., London, 1976), provide good brief overviews. More specific studies of segments of the life or the works include, for the early period, Rudolf Kókai, Franz Liszt in seinen frühen Klavierwerken (1933; reprint Budapest, 1968), Dieter Torkewitz, Harmonisches Denken in Frühwerk Franz Liszts (Munich, 1978), and Alexander Main's "Liszt's Lyon," Nineteenth-Century Music, IV (1981), 228–43, which also includes proposed new datings for many of Liszt's most important compositions from his twenties. Bence Szabolcsi's The Twilight of F. Liszt (English trans. London, 1968), a sympathetic if somewhat chauvinistic study of the late years, contains a musical supplement.

Many analysts disagree in describing Liszt's formal structures. I have analyzed the B minor sonata more extensively than here in Music Review, XXXIV (1973), 198–209; differing analyses include Newman's in The Sonata Since Beethoven and (with an extensive manuscript study) Sharon Winklhofer's in her Liszt's Sonata in B Minor (Ann Arbor, 1980). In his article "Sonata Form in the Orchestral Works of Liszt," Nineteenth-Century Music, VIII (1984), 142–52, Richard Kaplan presents four different analyses of the first movement of the Faust Symphony; a still different one by Kate Covington and myself appears in Vol. IX (1985), 158–60, of the same journal, and more extensively in the Liszt issue (1986) of Studia Musicologica. Many other aspects of Liszt's style, especially melodic and harmonic ones, are ably explored in Serge Gut's *Franz Liszt: Les Eléments du langage musical* (Poitiers, 1975). Much of the recent research on Liszt is announced in the *Journal of the American Liszt Society*.

The thorny bibliographical problems occasioned by the scattering of Liszt's autograph manuscripts and his numerous revisions and rearrangements have hindered study and collection of his works. The older "Complete Works" (1907–36) is being supplemented by publications of the Liszt Society, a Russian edition of the complete piano works, and since 1970 the *Neue Liszt Ausgabe*. There is not yet even a complete thematic catalogue, and many problems of chronology remain to be solved. A sizable sampling of the letters, assembled by Marie Lipsius and published under her pen name of La Mara, has been reprinted in English translation (New York, 1968); other recent publications include letters in Hungarian collections (Kassel, 1969) and the letters to Olga von Meyendorff (Washington, 1979). The collected writings, the *Gesammelte Schriften* edited by Liszt's first "authorized" biographer, Lina von Ramann (Leipzig, 1880–83), suffer because all the writings were translated into German; a new edition of them, in their original languages, is needed. The question of their actual authorship may never be solved; at present most believe they are Liszt's ideas "as told to" Marie d'Agoult or Carolyne de Sayn-Wittgenstein, with Liszt's subsequent corrections.

Wagner. So much had already been written on Wagner and his music by 1900 that a separate classification in the Dewey Decimal System was assigned to "Wagnerian literature." This stream has shown no signs of abating. Certain studies, however, are highly valuable for further understanding of this complex composer. The most recent one-volume biography in English, *The New Grove Wagner* (in preparation), has a new biographical section by John Deathridge that replaces the one by Curt von Westerhagen in *The New Grove* article; the musical section by Carl Dahlhaus should be supplemented by his penetrating yet concise study *Richard Wagner's Music Dramas* (1971; English translation, 1978). For the student coming for the first time to the serious study of Wagner, such earlier studies as Chappell White's *An Introduction to the Life and Works of Richard Wagner* (Englewood Cliffs, N.J., 1967) and Ernest Newman's *The Wagner Operas* (New York, 1949) and *Wagner Nights* (reprint, London, 1968) give good preliminary orientations.

The bibliography in *The New Grove Wagner* contains the important biographies and studies of individual operas. Of the biographies, Martin Gregor-Dallin's *Richard Wagner* (Munich, 1980) deserves an English translation. Nearly all of the secondary biographical literature on Wagner is suspect because of alterations in the then-available primary sources by Wagner or members of his immediate family and descendents.

Special studies of Wagner's music are innumerable; only a few can be mentioned here. Analytic studies of Wagner's music are effectively summarized in David R. Murray's "Major Analytical Approaches to Wagner's Style: A Critique," *Music Review*, XXXIX (1978), 211–22; major subsequent investigations include Patrick McCreless's *Wagner's 'Siegfried'* (Ann Arbor, 1982) and the Wagner issues of the *Archiv für Musikwissenschaft* (XL, 1983) and *Miscellanea Musicologica* (XIV, 1985), all going well beyond the "plot and leitmotive" school of analysis. Sources of Wagner's style are discussed in Robert Laudon, *Sources of the Wagnerian Synthesis* (Munich, 1979).

John Deathridge and others have presented a detailed musical catalogue of Wagner's works and their variants in *Verzeichnis der musikalischen Werke Richard Wagners und ihre Quellen* (Tutzing, 1985), with a catalogue of the prose writings to follow. The English translations of the composer's autobiography *My Life* (*Mein Leben*, Cambridge, England, 1983) and the diaries of his second wife, *Cosima Wagner, Diaries 1869–77* (New York, 1978) provide vivid and direct, if not always trustworthy, narratives. Herbert Barth and others have prepared a fine iconographical study, *Wagner: A Documentary Biography* (English trans., New York, 1975), and Detta and Michael Petzet's *Die Richard-Wagner-Bühne König Ludwigs II* (Munich, 1970) is beautifully illustrated with pictures of costumes, sets, and performers in early productions of Wagner's operas.

Wagner's posthumous influence has occasioned many studies, with Raymond Furness's *Wagner and Literature* (Manchester, 1982) being concise yet comprehensive, and Stoddard Martin's *Wagner to 'The Waste Land'* (Totowa, N.J., 1982) more detailed in scope. The collection of essays edited by David C. Large and William Weber, *Wagnerism in European Culture and Politics* (Ithaca, 1984) shows the variety of interpretations that have been made internationally, from the United States to the early years of the Soviet Union, and embracing most of the century after Wagner's death. Eric Werner has revisited a very controversial topic in his essay "Jews Around Richard and Cosima Wagner," *Musical Quarterly*, LXXI (1985), 172–99.

Wagner's prose writings are not too well served by William Ashton Ellis's Victorian translations (1892–99; reprint, London, 1966). Important primary source materials on Wagner are now being published in Germany, particularly his letters, to appear in approximately 15 volumes, and various documents about his life and career in the series *19. Jahrhundert*. A new edition of Wagner's music, including his stage directions for his operas, is in progress.

Of the other composers discussed, the complete works of Peter Cornelius deserve to be reprinted. Selections of Alkan's music have been edited by Raymond Lewenthal (G. Schirmer, Inc.) and Georges Beck (*Le Pupitre*, XVI, 1969). Ronald Smith's popular biography *Alkan: The Enigma* (New York, 1977) is to be followed by a discussion of his music.

SEVEN

THE REBIRTH OF ABSOLUTE MUSIC

An observer of the musical scene in 1860 would have been forced to conclude that sonatas, symphonies, and string quartets would soon be as extinct as canzonas or trio sonatas, yet during the next four decades absolute music won a new lease on life even though it did not dominate the minds of composers as it had during the Classic period. Nor was this revival a repudiation of the aesthetic of Berlioz, Liszt, and Wagner, for the harmonic, structural, and orchestral resources of the "music of the future" were at least partially retained, and in France and the Slavic nations many composers demonstrated allegiance to both camps by writing both instrumental cycles and symphonic poems.

The principal composer to keep the ideals of absolute music alive during the heyday of Liszt and Wagner was Robert Volkmann (1815–83), a German who spent most of his life in relative obscurity in Hungary. Volkmann is best known for his light, tuneful chamber music, of which the best examples are the effusive B♭ minor Trio, Op. 5 (dedicated to Liszt), and the string quartets in G minor, Op. 14, and E♭ major, Op. 43. His two symphonies are interesting; the First, in D minor, furnished Borodin with the structural model for the first movement of his Second Symphony. Of greatest import for the future were Volkmann's serenades for strings, prototypes not only for Chaikovsky's but also for the Opp. 1 of two important twentieth-century composers, Leoš Janáček and Carl Nielsen. Such serenades reflected an important, if paradoxical, strain in the predominantly Romantic music of the nineteenth century, that of Neoclassicism.

NEOCLASSICISM IN NINETEENTH-CENTURY MUSIC

The term "Neoclassic" has sometimes been applied to the composers to be discussed in this chapter, especially Brahms, Franck, and Saint-Saëns. The term would seem to imply a return to the artistic canons of the period between 1750 and 1800, with its emphases on clarity, balance, and proportion, and its doctrines of simplicity, objectivity, and the elevation of form over content. These attitudes played a part in Neoclassicism after 1850. After this date Neoclassicism was almost as pervasive as Romanticism; yet, like Romanticism, it displayed so many individual manifestations that we should seek trends and tendencies to describe this movement rather than a universal definition.

Neoclassicism among nineteenth-century composers was a look back to the past, but not just to that period bounded by Pergolesi and Haydn. For the Romantics, the past was the entire remembered past of musical history, at least back to the sixteenth century, and in fact both Beethoven (for the *Missa Solemnis*) and d'Indy, composers at opposite ends of the nineteenth century, did research in Gregorian chant for their music.

Some Neoclassicism was evident early in the nineteenth century. Beethoven ventured occasionally into Neoclassic works, not just with "official" music like *The Ruins of Athens* but also with the F♯ major and G major piano sonatas (Opp. 78 and 79) and the Eighth Symphony, while some contemporaries of Spohr and Weber at the fringes of musical development, like Polledro in Italy and Alyabyev in Russia, retained a Classic orientation well into the new century. A genuine shift to a Neoclassic orientation, however, is not evident until the 1840's: Schumann's turning from the characteristic piano piece and the art-song, typically Romantic media, to the symphony and chamber music is one of the first decisive indications. From the standpoints of form and structural balance. Chopin's B minor and G minor Sonatas are more "classic" than his earlier B♭ minor Sonata, and the same is true of his later nocturnes and mazurkas. Berlioz jokingly tried to pass off his *L'Enfance du Christ* as the work of a seventeenth-century composer;

his operas *Les Troyens* and *Béatrice et Bénédict* are culminations of tendencies from the past, less "modern" than the contemporaneous operas of Meyerbeer, Verdi, Gounod, or Wagner. A data that is frequently cited as marking the firm establishment of Neoclassicism is 1860, the year in which Brahms signed a manifesto attacking the "New German School" of Liszt. After 1860, Neoclassicism was an important counter-tendency to Romanticism. It appeared in a wide variety of individual manifestations, and with a typically Romantic air of contradiction, but two basic themes can be associated with it (if not in the same composer at the same time or with equal emphasis): (1) an emphasis on musical forms and attitudes from the past and (2) a simplification of musical style.

The forms inherited from the Classic period—sonata, symphony, string quartet, and the rediscovered serenade—were the ones that most frequently embodied the idea of Neoclassicism, yet earlier forms were also revived. The Baroque suite of contrasting abstract dances (as opposed to the ballet suite or the musical travelogue) was discovered again, not just by obvious Neoclassics like Saint-Saëns or Raff but also by composers usually associated with late-Romantic nationalism like Chaikovsky, Dvořák, and MacDowell, whose two "Modern Suites" (composed 1880–82, published 1883) epitomize the idea of reconciliation of the legacy of the past with the musical ideas of the future. Preludes and fugues were written by composers from Mendelssohn to Hindemith in frank emulation of Baroque models, and the motet for unaccompanied chorus was a medium not just for antiquarians seeking to revive Renaissance and early Baroque church music but also for such progressive composers as Bruckner and Brahms.

Even in the works most closely fitted to Classic-era models one sees no slavish return to eighteenth-century styles; this is evident as early as the first six symphonies of Schubert. Yet in several respects the Neoclassic works are "simpler" than the original models; the slow movement of Bizet's youthful Symphony in C (1855) is "simpler" than its prototypes, the slow movement of Beethoven's Op. 18, No. 1 Quartet and the fugato in the second movement of his Op. 18, No. 4 Quartet. Bruckner, Saint-Saëns, and Chaikovsky present far more clearly articulated sonata-form movements than do C. P. E. Bach or Haydn; one senses that the Neoclassic composers had a self-conscious image in their minds of a standardized sonata form.

In the broader sense, one can even postulate the emergence of a Neoclassic ethos in a composer's deliberately setting himself a compositional problem to solve. Brahms' love for this is well known, yet virtually every composer of the second half of the nineteenth century shared it and regarded the subsequent work not as a student exercise but as a piece of music worthy to stand alone in its own right. Verdi's one string quartet, by a composer who had previously warned young Italians against following the model of the German *quartettisti*, is a striking example.

Another illustration, from a composer not especially famous as a composer of absolute music, is Bizet's *Variations chromatiques* (1868), wherein the theme, usually stated in the bass, consists simply of the ascending and descending chromatic scale; one is reminded of the *inventio* of Byrd and Sweelinck in their fantasias on abstract note-patterns. Yet if Bizet's attitude was old, his harmonies were as novel as Franck's.

Simplicity in Neoclassic music implies not only a return to clearcut musical forms but also to the simplication of other musical elements as well, for instance, harmony. Around 1860 a "diatonic reaction" against the altered chords and chromatic modulations of Liszt and Wagner became evident: the symphony in C major by Clara Schumann's half-brother, Woldemar Bargiel (1828–97) is one of the best illustrations. However, not all composers who have been called Neoclassic followed the path of harmonic simplification: Franck was one post-Wagnerian composer who developed a completely individual style of chromatic harmony (Example 7–5), and Bruckner, though his chromaticism is usually a shifting of microtonal planes (Example 7–2), became quite chromatically complex in his later works, especially the Eighth Symphony.

The return to diatonicism was genuinely a return to Beethoven's emphasis on tonality rather than harmonic color, a widened tonality in which natural or flattened mediants and submediants were significant tonal anchors or modulatory pivots. Added to this were Schubert's free interchange between major and minor harmonies, a renewed emphasis on secondary triads outside the dominant-tonic axis, and the utilization of altered or borrowed chords when desired. The result was a greatly widened harmonic vocabulary, diatonic in ethos, that permitted modulations to quite remote keys: both Brahms and Bruckner, for example, found that a modulation to the flattened submediant or mediant (a major triad) could be extended by using the minor form of this same chord as a further pivot, thus permitting modulation to even remoter keys. Even a purely diatonic harmony, as in the first theme of Saint-Saëns' Fifth Piano Concerto (Example 10–9), could be written in such a way as to avoid the dominant-tonic pull that had characterized Western music for the previous two centuries. Bruckner, Brahms, Saint-Saëns, and Fauré widened the vistas of tonality diatonically as Liszt and Wagner had expanded them chromatically. Even Wagner, in some of his later works—*Die Meistersinger,* the *Siegfried Idyl,* and the "Good Friday Magic" from the third act of *Parsifal*—returned to an essentially diatonic, triadic, and clear harmonic palette.

Other elements of music were also simplified. The term *clarté latine* is a very subjective expression with many interpretations; it can be best taken to mean not just "Latin clarity" in opposition to Wagnerian chromaticism and Germanic academic music, but also structural, harmonic, and melodic simplicity and an orchestration with many "open" places in the score.

Nor is this term limited to French composers, for it is also perceivable in several works by such disparate composers as Bruckner, Chaikovsky, Dvořák, and Grieg. A further aspect is the reduction of orchestral resources, strikingly seen in numerous serenades (Volkmann, Brahms, Dvořák, Chaikovsky, Elgar, and many others), in Wagner's *Siegfried Idyl*, and in the renewed interest in chamber music, quite often for large ensembles with unusual combinations of instruments. Even among composers who specified large orchestral resources, from Berlioz to Mahler, one finds many passages that are scored with a simplicity and delicacy appropriate to chamber music.

If Neoclassicism avoided the dangers of Romantic eccentricity (Alkan), grandiloquence (Liszt), seeming chaos (Wagner's *Tristan*), or excessive subjectivity (Chaikovsky, Mahler), its idiom had pitfalls of its own: epigonism, a sterile academicism, triviality, or a precious cuteness. One senses in much Neoclassic music at its most extreme a reversion to the Classic idea that composition was a craft and music a product: the result was much music that simply filled gaps in the repertoire, such as the instrumental solos that Fauré commissioned as jury pieces for the Paris Conservatoire, or the concertos for such relatively neglected instruments as flute, cello, harp, and clarinet by Reinecke—music that is well put together, sounds well, and never sinks below a certain minimum standard of quality, yet somehow lacks the vigor, spontaneity, individuality and freshness of even the worst music by such prolific early Romantics as Dussek, Auber, Weber, or Donizetti. Many Neoclassic composers were extremely productive and prolific, yet one can make the same criticism of their music that has been made of that by their eighteenth-century counterparts like Dittersdorf and Pleyel: it is written according to formula and thus its musical events are easily predictable, it lacks individuality because it is too close in spirit to that of a major composer of its time, and, frankly, it all sounds too much alike.

One aspect of Neoclassicism that prevailed throughout the nineteenth century and well into the twentieth is in fact strongly Romantic: Neoclassicism as nostalgia. The minuet movements in Schubert's A minor Quartet (D.804) and Mendelssohn's D major Quartet, Op. 44, No. 1, are not Classic minuets, but yearning looks back to a faintly remembered past; Schubert's minuet was taken from his earlier setting of portions of an equally nostalgic poem, Schiller's "Die Götter Griechenlands," with the words "Schöne Welt, wo bist du?" (Lovely world, where are you?). Examples of later and equally fervent longing for the past, using Neoclassic means, are the Ländler in Mahler's Second Symphony, his depictions of the child's view of heaven in his Third and Fourth Symphonies, and Strauss' yearnings for the ambience of Rococo and Classic times in *Der Rosenkavalier* and *Ariadne auf Naxos*.

In summary, nineteenth-century Neoclassicism is a paradox: it is a reaction against Romanticism, but also in its historicism a continuation of it. It exemplifies a return to principles of formal construction that had never really been absent from Romantic music, but places stronger, and often self-conscious, emphases on them. Its reliance on simplicity was not shared by all who have been called Neoclassics, and among composers from Schumann to Strauss, Berlioz to d'Indy, Glinka to Glazunov, there are oscillations, sometimes in the same composition, between Neoclassic and Romantic elements. As clearly seen in the music of Busoni and Reger, Neoclassicism was another ingredient in the turbulent pot of post-Romanticism, and the Neoclassicism of Stravinsky, Milhaud, Prokofiev, and Hindemith was a descendent from, but also a reaction against, its post-Romantic antecedent. Yet with the major composers discussed in this and subsequent chapters who committed themselves to or casually flirted with Neoclassicism, Romantic individualism remained paramount.

ANTON BRUCKNER (1824–1896)

A provincial schoolmaster in Upper Austria, cathedral organist in Linz, and finally professor of counterpoint in Vienna, Bruckner is known today chiefly through his church music and especially his monumental symphonies, nine of which are numbered, in addition to a "student symphony" of 1863 and a rejected "Symphony No. 0" (*"die nullte Sinfonie"*) of 1869. Although many of the anecdotes about his naiveté and self-effacement can be dismissed as *petite histoire*, his deep humility, piety, and personal integrity made him the most noble figure of nineteenth-century music. They also contributed to his lack of self-confidence in his musical ability, complicated by few opportunities to hear his music performed; he was thus led to consent to revisions, often disastrous, of many of his best works.

Bruckner is the direct descendant of the Beethoven of the Ninth Symphony and the Schubert of the Great C major symphony and the last chamber works and piano sonatas. Though he esteemed Wagner highly and dedicated his Third Symphony to him, Bruckner was influenced by the Bayreuth master in only a limited number of ways, chiefly in certain aspects of instrumentation, predilection for the sequence to expand a musical idea, and fondness for enharmonic modulations and third-related tonal progressions.

In his orchestral works of the 1860's, ranging from the Overture in G minor (1863) to the First Symphony, even in its revision of 1890, Bruckner's mature symphonic style is perceivable only embryonically or in scattered places, for instance, in the second theme-group of the first movement or the ponderous scherzo of the First Symphony. After major personal crises, Bruckner's mature style materialized with his Second Symphony in 1871. From this symphony onward, Bruckner utilized certain musical devices which are virtually fingerprints of his style, yet he gave them enough variety to avoid mannerism. One can almost reconstruct a "typical" Bruckner symphony—with the reservations that the Fourth and Sixth symphonies are "lighter" works and that the last three symphonies soar to a pinnacle of achievement. Bruckner begins his symphonies "out of nothingness," either with a string tremolo (Fourth, Seventh, Ninth Symphonies), a rhythmic pattern (Sixth Symphony), or, rarest of all, a slow introduction (Fifth Symphony, the allegro opening with a soft tremolo). With the significant exception of the chromatic opening of the Eighth Symphony, his longest, most fully scored, and most "philosophical" (in the Lisztian sense), Bruckner's first themes usually begin with a motive featuring the open fifth or triad; sometimes he will use many themes (six in the first movement of the Ninth Symphony, for example) in a theme-group. He called his second themes "song themes"; in slow movements and finales (Example 7–1a) as

EXAMPLE 7–1. Bruckner, Symphony No. 5, finale, recapitulation of second theme-group. Note the use of pseudo-imitation in the first section and double counterpoint in the second.

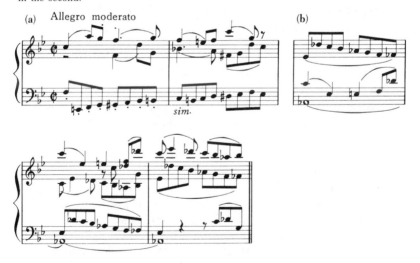

well as in first movements, the theme will be closely interwoven with a counterpoint which is an essential part of the theme-complex, and his love for exploring possible permutations of the themes in invertible counterpoint (Example 7–1b), adds to the length of the second theme-groups. The closing themes can be forceful (Fifth Symphony, finale) or quietly stark (Seventh Symphony, first movement). Bruckner's expositions are not cluttered with padded transitions; often, after a pause, he will begin a new theme-group without preparation, thus adding to the granitic effect of his symphonies. His expositions often include three or more structural key-centers instead of the customary two, a legacy from Schubert's three-key expositions.

Bruckner's developments are like Schubert's in that both composers rely on repeating themes in sequence; the great double fugue of the development in the finale of the Fifth Symphony is an exception. Bruckner's recapitulations are shorter than his expositions and his codas are modeled on Beethoven's. In these codas one often sees a favorite Brucknerian device: a crescendo consisting of an immense buildup out of nothingness, over a pedal point, frequently culminating in the glowing sonorities of the full brass section.

Except for the slow march in the Fourth Symphony, the slow movements are Bruckner's centers of symphonic gravity; they generally consist of solemn hymnlike adagios in a very free sonata form, with the contrasting "song theme" often a letdown in the mood of exaltation. The scherzos are often deliberate and ponderous, less often (as in the Sixth Symphony) fantastic; the trios range from the dance-like one in the Fourth Symphony to the mysteriously shadowy one of the Ninth.

Like the other composers of the century, Bruckner struggled with the problem of the finale; there is none for the Ninth Symphony, though Bruckner began this composition in 1887. Sometimes themes from previous movements are recapitulated in the finale, and there are sometimes sharp contrasts between themes, often with programmatic significance; in the last movement of the Third Symphony the juxtaposition of a dance-like melody with a trombone chorale symbolized for Bruckner a funeral ceremony inside a church with street life going on outside its portals. A climactic chorale is a frequent, but not essential, ingredient of the finales; that of the Fifth Symphony is treated in counterpoint with the fugue subject that figures in the first theme-group of this movement.

Bruckner's melodies tend to be long, based either on a triad or on wide leaps, and are often treated as "double sequences" a third apart; this leads, in notation, to what seems to be a frightening enharmonic thicket, since part of the sequential treatment includes a Schubertian love for contrasts between major and minor. A sequence from A major, for example, can include F major, D♭ major, and C♯ minor. In the passage shown in Example 7–2b, Bruckner begins his melody in the tonic, modulates to distant areas, and returns securely to his home key; here one can see the roots of Hindemith's melodic-harmonic style. Bruckner's rhythmic fingerprint is the contrast of triplets and duplets in a given melody; when they occur in cross-rhythms (Fifth Symphony, second movement; Sixth Symphony, first movement), they create an effect of intricacy.

EXAMPLE 7–2. Bruckner, Symphony No. 3, second movement.

(a)   Adagio bewegt, quasi andante   **(b)**   Andante quasi allegretto

When Bruckner uses rich altered chords, he usually employs them as functional harmonies to go from one tonal center to a transient internal center. Often, after a pause, Bruckner shifts his tonal planes abruptly, a device derived from Beethoven's late works. His orchestration has been criticized as "organist's scoring": frequently one hears an effect comparable to changing organ manuals (from pure string color to woodwind color to another "manual" of glowing brass), in tutti passages he uses the contrabass tuba like an organ pedal playing an active bass line, and his tremendous octave passages, either against string figurations or powerful unisons with 32', 16', 4', and 2' "registrations," produce a massive organlike effect. Yet he eschewed the reedy, flutey, or "voix céleste" sonorities of his fellow organist-composer César Franck.

Bruckner's well-meaning but hopelessly misguided pupils persuaded their mentor to agree to many disastrous cuts in his symphonies; after his death they changed his orchestration to achieve a more Wagnerian blend and committed mayhem on his music, for example, hacking out most of the recapitulation of the finale of his Fifth Symphony. In explanation, but not defense, one should mention that this was a period when musicians often "improved" the works of their predecessors: thus Grieg's second piano parts for some of Mozart's sonatas, MacDowell's reharmonizations of pieces in the "Anna Magdalena Book" once attributed to J. S. Bach, and the differing versions of Monteverdi's *Orfeo* by d'Indy and Respighi.

Much of Bruckner's church music, especially the motets, derives from the ethos of the Cecilian reformers who sought to restore Catholic church music to a pristine *a cappella* purity, but his Masses in D minor and F minor and his *Te Deum* are in the tradition of Viennese symphonic church music; despite many lovely passages, especially the Benedictus of the F minor Mass, these works sound overwritten. A magnificent synthesis of symphonic and Cecilian trends in church music is the E minor Mass (1866, revised 1882), which succeeds where Spohr failed in his attempts to unite sixteenth-century counterpoint and nineteenth-century harmony.

Bruckner failed to found a "school" of composition, and during his lifetime he seldom heard his symphonies in their entirety or without some kind of fiasco. Although his influence on Mahler was strong, it was not overwhelming, and linking the two composers together, as is often done, is as unjustified as bracketing Bach with Handel or Debussy with Ravel.

JOHANNES BRAHMS (1833–1897)

Writers have disagreed on an exact periodization of Brahms's creative life, but there is a consensus as to an early period ending in early 1854 with the first version of the B Major Trio, Op. 8, and a final period beginning in 1891. The intervening demarcations usually involve groups of works: those marking his "first maturity" attained in the early 1860's with the two Piano Quartets and Piano Quintet; the *German Requiem* and several important songs of 1868; the final version of the First Symphony in 1876 followed shortly by the Second Symphony and Violin Concerto; and the duet sonatas of 1886. Identifying these "periods" firmly is a difficult task since Brahms's first work for any medium (even as late as the First Symphony and G Major Violin Sonata) often has a certain tentative and experimental quality to it, whereas even in the earliest published works one easily discerns many salient traits of his mature style. One can best identify periods within each of the forms and media for which Brahms wrote.

Piano Music. Brahms's first published works include a magnificent Scherzo, Op. 4 (his earliest work he deemed worthy of publication), and three taxing solo sonatas, the main works that inspired Schumann's extravagant praise of the twenty-year-old composer. Schumann's influence, especially in the inner movements of the sonatas, is the most pronounced, but there are traces also of Schubert, Hummel (the F♯ minor sonata), Chopin, and even Liszt (aspects of technical writing for the piano, a tendency to "apotheosize" themes, and some of the thematic transformation of the symphonic poems and B minor sonata). After the crisis of Schumann's attempted suicide in 1854 came the Op. 10 Ballades and several sets of variations, crowned in 1861 by the Variations and Fugue on a Theme of Handel, Op. 24, one of the landmarks of the composer's "first maturity," and the virtuoso Paganini Variations, Op. 35, of 1862–63. Brahms thereafter limited himself to short piano pieces: those of Op. 76 (1878) are highly concentrated; the Op. 79 Rhapsodies of the following year display his "Sturm und Drang" piano writing.

The short piano pieces of 1892, from Op. 116 through Op. 119, are the culmination of his achievement as a composer for the piano and the conclusion of the golden age, beginning with Beethoven's *Bagatelles*, of the German Romantic character piece. These brief pieces bear such noncommittal titles as "capriccio," "rhapsody," and especially "intermezzo." Generally ternary in form, the individual sections show highly subtle internal links and are often interrelated. The few passionate pieces (e.g., Op. 116, Nos. 1 and 3) are restrained and concentrated in comparison with the Rhapsodies of Op. 79; others, like Op. 116, No. 5 and Op. 118, No. 4, are highly abstract plays on rhythmic motives. Such warm and contemplative pieces as Op. 118, No. 2 and Op. 116, No. 4 may be contrasted with the somber Op. 118, No. 6, the songful Op. 117, No. 1, and the reflective Op. 119, No. 1. These late pieces are the complete antithesis of the Romantic "salon piece"; comparing them with Liszt's *Consolations* shows a striking contrast between the aesthetics of two different composers working within the same self-imposed limitations.

Brahms often sketched his larger chamber or orchestral works for two pianos; the scanty original literature for this medium counts among its cornerstones the two-piano versions of the Piano Quintet and the Haydn Variations. Among the fine works for piano duet are the Waltzes, Op. 39; the intricate and difficult Variations on a theme by Schumann, Op. 23; the Liebeslieder Waltzes, to which vocal parts were later added; and the familiar Hungarian Dances, which helped start a virtual avalanche of "national" dances for piano duet of which those by Dvořák, Grieg, Moszkowski, and Gilbert are the most worthy successors.

Chamber Music. This medium occupied Brahms during all his creative life and contains perhaps his best work. In number of performers, the range is from duet sonatas to string sextets, and there are interesting contrasting timbres in the Trio for horn, violin, and piano (Op. 40) and the Trio for clarinet, cello, and piano (Op. 114).

In all the media except for quintets, the first work reveals not only a certain tentativeness, as if Brahms were exploringly feeling his way, but also a certain expansiveness, for each first work tends to be longer than its successors. The B major Trio, Op. 8, the first of his chamber works, was originally so long that Brahms later condensed it drastically, but it is still his longest chamber work. These first works often have a serene contemplativeness, as in the B♭ String Sextet (Op. 18) and E minor Cello Sonata (Op. 38), but the extremely somber C minor String Quartet (Op. 51, No. 1) is a striking exception. As a rule, the second work in each medium is quite frequently paired with the first, is often the best constructed, and may be either the most lyrical (A major Piano Quartet, Op. 26,) or most "romantically" effusive (A minor String Quartet, Op. 51, No. 2; A major Violin Sonata, Op. 100). The third work in each medium can either be the most "Classical," like the B♭ major String Quartet (Op. 67), or the most abstract, like the D minor Violin Sonata (Op. 108).

The growth of professional string quartets stimulated Brahms's muse; his chamber works, unlike Volkmann's, are not for amateurs playing *Hausmusik*. Generally his chamber music is highly restrained, disciplined, and even somber (C minor Quartet, B minor Clarinet Quintet), but few more exuberant chamber works exist than the gypsy rondo which closes the G minor Piano Quartet (Op. 25) or the light-hearted first movement of the B♭ String Quartet. A few of the chamber works have an almost "orchestral" sound, especially the two string quintets, and Schoenberg later gave the G minor Piano Quartet an orchestral garb (though anachronistically inappropriate). Many performers of the duet sonatas complain that the competition with the piano is an unequal one, and that the close relationship between solo instrument and piano is uncongenial to the kind of virtuoso who considers his instrument the center of a duet sonata.

Orchestral Music. Though Brahms wrote only four symphonies and four concertos, they are among the major orchestral works of the nineteenth century. The concertos—two for piano, one for violin, and the "Double Concerto" for violin and cello, Brahms's farewell to writing for the orchestra—firmly uphold Beethoven's tradition of the concerto as a symphony with obbligato solo instrument. The two early Serenades (D major, Op. 11, with six movements, and A major, Op. 16, with five), the "Tragic" and "Academic Festival" overtures, and the orchestral version of the Haydn Variations, apparently the first independent variation cycle written for orchestra, complete the short list.

Not only does the first work in each orchestral genre seem tentative and exploratory, whether serenade, concerto (D minor, Op. 15), or even symphony (C minor, Op. 68), but the second work in each genre shares the expansiveness of the first and counteracts its tempestuousness with lyrical expressiveness. Brahms's orchestration, stemming from that of Beethoven and Schumann, is characterized by great restraint in using orchestral "heavy artillery" and by a rather dark brown, somber coloring thanks to the importance of the violas, the blended tone colors, and the doubling of notes, particularly the thirds of chords, in the low registers (a characteristic also of his piano and chamber music). Only in the D minor Piano Concerto does he write poorly for his instruments. The serenades are works for chamber orchestra: in the second, in A major, he even (as in the first movement of the *German Requiem*) omits violins.

Songs. Brahms wrote over two hundred songs in the tradition of the German Lied. Except for the romances from *Magelone* (Op. 33), settings of a poetic cycle by Ludwig Tieck, and the *Four Serious Songs* (Op. 121) on Biblical texts, Brahms avoided the song cycle, preferring to write a group of songs to texts by a variety of poets.

From a strictly evolutionary standpoint Brahms's songs are regressive, for he limited the role of the accompaniment to short preludes and postludes, occasional interludes, and to doubling the vocal melody or playing arpeggiated chords, often in cross-rhythms, without, however, any semblance of hackneyed accompanimental patterns. The voice is the center of attention; the occasional wide leaps demanded are generally triadic, and irregular (three- or five-measure) but balanced phrases frequently occur. The most typical songs are either those in folk song style ("Sonntag" from Op. 47, or the German folk songs with piano accompaniment) or are slow and contemplative, like "Sapphic Ode," "Feldeinsamkeit," or "Wie bist du, meine Königin." When he examined a song by another composer, Brahms would cover all the parts except the vocal melody and the bass, evidence that he considered these the most important elements of a song.

Choral Music. Only Handel and Mendelssohn can be said to have written as grateful music for choral voices as Brahms, a choral conductor who thoroughly understood the medium. His choral music is the culmination of the German tradition, embracing not only the large festival chorus but also the small mixed, male, or women's choruses that fulfilled important social as well as musical functions. Brahms's largest accompanied choral work, the *German Requiem*, is based on Biblical rather than liturgical texts and contains not only dramatic fugal passages and a song-like soprano solo in the fifth movement but also, in the outer movements (in F major, one of the composer's favorite keys), and the fourth, the finest choral writing of the century. Among the shorter acompanied works the *Song of Destiny* and the exquisite *Nänie* deserve particular mention. His *a cappella* choral works include not only motets based on Renaissance and early Baroque choral traditions, which Brahms thoroughly had mastered through his musicological studies and by having conducted these works as well as several of J. S. Bach's cantatas, but also delightful arrangements of folk songs.

Musical Style. As with any major composer, a capsule description of Brahms's musical style is difficult to make, but several stylistic traits are prominent in his music. His melodies emphasize the triad (characteristic also of German folk song in which he was deeply interested), and triadic leaps give a virile strength and energy to even the most contemplative passages. When the melodies tend to be long, as in reflective works like the B major Trio, E minor Cello Sonata, and B♭ major String Sextet (like the opening melodies of Beethoven's "Archduke" Trio or Schubert's B♭ Piano Sonata, D. 960), they indicate that the work is to be on an extensive timescale. Brahms's long melodic arches are evident even when interruptions must be taken for breath, as in the songs or the slower movements of the works for clarinet, or when the melody itself is seemingly broken up by rests, as in the third movement of the Op. 108 Violin Sonata. As Examples 7–4 and 10–2a will show, his handling of simple phrases by extending them motivically is magnificent.

Brahms's secret for the motivic extension of phrases was given the term "developing variation" by Schoenberg to illustrate the practice of building a theme from small motivic cells, melodic and rhythmic, that are continuously being modified; an idea seems to grow out of the one that preceded it, in contrast to Wagner's technique of applying sequence to a leitmotive or Liszt's of transforming themes, wherein the original motivic outline is still retained though the mode or meter may be changed. Though Brahms freely utilized both sequence (especially in his development sections) and thematic transformation (as in the finales of the Violin Concerto or the F major viola quintet), developing variation in a variety of structural levels and media is an important key to his achievement. The technique can be seen in an expansive melody, as in the slow movement of the Second Symphony (see Example 10–2a), or in Brahms's most abstract, untuneful, and uncompromising motivic writing, such as the first movement of the C minor String Quartet.

Rhythm is Brahms's driving force, and his treatment of this element, which he shared with Beethoven, Schumann, and Berlioz, raises his music far above that of his contemporaries like Raff and Reinecke, who were too easily satisfied with static or jog-trot rhythms inseparable from the meter. Although Brahms occasionally used irregular meters or (like Schumann) added another beat to a measure to extend a phrase or delay a cadence, he generally relied on syncopation, sometimes united with a syncopated harmonic rhythm (as in the first movement of the Third Symphony or Example 7–3c) that helps to remove or displace the usual points of reference that determine where the listener hears "downbeats" and "upbeats" in the music. Cross-rhythms, with triplets in one hand and duplets in the other, are most obvious in his piano music and song accompaniments and are one of his favorite ways of giving added interest to a homophonic passage.

Brahms's most striking rhythmic device is his use of hemiola, which pervades most of his movements in 3/4 or 6/8 meter. Quite often this is a "sprung rhythm" wherein a prevailing pattern in 3/4 will give way to measures of 6/8 or vice versa (Example 7–3a) and there are also combinations

EXAMPLE 7–3. Selected rhythmic devices in Brahms's music: (a) 3/4 and 6/8 meters within a theme (Horn Trio, Op. 40, last movement); (b) Hemiolar cross-rhythms (Violin Sonata, Op. 78, first movement); (c) Syncopated harmonic rhythm (Handel Variations, Op. 24; end of second variation leading into third variation).

of the two meters to provide another variety of cross-rhythm (6/4 and 3/2 in Example 7–3b).

Though Brahms was the most contrapuntal composer of the century, he was the least ostentatious about it and in this respect is surpassed only by Mozart, for even in Beethoven's music one often senses that the composer is deliberately calling attention to his use of a "learned" device. Especially in the large choral works Brahms's fugues are "accompanied," perhaps to keep the rhythmic propulsion from sagging (the fugues in the third and sixth movement of the *German Requiem* are excellent illustrations), but in the motets he reverts to more archaic techniques. The best instrumental fugal finales conclude the E minor Cello Sonata and F major String Quintet; Haydn's and Beethoven's fugal finales, especially those that reconcile both fugal and sonata form, are the most obvious models, but the ultimate ancestor is J. S. Bach's *Well-Tempered Clavier* rather than the organ fugues of the Weimar epoch which Liszt and his disciples were transcribing as virtuoso piano solos. In his variations Brahms took great delight in canonic problems, as Bach did in his "Goldberg" Variations, and in setting compositional limitations for himself, especially in the use of invertible counterpoint, where soprano and bass melodies may exchange places, or of such difficult tasks as occur in the tenth of the Schumann variations, Op. 9, where the bass line is the mirror image of the soprano melody. Occasionally Brahms utilized ground bass techniques, as in the finales of the Haydn Variations and the Fourth Symphony.

Although Brahms used many of the harmonies of the "new German school," particularly the half-diminished seventh chord as dominant preparations in cadences, to him harmony was strictly functional, neither coloristic nor rhetorical. Along with his love for folk song came a desire for authentic sounding harmonizations requiring a lavish use of secondary triads, even to the point of blurring the tonal center of the melody, as in Example 7–4; the beginning sounds like F major but the middle A minor or major. Brahms's rather somber harmonic coloring derives from his fondness for subdominant harmony, the "dark" side of the circle of fifths as opposed to the "brightness" of dominant harmony. Often when Brahms goes to the dominant side of the circle of fifths he returns via the subdominant to the tonic. The minor forms of the subdominant and the tonic are his favorite pivots for modulation, and many of his diminished-seventh chords consist of the third of the minor subdominant (B♭ in the key of D) added to an incomplete dominant harmony (C♯–E–G) and are thus functional; similarly, chords of the augmented sixth are not used as color harmonies but serve as intensified dominants to reinforce the tonic (F♮–A–B–D♯ to an E major triad, as in the seventh and eighth measures of the finale of the Fourth Symphony), and chords of the half-diminished seventh, usually in first inversion (G–E–B♭–D in the key of D major) as dominant preparations in cadences.

Key ambiguity is one of Brahms's most forward-looking tonal de-

EXAMPLE 7–4. Brahms, Quartet, Op. 51, No. 1, third movement, trio.

vices, one which he inherited from Schumann. We have seen one type in
Example 7–4, where this ambiguity occurs between firm tonal anchors, but
sometimes, as in the first movements of the B♭ major String Sextet, Op. 18
(between D major or minor and F major) or the Second Symphony (between F♯ minor and A major), the ambiguity will extend over the entire second theme-group, not to be resolved until the opening of the closing
theme.

In his sonata-form movements Brahms follows the models of middle-
to late-period Beethoven, late Schubert (especially the chamber music and
sonatas), and Schumann and Chopin (but to a lesser extent). Sometimes the
articulations will be clear-cut, with considerable contrast between themes,
but in the more abstruse works he tends to blur the boundaries between
sections. There is generally a complex segmentation of theme-groups,
which often consist of two basic short ideas, sometimes very subtly related,
that are subject to constant reinterpretation. When Brahms does not indicate a repeat of the exposition (which should always be observed in performance in order to retain the carefully crafted tonal integrity and balance of

the movement), his developments then usually begin with a restatement of the opening theme in the tonic to give the impression of a repeated exposition. Often in the developments, even as early as the piano sonatas, there are one or more areas of great tonal stability in which one of the themes is given an apotheosis.

The recapitulations are often ambiguous, especially when thematic and tonal recapitulations do not coincide, and may begin with an interior portion of the first theme-group, the second theme, or even a reordering of the appearance of the themes. In the recapitulations, or even in reprises in simple ternary forms, Brahms does not merely repeat themes but rather "reinterprets" them. The slow movements, like Schubert's (and, later, some of Mahler's), are modeled on the art-song rather than the aria, hymn, or romance; this is especially evident when the "accompanying" instruments open the movement with a ritornello. The form is generally ternary on a large scale, although some of the movements are in free sonata form, with or without development.

Brahms's scherzo movements are seldom of the bumptious sort; only that of the Fourth Symphony really fits that description. Sometimes the scherzo is mysterious, deft, and fantastic, as in the Trio, Op. 87; sometimes it is a sturdy movement in 6/8 meter replete with duplets, as in the Horn Trio or the Op. 99 Cello Sonata. In the Op. 88 String Quintet and Op. 100 Violin Sonata the slow and scherzo movements are "telescoped" into one movement. But the most typical kind of third movement is a contemplative intermezzo, sometimes with varying tempos and thematic transformation as in the Second Symphony, most often highly poignant as in the Op. 67 Quartet or any of the late instrumental cycles; the comparable movements in Beethoven's Op. 130 and Op. 132 Quartets are the most evident models.

Considerable variety exists among Brahms's finales. One exciting kind, which Liszt appreciated most in Brahms's music, is the Hungarian rondo, at its most fiery in the G minor Piano Quartet and also found as a highly effective close to the Violin Concerto and the "Double" Concerto. A relaxed and expansive conclusion, often a rondo or set of variations, is characteristic of such works in B♭ major as the Op. 18 Sextet, the Op. 67 Quartet, and second Piano Concerto. Some of the finales are contrary to the "optimistic" and "victorious" instrumental cycle by being in minor, even when the first movement is in tonic major. Most of the finales are in sonata form, but the conclusion of the Fourth Symphony freely utilizes ground-bass techniques with numerous variations, refinements, motivic play, and harmonic substitution; it is unique, not only in Brahms's *oeuvre* but also for the century as a whole.

Though writers disagree about the actual amount of thematic or psychological interrelationships there is between movements of his instrumental cycles, Brahms occasionally uses material from the opening movement in a finale, ingeniously in the seventh variation and coda of the Op. 67 String Quartet, with possibly hidden programmatic significance in the endings of the Third Symphony and Clarinet Quintet. The introductions to the outer movements of the First Symphony contain most of the salient thematic material. Most frequently Brahms creates cyclic links within his movements, especially by using crucial motives in transitional passages or by transforming a theme from one section and using it in another.

Brahms's sets of variations, whether movements of an instrumental cycle or independent compositions, are an important portion of his work. They derive more from J. S. Bach's "Goldberg" Variations and Beethoven's later variations than from the free variations of Schumann's *Symphonic Etudes,* and are generally called "character variations" in that each individual variation is an alteration of the "character" of the theme. To use a mathematical analogy, the "constants" are the structure of the theme (number of phrases, binary or ternary organization) and the harmony in the broadest sense, allowing for substitutions of chords especially in changes of mode; the variables are the other elements—melody, rhythm, pitch location, and texture. Figure 7–1 shows the organization of Brahms's most familiar set of variations, the Variations on a Theme by Haydn, Op. 56. This analysis should be regarded as a point of departure for an intensive study of the motivic development and harmonic substitution typical of the composer's other mature variations.

Brahms's Achievement. It is generally thought today that Brahms's contemporaries viewed him as a pedantic musical reactionary who eschewed program music and music drama in favor of writing overly complex and inaccessible music in Classic-era forms. Yet Wagner remarked, on hearing Brahms play his Handel Variations, that there was still life in the old forms when one knew how to handle them, and Liszt, though cool to most of Brahms's music, enjoyed his Hungarian finales. Actually, Brahms used Baroque attitudes toward counterpoint and exploitation of all the possibilities of a musical idea and Classic techniques of musical craftsmanship with the Romantic views of musical expressiveness through harmonic and sonorous resources; he thus synthesized the best elements of the music of the past, from the late Renaissance through Schumann, with the music of the present that he was willing to accept, while avoiding stylistic incongruities or having to rely on antiquarian devices divorced from a living musical language. Brahms was the greatest composer of Protestant church music after J. S. Bach; his arrangements of folk or popular music, either as solo songs, in choral settings, or for piano duet, provided models for future composers; and he revived the duet sonata, the independent set of variations, and chamber music as viable artistic forms. Especially in the variation form, Brahms's influence strongly affected such twentieth-century composers as Reger, Dohnányi, and Hindemith, and Schoenberg not only

FIGURE 7-1. Brahms, Variations on a Theme by Haydn, Op. 56.

VARIATION	TEMPO	METER	STRUCTURE				REMARKS
			A	B	A	Coda	
Theme	*Andante*	2/4	5+5	4+4	4	Coda (prolongs tonic) 7	
I	*Poco più animato*	2/4		The same			Essentially the same harmony.
II	*Più vivace*	2/4		The same			5-measure phrase of A 1+4. Essentially the same harmony but in minor.
III	*Con moto*	2/4	10+10	4+4	4	Coda 7	Major. Written-out repeats with changes of orchestration and pitch-location.
IV	*Andante con moto*	3/8	5+5	4+4	A' 4	Coda 2+2+4	Written-out repeats with second statement in invertible counterpoint at the twelfth. Minor.
V	*Vivace*	6/8	A A 10+10	B+A 12+7	B+A 12+7		Diminution and distortion of theme, often using hemiola. Major.
VI	*Vivace*	2/4	5+5	4+4	4	Coda 3+3	Reversion to original structure with repeats. Theme recognizable but changes in harmony, especially at cadences. Major.
VII	*Grazioso*	6/8	5+5	B A Coda 8+4+7			Richer harmony; oscillation between 6/8 and 3/4, especially in section B. Major.
VIII	*Presto non troppo*	3/4	10+5+5	B A Coda 4+4+4+7			Minor. Variation farthest removed from theme.
Finale	*Andante*	2/2	Five-measure ground bass derived from harmony of theme.				Bass pattern repeated 11 times; 12th time ornamented; 13th through 15th time in minor and in upper parts; 16th time as before. Concludes with statement of theme and coda.

hailed "Brahms the progressive" as "a great innovator in the realm of musical language" but also incorporated his constructive techniques in his early works and even as late as the Fourth String Quartet of 1936. One might even say that virtually every composer of the twentieth century from Reger onward who sought or seeks to write "absolute music," whether sonata, string quartet, symphony, or concerto, has had to contend with the heritage of Brahms as well as that of Beethoven. Therefore Brahms, in his own way, also wrote a kind of "Music of the Future."

Composers in Brahms's Orbit. Perhaps the most neglected among all nineteenth-century composers are the German and Austrian representatives of the conservative wing of late Romanticism in music. As conservatives, they have been referred to, if mentioned at all, as minor Neoclassicists, academics (many were excellent teachers), epigones, and also-rans: composers whose music is too derivative from Mendelssohn or Schumann, or stylistically too close to Brahms, to have, at least by present-day standards, much individual identity. Yet among the works of these composers the conductor of the male or female chorus, the violist, the cellist, the flutist, and the clarinetist will find many compositions that are worthy additions to a rather limited repertoire.

Of all the composers in this group, the one with the best chance of having his music revived is Joseph Rheinberger (1837–1901), whose twenty organ sonatas are a worthy Germanic counterpart to Franck's organ music but who was active in several other spheres of activity, especially Catholic church music, piano works, and chamber music with or without piano. Rheinberger's Nonet, Op. 139 (1884), and Horn Sonata, Op. 178 (1894), are particularly effective works though not as permeated by contrapuntal thinking as the organ sonatas, and his symphonic poems were a post-Lisztian influence on those of a fellow-resident of Munich, Richard Strauss. Rheinberger was an internationally famous teacher of organ and composition, and included among his pupils Engelbert Humperdinck, Ermanno Wolf-Ferrari, Horatio Parker, and George W. Chadwick. Another meritorious if predictable composer, Carl Reinecke (1824–1910), was highly prolific in all media, with 288 opus numbers; of greatest possible interest today are his concertos for relatively neglected instruments (flute, harp, clarinet), his duet sonatas, and his chamber works that include wind instruments. If his music does not rise to the heights of Brahms, it is nevertheless idiomatic, euphonious, and skillfully written with considerable craftsmanship. Max Bruch (1838–1920) is best known today for violin works like his G minor Concerto and Scottish Fantasy; his "Kol Nidre" for cello and orchestra gave rise to the erroneous claim that he was Jewish. Although Bruch wrote symphonies and chamber music, his chief achievement lies in choral works written for Rhenish and other music festivals. Karl Goldmark (1830–1915), a Jewish composer who grew up in Hungary, was in his operas a neo-Wagnerian influenced by French *opéra lyrique*, but he was also an heir of the various German Romantic traditions in his instrumental compositions, especially his well-written Violin Concerto. His orchestral suite (not a symphony) *The Rustic Wedding* (1876), a melodious and very accessible work, contains several anticipations of Mahler's village-band style of orchestral writing.

THE "FRENCH MUSICAL RENAISSANCE"

Berlioz died, broken and embittered, in 1869. In the following year Prussia crushingly defeated France, and in 1871, shortly before the victorious German armies paraded through Paris, the Société nationale de musique was founded with the slogan *Ars gallica*—French art; its establishment marked a rebirth of French instrumental composition that was soon to provide musical alternatives to German symphonic thought or music drama.

The superficial impression given by the term "French Musical Renaissance" is that instrumental music finally became appreciated by Parisian audiences. In reality, quartet societies and symphony orchestras had been founded between 1850 and 1870, but the dislocations of the Franco-Prussian War and the insurrection of the Paris Commune caused a temporary suspension of musical activities; after the war instrumental organizations found it easier to resume their schedules than did opera companies. Besides Berlioz, other though lesser instrumental composers were active in France before 1870: the expatriate Englishman George Onslow (1784–1853), for example, turned out a prodigious amount of chamber music in a style resembling Weber and Mendelssohn, and Louise Farrenc (1804–75), probably the best woman composer of the nineteenth century, produced a group of piano works, mostly variations, and high-quality chamber-music, particularly piano trios and a skillfully effective nonet (1849). Gounod and Bizet, as well as Franck and Saint-Saëns, wrote instrumental music before 1870. Absolute music, furthermore, was only one facet of the activity of French composers after 1870, for all of them at least dabbled in opera, and in their instrumental compositions they were influenced not only by Beethoven and Schumann but also by the "new German school," especially Liszt. Wagner's influence on French composers, however, has been overstated, and the French cult of Wagner consisted of literary or even political figures rather than musicians.

The principal musical change in France after 1870 was the acceptance of French composers in more than one field of music. Although there was a significant school of French composers of symphonies, *symphonies concertantes*, and chamber music during the Classic period (including the first significant black composer, Joseph Boulogne, Chevalier de Saint-Georges, 1739–99), between 1750 and 1870 foreign composers tended to dominate absolute music and serious opera in France, whether Germans like Schobert, Gluck, and Meyerbeer or Italians like Cherubini, Salieri, Spontini, and Rossini. Between 1780 and 1870 the proper province for the French composer was a certain kind of opera: the rescue opera, *opéra comique*, or *opéra lyrique*. After 1870, however, critics and audiences accepted the absolute music of French composers, showing them an appreciation which had only hesitantly been granted Berlioz. During the first stage (1870–90) of the "French Musical Renaissance," influences from across the Rhine were strong, especially those of Beethoven, Schumann, and Liszt; furthermore, Franck was born in Belgium and Lalo was of Spanish descent.

César Franck (1822–90) was not a prolific composer, and most of his major works date from the last decade of his life. The organ was his principal instrument, which accounts for his polyphonic writing; the improvisatory nature of much of his music, especially in its developments and transitions; the awkwardness of his piano music; and the "registration changes" of his orchestration. In contrast to his organist-contemporary Anton Bruckner, Franck's orchestra stresses the reed- or flue-pipe sounds of the oboe, English horn, and bass clarinet.

Chromaticism and cyclic form are usually cited as the two salient characteristics of Franck's style, but like most attempts to summarize a composer's style in a few words, such statements have resulted in oversimplified generalizations. Franck used chromaticism as a source of contrast to a diatonicism with modal undercurrents, best seen in the central movement of his *Prelude, Chorale, and Fugue* for piano; his chromaticism is often the result of melodic chromaticism in many parts rather than either a functional or coloristic harmony. Typical devices are sequences, either stepwise or by thirds; sinuous chromatic motion within a narrow melodic ambitus, often centered around the third degree of the scale; and an intensification of the chromatic effects through modal interchange (shifts back and forth between major and minor), abruptly juxtaposed third-related chords, sometimes with a jarring effect (a D♭ major chord followed immediately by one in A minor), or a side-slipping of chords that often have sevenths attached. Franck's surface chromaticism seems to move much more rapidly and less directionally than Bruckner's, but at important structural points it is firmly anchored tonally. Example 7–5 is a good illustration of Franck's harmonic style; note the third-related chords, the enharmonic use of augmented triads, and the irregular resolution of chords of the augmented sixth.

Although Franck gave hints of his future reliance on cyclic form in his F♯ minor Trio (1841), he did not set his ideas definitely forth until his *Grande pièce symphonique* (1860–62) for organ. His cyclic form consists of

EXAMPLE 7–5. Franck, Organ Chorale in B minor.

thematic transformation and the recapitulation of salient motives, full
themes, or combinations of motives and themes, in subsequent movements; the technique is derived more from Schumann and the "thematic
transformation" of Liszt's Weimar works rather than from Wagner's treatment of leitmotives. Cyclic forms are most evident in *Le Chasseur maudit*
(1882, his noisiest work), the Piano Quintet (1879), and the Symphony in
D minor (1889), but are subtly stated in his *Prelude, Chorale, and Fugue*.
Franck frequently used not one but two "germ-cells" to create a contrast
and duality of expression, often with a mystic connotation of light opposed
to darkness; the best examples of such usage are the Symphony and the

Variations symphoniques (1885), in which he also contributed to the re-assessment of the solo piano as a participatory rather than the dominant in-strument in a concerto. Cyclic form for Franck was an effective means of unifying an often loose, rhapsodic, and rambling musical structure, but it remained for his pupil Vincent d'Indy to carry this device to its most logical conclusion (see Example 9–10).

Though Franck's students called him "Pater Seraphicus," the line between the sacred and the secular elements in his music is most difficult to draw, and there are few more voluptuous compositions than the first movement of his Violin Sonata. Franck's church music stands midway be-tween the unashamedly operatic expressiveness, sometimes bordering on sentimentality, of Gounod's *St. Cecilia Mass* and *The Seven Last Words* of the young Théodore Dubois (1837–1924) and the relative austerity of Fauré, d'Indy, and Dubois' twentieth-century works.

Supporters of Franck's music have hailed him as the only French composer of the century who was able to follow the path set by Beethoven's late works (and Franck's one string quartet is a worthy successor to Beetho-ven's last quartets), and as being one of the very few nineteenth-century composers after Wagner who was able to develop a completely original and underivative harmonic idiom. Though his highly individual style did not permit imitation, he attracted a devoted yet diverse group of students, some of whom will be discussed in Chapter 9, and passed on to them a sense of high seriousness about music with patriotic and religious over-tones, also an interpretation of chromatic harmony and musical structure which contributed to the breaking-down of nineteenth-century concepts of tonality and form.

Edouard Lalo (1823–92) spent most of his life as a violinist or violist in orchestras or chamber ensembles and was second violinist in a string quartet that introduced Wagner to Beethoven's late works in this genre. Strongly influenced by Schumann, Lalo wrote little music but it is of high quality, sound technique, and appropriate for its purpose. His Symphony in G minor (1889) is exceeded only by Brahms's C minor String Quartet as the most somber instrumental work of the century, but the soberness of the Cello Concerto (1877) is relieved in the second and third movements by delightful Spanish intermezzi, a vein Lalo had previously exploited in his best-known work, the *Symphonie espagnole* (1875) for violin and orches-tra. Lalo was not successful as an operatic composer until his best work, *Le Roi d'Ys* (1888), which still enjoys occasional performances and is among the midpoints between *opera lyrique* and Debussy's *Pelléas et Mélisande*.

Camille Saint-Saëns (1835–1921) was the most prolific and universal among his contemporaries, for he wrote in virtually every musical medium. In 1871, when he was thirty-six he was considered the dean of French com-posers and became the most important founder of the Société nationale de musique. Though he wrote some significant works before 1870, especially the intimate *Oratorio de Noël* and G minor Piano Concerto, his reputation rests mainly on his works of the 1870's since his later music was eclipsed by the new developments of the 1890's.

Among his instrumental works are four symphonic poems, modeled on Liszt's but with a much simpler structure: *Danse macabre* (1874) is the best known. His most popular chamber work is the Septet for strings, piano, and trumpet (1881); its movements, entitled "Préambule," "Minuet," "Intermède," and "Gavotte et final," hearken back in spirit to the chamber suites of Couperin and Rameau rather than to the instrumental cycles of the High Classic and Romantic period (see Example 9–9b), and his six preludes and fugues for organ pay an effective end-of-the-century homage to those of Bach. His Third Symphony in C minor (1886) for orchestra and organ is from a technical standpoint the best synthesis of the expressive resources of the "music of the future" with the ethos and techniques of absolute instrumental music, for Saint-Saëns uses thematic transformation and reminiscence as effectively as Liszt and with more technical surety than Franck, and he links the sections together with thematically connecting material, often contrapuntally treated, with almost as much finesse as Brahms. The elegance, unpretentiousness, and skillful craftsmanship characteristic of his best work may be seen in his finest concertos: the A minor Cello Concerto (1873), C minor Piano Concerto (1875), and B minor Violin Concerto (1880). However, his fluency and Gallic wit could lead him into triviality, as shown by some wag's comment that the G minor Piano Concerto "begins like Bach and ends like Offenbach," or preciousness, as in the gavotte of the Septet.

Saint-Saëns strove for years to make a reputation as an opera composer but with little success. *La Princesse jaune* (1872) has a delightful overture replete with pentatonic exoticism. *Samson and Delilah* (completed 1877) was originally conceived as an oratorio and betrays many characteristics of this genre: considerable use of counterpoint (the canon in the final scene between Delilah and the Philistine priest, for example), the important position of the chorus, and the consistently static action. Yet the choral writing is extremely idiomatic if neo-Handelian, and the mezzo-soprano arias are as voluptuous as those for Massenet's heroines.

Saint-Saëns was one of the major forerunners of twentieth-century music. In Example 10–9, from his Fifth Piano Concerto, we can see how his diatonic harmonizations, avoiding leading-tone or dominant-tonic tendencies, weakened the force of traditional tonality as much as the chromaticism of Liszt and Wagner or the empiricism of Musorgsky and led to the pan-diatonic writing which characterizes twentieth-century Neoclassicism. Equally important was Saint-Saëns's attitude toward music in stating his credo of musical objectivity toward the end of his life: "He who does not feel wholly satisfied with elegant lines, harmonious colors, and a fine series of chords does not understand art."[1] The subjective approach to music which had continued from the Baroque through the *Sturm und Drang* and culminated in nineteenth-century Romanticism ended with Saint-Saëns far more than with Brahms, whose music is full-bloodedly Romantic despite its composer's technical mastery and reliance on what Baroque composers called "invention." Saint-Saëns's music is objective: an orderly, disciplined kaleidoscope of sonorities lacking both the cosmic message of Beethoven, Wagner, Franck, or d'Indy and the sublimated personal emotions of Schumann, Liszt, or Brahms. Saint-Saëns's use of musical parody, best seen in his *Carnival of the Animals* (completed in 1886 but suppressed during his lifetime lest it damage his reputation as a serious composer), stemmed from Rossini's "secret" piano compositions but (in contrast to Beethoven's "Romantic irony") is an important transition to the anti-Romantic parody and caricature of Chabrier, Satie, Poulenc, and Milhaud. Saint-Saëns was a great admirer of earlier French music; he edited the music of Gluck, Rameau, and the *clavecinistes*, and incorporated their aesthetic into his works through his use of restraint and simplicity. He may be therefore considered the chief forerunner of the Neoclassic revival transmitted by his pupil Fauré to Ravel, and ultimately to others like Stravinsky and Piston.

BIBLIOGRAPHICAL NOTES

Bruckner. Winfried Kirsch's extensive survey of Bruckner research from 1945 to 1980, "Die Brucknerforschung seit 1945," extends over four issues of *Acta Musicologica* (1981–84); it shows that much has been written but also that much remains to be done to achieve a genuinely sound study of Bruckner's life and works. Of English-language studies, the most recent biography is by H. H. Schönzeler (London, 1970), with the most extensive studies of the symphonies being Erwin Doernberg's *The Life and Symphonies of Anton Bruckner* (London, 1960) and P. G. Langevin's *Anton Bruckner: Apogée de la Symphonie* (Lausanne, 1977). Dika Newlin's *Bruckner, Mahler, Schoenberg* (1947; 2d ed. in progress) relates the composer to his successors in Vienna.

Brahms. Karl Geiringer's classic biography of Brahms (3d edition, New York, 1982), is still the best one-volume study of the life and works available. A thorough thematic-bibliographical catalogue of the works, edited by Margit McCorkle, has been published by Henle-Verlag in Munich (1985) and will provide the source material for new studies, especially since it includes hith-

---

[1]*Les Idées de M. Vincent d'Indy* (Paris, 1919), cited in James Harding, *Saint-Saëns and His Circle* (London, 1965), p. 219.

erto unpublished works and a revised chronology of Brahms's compositions. Although several studies appeared during or near the 150th anniversary of Brahms's birth in 1983 (notably special issues of *The Musical Quarterly* and the *Hamburger Jahrbuch für Musikwissenschaft*), Imogen Fellinger's verdict was ". . . considering the great quantity of contributions . . . the number in which new research outcomes are reported is in the minority" ("Das Brahms-Jahr 1983. Forschungsbericht," *Acta Musicologica*, LVI (1984), 145–210). The *Brahms Society Newsletter* (1983–) presents news of ongoing research.

The old school of measure-by-measure analysis represented in the four-volume study by Edwin Evans Sr. (London, 1912–36) is being supplanted by a number of extensive and detailed studies pointing out appropriate strategies for further research. Among the most notable are Walter Frisch, *Brahms and the Principle of Developing Variation* (Berkeley, 1984), which heavily emphasizes the composer's motivic development and phrase syntax and includes songs as well as instrumental music in the discussion; Allen Forte, "Motivic Design and Structural Levels in the First Movement of Brahms's String Quartet in C minor," *Musical Quarterly*, LXIX (1983), 471–502, a very detailed analysis which includes rhythmic motives as well as those of pitch; James Webster, "Schubert's Sonata Form and Brahms's First Maturity, (II)," *Nineteenth-Century Music*, III (1979), 52–71, which takes Brahms to 1865, and four examples of micro-analysis with a Schenkerian orientation (including the Handel variations and first movement of the Fourth Symphony) in Jonathan Dunsby, *Structural Ambiguity in Brahms* (Ann Arbor, 1981). The volume in the *Norton Critical Scores* devoted to Brahms's Haydn variations contains a collection of essays as well as both the two-piano and orchestral versions.

Among recent studies, Virginia Hancock's *Brahms's Choral Compositions and His Library of Early Music* (Ann Arbor, 1983) shows the results of Brahms's study of the music of the past, and Schoenberg's essay "Brahms the Progressive" in *Style and Idea* (New York, 1975) is supplemented by two stimulating essays on Brahms's influence on the future: Peter Gay's "Aimez-Vous Brahms?" in his *Freud, Jews, and Other Germans* (New York, 1978) and J. Peter Burkholder, "Brahms and 20th-Century Classical Music," *Nineteenth-Century Music*, VIII (1984), 75–84. William S. Newman's *The Sonata Since Beethoven* (3d ed. Chapel Hill, 1983) presents an extremely comprehensive survey not only of the sonatas of Brahms and his major French contemporaries but also of the many composers in Brahms's orbit.

France. Bea Friedland's *Louise Farrenc* (Ann Arbor, 1980), is the standard study of this important forerunner of the "French Musical Renaissance." Jeffrey Cooper's *The Rise of Instrumental Music and Concert Societies in Paris, 1828–71* (Ann Arbor, 1983) documents the vitality of French musical life before the "French Musical Renaissance" in instrumental music; Chapter 6 contains a survey of lesser-known composers of instrumental music which can be profitably examined by performers seeking enlarged repertoires. Martin Cooper's *French Music from the Death of Berlioz to the Death of Fauré*

(London, 1951) and the second volume of Paul Landormy's *La Musique fran-çaise* (1945) are old but still useful surveys of French music under the Third Republic, and an excellent cultural perspective is given in Ursula Eckart-Bäcker's *Frankreichs Musik zwischen Romantik und Moderne* (Regensburg, 1965).

Laurence Davies's *César Franck and His Circle* (New York, 1970) is the best available biography in English; Rollin Smith's *Toward an Authentic Interpre-tation of the Organ Works of César Franck* (New York, 1983) includes many reminiscences by Franck's organ pupils. Wilhelm Mohr's thoughtful German-language biography (Tutzing, 1969, 2d ed) includes a thematic catalogue (which, however, needs revision). Systematic study of the music is enhanced by two studies of Franck's harmony, Jørgen Jersild's *Romantikkens Harmonik* (Copenhagen, 1970, in Danish), with an overly functional approach, and the more descriptive study by Bernd Wegener, *César Francks Harmonik* (Cologne, 1976, in German).

Lalo's music deserves an up-to-date study. Though James Harding's *Saint-Saëns and His Circle* (London, 1965) is a useful biography, the sheer amount of Saint-Saëns's music has hitherto daunted prospective students of his works. Many of his polemical writings have been translated as *Outspoken Essays on Music* (1922; reprint, London, 1970), and Jean-Marie Nectoux has edited Saint-Saëns's extensive correspondence with Fauré (Paris, 1973).

Whereas there is a nearly complete edition of Bruckner's music and a new edition of Brahms's complete works in progress that will incorporate the lat-est critical methodologies, no such undertaking is in view for the French composers, though Da Capo Press has reprinted some of Louise Farrenc's music.

EIGHT

NINETEENTH-CENTURY
NATIONALISM IN MUSIC

Nationalism is a concept better described than defined. It includes a feeling of political or cultural inferiority, a seeking for identity among the folk arts, of the common people and especially the "unspoiled" peasants, and a search for particular national means of expression different from the cultural norms of the dominant group. Music played an important role in the cultural nationalism that swept Europe during the nineteenth century. The opposite side of musical nationalism was exoticism, a search for new effects from the folk music of other lands and peoples, generally those considered to be less spoiled by civilization; this even led to the phenomenon of Russian nationalists who proclaimed their musical independence from western European models by exploiting the exotica of the peoples of central Asia who had recently been conquered by the Tsarist imperium.

Nationalism in the nineteenth century is first evident in western Europe. The reaction against the French literary and Italian musical culture of the eighteenth-century German courts culminated in the temporary unification of the Germanic peoples at the "Battle of the Nations" near Leipzig in 1813 against Napoleon, whose downfall was celebrated by cantatas or battle pieces by Weber and Beethoven, who at this time began to use German tempo and expression markings rather than the customary Italian indications. The male chorus (Männerchor) movement played an important role in the drive for German unification, and Wagner's writings, with their anti-Semitism and mythologizing, reflect the souring of German liberalism into a perverse nationalism after 1848.

We have already seen the important roles played by Verdi in the Italian *Risorgimento*, which culminated in the unification of Italy in 1870, and by nationalism in French music after the Franco-Prussian War. Perhaps inspired by French colonial adventures in the Near East and North Africa, French composers turned to exoticism, as seen in the Near Eastern motives in *Le Désert* and *Lalla Roukh* by Félicien David (1810–76) or Saint-Saëns's *Samson and Delilah, Suite algérienne*, and Fifth Piano Concerto. Imperialism is occasionally reflected in French operas such as Délibes's *Lakmé*. Spain was a favorite topic for French exoticism, from Auber's *Le Domino noir* (1839) to such masterpieces of local color as Bizet's *Carmen*, Chabrier's *España*, and Debussy's *Ibéria*. As we shall see, Hungary was a similar source of exotica for German composers. Yet nationalism was at its strongest in the countries east of Germany or in areas peripheral to the musical centers of the eighteenth century.

Not all the composers mentioned in this chapter were deliberate nationalists. Such composers as Anton Rubinstein and Horatio Parker wrote in an "international" Romantic style; Berwald, Chaikovsky, and MacDowell are unique musical figures, not locatable in convenient pigeon-holes, who included musical materials or at least topical themes from their homelands in their works and can thereby be subsumed under the heading of musical nationalism.

By 1900 virtually every ethnic group in Europe had developed its own national art music; let us concentrate on only the principal cultural areas of musical nationalism that had attained an international significance: Russia, Bohemia, Scandinavia, Hungary, England, and the United States.

RUSSIA

Tsar Pyotr the Great (1672–1725) opened a "window on the West" with his conquest of the eastern shores of the Baltic and the construction of his new capital, St. Petersburg, by Western architects. Throughout the eighteenth century many foreign musicians and composers came there, among them Galuppi, Paisiello, and finally Boïeldieu and John Field. Catherine the Great (1729–96) attempted to create a "national opera" by writing opera librettos in Russian and having them set by court composers. The opposition of East and West in Russian music is discernible at the end of the eighteenth century: Evstigney Ipatovich Fomin (1761–1800) sought to incorporate Russian folk melodies into his operas, whereas Russia's principal composer of the time, Dmitri Bortniansky (1751–1825), wrote Italianate operas and keyboard music, although Russian elements are present in the church music by which he is best known today. Ventures were also made at this time by Western composers in utilizing Russian folk song in the context of Western tonal harmony; the best known specimens are the *thèmes russes* in Beethoven's Op. 59 Quartets (see Example 8–3a).

In 1802 Spohr described the singing of Russian soldiers which he heard near Mitau:

> They howled frightfully, so that one would almost have to cover his ears. The songs are rehearsed by a cudgel-wielding noncom. The melodies of the songs were not bad, but were accompanied by nothing but false harmonies.[1]

Such views of their native music were shared by many of the Russian connoisseurs. It remained for Mikhail Ivanovich Glinka (1804–57) to synthesize authentic Russian folk idioms with the heritage of Western music and to achieve international stature, with Berlioz and Liszt the principal Western advocates of his music.

A dilettante like most of his Russian successors, Glinka was influenced by Italian music, especially Bellini's, and loved the folk music of Spain. His output was not large; it consists chiefly of short orchestral pieces utilizing either Russian or Spanish folk and popular music, some piano pieces and songs, and two operas, the historical *A Life for the Tsar* (1836) and the fairy-tale *Ruslan and Lyudmila* (1842).

Glinka's operas show, respectively, two of the three basic trends of east European opera during the nineteenth century (the third trend, the parody of the French Grand Opera with a libretto based on western European literature, like Dargomÿzhsky's *Esmeralda* and Chaikovsky's *The Maid of Orleans*, need not detain us here). *A Life for the Tsar* is a historical opera calculated to arouse strong national or patriotic feelings, with the peasants or popular heroes as the central figures, their music in the style of folk song and folk harmony. This harmony is diatonic and utilizes a large number of secondary triads, especially in the minor mode, which has led many to refer to it as "modal" harmony; Glinka often gives his folk-like melodies contrapuntal treatment, as Example 8–1 shows. The enemy are depicted by their own national music, Polish dances like the krakowiak,

---

[1]Louis Spohr, *Selbstbiographie (Kassel and Göttingen*, 1860–61, 2 vols.), I, pp. 36–37.

EXAMPLE 8–1. Glinka, *A Life for the Tsar,* Act I.

mazurka, and polonaise, and the opera concludes with the patriotic cannon-shots-*cum*-Kremlin-bells finale later epitomized in the conclusion of Chaikovsky's *1812 Overture. Ruslan and Lyudmila,* on the other hand, is a fairy-tale opera with brilliant orchestration and strange melodies and harmonies for fantastic episodes: Example 8–2 accompanies the cortege of the wicked magician Chernomor. Exoticism, through the use of Persian dances or the Caucasian *lezginka,* plays an important role. (Glinka's version of the latter dance surprisingly anticipates Khachaturian's melody, harmony, and orchestration a century earlier.) Noteworthy in both operas are the important role of the chorus, the exotic ballets, and the use of the alto and low bass voices for principal characters. Folk idioms and intonations appear

EXAMPLE 8–2. Glinka, *Ruslan and Lyudmila*, Act IV.

most frequently in the choruses, less in the arias for male voices, and least of all in the soprano arias, which are strongly influenced by Bellini and Donizetti. Glinka's remarkable orchestration deserves comment for its extensive use of the "primary" or unmixed colors of the orchestral palette rather than the blended sounds of the Germanic composers.

Glinka's piano music, the most uneven corpus of his work, spans his entire creative lifetime from the mid-1820's to 1855. Variations on themes by Mozart, Cherubini, Donizetti, and Bellini; popular dances such as the waltz, contradanse, and polka; and characteristic pieces which sometimes contain folk elements (the "Tarantelle" on a folk tune later used by Balakirev in his *Overture on Russian Themes* and by Chaikovsky in the finale of his Fourth Symphony is a good illustration) form the bulk of his work for the piano. Although almost all of these compositions are well-written salon pieces, the best of them share the sensitive and refined so-called *morbidezza* of Field, Bellini, and especially Chopin. The Barcarolle, the F Minor Nocturne, the later mazurkas, and especially the Valse-Fantaisie in B minor exemplify this *morbidezza* and embody a strain of pessimism and world-weariness that was to reach full flower in Chaikovsky's last three symphonies. To some extent this tendency is shown in Glinka's romance-like songs, with their predilection for the minor mode.

Glinka's treatment of folk song influenced composers throughout the century. Usually he repeats the short, almost fragmentary, tunes several times, but constantly varies the repetitions through changing the harmonies, placing the song in different voices, or contriving effective counter-melodies, all of which gave variety to repeated melodic material. One of his favorite devices, the use of sinuous chromatic inner parts, is found also in Cherubini, Beethoven, and Auber but became even more of a hallmark of various "national" composers' treatment of folk-like melodies, as Example 8–3 shows.

Glinka's work was continued by Aleksandr Sergeyevich Dargomÿzhsky (1813–69), whose lyrical romances reflect the domestic music making of the landowning class (gentry) as it became increasingly urbanized; at its best, this style, seen also in his opera *Rusalka* (1856) (Example 8–4), anticipates the soaring melodies of Chaikovsky. Beginning with the "mad scene" in the third act of *Rusalka*, the Overture on Finnish Themes, and some late romances, Dargomÿzhsky intensified Glinka's dissonances and linear writing and sought a more realistic vocal style which culminated in his unfinished opera *The Stone Guest*, Pushkin's version of the Don Giovanni story. The opera, with Pushkin's play almost intact, is sung in a declamatory arioso following speech rhythms and inflections and unified by the accompaniment; one of its more striking devices is the use of the whole-tone scale harmonized by the augmented triad as the "signature tune" of the statue. Dargomÿzhsky strongly influenced the speech-dominated vocal writing in Musorgsky's operas and songs.

Five quite dissimilar Russian composers—Cui, Borodin, Balakirev, Musorgsky, and Rimsky-Korsakov—have frequently been arbitrarily grouped together under the headings of "the New Russian School," "the mighty handful," (*moguchaya kuchka*), and erroneously as "The Five." All of these composers were essentially self-taught and were frequently engaged in other than musical occupations: Musorgsky as an army officer and civil servant, Rimsky-Korsakov as a naval officer, Borodin as a research chemist, and Cui as a career army officer who eventually became a lieutenant general of engineers.

César Cui (Kyui, 1835–1918) is known today, if at all, only as a writer of good salon music (Example 8–6a). Aleksandr Porfirievich Borodin (1833–87), the least productive composer of this group, is the most famous for his Oriental exoticisms in such works as the Polovetsian Dances from his unfinished opera *Prince Igor*, his symphonic sketch *In the Steppes of Central Asia*, and his Second Symphony. Mily Aleksandrovich Balakirev (1837–1910), the mentor of this group, was the principal generator of new musical ideas which were, however, treated more effectively by others in his circle. The Orientalia of his brilliant piano fantasy *Islamey* (1869) were more strikingly exploited by Borodin in his exotic works, and one need but compare Balakirev's symphonic poem *Tamar* (1867–82; Balakirev would often spend several years on one composition) with Rimsky-Korsakov's *Scheherazade* (1888) to see that Balakirev had the original ideas but that Rimsky-Korsakov could treat them in a slicker and more popularly effective manner.

EXAMPLE 8–3. (a) Beethoven, Quartet Op. 59, No. 2, third movement; (b) Glinka, *Kamarinskaya;* (c) Grieg, Ballade, Op. 24 (Copyright 1918 by G. Schirmer, Inc. Reproduced by permission); (d) Delius, *Appalachia* (Copyright 1906 by Harmonie, Berlin. Copyright 1927 by Universal Edition. Reproduced by permission).

(d) Andante

Balakirev's *Overture on Russian Themes* (1858, rev. 1881) and *Second Overture* (1864, rev. 1884; known also as "A Thousand Years" and later "Russia") were not only attempts to reconcile Western sonata form with Glinka's folksong treatments from *Kamarinskaya* and Russian folk-style harmonies (avoidance of secondary dominants in the major mode and dominant harmonies in the minor mode), but were seminal works for the rest of the century, not only for Russian composers but for others, like Gustav Holst or Henry F. Gilbert, who sought new ways of symphonically treating folk music. One of Balakirev's more striking harmonic progressions occurs in his *King Lear* overture of 1859, wherein a Schumannesque closing theme is followed by a storm scene in which the juxtaposition of two chords an augmented fourth apart (Example 8–5b) produces a sense of tonal dislocation. Glinka had done this earlier in the third act of *Ruslan and Lyudmila* for comic effect, at the moment when the sorceress Naina reveals herself to the cowardly Farlaf (Example 8–5a), but harmonically it is a coloristic elaboration of B♭ much as the first four measures of Example 10–7a are an elaboration of C. Example 8–5c shows Musorgsky's later use of this harmonic effect; here the key outcome is in doubt until it is finally revealed as C major (in Example 8–5d). In contrast, almost all of Balakirev's later piano music, published during the opening years of the twentieth century, is a nostalgic summing-up of the Romantic melancholy that we have previously seen in Field, Glinka, and Chopin.

The greatest and most original composer of this group was Modest Petrovich Musorgsky (1839–81), the composer of operas in various states of completion or revision (*Boris Godunov, Khovanschina, The Fair at Sorochinsk*), some piano music, and a number of superb songs. An army officer or civil servant for most of his life, he deplored his lack of "polish" and

EXAMPLE 8–4. Dargomÿzhsky, *Rusalka*, Act III.

"craftsmanship" yet assailed the techniques of the academic German symphonists; many of the supposed "crudities" in his music resulted not from his lack of musical knowledge (he had studied, albeit informally, with both Balakirev and Dargomÿzhsky) but from his strong conviction that art was a means of communicating with people in a spirit of truth and realism and not (as the aesthetes and Symbolists were to preach) an aim in itself. It is his distance from Western constructive techniques and harmonic practices that gives his music such power and directness.

Musorgsky's harmony is the most empirical of any composer since Monteverdi. Among his more interesting effects are sudden enharmonic juxtapositions (Example 8–5c, much more abrupt and sustained for a longer

EXAMPLE 8–5. (a) Glinka, *Ruslan and Lyudmila* (1842), duettino, Act III; (b) Balakirev, Overture to *King Lear* (1859); (c),(d), Musorgsky, *Boris Godunov* (1869), Prologue.

(a)

I -tak,   uz - nai   vol - sheb - ni - tsa   Na - i - na   ya!

(b)

Allegro moderato

(c)

(d)

period of time than the examples by Glinka and Balakirev); use of incomplete or augmented triads (Example 8–6b); extensive pedal points; harmonic ambiguity at close range (between A minor and F major in the Simpleton's song in *Boris*, for example) and scales avoiding or minimizing the leading tone, especially in minor. One need only compare Beethoven's harmonization, with its secondary dominant sevenths, of a Russian folk melody (Example 8–3a) with Musorgsky's diatonic treatment with secondary triads (Example 8–5d) to see the difference between Western and Russian harmonic practices.

In *Boris Godunov* Musorgsky contrasts Western and Russian idioms in the third (Polish) act, added to provide a love interest to the opera, and in the powerful "Revolutionary" scene with which the second version of the opera ends—where the tonal chant of the Jesuits is contrasted with the interjections of Russian peasant song (many here, as elsewhere, not genuine folk songs but melodies in folk style) or the more modal Russian hymnody of the rascally monks Missail and Varlaam. Echoes of Russian folk or ecclesiastical music dominate the choral scenes (as also in *Khovanshchina*), and folk song idioms characterize the charming scene between Boris's son Fyodor and his nurse. The soloistic high points of the opera, written in Musorgsky's declamatory style, are Boris's soliloquies; the confrontation scene between Boris and Prince Shuisky, followed by the "Clock Scene" in which Boris imagines he sees the corpse of the murdered child Tsarevich (it is quite probable that Alban Berg had this scene in mind when he wrote his more brutal passages in *Wozzeck*); and Boris's death.

Musorgsky finished the first version of the opera in 1869, revised it in 1871 and orchestrated it the following year, and oversaw the publication of the piano-vocal score in 1874 (on which Rimsky-Korsakov based his two subsequent revisions, undertaken after the composer's death). Concern not to lose any of Musorgsky's original music has led to attempts to combine both the 1869 and 1874 versions in trying to create an "authentic" version, but recent scholarship has advocated the 1874 version as representing the composer's final intentions.

Musorgsky, building on Dargomÿzhsky's unsuccessful experiments, succeeded in creating a speech-dominated Slavic musical language much as Caccini, Schütz, Lully, and Purcell had done for Western European languages during the Baroque era. The Slavic countries had lagged in achieving this kind of declamation possibly because of the widespread performance of Western operas in translation, the reluctance of many singers to try anything new, and the pervasiveness of Western melodic idioms which could not readily be adapted to Slavic or Magyar languages; other Eastern countries did not develop their own speech-dominated musical languages until the time of Janáček and Bartók early in the twentieth century. Musorgsky succeeded because he combined realistic declamation with a compelling musical expression that is more declamatory than lyric, interjectory rather than melodically continuous, motivic rather than phrase-dominated, variable rather than symmetrical; it sometimes relies on irregular or complex musical meters, and is often reinforced by empirical harmonies and snatches of folk or ecclesiastical motives.

In both his operas and songs Musorgsky achieves a realism comparable to Courbet's in painting or Zola's in literature. Like his contemporary Fyodor Dostoyevsky (1821–81), Musorgsky excels in the psychological portrayal of character and thus anticipates twentieth-century realism and expressionism. Compare, as an illustration, a sentimental romance by Cui with an example of "slice-of-life" realism by Musorgsky, who wrote the text as well as the music for his song "Kozel" to describe a girl frightened by a dirty, hairy goat yet who has no qualms about marrying an old man with the same unattractive qualities (Example 8–6). The unprepared, dissonant augmented triads help communicate the atmosphere of distaste and revulsion. In both text and music one can see the sharp contrast between Cui's (and Pushkin's) Romanticism and Musorgsky's brutal rejection of these conventions. Musorgsky's posthumous influence was strong not only on Janáček and Bartók but also on Debussy, who spent a brief time in Russia, and who continued Musorgsky's work in using coloristic harmonies, seemingly unrelated chords in succession, and declamatory expression.

Nikolay Andreyevich Rimsky-Korsakov (1844–1908), the most professionally trained musician of the *kuchka,* has undergone much abuse for having arranged, orchestrated, completed, and otherwise "improved" many of the works of his colleagues. His version of Musorgsky's orchestral sketch (later the choral dream sequence in *The Fair at Sorochinsk*) "Night on Bare Mountain" is a travesty of Musorgsky's ideas, and his version of *Boris* does not do justice to the original. In extenuation, Rimsky was not seeking to create an "archaeological" document but rather to get the music in shape for performance in practical editions in order to make Musorgsky's talent known.

Though he composed in a variety of media, Rimsky is best known for his brilliantly scored orchestral works (the earlier ones went through several revisions) culminating in the late 1880's with *Capriccio espagnole, Sheherazade,* and *Russian Easter Overture,* and his eleven operas, the genre to which he devoted the last twenty years of his life and the one which contains his most imaginative and original music. Rimsky-Korsakov excels in continuing Glinka's portrayals of the exotic, fantastic, and grotesque, often through the use of artificial scales; this is best shown in his last opera, *Le Coq d'Or* (1907). In his best and most varied opera, *Sadko* (1898), the composer juxtaposes fantasy with portraits of medieval Russia (including a chorus in rapid 11/4 meter), folk-like scenes to represent the "real" world, and some of the best musical portrayals of the ocean ever composed. Example 8–7 shows (a) the "real" diatonic world of the clowns; (b) the free-floating chromatic harmony of the *rusalky* (water-maidens), aquatic but hardly musical kin of Wagner's Rhinemaidens; and (c) an octatonic scale (the octave divided symmetrically) for the leitmotive of the sea-king's daughter. Such scales and the variety of non-functional harmonizations that they evoked led quite directly to Stravinsky's early style.

Other Russian composers had a more "professional" and cosmopoli-

tan orientation than the nationalistic amateurs of the *kuchka.* Anton Grigo-
rievich Rubinstein (1829–94), who spent most of his adolescence in the
West and inherited the fluency of Mendelssohn and Meyerbeer, founded
the Russian Musical Society in 1859 and the St. Petersburg Conservatory,
Russia's first professional music school, three years later. Rubinstein was a
formidable pianist regarded as Liszt's equal, his D minor Concerto was
once a staple of the repertoire, and one can trace a line of descent from his
early "Melody in F" to the American popular songs of George Gershwin
(1898–1937) and his contemporaries.

Pyotr Ilyich Chaikovsky (1840–93), one of the first graduates from
Rubinstein's conservatory, was more oriented toward Germanic models (especially Schumann) than the composers of the *kuchka,* yet incorporated
Russian music within an essentially Western framework in his first two
symphonies and his ever-popular B♭ minor Piano Concerto. His lyricism, inherited from Dargomÿzhsky, is best seen in the slow movements of his
symphonies, his operas (especially *Eugene Onegin,* probably his finest
work), and in his ballets; *Swan Lake* is a direct successor of the underwater
ballet in Act IV of Dargomÿzhsky's *Rusalka.* In his music Chaikovsky displayed a strong if not subtle harmonic sense, obtaining his effects chiefly
through oscillations around the mediants or submediants (compare mea-

EXAMPLE 8–6. (a) Cui, "Zhelanie" (Desire), Op. 57, No. 25; (b) Musorgsky, "Kozel"
(The He-Goat).

(b)

znat, pri-shla po - ra ei za - muzh. Nu, i vui-shla!

Muzh i sta - rui, i gor - ba - tui,

li sui; zloi i bo - ro da - tui, su - shchi chyort!

sures 1–3 of Example 8–8 with measures 1–2 of Example 8–2b) or through clustered non-harmonic tones.

Chaikovsky's best instrumental works are his ballets and his instrumental cycles based on Western forms of absolute music; in some of them one can even see a Neoclassic influence. Chaikovsky admired Mozart above all other composers, and in contrast to the extreme subjectivity of his last three symphonies and the four-movement symphonic poem *Manfred*, he shows an almost Classic restraint and balance in such works as the Op. 11 String Quartet (the slow movement the famous "Andante Cantabile"), Third Symphony, Second Piano Concerto, and Serenade for Strings—these

EXAMPLE 8–7. Rimsky-Korsakov, *Sadko*.

EXAMPLE 8–7. Rimsky-Korsakov, *Sadko* (continued)

(c)

Dye - vi - tsa vye - shcha - ya zna - yu ya, vye - da - yu

ne si - nyu mo - ryu ya pro - sva - ta - na

works, incidentally, being his principal instrumental cycles in the major mode, in contrast to the prevailing minor tonalities in most of his compositions.

Like Glinka, Raff, and Rimsky-Korsakov, Chaikovsky created brilliant settings of the folk or popular music of other nations, as in his *Capriccio Italien* or the musical travelogues in the ballets *Swan Lake* and *The Nutcracker*. Russian nationalism was only one of the many colors in his musical palette.

Several composers born in the 1860's and early 1870's continued Chaikovsky's essentially conservative idiom. Aleksandr Konstantinovich Glazunov (1865–1936) is best known for his symphonies, violin concerto, and ballets *(The Seasons, Raymonda)*, in which his scintillating orchestration and emphasis on the lyric over the dramatic are most pronounced. The lyrical refulgence of the piano works of Sergei Rakhmaninov (1873–1943) is also shown in his three symphonies, and his Russian church music is the capstone of the genre. Paradoxically, the Russian composers of the 1860's and 1870's generation (except for Skryabin, who belongs in a study of twentieth-century music) were less progressive around 1900 than Rimsky-Korsakov had been.

The polemics in which the Russian composers and their supporters engaged has led to some confusion as to the actual extent of Western influ-

EXAMPLE 8–8. Chaikovsky, *Eugene Onegin*, Act I.

ences in their music. In reality, all of the Russians were influenced by major Western composers, especially Beethoven and Schumann, with Berlioz and Liszt important for the *kuchka*. The finale of Borodin's First Symphony seems a frank imitation of Schumann's orchestral style, whereas Rimsky-Korsakov's Third Symphony (first version 1873), second and better version 1886) has themes as splendidly diatonic as any Neoclassic work by Reinecke or Saint-Saëns—but they are handled with a freshness that derives more from Glinka than from Beethoven or Mendelssohn. In contrast, the finales of Chaikovsky's Second Symphony and Glazunov's Third are as *kuchkist* as anything by Balakirev.

In the field of opera, the tendency of Glinka was to include French and Italian elements, while Dargomÿzhsky later aimed for an opera that would be a sung play based on the aesthetic of the through-composed art song rather than the Wagnerian sung symphonic drama based on principles of thematic development. Russia being the country second only to France in the cultivation of the ballet, Russian opera, especially of the domestic or fairy-tale variety, utilized dance and dance rhythms for many of its most memorable moments. The waltz holds the Act II finale of Chaikovsky's *Eugene Onegin* together much as the minuet does the Act I finale of Mozart's *Don Giovanni*, and Rimsky's *The Snow Maiden* is best known not for its arias but for its dance-like excerpts like the "Dance of the Buffoons." In sum, Russian music of this epoch strikingly exhibits in microcosm the paradoxes, chronological overlapping, and contradictions typical of the nineteenth century as a whole.

BOHEMIA

Bohemia, the westernmost of the Czech provinces, was musically dominant in this region during the nineteenth century. After the Thirty Years' War (1618–48) the Austrians subjugated Bohemia and overlaid its culture with Germanic influences to which the natives had to adapt. During the eighteenth century there was a great efflorescence of musical education in Bohemia, for since the Slavs were to be servants, the Austrian authorities thought that music would be a useful trade for them, and the products of the instrumental music programs of the Jesuit schools were disseminated throughout Europe because of the over-supply in Bohemia of musicians and the shortage of worthwhile positions. Noteworthy among the emigrés were Jan Stamic (Johann Stamitz), Anton Filc (Filtz), and Franz Xaver Richter in Mannheim; the Benda brothers, Jiří (Georg) in Gotha and František (Franz) in Berlin; and Koželuch, Tomašek, and Voříšek in Vienna. Bohemian music remained dominant during the nineteenth century, with that of the other West Slavic peoples (Moravians and Slovaks) regarded as exotic rather than national products; the reason may have been that the Austrian rule over Bohemia was less restrictive than the Hungarian dominance over Slovakia. Tuneful homophony was characteristic of both Baroque and Classic music in Bohemia; combined with a long tradition of instrumental, especially string, performance, this gave birth to the Mannheim school and was a strong influence on Viennese composers from Haydn to Schubert. Yet not until the nineteenth century could Bohemian composers obtain recognition at home and devote themselves to a particularly national style.

František Škroup (1802–62), the founder of Bohemian musical nationalism, wrote operas to librettos in Czech which contain some of the most technically simple music ever written. His most famous work, *Fidlovačka* (1834), includes folk song, quotations from *Der Freischütz*, and the aria "Kde domoj muj" which later became the Czech national anthem. The models for this work were evidently Rousseau's *Le Devin du village* and the simpler *Singspiele*.

Bedřich Smetana (1824–84) founded the most viable school of Bohemian national music. His musical development was late, and his first significant compositions date from the late 1850's—tone poems for Göteborg in Sweden, where he was musical director. One of them, *Wallenstein's Camp*, is based on a Bohemian subject and contains almost all of the composer's stylistic traits: passages in fast harmonic rhythm with considerable chromatic activity to create a sense of excitement; dance motives; and a triumphal conclusion. The apex of his orchestral achievement is the cycle of six symphonic poems *Má Vlast* (My Country), of which *The Moldau* is best known. His historical operas dealing with Czech topics *(The Brandenburgers in Bohemia, Dalibor, Libuše)* are virtually unknown outside of Czechoslovakia; they contain many striking passages and show the influence of German Romantic opera, especially in the prevailingly continuous texture and the important role given to the orchestra. On the other hand, his internationally popular *Bartered Bride*, essentially (like *Fidlovačka*) an *opéra comique* transferred to a Czech village, is one of the masterpieces of national opera, with its humorous intrigue, natural characters, tuneful and delightful music (in the opening chorus, authentic folk music). His best keyboard compositions, technically quite difficult, frequently utilize folk dances.

Conversely, his chamber music works are intensely personal and autobiographical, reflecting personal tragedies in his life. The G minor Piano Trio, Op. 15 (1855), written after the death of his oldest daughter, is rhapsodic, effusive, and the best continuation of Schumann's experiments in form in the piano sonatas of the 1830's. The E minor String Quartet (1876), which he entitled "From My Life," contains a turbulent first movement, a polka-like second movement, a slow movement depicting Smetana's love for his first wife, and a finale that begins triumphantly; the extremely high E with which the coda begins, representing the ringing sound in his ear that signalled the onset of permanent deafness, inaugurates flashbacks of earlier themes, and its emotional impact seldom fails to affect an audience. The second quartet, which Smetana finished the year before his death, is one of the most curious works of the century, for it departs from traditional sonata form and seems to be an application of the free form of Berlioz to the narrative structures of the individual tone poems of *My Country*, though there is no stated program to the quartet. One wonders whether the work is an application of "stream of consciousness" techniques to absolute music (as later with Mahler) or a harbinger of the supposed "formlessness" of such post-Romantic works as Schoenberg's and Bartók's First String Quartets.

Antonín Dvořák (1841–1904) is the most important Bohemian composer of the nineteenth century. In many ways his career parallels Haydn's: humble peasant beginnings, struggling musical apprenticeship, the slow growth of an international reputation with great acclaim in later life, a deeply fervent religious faith, and a reputation among the mass audience based on only one creative period. Dvořák is one of the few truly "universal" composers of the century in the sense that he wrote in all existing genres; though known primarily as a symphonist, he was both active and skilled as a composer of operas, chamber music, songs, choral works, and piano music.

Dvořák's development as a composer was slow, and his early works are marked by a spaciousness that borders on diffuse prolixity; this is evident in the best large work of the time, the Third Symphony, Op. 10, of 1873. The main works of the year 1875—the Fifth Symphony, Op. 24 (originally Op. 76), in F major; the string quintet in G major, Op. 77, for string quartet and double bass, and the E major string quartet, Op. 80—mark Dvořák's first maturity as a composer; they were not published for several years after they were written (which accounts for their high opus numbers). In the late 1870's Dvořák gained an international reputation, which was reinforced by premiere performances in the early 1880's of the *Stabat Mater*, Sixth Symphony, and C major string quartet, Op. 61.

As a symphonist, Dvořák partook of the heritage of Beethoven and Schubert (to which one can add Haydn and Schumann for chamber music); the influence of his friend Brahms was chiefly in architectonic structure and the use of a quiet intermezzo rather than a scherzo in several works. Schubert's three-key expositions affected Dvořák's as well as those of Brahms. Frequent modal interchange (passing rapidly between major and minor) often extended the spectrum of keys available for Dvořák's transient modulations, and his propensity for cadencing on a minor-mode submediant or mediant in a major-mode melody (Examples 8–9a, 8–11) also widened his tonal resources.

The last three symphonies represent the peak of his symphonic achievement, with the somber Seventh, in D minor (1885), ranking with (and easily mistaken for) those of Brahms. The popular Eighth, in G major (1889), is a folklike work, with a quietly reflective intermezzo rather than a

EXAMPLE 8–9. (a) Dvořák, String Quartet, Op. 61, third movement; (b) Dvořák, Symphony No. 9, Op. 95, first movement; (c) Czech folksong "Ja ne, to ty" from Jan Seidel (ed.), *Národ v Pisni* (Prague, 1941), p. 175.

scherzo and a set of free variations for the finale. In the familiar "New World" Symphony, the Ninth (1893), Dvořák was not successful in his attempts to create a cyclic work, for his themes were not amenable to such treatment, the effect is rather blatant, and the so-called American Negro and Indian themes cannot be ascribed to indigenous American "intonations" since gapped scales and "Lombard" rhythms are also prominent characteristics of Czech folk music (Example 8–9c), as is also the lowered leading tone in the minor mode. In fact, the trio of the scherzo of the Op. 61 string quartet (see Example 8–9a), finished in 1881, long before Dvořák's transatlantic journey, sounds as "American" as any of the works from the early 1890's.

Of his other orchestral works, a series of concert overtures culminated in 1891 with the triptych *Nature, Life, and Love* (respectively *In Nature's Realm*, the popular *Carnaval*, and *Otello*). After his return from America Dvořák wrote a set of symphonic poems based on Czech folk legends, ranging from the prolix *Golden Spinning Wheel* to the concise *Midday Witch* (both 1896). Dvořák's contributions to the concerto literature include an early (1876) and rather unsuccessful piano concerto (the comment was made that it seems as if written for a pianist with two right hands), a more successful violin concerto with a furiant-like finale (1880), and a cello concerto (1894–95) in B minor that is the capstone of this instrument's literature, as successful as those of Brahms at being a truly symphonic concerto.

The chamber works from Dvořák's "American" period, the F major Quartet (Op. 96) and the E♭ String Quintet (Op. 97), have been overplayed at the expense of his finest chamber works, the Brahmsian F minor Piano Trio, Op. 65, the splendidly lyrical A major Piano Quintet, Op. 81, and the magnificent late quartets in A♭, Op. 105, and G, Op. 106. As a violist, Dvořák was a skilled performer of chamber music and showed great and sympathetic understanding of the true possibilities of this medium.

If Smetana's basic dance rhythm is the slow polka, Dvořák's is the furiant, a dance based on the use of hemiola rhythm. In many furiants, Dvořák gives the impression of alternating a pattern consisting of one measure of 3/2 meter with two measures of 3/4 meter, as in Example 8–10b, but sometimes entire sections in one of the two meters (sometimes with

EXAMPLE 8–10. (a) Smetana, *The Moldau;* (b) Dvořák, Symphony No. 6, third movement.

cross-rhythms between the two) occur, as in his Slavonic Dance, Op. 46, No. 1. The two collections of Slavonic Dances (Op. 46 and Op. 72), originally for piano four-hands but subsequently orchestrated, are the most popular of his dance pieces: in these he includes not only Bohemian but other Slavic dances. A favorite of Dvořák's is the Ukrainian-Polish *dumka* (plural *dumky*), a slow lament interspersed with faster sections, which he used as slow movements in his String Sextet, Op. 51 String Quartet, Piano Quintet, as well as six of them for piano trio, the so-called "Dumky" Trio, Op. 90.

With the exception of his oratorio *St. Ludmila*, Dvořák was least nationalistic in his large choral works, especially those to sacred texts. In these the composer eschewed dance and folk song idioms and permitted his personal melodic and harmonic styles, the latter marked by a frequent use of secondary triads, to come to the fore. The kinds of musical expression range from the "severe," as in the "Inflammatus" of the *Stabat Mater*, to the soulfully lyric, as in Example 8–11.

Though Dvořák's operas are frequently performed in his native land, they have not travelled well, probably because of the close connection of most of the librettos with Czech topics. The only one in the Western repertoire is his masterpiece *Rusalka* (1900), the lyric and folk-like culmination of the Romantic fairy-tale opera of the romance of water-nymph and mortal man. The comic opera *The Devil and Kate* (*Čert a Káča*, 1899) would be effective with a good English translation.

Dvořák's music demands comparison with that of his two best known contemporaries, Brahms and Chaikovsky; his universality, innate musical gifts, developing technical command of his material, and profusion of memorable melodies made him one of the outstanding composers of the late years of the century.

Dvořák's most important Czech contemporary was Zdeněk Fibich (1850–1900), chiefly remembered today as a composer of operas. His numerous works include extensive cycles of piano miniatures (the *Images, Impressions and Souvenirs*, Op. 41, being the best of these) which are seemingly a late Romantic counterpart of Mendelssohn's *Songs Without Words* but in reality are a very detailed account of his love affair with one of his students.[2] The important post-Romantic Czech composers are Dvořák's son-in-law, Josef Suk (1874–1935), and an unjustly neglected composer in the larger orchestral and choral forms, J. B. Foerster (1859–1951). The musical development of the great Moravian composer Leoš Janáček (1854–1928) was late and belongs in a study of the music of the twentieth century rather than in this volume.

[2]Gerald Abraham, "An Erotic Diary for Piano." *Slavonic and Romantic Music* (New York, 1968), pp. 70–82.

EXAMPLE 8–11. Dvořák, "Recordare" from *Requiem*, Op. 89.

SCANDINAVIA

At the opening of the nineteenth century, the major musical figures in Scandinavian countries were German emigrants. The most important was Friedrich Kuhlau (1786–1832), who moved to Copenhagen in 1810 and became a Danish citizen in 1813. Although he is remembered today by his easy sonatinas, which have become favorite teaching pieces for beginning pianists, his sonatas for piano duet and his flute music, highly esteemed by players of that instrument, show Weber's brilliance.

    The Swedish composer Franz Berwald (1796–1868) is one of the most original and interesting of the composers of the first half of the nineteenth century. Although he wrote chamber music and operas, his symphonies and other orchestral works, most of them dating from the 1840's, are the peak of his achievement. It is noteworthy that his *Tongemälde* (tone paintings), short orchestral compositions with names like *Memories of the Norwegian Alps*, anticipate Liszt's symphonic poems. Berwald's style is highly original, especially in its harmonic and rhythmic aspects, and his use of rhythmic surprise and silence can be compared only with that of Berlioz. As Example 8–12 shows, Berwald's music is very melodious, with a subtle and original use of harmonic colors, but the Stockholm audiences for which

EXAMPLE 8–12. Berwald, *Sinfonie sérieuse*, second theme of fourth movement.

he wrote had to be educated even to Beethoven's style, and Berwald—too progressive for them—had to support himself as a businessman. It is quite probable that Sibelius was well acquainted with such passages in Berwald's music as the opening of the *Sinfonie singulière* and the conclusion of the *Sinfonie sérieuse.*

Although the Danish composer Niels Wilhelm Gade (1817–90) is written about as the most important Scandinavian composer before Grieg, his music is seldom heard. A protegé of Mendelssohn whose music was popular in Germany and England as well as in his native Denmark, Gade devoted much of his life to developing Danish musical institutions. He is at his best in his miniatures, such as the *Aquarelles* for piano, and as a musical landscape painter, as in the opening movements of his choral work *The Erl-King's Daughter.* A preference for the minor mode, often in its natural form, and a certain austerity are the chief "Nordic" elements in his music.

Edvard Hagerup Grieg (1843–1907), the major figure of nineteenth-century Scandinavian music, insisted that he was a localized Norwegian rather than a generalized Scandinavian composer. In his early works, like the E minor Piano Sonata or the popular A minor Piano Concerto, the influence of Schumann is pronounced, but Norwegian national elements are discernible as early as the *Humoresques*, Op. 6, of 1865. The Ballade, Op. 24 (1875–76), his most extensive piano work, is a set of variations on a Norwegian folk tune which Grieg harmonized in a quite individual manner, with chromatically moving inner parts (Example 8–3c). His most important piano works are the harmonizations or improvisations on folk melodies, in which some of his most interesting harmonies occur, and ten books of *Lyric Pieces*, individual miniatures in ternary or five-part form which range from simple teaching pieces or salon melodies to folklike pieces and even such daring works as the impressionistic "Klokkeklang" (Bell Ringing, Op. 54, No. 6), with its superimposed pan-diatonic empty fifths. Of his orchestral music, the two suites compiled from his incidental music to Ibsen's drama *Peer Gynt* (1874) are deservedly popular, but his fine choral music, especially his settings of psalms for baritone solo and male chorus, is virtually unknown today.

There are several facets to Grieg's musical personality: there is Grieg the "Mendelssohn of the trolls," evident in "The Hall of the Mountain King" from the *Peer Gynt* music and in the piano piece "Småtrold" (Little Troll) (Op. 71, No. 3); Grieg the lyricist, seen in the A minor Concerto and the violin sonatas; Grieg the elegiac singer, at his best in the slow movement of the G minor Violin Sonata; Grieg the harmonist, whose effective use of altered chords and non-harmonic tones so strongly influenced MacDowell, Delius, and Gilbert; and finally Grieg the folklorist, whose transcriptions of the *Slåtter* of the Hardanger fiddle—characterized by a major scale with a raised fourth degree, ornamentation, and drone strings—have a very "modern" sound (Example 8–13) which subsequently was reflected in the folksong settings of one of his disciples, the Australian pianist-composer Percy Grainger (1882–1961). Debussy's G minor String Quartet of 1893 owes much in its sonorities, modalities (especially lowered leading tones), and patternings to Grieg's quartet in the same key (Op. 27, 1877–78), though Debussy is more subtle and less sentimentally effusive in his use of cyclic form.

EXAMPLE 8–13. Grieg, "Bridal March from Telemark," *Slåtter*, Op. 72 (1902). Compare this example with his popular "Wedding Day at Troldhaugen"!

Grieg is one of the most individual composers of the nineteenth century, and those whose knowledge of his music is based only on the song "Ich liebe dich," the *Peer Gynt* suites, or his easier *Lyric Pieces* will find an extremely innovative and harmonically imaginative composer who anticipated many devices of the early twentieth century in his folksong harmonizations (especially those of the *Norske folkeviser* of 1896), the *Slåtter*, the *Haugtussa* song cycle, Op. 67, and other less familiar works. Grieg led not just to Delius and Grainger, but also to Bartók.

HUNGARY

During the eighteenth and nineteenth centuries the Hungarians were the most culturally independent of the national groups of eastern Europe. Many Hungarian aristocratic families, of which the Esterházys are best known, were patrons of Viennese composers, who in turn reciprocated by using "Hungarian" motives in their works. The separation of Hungarian, Turkish, and gypsy elements in Hungarian music of the nineteenth century is an almost impossible task, inasmuch as Hungary was occupied by the Turks for nearly two centuries and gypsy musicians were the chief disseminators of what became known as the Hungarian style. As in most of eastern Europe, folk and popular music was transmitted by oral rather than written tradition, and those who wrote the music down or incorporated it into their compositions were often far removed from the origins of the oral tradition of this music. What Western composers wrote as "Turkish" music was characterized by tonal instability and a marked rhythmic emphasis, often helped by a lavish use of percussion. In Example 8–14a, note the tonal instability of the introduction, the major scale with the raised fourth in the melody after the introduction, and the strongly percussive rhythm. The vogue for "Turkish" music lasted until the early 1820's, when the general European revulsion against the Turkish atrocities in the Greek War of Independence abruptly terminated its popularity.

In the middle of the eighteenth century a new kind of Hungarian popular music appeared, the *verbunkos* or recruiting music, originally played by bands of gypsy string players which accompanied Austrian recruiting officers to peasant villages. This music, disseminated by gypsy orchestras and composers of light music, soon became the favorite music of the Hungarian bourgeoisie and lesser nobility and, through the works of Germanic composers from Haydn to Brahms, became known as "Hungarian" music in the West until Bartók's folk song researches in the early twentieth century. Highly ornamented slow passages, syncopations, a characteristic cadential pattern (Examples 8–14c, 15a, 15b), and fast passages in a fiery duple meter with much instrumental fioritura are characteristic of this style.

Although Liszt sought out the "uncivilized" gypsy musicians in Hungary rather than the Germanized ones who played from notated music, his Hungarian works are chiefly utilizations of the *verbunkos* style by a highly cosmopolitan composer, and his Hungarian Rhapsodies and book *The Gypsy in Music*, as well as the continued exploitation of the *verbunkos* style by Raff and Brahms (Hungarian gypsy music had the same influence on German composers that Spanish gypsy music had on their French colleagues), gave the West a false picture of Hungarian music. Although the

EXAMPLE 8–14. "Turkish" (a) and Hungarian (b), (c) influences in Western art music. (a) Mozart, *Die Entführung aus dem Serail*, Act I; (b) Beethoven, "Eroica" Symphony, last movement; (c) Schubert, *Divertissement à l'hongroise*, D. 818.

(a) Allegro

8th-note rhythm in bass, percussion

(b) Allegro
staccato

sempre *f*

molto
marcato

(c) Un poco più mosso

verbunkos style degenerated into the salon piece or "Csárdás Princess" operetta during the closing years of the nineteenth century, it won a new lease on life with Kodály's popular compositions like *Háry János* and the *Galanta Dances.*

As the Viennese school of composition declined in influence after 1820, French and Italian opera became popular in Hungary. Their influences were effectively combined with the *verbunkos* style by Ferenc Erkel (1810–1893), Hungary's most important composer of this period, whose principal achievements were grand operas based on Hungarian history. His best-known work, *Hunyádi László* (1844), utilizes a mixture of styles: the *verbunkos* in its slow aspects (the farewell duet cited as Example 8–15c) or in the coloratura fireworks of the "La Grange" aria of Act II for his sympathetic characters, and an "international" style, largely based on Meyerbeer's, for such unsympathetic personages as King László V. In his later operas, like *Bánk Bán* (1860) and *Dósza György* (1867), Erkel's development surprisingly parallels Verdi's in its increasing musical depth and use of harmonic and orchestral resources.

ENGLAND

England's prosperity throughout the nineteenth century attracted many foreign musicians and composers. London became a musical center second only to Paris, with high standards of orchestral playing, generous support, and sizable audiences that received most new music favorably. Not only Spohr and Mendelssohn but also Berlioz, Liszt, and Wagner visited London. Paradoxically, London's very eminence and prosperity hampered the development of a native serious art music until the very end of the century, though many meritorious composers strove to create one. Their developments were hampered by the prevalence of European (especially Germanic) influences: at the opening of the century the Viennese composers, in mid-century Mendelssohn and to a lesser extent Schumann, and at the end of the century Brahms.

Cipriani Potter (1792–1871) was praised by Beethoven in 1818 as having a "talent for composition"; as a pianist, he contributed many chamber works featuring his instrument and wrote several symphonies, nine of which survive, and concert overtures. William Sterndale Bennett (1816–75) was highly praised by Schumann and gave evidence of talent in such early works as his piano concertos and concert overture *The Naiads* (1837), a seascape resembling in many ways Mendelssohn's *Melusine* overture. Though his later works have not received as much acclaim, his five-movement G minor symphony (1864–67), chamber music (especially a fine cello sonata-

EXAMPLE 8–15. The *verbunkos* style in popular and art music. (a) "Saltus Hungaricus" from the Martonfi MS. (late eighteenth century),[3] (b) Márk Rószavölgyi, "First Hungarian Social Dance," 1842; (c) Ferenc Erkel, *Hunyádi László*, Act IV.

duo of 1852), and character pieces for piano (see Example 8–16) merit revival; he should not be judged solely by his choral works such as *The Woman of Samaria* (1867), from which the quartet "God Is a Spirit" is often performed as a church anthem. In explanation, oratorio and choral cantata were among the few media wherein English composers could have some certainty of getting their music performed. Another area was music for the Anglican church, which will be discussed in Chapter 12.

Arthur Sullivan (1842–1900) succeeded in creating a living English

[3]Cited in P. P. Domokos, "Magyar Táncdallamok a XVIII. Századból" in B. Szabolcsi and D. Bartha (eds.), *Az Opera Történetéből* (Budapest, 1961), p. 284.

EXAMPLE 8-16. Sterndale Bennett, *Suite de Pièces*, (1842), Op. 24, No. 3.

opera in the sparkling works he wrote in collaboration with W. S. Gilbert; they combine the heritage of Mozart's comic style with parodies of previous operatic conventions and derivations from the middle-class musical theatre, drawing-room ballad, and part-song. In such works as *Iolanthe* (1882) and *The Yeomen of the Guard* (1888) they created masterpieces of their kind which deserve to rank with any operas originally written in English. Sullivan, trained at the Leipzig Conservatory, had written several excellent youthful orchestral works (such as the "Irish" Symphony of 1866) but abandoned orchestral composition in 1870; his attempts at writing major serious works during the 1890's, after his break with Gilbert, were not successful.

The "English Musical Renaissance" is thought to begin with the activity of Charles Hubert Hastings Parry (1848–1918) and Charles Villiers Stanford (1852–1924), both prolific composers and eminent teachers. Parry's choral works have been highly praised: Vaughan Williams once called his short cantata *Blest Pair of Sirens*, the fugue subject of which is cited in Example 8–17 as an illustration of his pan-diatonic noble style, the best such piece ever written by an Englishman. Parry also wrote much chamber music and four symphonies, as well as other orchestral works, especially the *Symphonic Variations* of 1897. Stanford excelled in dramatic choral works—his setting of Tennyson's *Ballad of the 'Revenge'* (1886) is a splendid depiction of the British imperial mood at the end of the century—and his Clarinet Concerto (1902), his orchestral masterpiece, makes a splendid autumnal conclusion to Britain's musical nineteenth century. His excellent Anglican services are discussed in Chapter 12.

One has the feeling, on hearing Stanford's Clarinet Concerto or Parry's *Symphonic Variations*, of encountering highly meritorious works that seem to have been written about fifteen years too late, for they were

EXAMPLE 8–17. Parry, *Blest Pair of Sirens*, fugue subject.

soon to be superseded by the music of Edward Elgar (1857–1934), England's first major composer since Purcell. Elgar's musical development was delayed and only one of his principal works, the *Enigma Variations* of 1899, falls within the nineteenth century. As a composer of oratorios, of which *The Dream of Gerontius* (1900) is best known, Elgar excelled in the portrayal of a Christian heaven and the path there, musically at the opposite pole from the diabolism of Berlioz and Liszt.

Frederick Delius (1862–1934), another late-blooming composer, had only tenuous connections to England; he spent most of his life in France and during his lifetime was most celebrated in Germany. His rich harmonic sense was influenced to some extent by Grieg (compare Examples 8–3c and 8–3d), but his characteristic blend of lush chromatic harmony and static harmonic rhythm is an extremely individual sonority. His English national- ist music consists mainly of genre pictures of the English countryside (e.g., *Brigg Fair*, 1907), musical counterparts of the landscape paintings of John Constable (1776–1837). Delius' stay in Florida and Virginia during the mid- 1880's resulted in some of the finest musical portrayals of the American South in his *Florida* suite (1889); his tragic opera *Koanga* (completed 1897, first performed 1904), based on a story by George Washington Cable; and his *Appalachia* (1896, revised 1903), in its final form for baritone soloist, chorus, and large orchestra, a set of free variations on a Negro slave song (Example 8–3d).

UNITED STATES

In 1800 the concert life of the urban Eastern seaboard was a pale reflection of London's musical activities, but the opening of the continent, the rise of cities in the Midwest, and the streams of immigration provided an increased strength for American musical life. Not until the twentieth century, however, did the strains of American popular music—the "singing school" tune, the minstrel-show tune, the gospel hymn, and the martial or sentimental Civil War song—become incorporated into art music; most nineteenth-century American art music was based on European models by composers who had studied there, and American musical nationalism was based chiefly on exploring Afro-American and, to a lesser extent, Indian music.

Louis Moreau Gottschalk (1829–69) expressed the Creole culture of the Gulf coast and the Caribbean islands rather than that of Anglo-Saxon Protestant America. His use of Louisianan (Example 8–18a), Cuban, and Puerto Rican tunes and rhythms, his unusual piano sonorities which exploit the extreme upper ranges of the instrument, and a certain piquancy of ex- pression raise his best piano compositions above the level of the "salon piece," although his *Dying Poet* is the epitome of Romantic sentimentality.

The most important American composer at the end of the century was Edward MacDowell (1861–1908), a pupil of Joachim Raff who was also influenced by Grieg, especially in his harmony and musical miniatures. MacDowell's "Indian" Suite for orchestra is directly in line of descent from Raff's Hungarian travelogues, and his sonatas exploit a certain vein of Celtic nationalism. Though MacDowell has been most highly regarded for his genre pictures of the sea (Example 10–10) or the northeastern countryside,

EXAMPLE 8–18. Comparative treatments of Afro-American musical material by American composers: (a) Gottschalk, *Bamboula;* (b) Gilbert, "Br'er Rabbit" from *Three American Dances* (Copyright 1919 by The Boston Music Co. Reproduced by permission).

and for his finely wrought songs, his two piano concertos of the 1880's deserve to rank with the best of the late-Romantic works in that genre. Among his contemporaries whose musical activity centered around Boston, Rheinberger's pupil George Whitefield Chadwick (1854–1931) should receive special citation. He spans the nineteenth and twentieth centuries, his later compositions belonging to twentieth-century post-Romanticism; his nineteenth-century works include the Second Symphony (B♭ major, completed 1885), with a Negro melody in its scherzo, and a finely wrought E minor string quartet (1896) which can stand comparison with the best European quartets of that decade.

When Dvořák came to America in the early 1890's he advised the local composers to turn to Negro melodies for inspiration. The chief utilizer of Afro-American melodies and rhythms was MacDowell's pupil Henry F. Gilbert (1868–1928), both in his larger orchestral works like the *Dance in Place Congo* and in his collections of piano miniatures like the *Negro Dances* or *A Rag Bag*, which show the influences of the cakewalk and the new dance craze of ragtime (Example 8–18b), which was being raised to a near-art form in the piano rags of the black composer, Scott Joplin (1868–1917). Although Gilbert's treatment of black music may seem patronizing today, he was serious and sincere in trying to reconcile these popular idioms with art music. In contrast, Horatio Parker (1863–1919) is the best of the "international" American composers; his oratorio *Hora Novissima* (1893) is one of the finest works written for the English choral festivals, but the eclecticism of his operas *Mona* and *Fairyland* prevented them from surviving. Mention should be made of the Irish-born Victor Herbert (1859–1924), whose successful operettas have overshadowed his fine serious compositions, particularly his magnificent Second Concerto for violoncello.[4]

BIBLIOGRAPHICAL NOTES

Nationalism in general is effectively described in Florian Znaniecki's popular *Modern Nationalities* (Urbana, 1952), Boyd C. Shafer's bibliographical essay *Nationalism: Interpretations and Interpreters* (3d ed., Washington, 1966), and Ernest Gellner's philosophical *Nations and Nationalism* (Ithaca, N.Y., 1983). For the musical areas discussed in this chapter, only the most selective bibliography can be given.

Russia. A one-volume survey of Russian music is badly needed; of those existing, the best is R. A. Leonard, *A History of Russian Music* (1956; reprint, New York, 1968), based on secondary sources. Alfred Swan's *Russian Music* (New York, 1973) is based on notes left at the time of the author's death and contains some valuable insights, whereas Robert Ridenour's *Nationalism, Modernism, and Personal Rivalry in 19th-Century Russian Music* (Ann Arbor, 1981) deals with personalities and institutions rather than music. Russian music benefits historiographically from the series of monographs edited by Malcolm Brown, *Studies in Russian Music*, published by UMI Research Press, and philosophically from Richard Taruskin's article "Some Thoughts on the History and Historiography of Russian Music," *Journal of Musicology*, III (1984), 321–39. James Billington's *The Icon and the Axe* (New York, 1970) is an excellent cultural history of Russia that provides a context for understanding the music.

---

[4]The reader is referred for a much more comprehensive evaluation to H. Wiley Hitchcock's *Music in the United States: A Historical Introduction*, 3d ed. (Prentice-Hall, 1988) in this series.

Concerning individual composers, David Brown's very serviceable biography of Glinka (London, 1974) can be used with Richard Mudge's translation of the composer's memoirs (Norman, 1963). Taruskin traces the impact of Glinka's orchestral fantasias in "How the Acorn Took Root," *Nineteenth-Century Music*, VI (1983), 189–212. The scholarly literature on Dargomÿzhsky is almost entirely in Russian; helpful for his later operas is Richard Taruskin's *Opera and Drama in Russia as Preached and Practiced in the 1860's* (Ann Arbor, 1981). Musorgsky has been valuably served in the group of essays edited by Malcolm Brown, *Musorgsky In Memoriam 1881–1981* (Ann Arbor, 1982) and the documentary biography by Alexandra Orlova, *Musorgsky's Days and Works* (Ann Arbor, 1983). For others in the *moguchaya kuchka*, leading studies are Edward Garden's biography of Balakirev (New York, 1967), Sergei Dianin's of Borodin (London, 1963), Gerald Abraham's numerous articles on Rimsky-Korsakov from his *Studies in Russian Music* (London, 1935) onward, and Rimsky's autobiography, translated by Judah Joffe, *My Musical Life* (New York, 1942). The sources and consequences of Rimsky's unusual harmonies and scales have been traced by Richard Taruskin in his "Chernomor to Kashchei," *Journal of the American Musicological Society*, XXXVIII (1985), 72–142. An important primary source now available in English is Florence Jonas (ed. and trans.), *Reminiscences of Rimsky-Korsakov* by V. V. Yastrebtsev (New York, 1985).

David Brown has begun a multi-volume biography of Chaikovsky (London, 1978–   ), three volumes of which have appeared as of this writing, and John Wiley has done a manuscript study, *Tchaikovsky's Ballets* (London, 1984). The story of Chaikovsky's supposed suicide (Alexandra Orlova, "Tchaikovsky: The Last Chapter," *Music and Letters*, LXII [1981], 125–45) has been greeted skeptically by most Slavicists.

Bohemia. Rosa Newmarch's *The Music of Czechoslovakia* (London, 1942) is sadly out of date; Gerald Abraham's *Slavonic and Romantic Music* (New York, 1968) contains essays on Russian and Czech composers, including Fibich. Michael Beckerman has ably described the pitfalls of trying to define Czechness in music too closely in "In Search of Czechness in Music," *Nineteenth-Century Music*, X (1986), 61–73. The main biographies in English of Smetana are those by Brian Large (London, 1970) and John Clapham (London, 1972), which is focussed more on the music; Clapham's outstanding biography of Dvořák (London, 1979) is the standard one in English.

Other countries. John Horton's *Scandinavian Music: A Short Survey* (London, 1963) is still the best introduction to this topic. More detail is provided in Robert Layton's biography of Berwald (London, 1959) and in the numerous biographies of Grieg, of which a symposium edited by Gerald Abraham (1948; reprint Westport, Ct. 1971) and the excellent biography by John Horton (London, 1974) deserve special mention. Bence Szabolcsi's *A Concise History of Hungarian Music* (English translation, London, 1964) is an excellent overview; it is supplemented by the recorded anthology of Hungarian music up to Liszt released by Hungaroton records. Special investigations of aspects of

Hungarian music written in Western languages are best found in the journal *Studia Musicologica*, published by the music section of the Hungarian Academy of Sciences.

English music of the nineteenth century is superbly and thoroughly covered in several genre-oriented essays by specialists in Nicholas Temperley (ed.), *The Romantic Age 1800–1914* (London, 1981), volume five of *The Athlone History of Music in Britain*. The most significant subsequent studies of English composers of the period under discussion are Jerrold Northrop, *Edward Elgar* (London, 1984) and Arthur Jacobs's *Arthur Sullivan: A Victorian Composer* (London, 1984).

American music is treated extensively in H. Wiley Hitchcock, *Music in the United States: A Historical Introduction* (3d ed., Prentice-Hall, 1988) and *The New Grove Dictionary of American Music* (London and New York, 1986); the bibliographies in these volumes should be consulted for additional studies. Among recent titles deserving special mention is Charles Hamm's *Music in the New World* (New York, 1983), both a history of music in America and a history of American music, including indigenous, black, popular, and functional musics. Current research in American music is being reported in the journal *American Music* (1983–   ).

Musical editions. The complete works of Glinka and Rimsky-Korsakov have been published in the Soviet Union, and Kalmus has reprinted the complete works of Chaikovsky, including the church music. Complete editions of the works of Dvořák, Fibich, Dargomÿzhsky, Berwald, and Grieg are in progress, but only (at this writing) the piano works of Balakirev, Gottschalk, and Smetana are available in scholarly editions. The series *Musica Britannica* emphasizes British music before 1750, but volume 37 (1951) contains some of Sterndale Bennett's piano and chamber works and volume 49 (1982) Parry's songs; Garland Publishing's anthology *The Symphony 1720–1840* contains several volumes of English overtures and symphonies, including some by Cipriani Potter and Sterndale Bennett. For American works, Da Capo Press has initiated a series of reprints of scores, many from the nineteenth century, under the general title *Earlier American Music* (ed. H. Wiley Hitchcock), and several volumes of *Recent Researches in American Music* (A-R Editions) provide critical editions. A reprint of the music published by the Wa-Wan Press (Arno Press, 1970), makes much late- and post-Romantic American music available for study, and recordings of the music of many American composers were issued by the Society for the Preservation of the American Musical Heritage and in the New World Recorded Anthology of American Music, for which Elizabeth Davis has compiled an index (New York, 1981). Recordings of many rarely encountered Russian works have been issued on the Melodiya label. Supraphon and Hungaroton play comparable roles for Czech and Hungarian music.

NINE

THE TWILIGHT
OF ROMANTICISM

The terms "late Romanticism" and "post-Romanticism" are not interchangeable, though they have been used by different writers to describe the same composers, especially Franck, Mahler, and Hugo Wolf. "Late Romantic" has most frequently been applied to composers who reached musical maturity, or at least substantially changed their musical styles, during the 1850's, thus separating them from Glinka, Berlioz, Mendelssohn, Chopin, and Schumann. Liszt, Verdi, and Wagner underwent both Romantic and late-Romantic phases, with the composers who were born between 1820 and 1850 as the quintessential late Romantics. The most convincing determination of late Romanticism may well be whether or not the composer had ceased composing by 1900.

Post-Romanticism, on the other hand, is essentially a twentieth-century phenomenon though its antecedents were firmly planted in the preceding century. Scholars cannot say with certainty where it begins or where it ends, since the problem is not like that of the geographer determining a continental divide by tracing the watersheds of streams, but rather resembles the task of finding the boundary between yellow and orange in the color spectrum: the task is to define colors not by their boundaries but by their extremes. As Liszt, Verdi, and Wagner were both Romantics and late Romantics, Puccini, Mahler and Richard Strauss could be both late and post-Romantics.

Even in the use of "Romantic" as a descriptive title one can see the difference between late- and post-Romantic by comparing Bruckner's "Romantic" symphony (final version 1886) and Rheinberger's "Romantic" piano sonata (c. 1895) with the "Romantic" piano concerto (1920) by Joseph Marx (1882–1964) and the "Romantic" symphony (1930) by Howard Hanson (1896–1981). Though this fascinating period deserves further investigation, the present volume is not the place for it, for the manifestations of post-Romanticism looked to the future: not only the novel ventures in harmony and tonality that Debussy had begun by 1890, but also the new paths for the symphony found by Carl Nielsen (1865–1931) and Jan Sibelius (1865–1957), the searches for ways of combining Baroque contrapuntal techniques and Classic formal structures with new expressive means made by Ferruccio Busoni (1866–1924) and Max Reger (1873–1916), or the logical progression from exaggerated hyper-Romanticism to serial music achieved by Arnold Schoenberg (1874–1951) and his disciples Anton Webern (1883–1945) and Alban Berg (1885–1935), whose early compositions were also post-Romantic.

The inescapable conclusion is that the 1890's saw not only the last works of Verdi and Brahms but also the first mature works of Debussy and Schoenberg, and it is therefore one of the more tangled decades of the history of music as well as one of the least explored. It is hoped that the remainder of this chapter will provide some incentive for further study of this period.

ITALIAN OPERA AFTER LA TRAVIATA

Verdi, after writing *La Traviata* in 1853, went through a creative hiatus shorter than Wagner's fallow spell between *Lohengrin* and *Das Rheingold*, for he was now writing operas for France and thus came under the influence of the best elements of Meyerbeer's style—harmonic richness and appreciation of the dramatic and gestic functions of the orchestra. Verdi's first opera in this vein, *The Sicilian Vespers* (1855), has vanished from the repertoire although its overture, one of Verdi's last full-scale works in this genre, is a magnificent example of the "old warhorse" overture once a staple of outdoor band concerts. *Un Ballo in maschera* (1859), based on the libretto Scribe wrote for Auber about the assassination of Gustav III of Sweden in 1792 but with the locale changed by censor's decree to colonial Massachusetts, looks back to the melodrama of *Rigoletto* but also ahead, in the Act II finale, to the comic genius of *Falstaff*. *Simone Boccanegra* (1857, revised 1881) is reminiscent in some respect of Verdi's earlier works and is chiefly a psychological drama in historical garb; psychological portrayals in Verdi's new harmonic language underscore his revisions for the Paris version in 1865 of *Macbeth* (1847). *La Forza del Destino* (1862, revised 1869) and *Don Carlo* (French version 1867, Italian revision 1884) are the most representative operas of this "experimental" period, which ended in 1871 with *Aïda*, the culminative synthesis of Italian and French Grand Opera.

Several features are common to these operas. Most of them were given their first performance outside of Italy. Except for *Un Ballo in maschera*, they are long and contain many divertissements, either unrelated to or tenuously connected with the plot, which are frequently omitted in performance (even the entire first act of *Don Carlo*). The musical inspiration of these operas is uneven, with *Don Carlo* the most consistently good, and they are appreciated more by singers and connoisseurs of opera than by the general public. Spectacle plays an important role in many of them, and in all the tenor-baritone duet is a climactic moment, especially in *Don Carlo* where the "reminiscence motive" of freedom is grandiloquently proclaimed. The conclusion of the grandest soprano arias is often a magnificent soaring melody, a kind first introduced in Act II of *La Traviata* and brought to its heights in *La Forza del destino* (Example 9–1), *Don Carlo*, and the first act of *Aïda;* such melodies are accompanied by string tremolos and effectively utilize non-harmonic tones. Also retained from the period of *La Traviata*, but abandoned by Verdi after *La Forza del destino*, is the set-number in a closed form, usually a duet, characterized by square construction and an even quarter-note rhythm in the style of Example 5–4c, from the third act of *La Traviata*. In these operas between 1855 and 1871 Verdi's harmony is much richer than formerly, his tonality is broader, and his orchestra plays a more important part in the musical dramaturgy.

The musical forms that Verdi used also became freer and more flexible, with duets more prominent than solo arias, which shed their cabalettas in favor of expressive cantabiles in modified ternary forms. The large-scale concerted finales of the grand operas, such as those to Act III of *Don Carlo* and Act II of *Aïda*, tend to assume the structure of a rondo, whereas powerful duets or trios on a large scale conclude other acts. Verdi showed a quite free conception of the role of tonality, although he did institute penalty clauses in many contracts to go into effect if there should be transpositions or tampering with the instrumentation; one should not seek the kind of large-scale organizing tonality in his operas that characterizes those of

EXAMPLE 9–1. Verdi, *La Forza del destino*, Act II.

Wagner. Yet even in his final works the outlines, at least, of earlier structures and operatic conventions are discernible.

Verdi's final creative period includes not only a delightful string quartet, written while *Aïda* was in rehearsal, and the magnificent *Requiem* (1874) and other sacred choral works, but also the two glowing sunsets of Italian Romantic opera: *Otello* (1887) for the serious style and *Falstaff* (1893) for the comic. These two operas display the quintessence of Verdi's harmonic, orchestral, and psychological development; in them his enthusiastic vulgarity, which persisted as late as the Act II finale of *Aïda*, was finally purged; and the character portrayal in *Otello* is equaled in musicopsychological insight only by Musorgsky. *Falstaff* is actually the epitome of Wagner's theories of opera, for plot and music, orchestra and singers, are on an equal footing; the demarcations between set-numbers are dissolved; and the aria, except for Falstaff's declamatory soliloquies, is replaced by deft ensemble writing. One need but compare Falstaff's soliloquies or Iago's "Credo" in Act II of *Otello* with Example 5–5 to see the range of Verdi's development.

Verdi overshadowed, yet learned much from, his younger contemporaries. Posterity has termed them "one-opera" composers who wrote only a single work that attained any popularity, even enough to survive on the fringes of the repertoire, yet these composers effected basic changes in the native Italian tradition while also adopting French operatic ideas (many of the operas of Meyerbeer, Gounod, and even Bizet and Massenet were highly popular in northern Italy after 1870) and flirting with the German tradition of Weber and Wagner's Romantic operas.

Arrigo Boito (1842–1918) may have made his best contributions to opera by writing the librettos for *Otello* and *Falstaff;* his one completed opera, *Mefistofele* (1866, more successful in its 1875 revision) is a grandiose and impressive work, superior from a literary standpoint to the other operas based on Goethe's *Faust*. Yet it is one of the triad of "magnificent failures" in nineteenth-century opera that includes also Berlioz's *Les Troyens* and Cornelius's *The Barber of Bagdad*, probably (as could be said in the preceding century of Mozart's *Idomeneo*) because it contains too much music that requires the attentive involvement of the audience.

The tradition of Grand Opera with sizable instrumental resources (often including a band on or off the stage), ballet, concerted finales for all the singers and others, and a historical or exotic setting, was exemplified by Verdi in works from *Nabucco* to *Otello*. The first to continue this style successfully was Antônio Carlos Gomes (1836–96), a Brazilian composer living in Italy, whose *Il Guarany* (1870) contains intonations of Amazonian Indian melodies woven into an operatic canvas comparable to that of *Don Carlo*. More innovative and influential for the future was Amilcare Ponchielli (1834–86), whose *La Gioconda* (1876), his one opera to attain international success, is not about Leonardo da Vinci's painting of Mona Lisa but instead a violent melodrama by Boito based on a Rigoletto-like play by Victor Hugo. The most successful exponent of the "grand" rather than the "intimate" side of Italian opera, Ponchielli's music is characterized by a predominance of duets over arias (though the latter provide some of the most memorable moments), effective concerted finales, and a high level of dramatic intensity that influenced the later composers associated with the so-called "verismo" school. Iago's Credo in Act II of Verdi's *Otello* seems to have been strongly influenced by Barnaba's monologue in Act I of *La Gioconda*.

An "intimate" school of Italian opera, with its roots in the pastoral works of Donizetti and Bellini, is characterized by similarities to French *opéra comique*, with a kind of *parlando* recitative instead of spoken dialogue, and often with a tragic ending in the style of Bizet's *Carmen*. The best composer of such "intimate" Italian operas was Alfredo Catalani (1854–93), whose masterpiece *La Wally* (1892) is the best illustration of his refined style. His harmonic richness and extensive use of the orchestra has occasioned comments of "Wagnerian" writing; the subtleties of his harmonic writing include planing of triads or unrelated parallel thirds, climactic uses of augmented triads, and ambiguities between major and minor modes. *La Wally*'s Alpine setting includes distorted waltzes and Ländler which remind the listener of Dvořák and even Mahler. The somber, bittersweet quality of Catalani's music and its refined expressiveness make his works operas for connoisseurs; his early death ended a career as promising as those of Bellini or Bizet, with whom he can justifiably be compared.

Competing with Catalani's operas were the products of *verismo* (realism), the generic term for a short-lived operatic movement which attempted to combine the traditional operatic portrayal of raw emotions and shocking incidents, best seen in *Il Trovatore* and the last act of *La Gioconda*, with the literary realism of such authors as Émile Zola (1840–1902) and Giovanni Verga (1840–1922) and even crime news as reported in the sensational press. Only two lasting Italian successes resulted: *Cavalleria rusticana* (1890) by Pietro Mascagni (1863–1945) and *I Pagliacci* (1892) by Ruggiero Leoncavallo (1858–1919). Neither composer was able to repeat his success and their other operas have sunk into oblivion, though there are many beautiful portions in Mascagni's *L'Amico Fritz* (1891), an excellent example of "intimate" Italian opera at the end of the century. The best example of *verismo*, dramatically and musically, is actually Czech: Janáček's *Jenufa* (completed 1903), one of the initial masterworks of twentieth-century opera.

Since the operas of Giacomo Puccini (1858–1924) span both the nineteenth and twentieth centuries and his two masterpieces, *Gianni Schicchi* (1918) and *Turandot* (incomplete at his death), are outside the chronological confines of this volume, attention need be paid only to the genesis of his style represented in his most important works of the nineteenth century, *Manon Lescaut* (1893) and *La Bohème* (1896), in which he created most effective syntheses of intimate Italian opera, French opera with its sentimental and comic elements and wayward heroines, and the pathetic (though at least nonviolent) endings of the *verismo* operas. There are even Wagnerian touches, such as the continuous textures without tonal closures at the end of solo passages and melodic reminiscences which (as with Catalani also) fall just short of being considered leitmotives; the intermezzo before Act III of *Manon Lescaut* could not have been written without Wagner's *Tristan* prelude.

Puccini's writing for the voice and his operatic orchestration deserve detailed study by today's opera composers. His harmony is a delicately pastel synthesis of all the effective devices from Liszt through Debussy, especially an employment of augmented triads, a wide variety of seventh chords, and streams of parallel triads; his "modal" harmony, which he shares with Fauré, may well stem from the organ accompaniments to Gregorian chant which became increasingly used during the nineteenth century. The most memorable moments of his operas are often the arias and the love

duets, usually containing an intense and climactic melody, subtly harmonized and closely bound to the orchestral accompaniment (Example 9–2).
Whereas critics may disagree about the integrity of Puccini's music, no one
can deny his fine sense for the theatre or his attention to subtle musical
details.

EXAMPLE 9–2. Puccini, *La Bohème*, Act I.

CENTRAL EUROPE

During the closing years of the nineteenth century Vienna again became a musical capital. Brahms and Bruckner were still active, Wagner's
music had gained impressive support despite the opposition of the critic
Eduard Hanslick (1825–1904), and despite the decline of the Austro-Hungarian Empire Vienna was virtually the crossroads of Europe, famous not
only for music but also for advances in art, science, architecture, literature,
philosophy, medicine, and economics. On the other hand, the unification
of Germany after 1870, though it resulted in centralizing political and financial power in Berlin, saw a qualitative decline in Germany's musical energies although an immense amount of music, now mostly forgotten, continued to be written and performed.

Hugo Wolf (1860–1903) came from a border province of the Austro-
Hungarian Empire and is said to have been partially of Slavic (Slovene) descent. His reputation rests almost exclusively on his songs, though he made
ventures into opera, the symphonic poem, and chamber music. His creative process consisted of short bursts of intense activity, during which he
wrote as many as three songs in a single day, followed by extensive periods
of fallowness. One writer has speculated that the works on which Wolf's
reputation rests were the product of only eighteen months of effort spread
over ten years: his first major songs date from 1887 (of the more than hundred songs he wrote before then, he considered only twelve worth publishing) and he became incurably insane in 1897.

To explain the frequently made claim that Wolf set the "inner meaning" of a poem to music is a difficult task. One writer has suggested the
concept of "song as an extension into musical terms of the essence of the
poem," with the central issue not the poem's literal meaning but "its connotations, its ambiguities, its paradoxes."[1] Frequently Wolf entitled his collections of songs "Poems for solo voice and piano," showing that the poem
was paramount in his thinking, and he wanted the poem to be recited before the song was performed. Wolf's ideal was as complete a synthesis as
possible of word and tone, with the vocal declamation corresponding to the
rhythm of the poem and the depiction of its imagery while the piano part
(comparable to the way in which Wagner had treated his orchestra) was the
source of the musical atmosphere, serving to create a background for the
poem and to express emotions that the singing voice alone cannot suggest.

Wolf had the best literary taste of all the composers of nineteenth-

---

[1]Jack M. Stein, "Poem and Music in Hugo Wolf's Mörike Songs," *Musical Quarterly*,
LIII (1967), 22–23; see also his *Poetry and Music in the German Lied* (Cambridge, Mass.,
1971), pp. 155–202.

century song, and his major works in this genre consist of a prodigious number of settings of poems by Mörike, Eichendorff, Goethe, and lesser poets as far back as Luís de Camões and Michelangelo, and of German translations of Spanish and Italian poetry; Wolf gathered virtually all of these into collections designated by the name of the poet or locale of the collection. The songs show a great variety of mood and emotional intensity, ranging from deep pathos to ironical humor; from placid contemplativeness, seen in the songs dealing with nature, to rollicking waltzes or songs in a popular style (on the evidence of "Auftrag," Wolf could have made a fortune as a composer of light music); from deeply mystical religious ecstasy, best seen in the *Spanish Songbook*, to a realism exceeding even Musorgsky's, as in "Zur Warnung," Mörike's description of a hangover, in setting which Wolf pushed nineteenth-century tonality to its limits.

Wolf's songs are frequently described as being piano-dominated and filled with chromatic harmony; like all generalizations, this one has its exceptions. One may profitably compare the songs "Peregrina I" and "Peregrina II" from the Mörike songs: the former contains one of Wolf's finest vocal melodies, supported by the piano, whereas the other is a piano-dominated song with the voice declaiming the text; both songs are linked by a common ritornello. Even as late as the *Italian Songbook* some of the songs, e.g., "Mein Liebster singt," are independent piano pieces with words attached. The most common kind of song has an ostinato-like accompaniment, often subtly varied in the course of the song. Many of the songs are declamatory with a chromatic substructure, but some are quite diatonic, yet with the phrases extended to avoid square-cut writing, e.g., "Fussreise" from the Mörike songs.

Wolf's rich harmonic palette derives from that of Liszt and Wagner. His sharpest dissonance is the chord of the major seventh, chiefly associated with the more tortured aspects of religious mysticism, as in Example 9–3. Actually, most of Wolf's harmonic vocabulary and turns of expression may be found in the miniatures of MacDowell and Grieg. Although some of the songs, especially the narrative ballads, are rather long, almost all of the finest are extremely concentrated and show great restraint and economy of means; in structure they are through-composed but unified by the musical patterns of the accompaniment. Wolf's modulations within a single song are often as extensive, far-reaching, and significant as those within an entire act of one of Wagner's operas.

Wolf is a major forerunner of the twentieth-century Viennese school. The intense concentration of many of his songs inspired the similarly condensed instrumental compositions of Schoenberg and Webern; and the extended tonality, with several changes of key-signature and even with a song's ending in a different key from its opening, as well as the harmonic and tonal ambiguity in several songs, contributed in no small degree

EXAMPLE 9–3. Wolf, "Herr, was trägt der Boden hier" from the *Spanish Songbook* (1889–90).

to the breakdown of traditional tonality. Wolf's realism also anticipates the expressionism of Schoenberg's *Erwartung* or Berg's *Wozzeck* and *Lulu*.

Gustav Mahler (1860–1911), like Wolf, came from a border province of the Austro-Hungarian empire; of Jewish descent, he was baptized a Catholic in 1897. Except for an early secular cantata, *Das klagende Lied* of 1880, Mahler limited himself to two musical genres, the song and the symphony, and described himself as a "holiday composer" since so much of his life was spent in conducting. But whereas Wolf aimed toward an increasing condensation of musical space in his songs through economy of means and a corresponding heightening of intensity, Mahler endeavored to create the "symphonic song," not only through the use of orchestral accompaniments in the *Songs of a Wayfarer* (1883–85) and several settings of folk poems from *Des Knaben Wunderhorn* (his chief source of texts) but also in expanding the scale of the song and elaborating its accompaniment. Certain topics appealed to him: the ironic and sardonic ("St. Anthony's Sermon to the Fish," later used as the third movement of the Second Symphony), the macabre ("Reveille," 1899), or the child's pictures of heaven in the Third and Fourth Symphonies. The culmination of Mahler's symphonic songs came in the first decade of the twentieth century with his songs to Rückert's texts, especially the moving *Kindertotenlieder*, and the most massive and symphonic of song cycles, *Das Lied von der Erde* (1907–8), to German translations of pessimistic Chinese poems. Mahler led the art-song on a grand scale (as opposed to the ballad), originally exemplified by Schubert's "Der Zwerg" and "Ganymed," to a point from which further development was impossible.

Mahler's first four symphonies belong chronologically as well as aesthetically to the nineteenth century. They are all on a massive timescale, though the intimacy and light orchestration of the Fourth Symphony (1899–1900) make it seem like a chamber work in comparison with the others. Of this group, only the First Symphony (1884–88, revised 1893–96), which Mahler originally conceived as a symphonic poem in five movements and two parts, is purely orchestral; the others use voices in at least one movement. Except in the Fourth Symphony, Mahler uses a large orchestra, with quadrupled woodwinds (many doubling on piccolo, English horn, E♭ or bass clarinet), eight horns, occasional offstage brass choirs, and the heaviest artillery of the brass and percussion to emphasize his climaxes. Added woodwind color is used for doubling melodic lines in high registers to provide a "military band" effect. The scores are liberally sprinkled with explicit directions to performers and the conductor and are an excellent source for the study of orchestral performance practice around 1900. Far more than Schubert or Brahms, Mahler relied on songs to provide movements for his instrumental cycles, either pre-existing songs expanded as instrumental symphonic movements or newly composed, orchestrally accompanied solo songs. To Mahler the symphony was a kaleidoscopic world, calling for a mixture of a variety of styles and often incongruous musical elements and moods; the immense Third Symphony (1893–96; revised 1906) in six movements, originally conceived as a series of fantastic dream-episodes during a summer noonday, is the epitome of this idea.

Though Bruckner taught and befriended the young Mahler, the

principal similarities between them are not their long symphonies with apocalyptic climaxes but certain harmonic devices, especially the use of shifting tonal planes (but for different reasons) and certain effects like the slow march, which Bruckner used in his Fourth Symphony and which Mahler adopted even more extensively. Mahler's symphonies are really continuations of the symphonic ideal established by Liszt in his *Dante* and *Faust* Symphonies, with reliance on thematic transformations, sharp contrasts between diatonic and chromatic writing, an expanded time-scale, rhetorical and even sensational passages for dramatic effect, and sardonically diabolic distortion of melodic materials—the last-named deriving from the finale of Berlioz' *Symphonie fantastique* and fully established in Liszt's *Totentanz* and the third movement of his *Faust Symphony*. Liszt's funeral marches, especially that of *Héroïde funèbre*, also influenced Mahler, and the climactic apotheoses of Liszt's symphonies and tone poems were further intensified by Mahler through expanded orchestration and sudden shifting of tonal planes, as in Example 9–4. As a harmonist, Mahler was

EXAMPLE 9–4. Mahler, Symphony No. 1, finale (string and most woodwind parts omitted) [Copyright assigned 1952 to Universal Edition (London), Ltd. Reproduced by permission].

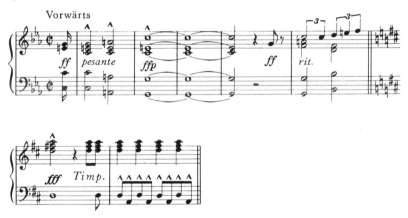

more conservative than such contemporaries of his as Wolf, Grieg, or Fauré; his chromaticism consists chiefly of melodic non-harmonic tones, often accented, with delayed resolutions imparting an intense yearning to his lyrical melodies. He relied heavily on wide melodic leaps, especially in violin melodies, and on sudden changes of tonal plane for dramatic effect (Example 9–4); in Mahler's words, he wanted the D major harmony to sound "as if it had fallen from heaven." His often linear counterpoint has several precedents, not just those of late Beethoven or Wagner's *Die Meistersinger* but others as far back as the varied countersubjects that Bach used in his chorale settings.

Mahler's form and use of tonality have perplexed many analysts, who either consider his attitudes to these compositional features to be overly casual and empirical or (the view most commonly found today) as part of a scheme of "interlocking" or "progressive" tonality. In assessing the structure of his symphonies, we must recall that Mahler (like many other composers) did not necessarily compose his music in the order that we hear it today. The first four symphonies had original programmatic scaffoldings that were often changed (about seven different programs for the Third Symphony, for instance, during its gestation period); the finale of the Fourth Symphony was composed in 1892 as a finale for the Third Symphony; and the order of the three inner movements of the Second Symphony was not decided until late in the work's composition.

Mahler, like many of his contemporaries and even precursors of the Wagner-Liszt generation, seems to have thought of a circle of thirds, major or minor, as replacing the circle of fifths in both small- and large-scale tonal organization; his return to the circle of fifths and dominant-oriented directional harmony in the Fourth Symphony is one of the main ingredients of its "Neoclassic" sound. This circle of thirds explains, for instance, why in the first movement of the Second Symphony such keys as E major (second theme-group) and E♭ minor (a main tonality in the development) are both significantly related to the home tonic of C minor. The tonality of the last movement of the First Symphony is not the expected D major but F minor-major, which is dramatically overridden by D major both in the tonal recapitulation (Example 9–4) and, after the thematic "mirror" recapitulation (where second theme precedes first theme) in F major-minor, in the coda. Mahler seems to have thought of large-scale tonality in terms of eventual outcome rather than initial or intervening events.

Mahler's sonata-form structures, as well as his sonata-rondo movements, are very logical if we consider that he abhorred exact repetition and that he was influenced by the free-style tonal recapitulations or recapitulatory codas in such works as Beethoven's second and third Leonore overtures, Wagner's *Flying Dutchman* and *Meistersinger* preludes, and symphonic poems by Liszt like *Tasso* and *Les Préludes*.

To give a few examples of Mahler's free-wheeling structures, in the first movement of the First Symphony a horn fanfare (which may have programmatic significance) replaces the opening of the first theme-group in the recapitulation, a procedure that seems more appropriate to the narrative symphonic poem than for the first movement of a symphony. In the first movement of the Second Symphony, originally conceived as a massive funeral ceremony *(Todesfeier)*, there is a kind of double exposition before a massive development; the recapitulation begins with a truncation of the first theme in C minor while the second theme is given a chromatic exegesis, mostly in E major, that Hugo Wolf would have envied, but the transition between the keys is only six measures long and pivots through the key of A♭ minor. The chief ways in which Mahler achieves coherence in symphonic movements extending over hundreds of measures are directional tonal organization, melodic reminiscence and transformation not only within movements but among movements and even entire symphonies, and (at least in the earlier works) a program, later suppressed.

Mahler's symphonies are the culmination of the tradition of the extended symphony with more or less programmatic content, extending from the Third and Ninth of Beethoven through the program symphonies of Berlioz and Liszt and Bruckner's Fourth and Eighth symphonies. The five-movement program symphony, from Beethoven's *Pastoral Symphony* and Berlioz's *Symphonie Fantastique* onward, seems to have been Mahler's basic conceptual symphonic structure until the Sixth Symphony. (A "Blumine" movement, originally the second movement of the First Symphony, was later suppressed by the composer.) Other influences are less obvious, such as Beethoven's late quartets, some of which Mahler conducted using the entire string section of the orchestra. Mahler's works have been perceived by many writers as autobiographical; they also seem to reflect many external stimuli such as childhood or youthful memories (from impressions of nature to domestic disputes), village bands, or spectacular Alpine scenery encountered during his summer vacations.

With the Rückert songs and the Fifth Symphony (1901–2) Mahler crossed the line from nineteenth-century late Romanticism to twentieth-century post-Romanticism. Although his forms became more rigorous (two of his strictest sonata-form movements are found in his Sixth and Seventh Symphonies), his time-scales became more massive; he oscillated between the huge resources demanded for his Eighth Symphony and the extremely restricted scoring (strings and harp) of the adagietto of the Fifth Symphony or the delicate opening of the Ninth Symphony; his sardonic diabolisms became more and more distorted, especially in his scherzos; and his climaxes, though even more apocalyptic, soon petered out to be succeeded by moods of deep pessimism. He brought the expanded programmatic symphony to its fullest possible development and, as with the art-song, concluded a chapter in the history of this genre.

The early development of Richard Strauss (1864–1949) is almost as astounding as those of the young Mozart or Mendelssohn. Among the magnificent works of this early period (1881–88) are the Cello Sonata, Op. 5; the Serenade for wind instruments, Op. 7; the First Concerto for horn; the *Burleske* for piano and orchestra; some of his finest songs; and the concluding work of this period, the Violin Sonata, Op. 18. These works have erroneously been called "classical"; they are really in the tradition of Romantic

Neoclassicism as exemplified by the duet sonatas of Schumann, Brahms, and other German composers of absolute music, and it is significant that Strauss wrote these compositions before Brahms's "late" period, which began in 1891. They all contain a virile and sturdy expression, strong and forceful harmonies, and fine construction leavened with a vein of piquant humor, most evident in the *Burleske* and the finale of the Cello Sonata.

Strauss is said to have changed his musical style under the influence of Alexander Ritter, who introduced the young composer to the works of Liszt and Wagner. In the first works where this change is evident, the symphonic fantasy *Aus Italien* (1886) and the first version of the symphonic poem *Macbeth* (1888, revised 1890), the influences seem also to include, respectively, Raff's musical travelogues and Chaikovsky's tone poems. *Aus Italien* particularly contains harbingers of Strauss's later styles: soaring, fortissimo string melodies, brass fanfares, bubbling horns in the first movement, and intimations of *Der Rosenkavalier* in the third movement. In the finale, the popular song "Funiculì-funiculà" (in using which Strauss had some trouble with copyright laws) is contrasted with a *Meistersinger*-like second theme. *Macbeth*, on the other hand, is too much influenced by Liszt's and Chaikovsky's tone poems, too experimental, and often too gloomy and lacking in contrast and variety to be popular.

The pivotal year for Strauss was 1888, for during it he not only completed the Violin Sonata but also *Don Juan*, his first successful symphonic poem; *Death and Transfiguration* was finished in the following year. Both works owe much to Liszt and something to Raff, but the influence of two other composers is also evident: Josef Rheinberger and Moritz Moszkowski (1854–1925), best known for his "Spanish dances" and salon music for the piano but who also wrote in the larger forms. *Don Juan* is written in a free but recognizable sonata form with its most striking theme (initially stated by the horns) first appearing in the development; its recapitulation is truncated and its coda is wry, a direct contrast to Liszt's optimistic conclusions. *Death and Transfiguration*, influenced by Moszkowski even to its title, is a sonata-form movement with long introduction and coda and drastically shortened recapitulation, and represents a fine continuation of Liszt's best ideas of thematic transformation (see Example 9–5) as well as Liszt's tendency to anticipate his apotheoses. *Till Eulenspiegel's Merry Pranks* (1895), an orchestral scherzo "after the old rogue's tale in rondeau form," is a later work but in its spirit and brevity belongs with Strauss's earlier tone poems. Its structure is akin not to the High Classic rondo of Haydn and Mozart but to the rondos of C. P. E. Bach in which the theme itself undergoes transformations and statements outside the tonic.

Example 9–5 illustrates an important ingredient of Strauss's thematic transformation: his use of the original theme as a counterpoint to new ideas which have strong programmatic and structural significance. From a

EXAMPLE 9–5. Thematic transformation in Strauss's *Death and Transfiguration*.

programmatic standpoint, the theme cited in this example follows the protagonist of the tone poem from his deathbed reverie (Example 9–5a) to flashbacks from his childhood (Example 9–5b) and young manhood (Example 9–5c), then is combined with motives from his mature manhood (Example 9–5d), his struggle against death (Example 9–5e), and the apotheosis theme of transfiguration (Example 9–5f). From a structural standpoint, the themes cited in Example 9–5 occur in (a) the introduction; (b) the second theme-group of the exposition; (c) the closing group of the exposition; (d) the development section; (e) a signal of the first theme-group in the development section; and (f) the coda. The clash between the exigencies of sonata form and the narrative structure is most evident in the first theme-group, in C minor, which depicts the first death-struggle in the exposition and the final death-struggle in the extremely shortened recapitulation. Tonally, the most striking events are the extensive three-key exposition with the tonal structure C minor—G major—E♭ major and the pan-diatonic confusion at the opening of the coda out of which the transfiguration theme (Example 9–5f) emerges.

Don Juan, Death and Transfiguration, and *Till Eulenspiegel's Merry Pranks* represent the peak of Strauss's career during the nineteenth century. The next group of tone poems, from *Also sprach Zarathustra* (1896) to the *Symphonia Domestica* (1903), shows not only Strauss's shift from late- to post-Romanticism but also displays a steady decline in his creative powers and especially a marked lessening of the feeling of freshness and spontaneity that characterizes his earlier compositions. Although each of these new works is triple the length of the earlier tone poems, they do not have an equivalent amount of the earlier verve, élan, and dash, which appear only occasionally. Strauss at this time also began a kind of "role-playing," like Berlioz more than sixty years previously, in setting himself up as a "bad boy of music." He provoked indignation by imitating, in muted brass, the bleating of sheep and even calling for a real wind machine in *Don Quixote* (1897), a free set of variations analogous to Franck's *Variations symphoniques* in its use of a double theme and inclusion of concertante elements (solo cello and viola); and he aroused critical wrath with *Ein Heldenleben* (1898), an autobiographical tone poem of large dimensions in which he utilized several quotations from his earlier works to make the hero's identity clear, with the carpingly chattering woodwinds unmistakably setting forth Strauss's opinion of his critics.

Comparisons have been made between Strauss's expansion of his musical and orchestral dimensions and the ethos of Germany after the accession of Kaiser Wilhelm II in 1888 and the subsequent transformation of German life into emphasis on armaments and imperialist adventures. It is more appropriate to compare Strauss's change of style and his attitude toward the orchestra with the industrialization of Germany and its concentration not only on armaments but also on precision machinery, for Strauss's orchestra relies not so much on the heavy artillery of brass and percussion, which he uses with much more restraint than Mahler, as on efficient, meticulous precision, best seen in the difficult string passages which entire sections must execute cleanly (Example 10–2b). Strauss's orchestra became a precision instrument like a Siemens dynamo or Zeiss camera, with a corresponding loss of status for the individual musician, who became a cog in a remarkably efficient mechanism. It should be added that Strauss's orchestral music must be heard in live performance to be fully appreciated.

The active inner parts in Strauss's orchestral music have been praised as the continuation of Wagner's counterpoint and attacked as a cluttering of the texture; the latter is true only in a few passages such as the introduction to *Don Quixote,* in which the composer tried to create an atmosphere of confusion for deliberate effect. The function of these inner parts is either to sustain a mood of drive and excitement, through intricate string passages of a sort derived from Wagner, or to give a restful or propulsive effect, through countermelodies or active accompaniment patterns, often in involved rhythms. In the middle of *Don Juan,* for example, the quiet pattern which accompanies the yearning oboe solo is transformed into the driving transition to the exuberant horn melody. When Strauss used genuine counterpoint it was to create a mood of archaism or "learnedness," as in the fugue "Science" in *Also sprach Zarathustra,* or for a realistic depiction of domestic controversies, as in the double fugue in the "Finale" of the *Symphonia Domestica,* which sounds quite similar to the contrapuntal writing in the finale of Mahler's Fifth Symphony. Strauss's melodies, for the most part, are motives rather than themes, but there are many memorable examples of the latter, like the horn themes in *Don Juan* or *Till Eulenspiegel,* the apotheosis of *Death and Transfiguration,* or the conclusion of *Also sprach Zarathustra,* accompanied with parallel thirds, which can be considered a poignant farewell to the nineteenth century.

Strauss's harmonies, once stripped of their non-harmonic tones and linear counterpoints, seldom are more adventurous than those of his contemporaries. One of the more striking examples of his style frequently cited is the enigmatic ending of *Also sprach Zarathustra,* where there is an apparent conflict between B major, ethereally stated in the high strings, and C major with an added F♯ in the low brass and the low string pizzicatos; yet that "C major" is really an incomplete French sixth (with the A♯ missing) which would normally resolve to B major. Strauss achieved most of his harmonic surprises through unexpectedly side-slipping from one tonal area into another, then smoothly back, or into still another tonal orbit.

Structural organization through motivic reminiscences, ingenious tonal organization, and creative use of older forms like rondo, variation, and sonata form, provide coherence in even the longest of the tone poems. Most fit a traditional form: *Ein Heldenleben* a massive one-movement sonata-form, with the "Critics" section corresponding to the transition and the "Battle," with its pounding rhythm, to the development; the *Symphonia Domestica* a one-movement double-function form akin to Liszt's B minor Sonata in which Strauss labelled, or at least authorized, the indication of sub-"movements" like scherzo, lullaby, and finale. *Also sprach Zarathustra* is the only one that does not fit a pre-existing traditional form, but Strauss achieves coherence by motivic transformations and repetitions (especially the C–G–C idea) and an interlocking tonal structure of C and B, C dominating the first half and B the second, with a "reconciliation" at the very end. The key-relationships are widely expanded: that of the "exposition" part of the *Symphonia Domestica* is that of F major for the first theme-group, B major for the second, and D minor for the closing group.

Strauss's abandonment of nineteenth-century Romanticism is shown in his change of emphasis from the symphonic poem to opera. He had begun this shift of interest with *Guntram* (1887–93), but his successes in this medium did not occur until the first decade of the twentieth century with *Salome* and *Elektra*, with their monster orchestras and "theater of cruelty" effects; these actually are an aberration in his stylistic development (his songs, for instance, show improvement but little change in style throughout his career), for he later found the vein of a post-Romantic nostalgia in *Der Rosenkavalier* and *Ariadne auf Naxos* most congenial to his muse.

FRANCE

French music during the closing years of the nineteenth century presents a complex picture of overlapping styles. The pioneers of the "French Musical Renaissance" continued their activity—Franck until 1890 and Saint-Saëns until 1920—Fauré's first major works date from the late 1870's, and Franck's best pupils, Chausson and d'Indy, wrote their first significant compositions during the 1880's. The music by all these composers except Franck overlapped to some extent Debussy's revolutionary works of the 1890's; hence chronology alone is no guide to this period, for French music after 1880 moved along several different paths.

Many of the composers in France had made a pilgrimage to Bayreuth or Munich to hear Wagner's operas, and almost all found the program of instruction at the Paris Conservatoire to be musically stultifying since it centered around operatic composition and the acquisition of mere technical skills in performance; this did not change until Fauré became director in 1905. A number of composers sought alternate means of instruction: private lessons with Franck; study at the École Niedermeyer (originally a school to train organists and church musicians), which included Saint-Saëns on its faculty and Gounod and Fauré among its distinguished alumni; and even, in the case of d'Indy and his friends, the founding of a new school of music, the Schola Cantorum, which placed considerable emphasis on the history of music in its curriculum. All four of the major French post-Romantic composers discussed in this chapter were outside the prevailing musical "Establishment," which stressed opera as the highest form of musical expression; all followed different paths; and all had significant influence on twentieth-century French music.

Emmanuel Chabrier (1841–94) was a minor bureaucrat who heard a performance of *Tristan* when he was thirty-eight and decided to devote himself to composition. Though his reputation today rests largely on a single orchestral work, *España* (1883), an exciting musical travelogue, his genius is best revealed in his light, unpretentious compositions, with the *op-*

éra comique Le Roi malgré lui (1887) his masterpiece in this genre. As a musical parodist, he was a significant forerunner of Satie, Milhaud, and Poulenc; one of the best of his parodies, a milestone in the French rejection of the more turgid aspects of Wagnerian Romanticism, is the *Souvenirs de Munich* (1886) in which he arranged a series of quadrille dances based on motives from Wagner's *Tristan und Isolde*. Chabrier has erroneously been called a Wagnerian because of his opera *Gwendoline* (1886), but Wagner's influence is felt more in the libretto than in the music, which contains much modal writing or emphasizes the tritone. Chabrier's rhythm is quite free and supple, as *España* or the parodistic *Trois valses romantiques* for two pianos will show; his phrases are often irregular in length and avoid the square-cut four-measure symmetry so common during the century. An anticipator of twentieth-century pan-diatonicism, he uses lush harmonies generally in a parodistic context. In Example 9–6, quite representative of his style, he delays the tonic chord until the end of the five-measure phrase. Chabrier's musical innovations have been frequently overlooked or

EXAMPLE 9–6. Chabrier, "Idylle" from *Pièces pittoresques* (1881).

misunderstood because they occurred within the context of "light" music rather than within the more "serious" frameworks of symphony, sonata, or neo-Wagnerian opera. Throughout his career Ravel proclaimed his debt to Chabrier, whom he considered "the most profoundly personal and the most French of our composers."

Gabriel Fauré (1845–1924), Saint-Saëns's pupil, strayed the farthest of all these composers from the musical language of Romanticism, and to many writers he is no Romantic at all. He excelled in works on an intimate scale, like piano pieces, chamber music, and songs; friends or pupils scored most of his few orchestral works. As a composer of absolute instrumental music, he followed the leadership of Schumann as transmitted through Saint-Saëns, but in a very original manner, as can be seen in his two most important early works, the Violin Sonata in A major, Op. 13 (1876), and the First Piano Quartet, Op. 15 (1876–79, revised 1883); it is interesting to note that his Violin Sonata precedes Franck's by a decade and that the Piano Quartet stems from the same time as Franck's Piano Quintet. Fauré's melodic lines are as long, unsymmetrical, and unpredictable as those of Berlioz; his slow movements are derived from song, but from the French *mélodie* rather than from the German Lied; and his music has a grace, elegance, and lightness, especially in his scherzos, that is often mistaken for lack of depth by those oriented toward German music.

Fauré's piano writing, deriving from Chopin's, is centered around expansions of small forms with such noncommittal titles as "Barcarolle" or "Nocturne," with melodies floating above or within arpeggiated accompaniments. Among his most delightful works for piano is the suite *Dolly*, Op. 56 (1894–97), for piano four-hands, in which the composer showed himself as adept in portraying the child's world as Schumann, Bizet *(Jeux d'enfants)*, Musorgsky *(The Nursery)*, or Debussy.

Fauré's chief achievements are his songs, and in them the contrast between the German Lied and the French song is most evident. Only in the late years of the nineteenth century did France enjoy a school of poets comparable to those between 1770 and 1850 in Germany; their poetry was evocative, hinting, suggesting, hesitant, and restrained in its declarations. Similar are Fauré's settings of these poems; they lack the exuberance of Schubert or Schumann, the idealized, sublimated sensuality of Brahms, or Wolf's musical "close reading" of a poem. Typical of Fauré's songs is an active yet subordinate piano accompaniment that establishes an atmosphere over which floats a vocal melody that sedulously avoids any suggestion of the square-cut popular song or of the strophic style; sometimes the piano participates with the voice in dialogue. The nearest German equivalents are Schumann's "Der Nussbaum" and his *Frauenliebe und Leben* songs; the French precedents are the finely wrought songs composed between 1868 and 1884 (e.g., the setting of Baudelaire's "L'Invitation au voyage") by Henri Duparc (1848–1933).

The French song melody is neither wholly tuneful nor wholly declamatory; it characteristically moves within a fairly limited ambitus and is principally devoted to bringing out the limited vocal sonority of the French language with its diphthongs and mute "e" sounds, and is written to be sung in an elegant salon frequented by a cultured elite rather than in a concert hall. Not until Debussy's *Pelléas et Mélisande* was the technique of French song transferred to opera.

Fauré's restrained musical language is the antithesis of German Romanticism. Fauré eschewed *Sturm und Drang* tempestuousness (note the opening of the First Piano Quartet), unbridled exuberance, or obvious wrestling with knotty compositional problems, though his secure contrapuntal technique is evident in such disparate works as the *Requiem* (1887–1900) and *Dolly*. Fauré's supple and flexible rhythm, like that of most French composers at the end of the nineteenth century, is quite different from that of Schumann or Brahms, for the latter two composers wrote "barline" music even though the impression of the bar-line is different from that which appears on the printed page, and the idea of a four-measure phrase in the background, to be extended or elided, was ingrained in their thinking. However, the suppleness of the rhythm and phrase-structure of the second acts of *Tristan* and *Parsifal* contributed, as did Berlioz' rhythmic flexibility, to the freedom of French rhythm and phrasing. One may contrast Example 9–7 with Examples 4–1 and 7–4 to see the difference between sophisticated French and German rhythm and phrase-structure.

EXAMPLE 9–7. (a) Fauré, Piano Quartet, Op. 15, second movement; (b) Chausson, Symphony in B♭ major, Op. 20, first movement.

Fauré was one of the most revolutionary harmonists of the century, a fact which may be surprising because of his constant understatement which avoids the rhetorical gestures, attempts at surprise and pathos, or dramatic contrasts so characteristic of both German and nationalist composers. A major ingredient of Fauré's harmony, its modality, stems from his study of Gregorian chant accompaniment at the École Niedermeyer and his years as organist in Parisian churches; this style of chant accompaniment, though frowned on by the purists of Solesmes, conformed to the inherent modality of the chant through using many secondary triads, especially in minor, rather than forcing it into a major-minor straitjacket. Especially in minor, Fauré's melodies are also modal, with much use of the lowered leading tone, as often in the C minor Piano Quartet or the *Requiem;* in a piece in the major mode Fauré minimizes the leading tone or even omits it altogether.

As did Puccini to a lesser extent, Fauré discovered the effectiveness of two chords of the seventh which had been neglected during the century, perhaps because of their lack of tonal directive properties: the minor seventh (C–E♭–G–B♭) and the major seventh (C–E–G–B♮). These differ from what Suckling has called the "straightjacket of leading-note diatonicism" characteristic of German music and evident in the chords of the dominant seventh, augmented sixth, and the juicier "altered" chords in which "tendency" tones, resolved (or seeming to demand to be resolved) as if they were leading tones or dominant sevenths, are prominent. With Fauré the major seventh chord is not a tortured dissonance, as in Hugo Wolf's music (see Example 9–3) but rather a passing dissonance, as in measure 6 of Example 9–8. The minor seventh, either in root position or inverted, is flexibly used not only as a harmonization of modal melodies but also as a pivot to or from remote key centers since it lacks the "pull" of a dominant harmony with a leading tone. It is as if the chords of the seventh and ninth are no longer dissonances, but virtually consonances.

Fauré's tonality is usually clear but in his works of the 1890's he often delighted in the ambiguities possible through third-related harmonies, achieved through the "mobility of the mediant" when it can be raised or lowered without any real change in the tonality. In two works his flexibly ambiguous tonal sense is quite evident: the first section of the Fifth Barcarolle (1894) and the "Offertory," added in 1900, of the *Requiem*. In the first section of the former work, the tonality at first seems to waver between F♯ minor and the tonal orbit of G major, but is then followed by juxtapositions of F♯ major and C major, sometimes with a seventh attached, with planed dominant and diminished seventh chords preparing F♯ major again, the effect being one of horizontal polytonality. The remaining sections contain striking tonal juxtapositions that are subtly stated through veiled piano sonorities, gentle syncopations, and restrained dynamics.

The "Offertory" of the *Requiem* is equally remarkable and striking in its tonal ambiguity. The tonal goal is in doubt as it opens, for the dominant of C major is implied, but the end of the orchestral introduction establishes B minor through its subdominant (with a seventh attached) and dominant chords; the ambiguous tonality of the choral entrance (B minor or D major?) is enhanced by cross-relations. Subsequently the emphasis on the chord of the major ninth sounds like an anticipation of Ravel's style. The ultimate goal of the first section of the "Offertoire" is not B minor but D major, with a quite dissonant augmented triad serving as the pivot chord between the two keys. The middle section ("Hostias et preces tibi") features mediant-related oscillations between D major and F major with a sev-

EXAMPLE 9–8. Fauré, *Requiem*, Offertory.

enth attached, and later one of Fauré's most striking modulations, from C♯ major through a dominant seventh of A major to F major, with the latter key enriched by both minor and major sevenths, and through a non-functional modulation back to D major (Example 9–8).

A love for Fauré's music is an acquired taste generally found among those with a conspicuous lack of enthusiasm for Wagner and Brahms. Although Maurice Ravel (1875–1937) was the only one of Fauré's pupils to become a major composer, his influence was transmitted well into the twentieth century by the teacher Nadia Boulanger (1887–1979), another of his pupils, and he can be considered one of the principal sources of French Neoclassicism with its emphasis on restraint, long melodic lines, and modal-sounding harmonies.

Ernest Chausson (1855–99) is both one of the most derivative and one of the most progressive of this group of composers. Independently wealthy, he was not a professional composer, and his music suffers from a certain amateurishness. He is at his most derivative in such Franckian works as *Poème* for violin and orchestra (1896) and the first movement of the Concert, Op. 21, for piano, violin, and string quartet; this work is not a "violin concerto" but an attempt to recreate the *concerts* for mixed instrumental groups of François Couperin and Rameau. In his best instrumental composition, the Symphony in B♭ major, Op. 20 (1889–90), Chausson recapitulates material in the finale from the preceding two movements in the manner of his mentor Franck's D minor Symphony. Chausson constantly wrestled with what he called "the red spectre of Wagner which does not let go of me" (see Example 6–5d). The Wagnerian influence was the evocative, atmospheric mood of most of the second act of *Tristan*, the last act of *Parsifal*, and the *Siegfried Idyl*, and it is chiefly evident in the symphonic poem *Vivianne* (1882, revised 1887), the extended song-cycle, *Poème de l'amour et de la mer* (1882–92), and the posthumously performed opera *Le Roi Arthus*, on which Chausson worked between 1886 and 1895 but which was not performed until after his death.

Chausson's most progressive ideas are to be seen in his use of a Neoclassic style, most evident in the delightful Sicilienne of his Violin Concert, the Piano Quartet (1897), and the *Quelques danses* (1896) for piano, of which the Sarabande (Example 9–9c) is cited as an illustration. Note, in Example 9–9, the difference between Raff's diatonically oriented harmony, Saint-Saëns's extensive use of secondary triads, and Chausson's free modality, avoiding dominant harmonies. Chausson seemed to be on the verge of creating a highly individual style when he was killed in a bicycling accident at the age of forty-four.

Vincent d'Indy (1851–1931) made the best synthesis of French and Germanic musical styles in creating works of strong originality and masterly workmanship. Though in his later music he used such Debussyesque devices as whole-tone scales and unrelated parallel fifths or triads, chiefly for coloristic effects (as in his *Sept chants de terroir* of 1918), in spirit he was of all French composers the most antithetical to Debussy's music and the newer French trends; yet his influence extended into the twentieth century in the larger works of Albert Roussel (1869–1937) and Arthur Honegger (1892–1955) as well as in the French version of *Gebrauchsmusik*, the Paris Conservatoire contest solo. An ardent and contentious polemicist not only for his musical ideas but also for a conservatively ultramontane Catholicism and a chauvinistic nationalism, his ideas may be compared with Wagner's.

EXAMPLE 9–9. (a) Raff, Sarabande from Suite, Op. 207 (*ca.* 1880); (b) Saint-Saëns, trio of minuet from Septuor, Op. 65 (1881); (c) Chausson, Sarabande from *Quelques danses*, Op. 26 (1896).

D'Indy's logical, systematic, intellectual view of music was expressed not only in his compositions but also in his work as a teacher and in his monumental *Cours de composition musicale* (1903–33, the last part published posthumously).

One of the few "universal" composers of the century, d'Indy wrote in many different media. His atmospherically Wagnerian operas belong to the twentieth century, and his choral works include not only much church music (which increased in austerity during the course of his career) but also an early statement of his artistic credo in *Le Chant de la cloche* (1885), in which he overlaid Schiller's poem with a sturdy uncompromising Catholicism and the artistic ideas expressed by Wagner in *Die Meistersinger*. D'Indy's absolute instrumental music was strongly influenced by the architectonic principles of cyclic form and the melodic styles of Gregorian chant and French folk song; his chamber music includes not only string quartets (the E major Quartet is based on a chant motive) but also chamber music with winds.

D'Indy began his career as an orchestral composer with symphonic poems, of which the best known is the trilogy based on Schiller's *Wallenstein* (1873–81). The *Symphony on a French Mountain Air* (1886), his most frequently performed work, follows the example of Franck's *Variations symphoniques* in having the solo piano prominent yet subordinate to the orchestra and contains ingenious thematic transformation. *Istar* (1896), based on an Assyrian legend in which Istar is gradually unclothed as she passes through the various portals of the temple, is a reversal of the standard variation form in that the theme, in a most effective orchestral unison, is stated toward the end of the composition.

D'Indy's crowning orchestral achievement was his Second Symphony in B♭ (1902–03); as Example 9–10a illustrates, the composer declined to add the term "major" or "minor" because of the ambiguity of the opening germ-motive. This symphony represents the culmination of the art of thematic transformation, for the germ motives, especially motive "A," permeate each movement, especially in transitional passages, and many of the themes that do not derive from the germ-motives can nevertheless be combined with them. With this work, the greatest French symphony since Berlioz's *Symphonie Fantastique*, the chronological discussion of the music of nineteenth-century Romanticism can be concluded.

EXAMPLE 9–10. Selected cyclic interrelationships in d'Indy's Symphony No. 2 in B♭, Op. 57: (a) First movement, introduction; (b) First movement, second theme; (c) Coda of first movement: combination of motive A with (1) transitional theme between first and second theme-groups and (2) transformation of first theme; (d) Second movement, second theme with oboe countermelody; (e) Fourth movement, fugue subject; (f) Fourth movement, chorale in coda. (Permission for reprint granted by Durand et Cie.; Copyright Owners of Paris, France; Elkan-Vogel Co., Inc., Philadelphia, Pa., Sole Agents.)

(b) Un peu plus modère   ♩ = 76

(c) Assez animé   ♩ = 104

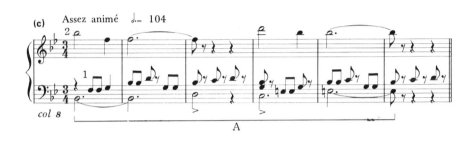

col 8

(d) Plus animé   ♩ = 52

(e) Modèrè et solennel   ♩ = 76

(f) Lent et largement chanté (♩ = 56)

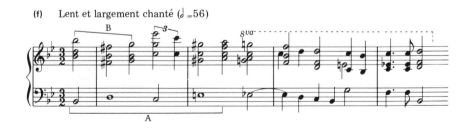

BIBLIOGRAPHICAL NOTES

The Turn of the Century. Edward R. Tannenbaum's *1900* (Garden City, N.Y., 1976) surveys social, political, and cultural trends in Europe as a whole. In recent years end-of-century Vienna has been the subject of numerous studies, with Frederic Morton's *A Nervous Splendor* (New York, 1979) limited to the years 1888 and 1889, William M. Johnston's *The Austrian Mind* (Berkeley, 1972) an intellectual history, and William McGrath's *Dionysian Art and Populist Politics in Austria* (New Haven, 1974) discussing Mahler's Third Symphony in the musical portion of this controversial interdisciplinary study. Though Carl Schorske's *Fin-de-Siècle Vienna* (New York, 1980), gives a fine cultural setting, its musical discussions are focussed around Schoenberg after 1908. Gordon A. Craig's *Germany 1866–1945* (New York, 1978) is a good corrective to the anti-German biases that have marred much earlier writing about the period around 1900. Unfortunately there are no good comparable works for Paris or Italy at this specific time.

It is even more difficult to find comprehensive studies of the music of this particular sub-epoch. Carl Dahlhaus's thought-provoking study *Between Romanticism and Modernism* (1974; English trans. Berkeley, 1980) is heavily oriented toward German music; Jim Samson's *Music in Transition* (New York, 1977) is chiefly focussed on the early twentieth century, with stylistic elements of the preceding century regarded as points of departure. In the *New Oxford History of Music* series, Martin Cooper (ed.), *The Modern Age 1890–1960* (London 1974), has a more balanced approach, with Gerald Abraham's essays on Romanticism's apogee, decline, and the reactions against it including excellent descriptions of post-Romantic musical styles.

Italian Opera. See the items on Verdi's operas listed in the bibliographical notes for Chapter 5. Marcello Conati (ed.), *Encounters with Verdi* (English translation, Ithaca, 1984), is almost entirely devoted to personal impressions of the composer (including his rehearsal techniques) from 1855 onward. Analytical methodologies for Verdi's late works are included in Roger Parker and Matthew Brown, "Ancora un bacio," *Nineteenth-Century Music*, IX (1985), 50–61. Jay Nicolaisen's *Italian Opera in Transition, 1871–1893* (Ann Arbor, 1980) is a challenging evaluation of this period with stimulating reappraisals of the composers between Verdi and Puccini; Ponchielli is further served by a volume of essays edited by Antonio Polignano, *Amilcare Ponchielli 1834–1886* (Casalmorano, 1984). Mosco Carner's *Puccini* (2d ed., London, 1974) and William Ashbrook's *The Operas of Puccini* (London, 1969) cover this composer's output. The rise of instrumental composition in late nineteenth-century Italy is described in Bea Friedland's, "Italy's Ottocento: Notes from the Musical Underground," *Musical Quarterly*," LVI (1970), 27–53, and in Sergio Martinotti's *Ottocento strumentale italiana* (Bologna, 1972).

Central Europe. Frank Walker's excellent biography of Hugo Wolf (2d ed., New York, 1968) is supplemented by Eric Sams's *The Songs of Hugo Wolf*

(London, 1983), which includes translations and discussions of each song. Deborah Stein's *Hugo Wolf's Lieder and Extensions of Tonality* (Ann Arbor, 1985) uses a basically Schenkerian approach where applicable, and includes valuable insights on central European tonality and harmony in general at the end of the century. Many of Wolf's polemical writings on music are contained in Henry Pleasants (ed.), *The Music Criticism of Hugo Wolf* (New York, 1978).

Mahler is presently served by two large-scale studies: the biography in progress by Henry Louis de la Grange (Vol. 1, New York, 1973) and Donald Mitchell's three-volume study (Berkeley, 1980–85), which concentrates more on the music. A number of Mahler's letters are available in English in Knud Martner (ed.), *Selected Letters of Gustav Mahler* (New York, 1982). The reminiscences of Mahler's friend Natalie Bauer-Lechner, *Recollections of Gustav Mahler* (1923; English translation, New York, 1980) is an excellent primary source for the composer's nineteenth-century career, preceding the memoirs of his widow, Alma Mahler, *Gustav Mahler: Memories and Letters,* in the most recent edition (3d enlarged edition, London, 1975). Significant recent German studies include Constantin Floros, *Mahler* (2 vols., Wiesbaden, 1977), which emphasizes the context of the symphonies; H. H. Eggebrecht explains many of Mahler's musical symbols in *Die Musik Gustav Mahlers* (Munich, 1982). I. A. Barsova's Russian-language study of Mahler's symphonies (*Simfonii Gustava Malera,* Moscow, 1975), with interesting analytical procedures, deserves to be translated into a Western language. Richard Strauss is well covered in Norman Del Mar's three-volume study (London, 1962–72) and by his designated biographer Willi Schuh in *Richard Strauss: A Chronicle of the Early Years 1864–1898* (Eng. tr. Cambridge, England, 1982) which deals with the composer's life rather than his music. Barbara Peterson's reappraisal in *Ton und Wort: The Lieder of Richard Strauss* (Ann Arbor, 1980), defends Strauss against the charges that he showed little improvement as a song composer and could not discriminate between good and poor poetry. A study of Strauss's orchestral works incorporating present-day analytical techniques and procedures would be welcome.

France. The books by Cooper and Landormy (less so Hastings's study of Franck and his circle) cited in the bibliographical notes of Chapter 7 and my study "Towards the 'Fin de Siècle': Stylistic Change and Symbolist Connotations in French Music" in *Miscellanea Musicologica,* XIII (1984), pp. 75–96, provide brief overviews of French music during the *belle époque.* Biographical studies of French composers include Jean-Pierre Barricelli and Leo Weinstein, *Ernest Chausson* (Norman, 1955); Rollo Myers, *Emmanuel Chabrier and His Circle* (London, 1969); Roger Delage, *Chabrier* (Paris, 1982), in the series *Iconographie Musicale,* a documentary biography with text in French and English; and Norman Suckling, *Fauré* (London, 1951), which also spiritedly points out many differences between French and German music. The numerous and more recent studies in French by the Fauré scholar Jean-Marie Nectoux will be summarized in his English-language *Gabriel Fauré and His World,* in preparation at the present writing. D'Indy, unfortunately, has not been well served in English either by the appreciative study of his American pupil Daniel Gregory Mason (in *Contemporary Composers*, New York, 1929) or Norman Demuth's defensive biography (London, 1951); Léon Vallas's *Vincent d'Indy* (2 vols., Paris, 1946–50) remains the most comprehensive source.

Complete editions of the music of Wolf and Mahler are in progress, and for Strauss's centennial year (1964) Boosey and Hawkes published his complete songs in four volumes. Müller von Asow's *Richard Strauss: Thematisches Verzeichnis* (Vienna, 1955–1974) shows how productive Strauss actually was. French music has not been as well served; the authentic text of Fauré's *Requiem* was not published until 1985. The fragile and crumbly paper used by most music publishers in the latter part of the nineteenth century is now rapidly deteriorating, making republication of the works of the other composers discussed in this chapter imperative.

TEN

ROMANTIC MUSICAL STYLES

After examining the tendencies of Romanticism in general and the various works of individual Romantic composers, it is appropriate now to investigate the musical styles of the nineteenth century. We must remember, though, that this Romantic era in music was a period of contrast and antithesis, discernible not only between generations or among different composers living at the same time, but even within the works of individual composers. Romantic musical style is also fluid rather than stable; in describing it one can speak only in terms of trends and tendencies rather than norms. Especially in the second half of the century, several differing styles existed at the same time and developed independently, and apparent "regressions," like the avoidance of chromatic harmony by Brahms, Saint-Saëns, and Fauré, proved to be "advances" in a different direction.

There is no sharp dividing line between Classic and Romantic styles, for most Romantic style-traits are based on the transformation and intensification of ideas present before 1800. Although Romantic composers, like

Romantic writers and artists, were extreme individualists and sought to proclaim their uniqueness in their music, there are some discernible tendencies common to musical Romanticism that separate this movement from Classic or Modern musical styles. Some writers have objected to the use of Romanticism as a virtual synonym for nineteenth-century music, yet one can justifiably ask, "Who were the composers active between 1785 and 1905 who entirely escaped or avoided Romanticism?"

In the first chapter we saw that it is virtually impossible to find a simple definition of Romanticism in general, and that examining some themes common to Romanticism—individualism, nationalism, interpenetration of the arts, escape into nature or a vaguely identifiable past—is the more serviceable approach. A study of the writings of nineteenth-century composers or critics discloses equally thorny problems in defining musical Romanticism, for the composers were as vague and contradictory as were their literary counterparts. Although one can find in the musical writings of the nineteenth century almost any definition of Romanticism, there are a few common themes that suggest the integrity of this period as a separate epoch in the history of music.

In the first chapter our discussion centered around the elements common to Romantic composers and their literary and artistic contemporaries. Now the main task is to delimit musical Romanticism in terms of its musical styles: how do Romantic and Classic musical styles differ, how do the individual elements of musical style change in the course of the nineteenth century, and what happens to these stylistic elements at the end of the century so that they can no longer be called Romantic? Our discussion, couched in the most general terms from the standpoint of style in general, is planned as an overview rather than as a series of detailed investigations.

ELEMENTS OF ROMANTIC MUSICAL STYLE

Melody and Periodicity. As in the Classic period, most Romantic melody is phrase-dominated, with the prevalent texture describable as "melody with accompaniment." Increased individualism is a hallmark of Romantic melody, and if one asks a layman to list ten "immortal" melodies, the chances are overwhelming that all those he cites will be from nineteenth-century works.

Two typical eighteenth-century melodies are cited in Example 10–1. Mozart's theme is concise whereas Haydn's theme is longer, but both are well balanced, closed rather than open, and with easily perceived inner relationships between the contrasting sections. Stepwise motion is dominant, and the skips and leaps are balanced by opposite stepwise motion.

EXAMPLE 10–1. (a) Mozart, String Quartet in C major, K. 465 (1784), first movement; (b) Haydn, Symphony No. 30 (1765), second movement.

In contrast, most Romantic composers sought to write long melodic lines, whether constructed from phrases (Examples 10–2a and 10–2d), motives (Example 10–2b), or, rarest of all, from a virtually seamless, unperiodic, exuberant melodic line (Example 10–2c). Instrumental themes especially tend to increase in length. The melodies of Examples 10–1a and 10–2c have similar functions: the opening allegro theme of a first movement in sonata form with the initial phrases repeated and spun out to lead the transition to the second theme group. Yet whereas Mozart's theme is nine measures long, Schumann's is thirty-two measures in length.

Other devices characteristic of Romantic melody include wide leaps for expressive purposes, often leaps of sixths, sevenths, and other intervals,

EXAMPLE 10–2. (a) Brahms, Symphony No. 2 (1877), second movement; (b) Richard Strauss, *Ein Heldenleben* (1899), opening; (c) Schumann, String Quartet in F major, Op. 41, No. 2 (1842), first movement; (d) Chaikovsky, Symphony No. 5 (1888), second movement.

285

diminished or augmented; this tendency becomes exaggerated in late-Romantic composers, as in Example 10–2b, which also shows, in its ambitus of four octaves, the tendency toward increasing the melodic range. One may compare the relative irregularity of Brahms's melody (Example 10–2a), with its avoidance of frequent internal articulations and constant mutation into new ideas, with the regular periodicity of Chaikovsky's (Example 10–2d); both are slow movement symphonic themes and can be considered each composer's epitome of melody *qua* melody.

Other Romantic melodies that do not correspond to the illustrations in Example 10–2 can be cited. The finely arched Classic melody, symmetrical, closed (*i.e.*, cadencing at its end) rather than open, phrase-dominated, vocally oriented, and with a stanzaic construction equivalent to that of poetry, can be found chiefly in the German Lied from Reichardt through Robert Franz; Italian opera from Rossini through middle-period Verdi; French operatic genres, including the operetta; and the short piano piece, whether abstract (Brahms's A major Intermezzo, Op. 118, No. 2) or based on dance forms (Chopin's mazurkas). Non-stanzaic melodies with loosely related phrases are one of the harbingers of musical Romanticism. A stanzaic melody and a non-stanzaic melody are shown in Example 10–3.

EXAMPLE 10–3. (a) Stanzaic melody: Beethoven, Symphony No. 4 (1807), trio of third movement; (b) Non-stanzaic melody: Koželuch, Piano Sonata in D minor, Op. 20, No. 3 (ca. 1787), first movement.

Instrumental color is often closely associated with Romantic melodies: Example 10–2a with the cello section, for example, and Example 10–2d with the solo horn. One coloristic procedure has been given the German name *Durchbrochene Arbeit* to describe a melody that is divided among various instruments; Example 10–4 is the epitome of this type. This may be compared with a late-Romantic exaggeration that is too long to cite here, the opening of the allegro moderato section of the first movement of Glazunov's Fourth Symphony (1893), in which the theme is divided among several registers as well as instrumental colors, from high violins and flutes to the lowest strings and woodwinds. Although the melody itself is longer than Beethoven's example, there is less contrast between motives because of the composer's trying to write as effusively lyrical an idea as possible. Another late-Romantic device, seen in such disparate works as Bruckner's late symphonies and Puccini's operas, is the intense, pregnant, soaring melodic climax (Examples 9–2 and 10–8d).

Less "melodic" but highly significant is a type of instrumental melodic writing that is abstract and motivic rather then tuneful and phrase-oriented; its epitomes may be found in the first movements of Beethoven's "Tempest" (Op. 31, No.2) and E major (Op. 109) sonatas. The most striking continuations of this kind of abstract design, as opposed to tune, are to be found as leitmotives in Wagner's post-*Lohengrin* music dramas and in several of Brahms's more abstruse compositions, such as the first movements of the C minor String Quartet (Op. 51, No. 1) and First Symphony. These melodies can be considered the ancestors of the highly abstract themes of Schoenberg and Webern. Another type of abstract melody derives from instrumental figuration; often based on a single rhythmic pattern, it might be called "étude melody," and can be artistic in the hands of Chopin, excitingly virtuosic with Paganini or Liszt, or, conversely, almost excruciatingly dull in transition passages of concertos or sonatas by minor composers.

The kind of motivically oriented thematic work characteristic of C. P. E. Bach and Haydn was effectively continued in the nineteenth century; its hallmark is its adaptability to a variety of transformations rather than to just ornamental variation. Even in the Classic period one can sense an underlying philosophical program behind the thematic transformation that occurs in minor-mode sonata-form movements, where second- and closing-group thematic material is stated in mediant major in the exposition and tonic minor in the recapitulation. A melody or motive that can undergo a wide variety of transformations is the underlying basis of Romantic cyclic form.

Associated with Romantic musical nationalism are melodies which are either borrowed folk tunes or original themes utilizing piquant characteristics of folk melodies, usually irregular phrase structures or alterations of the major or minor scales. Rarely can these melodies be subjected to development or transformation; variation, ornamentation, re-harmonization, or fragmentation are the only possible treatments. Several such melodies are cited in Chapter 8.

EXAMPLE 10–4. Beethoven, Symphony No. 3 (1804), first movement.

Rhythm. Freedom and flexibility are the chief elements that separate Romantic from Classic treatments of rhythm. Although Haydn had made occasional rhythmic experiments, as in the trio of the minuet of his "Oxford" Symphony (No. 92), it was Beethoven who overcame what he called the "tyranny of the bar-line" as early as 1800, as Example 10–5 demonstrates in its syncopations, rhythmic counterpoint, and unprecedented cross-accents. The liberation of the musical macrorhythm from its underlying metric structure was continued throughout the century; one need but cite such diverse orchestral scherzos as those of Schumann's First Symphony, Brahms's Second Symphony, Chaikovsky's *Manfred,* Dvořák's Seventh Symphony, and Chabrier's *España.*

EXAMPLE 10–5. Beethoven, String Quartet in B♭ major, Op. 18, No. 6 (ca. 1800), third movement.

Cross-rhythms are of three types in the Romantic period. The first and most common, duplets against triplets or other permutations of the concept of two beats in one part against three in another, occurs in some Classic music (the slow movement of Mozart's C major Piano Concerto, K. 467); though considered a hallmark of Brahms's style, it frequently occurs in the music of E. A. Förster, Berlioz, Chopin, Liszt, Bruckner, and many others. A second type of cross-rhythm, consisting of silvery washes of pianistic color with rapid, irregularly grouped notes in the right hand against a steady beat in the left hand, is considered typical of Hummel and Chopin but can be found as far back as C. P. E. Bach and as far ahead as Balakirev. The most complex type of cross-rhythm, the intersection of two or more rhythmic planes, usually a macrorhythmic plane enhanced with syncopation against a metric microrhythm, has been described in the preceding paragraph.

One typically Romantic rhythmic device may be compared with what the English Jesuit poet Gerard Manley Hopkins (1844–89) called "sprung rhythm," based on word stress rather than syllabic count. In music this was most frequently achieved by substituting occasional measures of meters different from the prevailing rhythmic organization (a measure of 3/4 or 6/8 in rapid 2/2 meter), syncopations, sforzando accents in the "wrong" places, and syncopated harmonic rhythms giving the effect of "misplaced" bar-lines, as in Example 7–3c.

Irregular and complex meters are sometimes present in Romantic music. Eastern European music, from Glinka to Rimsky-Korsakov, has been cited as the principal source of these meters, yet there are some curious and interesting Western counterparts in such diverse works as Boieldieu's *La Dame blanche*, Liszt's *Faust Symphony*, Cornelius's *The Barber of Bagdad*, Sullivan's *The Yeomen of the Guard*, and the finale of d'Indy's Second Symphony. By 1900 the most radical form of metric complexity consisted of changing beat-units as well as meters (Example 10–6).

EXAMPLE 10–6. Rimsky-Korsakov, *Tsar Saltan* (1900), Act I.

Rhythmic complications are one of the leading characteristics of late- to post-Romantic music. A thread of such complexities runs from Berlioz through Liszt to Chaikovsky, Richard Strauss, and (with Russian folk influences) Glière. Permutations of compound meters (especially 9/8), half-note triplets in 4/4 meter, constantly shifting meters, and interactions of rhythmic planes of increasingly great complexity all contribute to the establishment of twentieth-century rhythmic styles.

An apparently contrary and antithetical development in the nineteenth century is the close interpenetration of dance and art music. The idealized, stylized dance is as important to Romantic composers as it was to the writers of keyboard and orchestral suites in the Baroque. One need but cite the use of the waltz in Schubert, Schumann, Chopin, Brahms, and Richard Strauss; the quadrille in French *opéra comique*, the galop in Offenbach, the operatic processional march, or the numerous eastern European dances with their piquant rhythmic effects. Fascinating collections of Romantic dance-types are the ballet, especially among French or Russian composers, and the multitudinous collections of national or "exotic" dances for piano duet. One striking example of Romantic dance stylization is the steady dance-beat in the accompaniment with cross-rhythms in the melody.

A major failing of many of the lesser Romantic composers is that they rely on one rhythmic pattern to sustain interest throughout a major portion of a composition or symphonic movement. Another failing, often acute among late Romantics, is a lack of rhythmic imagination that causes the music to "sag," an effect that can be quite static and boring when combined with frequent repetition of melodic material.

Expression. Tempo and other expression markings increase in complexity and verbosity during the Romantic period; not for the Romantics such simple terms as "allegro" and "forte"! Yet the frequent clusters of modifying adverbs are not meant to restrict the performer, but to provide more freedom and interpretative license. Not until the close of the century, with such composers as Debussy and Mahler, did composers meticulously mark each effect and nuance, doubtlessly in a reaction against some of the overly subjective interpretations by performers and conductors. Extremes of dynamic gradations from the Classic outer limits of *pp* and *ff* began with the French "rescue opera" composers of the 1790's and reached, with late Romantic composers, extremes from *ppppp* to *ffff*, or even greater.

Harmony. Separate volumes would be needed to do proper justice to the concepts of harmony and tonality in the nineteenth century. Harmony was one of the greatest preoccupations of Romantic composers, as seen by the proliferation of treatises or textbooks on harmony between 1800 and 1914. Especially among German, German-influenced, or most late- or post-Romantic composers, harmony was the chief vehicle for musical individuality and striving for originality.

From the standpoint of harmony, the chief difference between Classic and Romantic composers is that the former used dissonant chords relatively infrequently and then in a functional manner, usually to enhance or intensify the progression of a dominant to a tonic or as a pivot in modulation, but Romantic composers frequently used the same chords in a coloristic sense and progressively elevated the milder dissonant chords, usually dominant and diminished sevenths, to the level of consonances. They also modified, or altogether dispensed with, the earlier conventions of preparing and resolving these dissonant chords. Throughout the century there was a steadily rising "dissonance threshold," especially among German and Russian composers or Franck and his disciples; a counter-reaction was the rejection of chromatic harmony for its own sake by the various kinds of "Neoclassic" composers who often used diatonic harmonies in radically different ways from those of their Classic models.

Only a few general typologies of chromatic microharmony (chords and their progressions) from the Romantic period can be cited. The chord of the *diminished seventh* (F♯-A-C-E♭, for example), usually an enhancement of the dominant in works in the minor mode during the Baroque and Classic periods, became elevated in the "rescue operas" of the 1790's to an all-purpose coloristic effect to depict emotional tension or storms. Early Romantic composers perceived that this chord, with its four equally possible resolutions, could open new vistas for modulation, need not be resolved if used for coloristic purposes, and could even be the first chord in a composition. Two of the many coloristic uses of this chord, one early and one late Romantic, are cited in Example 10–7: the first, from Schubert, is a coloristic expansion of tonic harmony that permits a major-minor interchange; the second, from Chaikovsky, is a programmatic use of this chord, unprepared and unresolved, to create an atmosphere of unsatisfied yearning.

EXAMPLE 10–7. (a) Schubert, String Quintet in C major, D. 956 (1828), first movement; (b) Chaikovsky, *Francesca da Rimini* (1876), opening.

Among the other chords of the seventh, the *half-diminished seventh* (D–F–A♭–C, for example) had been used functionally during Classic period in the minor mode as a cadential progression (ii°$^6_5$–V–i), but Romantic composers found it an effective color harmony because it had a different "flavor" in each of its four inversions. Chords of the *minor seventh* (C–E♭–G–B♭) and *major seventh* (C–E–G–B) were not fully discovered until the closing years of the century; with the post-Romantics they were treated as dissonant climaxes, whereas the French neoclassicists used them as passing chords in inversions, since they could fit without alteration into the minor or major scales respectively.

Altered chords represent one of the most ambiguous terminologies in the theorists' vocabularies. One must exclude from this category the so-called "borrowed" chords, whether taken from minor to major or major to minor, and the so-called "applied," "secondary," or "tonicizing" dominants, the most important means of harmonic sequence and modulation from Corelli to Schumann. Borrowed chords, chiefly diminished sevenths as enhancers of dominants, minor subdominant harmony, or the supertonic half-diminished seventh chord, all transferred from the minor to the major mode, are among the favorite harmonic devices of Beethoven's contemporaries, and their abuse (as early as Spohr) led to an insufferably cloying sentimentality that is one of the major ingredients of musical *kitsch* (see Chap. 12). Altered chords proper can be subsumed under the following headings:

1. *Chromatically altered triads, usually with the raised fifth* (the augmented triad). Whereas with Classic and even early Romantic composers this was a passing harmony from tonic to subdominant, from about 1850 onward it became a coloristic harmony for its own sake. Example 10–8 contains four highly varied, but all coloristic, uses of this harmony: 10–8a as a harmonization of a melody containing all twelve tones of the chromatic scale; 10–8b as a coloristic device to blur a traditional feeling of tonality; (see Example 8–6b for its use as a percussive dissonance); 10–8c, an augmented triad with an added seventh, to flavor a piece of musical *kitsch;* and 10–8d, unprepared and unresolved augmented triads leading to a musical and dramatic climax. Measures 4–8 of Example 8–7c show how the augmented triad can be the "tonic chord" of the whole-tone scale.

2. *Chromatic or enharmonic alteration of a chord containing a minor seventh,* the most frequently encountered such chord being the augmented sixth. Functionally, this harmony has enhanced dominant harmonies as far back as the mid-Baroque, but during the Romantic period it was often used coloristically, often with irregular or no preparation or resolution; it is a chief constituent of the lushness of Romantic harmony. The normal treatment of the two most critical members of this chord is to regard one as a leading-tone resolving upward, another as a seventh resolving downward, and to re-spell individual notes enharmonically in order to alter their basic tendencies of resolution; most familiar is the so-called "German sixth," an enharmonically re-spelled dominant-seventh chord. Examples 7–5 (Franck), 8–3c (Grieg), and 8–3d (Delius) show some of the varied late-Romantic uses of the chord of the augmented sixth. On a more popular

EXAMPLE 10–8. (a) Liszt, Faust Symphony (1854–57), first movement; (b) Liszt, "Unstern" (ca. 1883); (c) Ethelbert Nevin, "Mighty Lak' a Rose" (1901); (d) Puccini, *Madame Butterfly* (1904), Act I.

level, borrowed and altered chords are the essential ingredients of "barber-shop" harmony for male voices.

Non-harmonic tones in the Baroque and Classic period were mostly passing dissonances; when used on the beat they often intensified cadences, particularly a 7–8 melodic movement in a cadence in minor, or served as expressive "sighs." Although Beethoven as a rule eschewed non-harmonic tones occurring with chromatic alteration on the beat, his younger contemporaries delighted in them, even doubling them at the third or sixth below to enhance their effect. A prevalent tendency during the Romantic period was the delaying of the resolution of these accented non-harmonic tones in order to heighten the effect of yearning and longing which occurs, even in diatonic harmony, when the resolution of these tones is delayed (see Examples 6–5b, 6–5c, 6–5d).

Higher discords, a late-Romantic term, resulted from building chords upward by thirds. Whereas during the Classic and early Romantic period the upper level was the minor or major ninth, later Romantic composers built their chords farther upward (the major thirteenth has been called the "Chopin chord" because of his frequent use of this sonority) to the point where ambiguity resulted between, for example, chords of the minor thirteenth and augmented triads with an added minor seventh (see Example 10–8c).

Chord progressions during the Romantic period tend to differ from their Classic equivalents through the passage from functional to coloristic harmony, the increasing freedom in part-writing, and resolutions that are often enharmonic, delayed, or even non-existent. Precedents for nearly all of these devices can be found in the music of C. P. E. Bach. Among the late Romantics from Wagner and Liszt onward, many chords can be explained only in terms of their contexts. Any given note could be harmonized as a leading-tone, or as a seventh with a tendency to resolve downward, or the natural tendencies of given notes could be changed through enharmonic spellings. Principles of functional harmonic analysis (the "Roman numeral" system) gradually cease to be applicable because of microharmonic ambiguity and macroharmonic modulation; often only a descriptive or reductionist analysis is possible, since the hierarchical relationships between triads and between tonalities had been severely weakened if not destroyed.

The dividing line between the nineteenth and twentieth centuries, from the standpoint of harmony, comes when chords can no longer be described in tertian terms (Skryabin's famous "mystic chord" or the quartal chords, built by fourths, in the early songs of Alban Berg); when unresolved chromatic harmonies, often further complicated by enharmonic spellings and clustered non-harmonic tones, are a pervasive fabric and lack diatonic anchors as points of reference; when diatonic or chromatic harmonies pass from one to another in a kind of side-slipping in parallel or contrary motion; or when dissonant chords are used not as functional or coloristic harmonies, but as percussive sounds in the context of a musical "cultural primitivism."

Harmonic rhythm (the rate of chord change, expressed in terms of duration) is one of the subtlest aspects of a composer's musical style. Although a fast harmonic rhythm is typical of Baroque music and a slow harmonic rhythm is characteristic of Classic music, no such generalization is possible in the Romantic period. During this era a slow harmonic rhythm is often used to create an atmosphere of repose (for example, the first movement of Beethoven's Sixth Symphony), and Brahms and Dvořák frequently used syncopated harmonic rhythms to reinforce the effect of an interaction of rhythmic planes. On the other hand, the *longueurs* of much of the extended music of late Romantic composers arise from an insufficient control or understanding of harmonic rhythm, especially when coupled with the harmonic ambiguity and pervasive tonal flux of much post-Romantic music, thus weakening the principle of harmonic rhythm as a structural device.

Reactions against chromatic harmony took place in the course of the nineteenth century. One was a return to functional diatonicism with the emphasis on widening the spectrum of tonality to include various mediant and submediant harmonies, in their major and minor forms, as well as the traditional tonic, dominant, and subdominant; rooted in Beethoven's music, this "diatonic reaction" became the essential resource of nearly every composer who has been termed "Neoclassic." The non-functional equivalent consists of non-directional chord successions, a favorite device of Berlioz but one used with equal force by Liszt, Fauré, and Catalani among others. Still another reaction was the introduction of a so-called "modal" harmony with a strong emphasis on secondary triads (ii, iii, and vi in major; III, v, VI, and VII in minor) in the diatonic scales, treated in non-functional ways. Although this harmonic fabric is considered typical of Russian music (see Examples 8–1 and 8–5d), modal-type harmonies were applied to many melodies by Western composers as well, from Berlioz onward; it became a means of widening tonal spectra among various types of Neoclassic composers, especially Brahms (Example 7–4) and Saint-Saëns (Examples 9–8b, 10–9). A further influence on modal harmony was the revival of Gregorian chant, with its new organ accompaniments contrived to remove the earlier major-minor straitjacket into which the modes had previously been forced; this kind of modal harmony is evident in the music of Fauré and Puccini. Artificial scales with a modal import, ambiguity between tonal and modal sections within a piece, whether in the melody or the harmony, vitiation of the force of the leading tone by lowering or omitting it—all these contributed further to weakening the force of traditional tonality. The difference between nineteenth- and twentieth-century modality can be seen in the treatment of the leading tone; in late Romantic music the leading tone eventually surfaces in V-I cadences or tonicized dominants (Fauré, Puccini), whereas in the twentieth century the leading tone will be avoided (Ravel, Sibelius, Vaughan Williams, Respighi).

Example 10–9 shows a late example of the "diatonic reaction" in which the roots of twentieth-century "pan-diatonicism" are clearly visible. It represents a reaction against the "leading-tone" or dominant-seventh-oriented chromaticism of the century. Note (1) the leading tones that do not lead upward but are harmonized with mediants and descend, (2) the purely diatonic nature of the theme and its harmony, and (3) the composer's reliance on secondary triads that weaken the feeling of dominant or subdominant harmonies as essential structural elements.

EXAMPLE 10–9. Saint-Saëns, Piano Concerto No. 5 (1896), first movement.

Among the composers who relied on the diatonic reaction against Wagnerian chromaticism were Brahms, Raff, Saint-Saëns, Fauré, Chausson, and Rimsky-Korsakov, to list the few whose examples are cited in the text; all have strikingly different harmonic palettes. The dividing line between nineteenth- and twentieth-century diatonicism is most strikingly crossed in the music of Debussy and Ravel, with their use of parallel diatonic triads, sometimes with sevenths and ninths added in a kind of organum; extended non-functional sequences of diatonic triads; displacements of one diatonic scale by another; and the blurring of tonal centers by superposing unrelated tones or even other triads on the original chord, especially in final cadences, and often for coloristic or programmatic purposes.

Tonality. The expansion of the tonal frame of reference is one of the most crucial elements of Romantic musical style. In simple terms, the definition of a given key was substantially widened. The dominant as well as the tonic was a determining factor, with the mediant and sub-mediant degrees (often the flatted degrees of the scale) assuming an importance close to that which the dominant and subdominant had held in the Classic period. Many harmonies, when chromatically altered, could assume an even stronger functional character. There were new vistas in modulation through the use of the deceptive cadence (V–vi or V–♭VI), enharmonically spelled chords of the diminished seventh or augmented sixth, or "borrowed chords" (the flatted mediant or sub-mediant the most frequent) as pivots from one tonal center to another. Unprepared shifts, sudden and dramatic, from one key to another were increasingly tolerated. All these provided an enhanced and enlarged feeling of tonality that permitted a dramatic expansion of musical space itself.

Keys themselves were treated with greater freedom. Whereas during the Classic period the normative limitation was between E and E♭ in major and between F minor and E minor, any key could be and was used by the Romantics, and several composers, from Hummel and Chopin to Busoni and Skryabin, wrote sets of preludes or études in all the major and minor keys. Music for the piano was the first to be written outside the Classic key limitations, but the improvement of brass and wind instruments enabled chamber and especially orchestral music to be written in keys that were highly unusual by Classic standards. The key of F♯ minor can almost be called *the* Romantic key, especially in piano music.

The minor mode's increasing popularity between 1780 and 1800 is a major harbinger of Romanticism, a mode that rose to a position of near-dominance in Romantic music. Whereas approximately 5 percent of Classic symphonies are in the minor mode, during the second half of the nineteenth century approximately 70 percent of the symphonies are in minor, with Glazunov the only symphonist of consequence who strongly preferred the major mode. The natural instability of the minor mode permitted the admission of more chromaticism and altered harmonies; this can already be seen among some Classic composers, with most of the harmonic originalities of C. P. E. Bach, Haydn, and Mozart appearing in their works in minor. The interchange of harmonies borrowed from minor into major, or major into minor, was an important ingredient of early Romantic chromaticism (especially Schubert's) but became so prevalent in the course of the century that by 1902 d'Indy could simply state that his Second Symphony was in B♭

since the major-minor question was no longer operative (see Example 9–10a).

The expansion of tonality can be seen principally in the following areas:

1. Extended introductions that usually begin outside the key and eventually settle on the dominant (dominant preparations).

2. A modified concept of the contents of a key, fundamentally a change from twenty-four diatonic major and minor keys to twelve chromatic keys in which major and minor could be interchangeable or the mode ambiguous. The contrary reactions were (a) a "modal" or freely tonal diatonicism; (b) planed triads or consonant dyads (thirds or open fifths, sometimes with another voice in contrary motion; or (c) reversions to Classic-era harmonic and tonal archaisms, best seen in operatic attempts to recreate the eighteenth-century *divertissement* in such operas as Massenet's *Manon* and Chaikovsky's *Pique Dame*.

3. Defining a key not by explicitly stating and emphasizing its tonic but by implication, usually through enhancing its dominant (see Example 4–3 and Figure 6–1 for illustrations). The prelude to Wagner's *Tristan* is the standard culmination of this technique, where A minor is the tonic but it is not stated, yet D minor is almost as elusive in the third movement of Brahms's B♭ major String Quartet (Op. 67), though it is the tonic of the movement.

4. Tonal parentheses (sometimes called "transient modulations") separating the tonal cells that unify the work; Example 5–11 is an illustration of a simple tonal parenthesis.

5. A freer treatment of modulation, anticipated in many of the sonatas and especially the fantasias of C. P. E. Bach, with a wider spectrum of related tonal areas, and a greater variety of pivots with which to reach them, than during the Classic period. Instead of the circle of fifths that dominated eighteenth-century theory, a kind of circle of thirds developed. Minor and relative major (e.g., C minor and E♭ major) could be two sides of the same key almost as much as major and minor, a concept expanded in the course of the century through modal mutations and interchanges. A tonic could have not only dominant and subdominant as closely related keys but four others as well, two a third above and two a third below; thus structurally significant tonal areas (for example, the second theme-group tonality in the exposition of a sonata-form movement) in, say, a work in C minor could include E♭ minor (as early as Beethoven's "Pathétique" sonata) or E major (Liszt's *Faust Symphony*). A tonic thus became not the center of a kind of tonal solar system as it had been in the past, but rather a lowest common denominator through which the other keys could be related. Paradoxically, chromaticism was viewed by a few enlightened theorists early in the twentieth century not as making keys more distant, but as relating

them more closely to a central tonic or tonics while providing more opportunity for individual and original expression.

6. Entire sections of a late- or post-Romantic composition in purely
non-functional harmony, a technique which had earlier been limited to development or transition sections, where the key is defined only by occasional tonal cells. In pieces with such usage, the statement of the tonic
chord in root position is a signal that the key is to be quitted or that the
piece itself is over. Example 10–10 demonstrates such non-functional harmony with occasional tonal cells; the piece as a whole is an excellent example of late-Romantic harmonic practice with its altered chords, irregular
chord progressions, and non-harmonic tones, yet all of these effects are surface ornaments to a rather static A major background harmony.

EXAMPLE 10–10. MacDowell, "Starlight," from *Sea Pieces*, Op. 55 (1898).

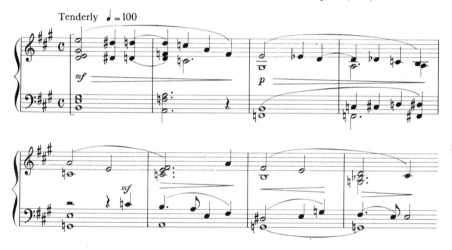

7. On the grandest scale, the expansion of tonality through the use
of unrelated keys as contrasting movements in instrumental cycles, seen as
early as Haydn's late sonata in E♭ (E♭–E–E♭); the use of third-related or step-
related keys for the second theme-groups of instrumental cycles; and the
architectonic design of given acts of Wagner's operas (see Figure 6–2) or
Liszt's double-function forms (see Figure 6–1), culminating in the interlocking tonalities of Strauss's later symphonic poems, Mahler's symphonies,
and (on a miniature scale) some of Hugo Wolf's more adventurous songs.

The dissolution of tonality is a topic that belongs to a study of twentieth-century music, with the reservation that many twentieth-century
composers have relied on tonality, but in a greatly widened sense. It
should be mentioned here, however, that the dissolution of the strong tonal

anchors that had characterized musical composition from Corelli through Mahler began during the nineteenth century through the exaggeration of all the tendencies of harmony and tonality that have been cited in this chapter. Chromatic harmony led eventually to the serializing of pitches with a deliberate avoidance of triadic implications; modulation became so frequent and far-reaching as to vitiate the structural role of tonality entirely. An individual section would not be "in" a given key, but—in a process that can be compared to the "stream of consciousness" writing in the novel of the time—would have as its musical anchors crucial associative references, usually some kind of chord (the so-called "referential sonorities" of late Skryabin or early Webern), rather than a tonal background that became increasingly harder to perceive. Conversely, diatonic harmony led to pan-diatonicism, with all the diatonic notes treated equally, or to polytonality; and composers strove to create new harmonic sonorities by constructing their chords from fourths rather than thirds.

Counterpoint. Although both the Classic and Romantic periods are regarded as dominated by homophonic musical textures, counterpoint played a subsidiary yet important role. The historicism that impelled Romantic composers to study the music of the past led them to explore the techniques of Renaissance and Baroque counterpoint and to regard this device as a legacy of the past, to be passed on with interest. *Canons* by Romantic composers are almost invariably accompanied, in order to provide euphony and enhanced sonority. *Ricercar* techniques provided an effect of particularly "severe" counterpoint and could be either tonal, deriving from Bach, as in Variation IV in the third movement of Beethoven's E major (Op. 109) piano sonata, or modal, inspired by Palestrina, as in Variation IV ("canonique") in Liszt's *Totentanz*. *Fugues*, obligatory for Classic and Romantic composers of church music and oratorio, sometimes appeared in Classic finales. Romantic composers soon found the fugue to be an important means of expanding the development of a large sonata-form movement, and later Romantic composers found the fugal treatment of a previously homophonic theme to be a striking element of dramatic rhetoric, best seen in the finales of Liszt's *Faust Symphony* and Chaikovsky's *Manfred*. Yet, among all the composers who continued Baroque contrapuntal techniques into the Classic and Romantic period, one has the feeling that only Mozart and Brahms were genuinely able to incorporate these techniques smoothly into their musical language; even with Haydn and Beethoven one senses a certain self-conscious parading of the ability to handle contrapuntal artifice, and often a deliberate archaism.

Linear counterpoint, often complicated by chromatic harmonies and non-harmonic tones, developed during the Romantic period. This kind of writing has been called "Meistersinger counterpoint" because of its most striking epitome, the prelude to Wagner's *Die Meistersinger* (Example 10–

11). There are several precedents for this type of linear writing: the irregularly resolving non-harmonic tones and independent lines of the slow movement of Mozart's E♭ Quartet, K. 428; Beethoven's contrary motion at the expense of euphony; Berlioz's combination of themes for programmatic purposes; and the active inner parts of Glinka, Chopin, and Liszt. Linear counterpoint, harmonically extended to include a free use of dissonance that often results from the interaction of chromatic contrapuntal lines, was frequently used by late- and post-Romantic composers. The use of a stark and open linear counterpoint (e.g., after 1904, Strauss, Mahler, d'Indy) marks another dividing line between nineteenth- and twentieth-century musical styles.

EXAMPLE 10–11. Wagner, *Die Meistersinger*, prelude *(1861–62).*

etc.

Sonority. The attitude toward sheer sound in Romantic music is one of the main constants in style that binds the Romantic era together and sets it apart from the Classic and Modern periods. Romantic sonority may be divided into two elements: (1) euphony, the Romantics' concept of "sweet and pleasing sound," and (2) color, the exploitation of instrumental and vocal timbres.

Euphony, for the Romantics, meant the avoidance of the relatively lean and spare sonorities of Classic writing by achieving a greater fullness of sound. This is seen at its extreme in the re-writings of earlier music, like the second piano parts that Grieg added to some of Mozart's sonatas. Even some early Romantic piano music by Weber and Schubert was reworked, mainly by adding octave doublings and fuller chords, to provide richer sonorities. Media that could provide the ultimate in rich, full, euphonious sound—the male chorus, the string quintet or sextet in chamber music, the brass section of the Wagnerian orchestra—reached a peak in Romantic music. The full, lush, rich euphony of Romantic music, whether seen in the multiplicity of eight-foot stops on the organ, the sustaining pedal to create fuller sounds in the piano, or the expansion of middle-register sonorities in the orchestra, is one of the chief strands binding together the Romantic movement in music, from Dussek, Weber, and Schubert through the epi-gones of Romanticism like Rakhmaninov and Dohnányi.

Yet reactions against Romantic euphony arose during the nineteenth century. The astringent sonorities in Beethoven's late sonatas and quartets, so often attributed to the deafness which precluded his hearing how the music sounded, is an early example. Musorgsky's "anti-Romanticism" is shown not only by the sharp and empirical dissonances in his piano writing but also in their frequently percussive treatment, blunted when his piano music is given orchestral garb. The "open" scoring of so many works with orchestra written toward the close of the century, including Saint-Saëns's last two piano concertos, Verdi's *Falstaff*, and Rimsky-Korsakov's *Sadko*, implies a rejection of the full sonorities of Wagner, Franck, Chaikovsky, and Brahms. Not only Debussy, but subsequently Mahler and Strauss, sub-stantially lightened their orchestral textures, and a striking feature of most orchestral music written between 1900 and 1914 is not a reduction of the size of the orchestra but a reversal of the trend to fill as much of the page as possible; an often stark, anti-euphonious, and linear writing, quite typi-cal of Mahler; and a search for more astringent orchestral sounds.

Color, whether on the piano or in orchestral writing, is such an indi-vidual property of each composer, even more so than his harmony, that it is difficult to sort out tendencies. The new resources of instrumental color would have been impossible without the technological improvements in all musical instruments. The principal vehicles for Romantic color were the clarinet, bass clarinet, French and English horns, and harp; the extended string sections with the individual sections often divided to achieve richer sonorities; comparable expansion of the woodwind and brass choirs to ex-tend their colors over a wide range; and the improved piano, particularly the Bösendorfer "Imperial Concert Grand" with its extra octave and non-percussive sound. Between 1800 and 1914 the orchestra nearly trebled in size, not for the purpose of expanding its volume but for enhancing sonor-ity: more winds to achieve homogeneous tone colors on a given chord, more strings to balance the number of winds, more percussion instruments for new colors or increasingly dramatic climaxes.

Perhaps the most succinct contrast, in terms of color, between Clas-sic and Romantic can be summed up as follows: few critics would attempt to differentiate, in performance style, between Haydn and Mozart, yet each performer must adapt his style not just from Classic to Romantic mu-sic but among each Romantic composer; the oboist, for example, must make subtle differences in his tone for Beethoven, Weber, Berlioz, Schu-mann, Wagner, Brahms, Chaikovsky, Saint-Saëns, Mahler, and Delius. During the period of overlap between Romantic and Modern music, the problem is characterized by the great variety of styles needed to play the music of each of the current composers between 1890 and 1914—even for the cymbal player!

Vocal timbres underwent equally far-reaching changes. Although the bulk of nineteenth-century operas were written with certain singers in mind, the operatic repertoire became increasingly varied and internationalized with a literally world-wide audience by 1914. Tenors, in particular, became increasingly specialized: one need but cite the light, agile tenor of *opera buffa* or *opéra comique;* the soulful light tenor of French *opéra lyrique;* the powerful dramatic tenor, with elements of the forced-up baritone, in Verdi's operas; the Wagnerian *Heldentenor* with his problems of sheer endurance; the sobbing tenor of Italian *verismo* opera; the smooth, sentimental, and even oily tenor of Russian opera. Mezzo-sopranos, contraltos, baritones, and basses were given increasing prominence on the operatic stage. The proliferation of opera houses and the immense quantitative expansion of oratorio and the art-song written for professional singers permitted this increased specialization.

THE CONTINUITY OF ROMANTICISM IN MUSIC

Some writers have attacked the idea that Romanticism was a continuing phenomenon during the nineteenth century. Among their concepts are Romanticism as an essentially Germanic phenomenon running through Wagner or, at the latest, Brahms, with the French version terminating in the middle of Berlioz's career; Italian opera or the various Neoclassicisms as anti-Romantic movements; or musical Romanticism as short-lived as its literary or pictorial counterparts. Yet eight elements provide the same continuity in Romanticism from its eighteenth-century beginnings to its twentieth-century dissolution that the recitative, thoroughbass, and *concertato* styles provide for Baroque music.

1. *Tonality*. Increasingly bent, masked, and blurred in the course of the century, it nevertheless constitutes the most vital motive and architectonic force of Romantic music. The basic element is a system of tonal hierarchy, considerably widened over that of the High Baroque and Classic periods, yet still rooted in tonic-dominant relationships that are at least implied.

2. *Tertian harmony*. Though more coloristically and less functionally treated in the course of the century, with more blurring through nonharmonic tones, it remains the essential harmonic fabric.

3. *Sonority*. With its emphasis on euphony and color, it avoids the spareness of Classicism and the astringency of Modern music.

4. *Music as a vehicle for personal and individual communication*. This applies to composer and performer alike. The audience might be the "happy few" that understood Beethoven's late quartets or as much a mass

audience as possible—whether reached for idealistic purposes (Berlioz, Wagner) or for commercial reasons (Meyerbeer, Puccini, touring virtuosi)—but musical esotericism *per se* was absolutely contrary to the Romantic temperament. Yet the communication was that of an individual who is purveying himself rather than a product.

5. *Rhythmic predictability.* This is a norm from which deviations can be expected. When complication and unpredictability are normative elements in themselves, the music ceases to be Romantic.

6. *Euphonious treatment of musical instruments and voices.* The growing technological improvements and the progressive escalation of orchestral technique had as a principal aim the enhancement of euphonious sonority. Percussive writing for piano or strings, extension of the extreme range of the instrument for strange rather than euphonious colors, and unusual combinations of instruments in chamber-music works to achieve astringent sounds are all counter to Romantic concepts of euphony, though a main basis of these effects (and especially affecting vocal timbres) lies in the Naturalistic side of Romanticism.

7. *Reliance by composers on Romantic literature* (including the works of Shakespeare, the author most esteemed by Romantics) as a stimulus for opera, song, or program music. The rejection of Romantic literature between 1890 and 1914 by many composers provides a break in the musical continuity; it is a topic deserving further exploration but can only be mentioned here.

8. *Acceptance of the legacy of musical form from the Classic period,* a topic so extensive that it must be considered separately in the next chapter.

BIBLIOGRAPHICAL NOTES

See bibliographical notes in Chapters 1 and 11.

In the recent general histories of music, the best treatments of the nineteenth century are in Donald J. Grout, *A History of Western Music* (3rd ed., New York, 1980), and Gerald Abraham, *The Tradition of Western Music* (Berkeley, 1974); older surveys providing valuable perspectives include Albert Smijers (ed.), *Algemeene Musiekgeschiedenis* (Amsterdam, 1940), Karl H. Wörner, *History of Music* (English trans., 1973), Jules Combarieu, *Histoire de la musique* (3 vols., Paris, 1913–19), and the nineteenth-century sections in Guido Adler, *Handbuch der Musikgeschichte* (1924; reprint, 2 vols., Tutzing, 1961).

Of the books devoted specifically to nineteenth-century music, Carl Dahlhaus's *Die Musik des 19. Jahrhunderts* (Wiesbaden, 1980; English translation in preparation) is a philosophical, intellectual, and conceptual approach to the music of the century; it is of greatest value to those intimately familiar with the century and its music. Dahlhaus's approach will be better appreciated after first reading his *Foundations of Music History* (2d ed., 1982; Eng. trans. Cambridge, Eng., 1983). The precursor volume to Dahlhaus's study is Ernst Bücken's still valuable *Die Musik des XIX. Jahrhunderts bis zur Moderne* (Potsdam, 1932), which follows a chronological approach. Dahlhaus has covered smaller segments of the century in two shorter studies, both thought-provoking: *Realism in Nineteenth-Century Music* (1982; Eng. trans. Cambridge, Eng., 1985) and *Between Romanticism and Modernism* (1974; Eng. trans. Berkeley, 1980).

Gerald Abraham's *A Hundred Years of Music* (3d ed., Chicago, 1964) has been partially supplanted by two volumes of the *New Oxford History of Music: The Age of Beethoven, 1790–1830* (Vol. 8, London, 1982), edited by Abraham, and Martin Cooper (ed.), *The Modern Age, 1890–1960* (London, 1974); a volume covering the years 1830–90 has not been published as of this writing.

Fine Italian perspectives are given in the series *Storia della Musica*, of which the pertinent volumes are Giorgio Pestelli, *L'età di Mozart e di Beethoven* (Turin, 1979), of which an English translation is in preparation; Renato di Benedetto, *L'Ottocento I* (Turin, 1982), covering the nineteenth century east of the Rhine and north of the Alps; and Claudio Casini, *L'Ottocento II* (Turin, 1983), which emphasizes music in France and Italy. A Marxist view of the period, limited to western and central Europe, is Georg Knepler's *Musikgeschichte des XIX. Jahrhunderts* (2 vols., Berlin, 1960–61). Of the textbook-type surveys, Leon Plantinga's *Romantic Music* (New York, 1984, with anthology) is superior to Kenneth Klaus's *The Romantic Period in Music* (Boston, 1970); both are organized chronologically by genres. Still worth reading, though more catalogue than history in its final chapters, is Hugo Riemann's *Geschichte der Musik seit Beethoven* (Berlin, 1901).

The German series *19. Jahrhundert*, with a large number of volumes of monographs, gives detailed coverage of several topics of nineteenth-century music, including several that are beyond the scope of this book such as musical journalism, aesthetics, and historiography. A counterpart series having the same title, containing much unpublished or hitherto unobtainable music, has been begun by Bärenreiter-Verlag in Germany. The *Norton Critical Scores*, a series of individual works from the standard repertory, include not only the score of the composition but also analyses and essays on the work by various writers. The journal *Nineteenth-Century Music* (1977–   ) contains a wide variety of essays on the music of this period.

One can spend fascinating hours in examining the musical periodicals of the nineteenth century. Space does not permit a complete listing of these, but those most significant for the reader are the *Allegemeine musikalische Zeitung* (begun in 1798), *The Harmonicon* (1823), *Berliner allgemeine musikalische Zeitung* (1824), *Cäcilia* (1824), *La Révue musicale* (1827), *Le Ménestrel* (Paris,

1833), *Neue Zeitschrift für Musik* (1834), *The Musical Times* (1844), *Dwight's Journal of Music* (1852), *La Guide musicale* (1855), *Signale für die musikalische Welt* (1843), *The Musical Standard* (1862), *The Monthly Musical Record* (1871), *Proceedings of the Royal Musical Association* (1874), *The Étude* (1883), and *Music* (1891). The periodicals of the time that were addressed to the general educated reader contain numerous articles on music: examples are the *Illustrated London News, Revue des deux mondes,* and *Deutsche Rundschau.* Nineteenth-century newspapers include contemporaneous musical criticism, reports of performances, and necrologies of composers.

Among the histories of musical style traits, those with significant sections on the nineteenth century are Bence Szabolcsi's *A History of Melody* (English translation, New York, 1965); Curt Sachs's *Rhythm and Tempo* (New York, 1953); Maury Yeston, *The Stratification of Musical Rhythm* (New Haven, 1976); Ernst Kurth, *Romantische Harmonie und ihre Krise in Wagners Tristan* (1920; reprint, Tutzing, 1968), which should be read in light of Patrick McCreless's "Ernst Kurth and the Analysis of the Chromatic Music of the Late Nineteenth Century," *Music Theory Spectrum,* V (1983), 56–75; and Graham George, *Tonality and Musical Structure* (New York, 1970). More detailed but still general studies of value include Lawrence Kramer, "The Mirror of Tonality," *Nineteenth-Century Music,* IV (1981), 191–208, and Robert P. Morgan's "Dissonant Prolongations," *Journal of Music Theory,* XX (1976), 49–92, and "Secret Languages: The Roots of Musical Modernism," *Critical Inquiry,* X (1984), 442–51. An updated revision of Adam Carse's *History of Orchestration* (1925; reprint, New York, 1964) would be welcome.

Analyses of nineteenth-century music according to the precepts of the Austrian theorist Heinrich Schenker (1868–1935) are listed in the comprehensive review article by David Beach, "The Current State of Schenkerian Research," *Acta Musicologica,* LVII (1985), 275–307. Some different approaches which embrace music of the nineteenth century can be found in Fred Lehrdahl and Ray Jackendoff, *A Generative Theory of Tonal Music* (Cambridge, Mass., 1983), influenced by linguistic theories of music; David Epstein's *Beyond Orpheus* (Cambridge, Mass., 1979); Eugene Narmour, *Beyond Schenkerism* (Chicago, 1977); and, from a semiological viewpoint, Janet Levy, "Texture as a Sign in Classic and Early Romantic Music," *Journal of the American Musicological Society,* XXXV (1982), 482–531.

Analyses of many specific pieces can be found in theory journals, of which the more recent ones include *In Theory Only* (1975–); *Music Analysis* (1981–), a British journal; and *Music Theory Spectrum* (1979–). Highly valuable, but more condensed, studies of individual style traits can be found in the standard musical encyclopedias and dictionaries, especially *The New Grove Dictionary of Music and Musicians* (London, 1980), *Die Musik in Geschichte und Gegenwart* (Kassel, 1949–79), and *The New Harvard Dictionary of Music* (Cambridge, Mass., 1986).

ELEVEN

FORM IN ROMANTIC MUSIC

Discussions of the elements of musical style—melody, rhythm, harmony, tonality, sonority—converge in the study of musical forms.

No new instrumental forms *per se* were created during the Romantic period: even the double-function one-movement form of Liszt represents a synthesis of elements of sonata form with the three- or four-movement instrumental cycle. The only new instrumental genre of the nineteenth century, the symphonic poem (or tone poem), was based on pre-existent musical forms but sometimes followed a literary narrative. The musical structures of the Classic period—sonata form,[1] the various kinds of rondos, binary and ternary forms, the symphony, concerto, overture, and chamber-music work—are the principal legacy of the eighteenth century to

---

[1]Throughout this volume I have used the term "sonata form" since the old terms "sonata-allegro" or "first-movement" form described poorly a large number of musical structures that are neither in fast tempo nor initial movements.

the Romantics. In vocal music the change from Classic to Romantic is more striking: the new vehicles are the German Lied and its offshoot, the French *mélodie*, with the through-composed opera gradually replacing the Classic "number" opera with its self-contained set-numbers separated by recitative or spoken dialogue.

ROMANTIC INSTRUMENTAL FORMS

The expansion of instrumental forms continued from the Classic throughout the Romantic period; one can trace a direct line of expansion from the operatic overtures of Alessandro Scarlatti (1660–1725), the principal "proto-Classic" composer, to the symphonies of Mahler. Beethoven must be credited with bringing the large instrumental forms to their peak (see the conclusion of Chapter 2), and his influence dominated virtually all instrumental composition until the early years of the twentieth century.

Instrumental Cycles. Whether these be symphonies, sonatas, concertos, or chamber works, they are the principal vehicles in the instrumental sphere for the major musical statement during the Romantic period, as well as the best vantage points for viewing the change from Classic to Romantic or the turn from late- to post-Romanticism.

The instrumental cycle, and to a lesser extent the Italianate "number" opera, during the High Classic period represents a peak of equilibrium, whether regarded as a whole or in their individual movements, between form and content; this is the real reason why the word "Classic" is applied to these works of Haydn's and Mozart's maturity. Only once before in the history of music had a comparable equilibrium been attained, in the High Renaissance mass and motet from Josquin to Palestrina.

This High Classic equilibrium implied at one end of the scale a certain invisible "floor" which maintained a certain minimum level of competence and interest, but also an equally palpable yet invisible "ceiling" at which Mozart particularly chafed, a ceiling which restricted the amount of individual expression and the extent of the emotions which could be represented, especially the heroic, the colossal, the tragic, and the pathetic. Within these limits an enormous amount of music could be and was written, as attested by the existence of at least ten thousand orchestral symphonies from the Classic period. It is the absence of this sense of equilibrium, balance, and control that makes the music of C. P. E. Bach, interesting as it is in individual details or innovations, seem somehow flawed; it is the presence of this equilibrium that permitted an immense amount of instrumental cycles to be created, almost as if by formula, all of which meet a certain minimum standard. That this equilibrium is evident though intangible and not susceptible to quantitative measurement in detail can be seen in various attacks on the High Classic style by those who *dislike* this music: the music, they say, lacks the strikingly obvious characteristics, signatures, and "fingerprints" of the individual composer; Classic composers produced their instrumental cycles not in individual births but in litters of six as if they were puppies or kittens; the Classic composer regarded his work not as an achievement of his inner spirit but as a *product*, as if it were a piece of furniture; or "all Classic music sounds alike."

Many composers strained against the limitations of the Classic equilibrium between 1780 and 1800. Mozart's struggles against the upper boundaries of these limitations resulted in some of his greatest achievements, and not only the young Beethoven, but also his contemporaries or even predecessors like Clementi, Dussek, Koželuch, and Viotti, pushed against the Classic equilibrium, with Spohr, Weber, Kuhlau, and Schubert working in parallel paths. By 1820 at the latest the Classic equilibrium had been irretrievably shattered, with the composer now freer to communicate his individuality to his audience and to express a wider range of emotion. Yet while freeing himself from the limitations that the Classic equilibrium had imposed, he in turn forfeited its support by destroying the grooves in which his musical imagination could coast, as it were, with a minimum of personal involvement. The Romantic composer was free to build a musical edifice which would soar into the clouds, but this edifice could also fall with a resounding crash. The principal structures most prone to soaring or toppling were the instrumental cycle, the opera, and the extended choral work, and these problems are all evident in Beethoven's *oeuvre*.

Virtually every nineteenth-century treatment of the instrumental cycle appears in Beethoven's works: (1) the cyclic idea, with recapitulation of themes from preceding movements; (2) contraction of the cycle to as few as two movements or expansion to as many as six real movements; (3) the performance of the cycle without pauses between movements; (4) drastic contraction or great expansion of individual movements, especially those in sonata form; (5) programs, whether expressly stated or internally implied, for the cycle; and (6) expansion of the overture to the level of a self-sustaining instrumental composition, emancipating it from its operatic or dramatic origins: a direct stage in the evolution of the symphonic poem. Precedents for almost all these devices can be found in the music of our "proto-Romantic," C. P. E. Bach, but it was Beethoven who decisively imposed them on the nineteenth century.

First Movements. *Slow introductions* frequently occur during the High Classic period, especially in Haydn's later symphonies, with Koželuch expanding his introductions to the dimensions of a short slow movement, and with both Haydn and Clementi using their introductions to state motivic material later to be heard as an integral part of the first movement proper. These practices were continued throughout the Romantic period, with an opposite tendency to reduce a slow introduction to merely a gesture of a few measures, as in Chopin's B♭ minor piano sonata. Occasionally (first movement of Schubert's "Trout" Quintet, Dvořák's *In Nature's Realm*) the introduction is a sort of "prelude" in the same tempo as the first theme which later appears. Yet whereas Classic composers opened their introductions with clear-cut statements of the tonic, many Romantic works, beginning with Beethoven's String Quartet, Op. 59, No. 3, have introductions with non-tonic beginnings, their main purpose being the preparation of the dominant so that the tonic's appearance will be a major event. Extensive introductions to variation sets or to large-scale piano works are Romantic developments. Even a few operatic preludes (Verdi's *Rigoletto* and Wagner's *Das Rheingold* and *Siegfried*, for example) resemble sonata-movement introductions rather than self-contained independent operatic overtures. Slow introductions for finales also appear in the Classic period and continue in the nineteenth century.

The first movement proper, as in the Classic period, is overwhelmingly fast in tempo and is in sonata form. Two kinds of sonata form had been prevalent in the Classic period: the kind exemplified by Mozart, with the form clear-cut, the themes phrase-dominated, and the different theme-groups[2] and sections clearly demarcated; and the kind favored by Haydn, with the form a vehicle for experimentation and surprise, based on motivic expansion and contrast. Two distinct theme-groups, usually separated by a clear articulation or even a pause, and an arietta-like closing group are typical of Mozart's expositions; in the movement as a whole, all sections are very clearly perceivable, with a generally short development, sometimes incorporating entirely new musical material, separating exposition from recapitulation. In contrast, Haydn's themes are usually highly motivic, the second theme-group is often more distinguishable by tonal shift rather than by thematic contrast as with Mozart, and a folk-like closing theme is strongly emphasized; the developments are longer and more intricate than Mozart's, and a sometimes truncated recapitulation is likely to contain several surprises.

Beethoven's sonata-form movements, which served as models for the entire nineteenth century and for much of the twentieth century as well, represent a certain coalescence between these two kinds, with consid-

---

[2]"Theme-group," rather than "theme," is the proper term, since often two or more separate themes occur. "Subject," the British term, is most applicable to the fugue and causes confusion in describing forms that are reconciliations of sonata form and fugal textures. Theme-groups are identified by position (first, second) and function (closing); the terms "principal" and "subordinate" to identify theme-groups apply to some but hardly to all sonata-form movements, and the usefulness of these terms collapses completely when one must speak of recapitulations that consist entirely of "subordinate" themes!

erable extremes in approach: the first movement of the B♭ major Piano Sonata, Op. 22, as clear-cut as any sonata-form movement by Mozart, that of
the Seventh Symphony as monothematic as any work by Haydn; that of the
E♭ major String Quartet, Op. 74, extremely motivic and athematic; that of
the A major Piano Sonata, Op. 101, a seamless structure without articulations between theme-groups or even sections; that of the E♭ major Piano
Sonata, Op. 31, No. 3, with an opening on supertonic rather than tonic
harmony. The keys of the second theme-groups in major can be in the
dominant or at extreme ends of the circle of fifths: the major submediant
("Archduke" Trio) or mediant ("Waldstein" Piano Sonata), or the flat submediant (B♭ major String Quartet, Op. 130), with the flat mediant reserved
for minor-mode works. Even when the second theme-group begins in the
expected dominant, there are frequently extended tonal digressions, usually in a related flat mediant or submediant, as early as the first movement
of the D major (Op. 12, No. 1) Violin Sonata. Sometimes the second
theme-group will quirkily begin in the wrong mode (A major Piano Sonata,
Op. 2, No. 2) or key (outer movements of the Eighth Symphony) and then
get into the "correct" mode or tonality. In terms of length, Beethoven's
sonata-form movements range between extremes of compression (F minor
String Quartet, Op. 95) and expansion ("Eroica" and Ninth Symphonies,
"Hammerklavier" Piano Sonata). The areas of expansion, with parallels and
even anticipations in sonata-form movements by Clementi and Dussek, are
the transitions between the first and second theme-groups, the development sections, and the codas. Figure 11–1 is an illustration of the normative sonata-form movement current in the nineteenth century.

The breakdown of the Classic equilibrium in the sonata-form movement was anticipated in the works of C. P. E. Bach and his successors.
The Romantic sonata form showed several lines of development: (1) the "academic" kind, which followed Mozart's example and resulted in a near-
"textbook" sonata form; (2) the kind containing extremes of contrast between the theme-groups, sometimes expressed as a "masculine" first theme
and a "feminine" second theme, providing a problem of reconciling oppo-
sites; (3) the opposite of (2), in which a lack of differentiation between the
theme-groups is perceivable, seen either in highly lyrical late-Romantic
compositions where all the themes "must sing," or in late- and post-Romantic sonata-form movements where the composer tried to use as few motives
as possible or even, following Haydn's example, tried to make one thematic
idea serve a variety of functions. Tonally, in addition to the two-key exposition there arose a "three-key exposition" in which the second and closing
groups are each in different keys from the first theme in the exposition.
Originally a minor-mode phenomenon (the second theme in the major mediant or submediant and the closing theme in the minor dominant) in some
keyboard sonatas of Jiří Benda, Clementi, and Dussek, Schubert trans-

FIGURE 11–1. Normative Sonata-Form Movement in the Nineteenth Century

SECTION	FUNCTION	KEY-CENTER
Introduction (optional)	Prepares first appearance of tonic	May fluctuate widely; usually enhances the dominant
Exposition	Statement of thematic material	Tonic, then modulation to related key
First theme-group	First group of themes or motives	Tonic
Transition	Modulation from tonic to related key	Modulatory
Second theme-group	May be very different from first theme-group or, in contrast, may be motivically related to it	Normally V in major, III in minor. May be in major-mode work III, VI, vi, iii, ♭VI, ♭III. At end of century may be in a distant key
Closing group	Concludes exposition	Usually in same key as 2d group but may be in different key (three-key exposition) or mode
Development	"Working-over" of some or all of the previously stated themes or motives; sometimes new themes	Tonally fluctuating; in longer developments a series of tonal plateaux sometimes related
Retransition	Return to tonic	Usually the dominant
Recapitulation	Restatement of thematic material	Tonic, expanded
First theme-group	As in exposition; may be abbreviated	Tonic
Transition	Balances comparable section in exposition; may be curtailed	Starts and ends in tonic, often with excursion to IV
Second theme-group	As in exposition	Tonic
Closing group	As in exposition	Tonic
Coda (optional)	Sometimes a "second development"; summary of and culmination of the movement or (in finales) of the entire cycle	Tonic, often with excursions to other keys

ferred this structure to the major mode and varied the keys in which the theme-groups could appear.[3] Development sections were the greatest problem for many composers because lyrical or folk-like themes were un-amenable to contrapuntal treatments and could only be repeated sequentially or artificially fragmented. The development sections of the outer movements of Dvořák's "New World" Symphony show nearly all the developmental problems of the Romantic sonata form.

The expansion of tonality provided the main structural anchors for the enlarged sonata-form movement, and it is the strong feeling of tonal directionality that provides the greatest element of success for such large-scale movements. In their individual ways, the major sonata-form movements of the century, from Clementi and Beethoven to d'Indy and Mahler, represent as much a triumph of structural engineering as do their contemporaneous counterparts in the Crystal Palace or the transcontinental railroads. Yet within this expanding tonality lurked the seeds of danger; themes which in themselves lacked a clear tonal definition, and were repetitiously treated in sequences or were separated by stretches of pervasive tonal flux, weakened the architectonic nature of sonata form itself. One may legitimately entertain the complaints about many post-Romantic sonata-form movements that they were "all development," with unclearly defined themes embedded in a slithering mass of modulation.

Some of the more interesting developments in sonata form occur in the recapitulations. Among the variants of the traditional recapitulations are: (1) omission of part or even all of the first theme-group, especially when motives from this group are extensively treated in the development (Chopin, Brahms); (2) symphonic recapitulations in which the themes are presented in entirely new guises through changes in orchestration and dynamics (Dvořák); (3) expressive countermelodies to the first theme (Mendelssohn); (4) "bonus" recapitulations in which new material is inserted (Beethoven); (5) substitution of new thematic materials for motives in the exposition, seen as early as the first movement of Rutini's sonata, Op. 3, No. 5, around 1755; these new materials may come from the development (Schumann's Fourth Symphony, first movement) or from the introduction (Glazunov's Fourth Symphony, first movement), from another movement altogether (Franck, D minor Symphony, last movement, where the second theme is replaced by the main theme of the slow movement), or completely new material (Mahler, First Symphony, first movement).

Tonal compensations in recapitulations for unusual features in the exposition range from restating everything in the tonic to repeating the un-

---

[3]This phenomenon should not be confused with the appearance of the transition in a different key, as in Beethoven's D major (Op. 10, No. 3) Piano Sonata, where the transition begins in B minor and works toward the expected A major in which the second and closing groups appear.

usual tonal relationships but a fourth higher, as when in Brahms's Piano Quintet the C# minor of the second theme's exposition is balanced temporarily in the recapitulation by F# minor. Quite often thematic and tonal recapitulations do not coincide: in some late-Romantic works (e.g., the first movement of Chaikovsky's Fourth Symphony) the first theme is recapitulated in the "wrong" key (here A minor in a work in F minor), with the "proper" key of F major not attained until the second half of the second theme-group.

The coda, from Beethoven onward, often was the climactic summary of the movement itself. Although extensive codas are not too frequent in the Classic period (the outer movements of Haydn's Symphony No. 44 or of Mozart's large works in C major are among the few Classic examples), they assume major importance in the Romantic period. Lesser composers found the applause-catching cabalettas and strettos from the Rossinian opera, with cumulatively faster tempos, effective in symphonic music, especially in overtures.

Throughout the century, sonata form became increasingly ambiguous. Problems of definition arise when one tries to use the terminology of Viennese Classic sonata form to describe events in the first movements of late- or post-Romantic instrumental cycles. Tonal directionality was weakened when a wider variety of keys, in which major and minor were interpenetrating and the character with which these modes is associated was vitiated, were substituted for the traditional dominant-tonic relationships in major or mediant-tonic relationships in minor. Though one can admire the tonally structural ingenuity practiced by many late-Romantic composers, one wonders whether many listeners in the audience could perceive aurally these large-scale tonal relationships.

Perhaps we should consider the basic principles of form at the end of the century simply in terms of areas of tonal stability and instability: stability in the theme-groups and instability in the transitional and development sections, with the tonal anchors in the stable sections becoming increasingly weak and less aurally discernible as the nineteenth century passed into the twentieth.

Slow movements in Classic music are of three basic kinds: (1) the aria-like movement, typical of Mozart, often an abridged sonata-form without a development; (2) the hymn-like slow movement, often an expanded ternary form or some kind of successive variation principle, typical of Haydn; (3) the romanza-like movement, often folk-like in character (see Example 10–1b), sometimes the locus of a set of variations, used by both composers.

Among the Romantics, Beethoven preferred the aria and especially the hymn, with his contemporaries often using the romanza-type movement. Schubert developed a slow movement analogous to the art-song, either ternary in form or a set of variations. The late Romantics exaggerated all these tendencies: Bruckner the hymn, Chaikovsky the aria and romanza, Brahms and Mahler the song. Toward the end of the century the slow movement was sometimes "telescoped" with a scherzo-type movement, as early as Berwald's *Sinfonie singulière* and seen at its best in Brahms's F major viola quintet and A major violin sonata.

Slow movements were sometimes in hybrid form: just as that of Haydn's Symphony No. 102 can be analyzed as a sonata-form with repeated exposition or as theme and variations, or that of Beethoven's Seventh Symphony as rondo or as theme and variations, so can the slow movements of Bruckner's last three symphonies be perceived either as Bar-form (AAB), with each section containing two strophes, or as sonata-form movements with the second A analogous to a development section.

By 1800 *scherzo-* or *intermezzo-type movements* replaced the minuet as the normative third movement of the instrumental cycle (see Example 10–5); when the minuet was used in the nineteenth century, it was generally as a nostalgic retrospection toward the bygone Classic era (Schubert, Mendelssohn, Brahms).

A bumptious scherzo in a very fast tempo, with one beat to the measure, was often necessary relief to the deep emotional profundity of the slow movement, and a line of development of such scherzos extends from Beethoven and late Schubert through Bruckner. A wide variety of scherzos developed during the nineteenth century, many quite extensive in length with two trios and a coda. Among the different kinds are the elfin (Mendelssohn), the daemonic (Chopin), the stylized national dance (Dvořák), the mysteriously ghostly (Brahms), and the distorted and sardonic (Liszt, Mahler). Some composers even reverted to the early Classic three-movement form by occasionally "telescoping" the scherzo with the slow movement, as mentioned above.

A directly contrasting tendency to the fast scherzo is the slowing down of the third movement to create an intermezzo-type movement, sometimes a reflective romanza (Mendelssohn, Brahms, Dvořák). A wider variety of meters than in the Classic era was used for both scherzo and intermezzo: 2/4, 2/2, 6/8, or even an occasional quintuple meter (Rimsky-Korsakov, Third Symphony; Chaikovsky, *Pathétique* Symphony) replacing the traditional 3/4 of the minuet or early scherzo.

In the Classic period, the minuet and outer movements were in the same key and usually the same mode. A minor-mode scherzo in a major-mode work is a typically early Romantic touch (Beethoven, Op. 69 cello sonata and Op. 74 string quartet; Weber), but as the century advanced the scherzo-type movement would often be in a key other than that of the outer movements—one contribution that led to both the enlargement and the weakening of tonality as a large-scale structural element.

Final Movements. The prevalent kinds of final movement in the Classic era, after the minuet had ceased to be the last movement, were usually of rondo character, often made more serious and complex as sonata-rondos in which the middle section was a true development, or sonata-form movements. Particularly intense finales were those incorporating fugal techniques or those in the minor mode. One senses in the finales of the High Classic instrumental cycle a feeling of balance and equilibrium which is disturbed by the developments in the finale during the nineteenth century.

Nearly every kind of Romantic finale—sets of variations, Hungarian-gypsy finales with some tonal ambiguity between tonic minor and a major mediant or submediant tonality, rondos, triumphant apotheoses, finales with "flashbacks" to earlier movements—occurs in Beethoven's instrumental cycles. Beethoven also firmly established the principal idea of the Romantic finale—that it be a conclusion on a note of triumph, thus reflecting the concept of Romantic optimism.

This is most clearly seen in finales in the major mode as conclusions to instrumental cycles in which the first movement is in minor. Some aestheticians, usually basing their conclusions on the most blatant example (Beethoven's Fifth Symphony), have concluded that such a finale represents the triumphant resolution or overcoming of a conflict that has been depicted in the minor-mode first movement. Most of the finales of instrumental cycles that begin in minor are in the major mode; even when the minor mode is used for the final movement, there is usually a triumphant coda in major (e.g., Mendelssohn's "Scottish" Symphony, Bruckner's Third Symphony), or at least an extended "tierce de Picardie" that provides the finale with prolonged tonic major harmony for its conclusion (e.g., Beethoven's String Quartet, Op. 131 and Dvořák's Seventh Symphony). The reverse process, a finale in minor for an instrumental cycle in the major mode (e.g., Brahms's Third Symphony, Bruckner's Sixth Symphony) almost invariably contains a coda or at least an extended close in major. Finales that are unmistakably in minor from beginning to end are usually in chamber music works (e.g., Schubert's "Death and the Maiden" Quartet, Brahms's Piano Quintet) or in compositions in which some kind of underlying pessimistic programs can be sensed (e.g., Chopin's B♭ minor Sonata, Chaikovsky's Sixth Symphony).

The idea of the triumphant finale led many composers to strive to make this movement the grand culmination of the instrumental cycle. The models for this idea were the finale of Mozart's "Jupiter" Symphony with its fugal coda and triumphant conclusion, and the last movements of Beethoven's Third, Fifth, Seventh, and Ninth Symphonies, "Hammerklavier" Sonata, and the original version of his B♭ String Quartet, Op. 130, which ended with the "Grosse Fuge." Although Beethoven's contemporaries and immediate successors shrank from this monumental kind of finale, the idea of the triumphant conclusion on the grand scale was revived by composers of the second half of the century. Liszt's apotheoses, Bruckner's chorales, and Mahler's choral endings are striking examples of these grand conclusions. Themes from previous movements, whether "flashbacks" to set the scene for the finale proper or as part of a rounded cyclic relationship (Brahms), intensified the summarizing quality of the finale. Extensive fugal sections in the finale contributed to its air of high seriousness. The last movement of d'Indy's Second Symphony almost epitomizes the triumphant, summarizing late Romantic finale: a slow introduction with reminiscences of themes from earlier movements, a massive fugue (see Example 9–10e), an animated sonata-form movement, and a triumphant chorale (see Example 9–10f).

The coda to many finales is a special case that shows in microcosm the contradictions in Romantic music. In the later symphonies of Mendelssohn and Schumann one often gets the impression that the codas of the last movements are not just conclusions of the finales, but of the symphony as a whole. Similarly, the coda to the last movement of Brahms's Third Symphony is a quiet epilogue to the entire work, a feature that was later expanded to movement length (e.g., the sixth movement of Mahler's Third Symphony).

A contrary type of Romantic finale is seen in some of the concluding movements by composers of the first half of the nineteenth century who seemed to deliberately avoid the triumphal or monumental finale by writing a gay, light-hearted, and unpretentious movement: Dussek and Schubert are the principal composers of such finales, and the last movement of Schumann's First Symphony is one of the best later examples. Analogous to the lighter kind of finale are the Hungarian-gypsy finales, often in rondo or even sonata-rondo form, that were occasionally written by Haydn and Beethoven but reached their peak with Schubert and Brahms. Sonata-rondo movements, with the form expanded to include closing themes and thus to become more like sonatas than rondos, were continued by Beethoven: particularly good and quite different examples are the finales of the C minor (Op. 30, No. 2) Violin Sonata and E minor (Op. 90) Piano Sonata, the former dramatic and the latter lyrical. One of the lightest types of rondo finale is the "perpetual motion" type which concludes a concerto or sonata and, like the finale of Weber's C major Piano Sonata, was often performed separately as a display piece.

Yet the successful finale was the principal problem for even the best Romantic composers of instrumental cycles. There are several "unfinished" Romantic cycles that end with slow movements, most notably Beethoven's Piano Sonatas, Op. 109 and Op. 111, Schubert's Eighth Symphony, and Bruckner's Ninth Symphony; note that three of these four works have first movements in the minor mode. Moreover, each of the three principal kinds of finale—the triumphal, the monumental, and the unpretentious—contained major pitfalls for the composer: bombast (Chaikovsky's Fifth Symphony), sprawl (many of Schubert's lengthy finales), or triviality (Dussek's Piano Sonata, Op. 25, No. 2). Finally, one subjectively senses that in a large number of Romantic instrumental cycles the final movements do not seem to be on an equal level with the other movements; it may be that the Romantic attitude of striving for the unattainable is best reflected in the finale of the extended instrumental cycle. Certainly the problem of the finale to the instrumental cycle has remained an equally difficult one for composers of the twentieth century.

Other Instrumental Cycles. The *Concerto,* though a major instrumental cycle, represents in the minds of some critics, past and present, a less lofty medium than the symphony. The synthesis of Baroque concerto and Classic sonata form attained in Mozart's mature concertos was continued by Beethoven, then by Henry Litolff (1818–91) in his "symphonic" piano concertos (Concertos symphoniques), and reached a late Romantic peak in the concertos of Brahms and Dvořák; the post-Romantic climaxes of the genre, the counterpart to Mahler's later symphonies, were Busoni's immense piano concerto (consisting of five movements, with a male chorus in the finale) of 1903–04 and Elgar's Violin Concerto of 1910.

Specifically Romantic developments in the concerto include written-out rather than improvised cadenzas; relocation of the first-movement cadenza from the coda to a place anywhere in the movement but usually as a transition between sections; eliminating the opening orchestral tutti in the first movement; expanding the cyclic fantasia into a full-length concerto; using national dances or folk songs in the finales; and either expanding the concerto to four movements by adding a scherzo-like movement or, at the other extreme, contracting it into a one-movement concerto following a double-function form.

Hybrid concerto types of the first half of the century include the operatic and other fantasies for solo instrument and orchestra that culminated in Liszt's fantasies and variations (such as his *Totentanz*), as well as such late Romantic hybrids as Franck's *Symphonic Variations,* which includes among its sections a theme and variations and a major-mode sonata-form finale, and d'Indy's *Symphony on a French Mountain Air* for orchestra and piano, with an underlying tonal macrostructure, replacement of the second theme of the finale in the recapitulation with the second theme of the second movement, and a folk tune that unifies the entire work in its cyclic transformations. Several programmatic works for orchestra feature an obbligato instrument serving as a "guide" through the narrative (e.g., Berlioz's *Harold in Italy* and Rimsky-Korsakov's *Sheherazade*).

The *concertino,* a short display piece for piano or other solo instrument (even bassoon or trombone), was a staple item of public concerts early in the century; the most familiar examples are the concert pieces and pot-pourris of Weber and Spohr. With the standardization of the concert format to favor concertos rather than concertinos after 1835, and the development of wind instruments leading to the growth of bands, such pieces came to be written for the outdoor band concert and often given pretentious titles (e.g., Herbert L. Clarke's *The Bride of the Waves* [1899] for cornet solo).

Soloist-dominated concertos were usually written by a virtuoso per-former for his own use to appeal to a mass audience. At their worst they consisted of displays of formidable technique and more-or-less naive at-tempts at writing attention-grabbing tunes (much as Meyerbeer, Donizetti, or Flotow were doing in opera); at their best they contributed to the idiom-atic development of writing for the instrument in question, for example Spohr's and Paganini's concertos or Joseph Joachim's Hungarian Concerto for the violin, or the piano concertos of Field, Hummel, Chopin, Liszt, and Rakhmaninov. Many concertos (except for piano concertos) were written for specific performers: the great cello concertos of the nineteenth century, those by Schumann, Lalo, Saint-Saëns, Brahms (the "Double Concerto" with violin), and Dvořák were not written by cellists but *for* cellists. Close consultation between composer and soloist went into such works, as also into the violin concertos of Beethoven, Mendelssohn, and Brahms. The dif-ferentiation between composer and performer that increased in the course of the century can be seen in the scarcity of cadenzas to be improvised by the performer in later Romantic concertos; almost without exception they are written out, usually after extensive discussion between performer and composer. A corollary was the increasing symbiosis between soloist and or-chestra to produce an effect of integration rather than polarity or opposition in many fine concertos.

Divertimento-type cycles, multi-movement forms sometimes called serenades, notturnos, or cassations, were frequently utilized for light music by Classic composers and were seemingly terminated by the early Roman-tics like Schubert, Hummel, and Field. Later in the nineteenth century, usually under the title of "Serenade," this cycle became the equivalent of an unpretentious symphony, often for a limited or unusual combination of instruments, and revealed several composers in their neoclassic phases (Volkmann, Brahms, Chaikovsky, Dvořák, Elgar). *Suites* after the Baroque model were revived as keyboard works as a vehicle for neoclassic or even Neo-Baroque expression (Saint-Saëns, Raff); orchestral suites were usually either musical travelogues or were carpentered out of ballets or instrumen-tal interludes from operas. After 1810 *groups of characteristic piano pieces* appeared as a favorite vehicle of Romantic expression; often the titles of the individual pieces have such vaguely indefinite connotations as Eclogue, Bagatelle, Impromptu, or Capriccio. Some of these groups of pieces, as seen from their succession of contrasting movements and their key-relation-ships, resemble the divertimento (Weber's four-hand piano pieces), are linked through cyclic thematic transformations (Schumann's *Carnaval*), or resemble sonata-type cycles (Brahms's Op. 119 piano pieces), sometimes with extra movements (see Figure 4–1, Schumann's *Kreisleriana*). The di-mensions of the individual pieces range from the extremely short frag-ment,[4] a short, pithy musical aphorism stated without any attempt at de-velopment, continuity, or narrative like those in Schumann's *Papillons* or Fibich's *Souvenirs*), through the finely wrought musical miniature of one or two pages in length, to the substantial piece in a fairly complex rondo or sonata form.

Variation cycles in the Classic period were chiefly individual move-ments, usually slow movements and less often finales, of instrumental cy-cles or they were independent piano compositions. Both were based chiefly on the ornamentation of a familiar melody, usually an operatic air, or an original theme. During the nineteenth century the variation cycle took two directions. One direction was toward a debasement that consisted of tech-nically brilliant piano variations on catchy operatic tunes or "national" airs; these became the stock-in-trade of the touring virtuoso. The other direction was toward an ennoblement of the variation cycle in which the structure and basic harmony of the theme were the "constants" and all the other ele-ments, including the melody itself, were the "variables." Such "character variation" cycles were written as orchestral compositions in the second half of the century (see Figure 7–1). A late- and post-romantic development was the very free variation cycle based on the development or transformation of motives from the theme itself, as in Strauss's *Don Quixote* or Delius's *Appalachia*.

ROMANTIC VOCAL FORMS

Although different kinds of vocal music are usually called genres rather than forms, the problem of musical form is inherent in all music. More innovations took place in the vocal than in the instrumental music of the nineteenth century, for Romantic vocal music had to keep pace in de-veloping a musical language to correspond with the lyrical or dramatic liter-ature of the time. Almost all the innovations in orchestration and many of the new harmonic developments took place first in vocal music rather than

---

[4]The "fragment" was also an important literary device of the Romantics and pre-Romantics; it was used in philosophy, criticism, and literature by Herder, Friedrich Schlegel, Novalis, Kierkegaard, and Machado de Assis, among others.

in the more abstract instrumental forms of the nineteenth century. The major areas of change in vocal music during the period were opera, the art-song, and choral music.

Opera. Points of operatic equilibrium in the Classic period were attained in (1) the monumental tragedies of Gluck; (2) the *dramma giocoso*, wherein serious and comic elements were brought together in a realistic plot that closely parallels the development of the eighteenth-century novel, with Mozart's mature Italianate works like *The Marriage of Figaro* and *Don Giovanni* representing the culmination of this genre; and (3) the lighter operas, whether called *opera buffa, Singspiel, opéra comique*, or ballad opera, all but the first consisting of isolated musical numbers separated by spoken dialogue.

Operatic equilibrium was disturbed even before 1800, chiefly in France and largely (though not exclusively) in the "rescue opera," a genre that reached its peak in Beethoven's *Fidelio*. The main problem of equilibrium was the relationship of the singers to the orchestra, which was increasing in importance. Sometimes composers gave sections of prominence now for the instrumentalists and now for the singers, whether in the grand tableaux of the French opera from Salieri to Berlioz or in the Italianate operas with their ritornelli and interludes as showpieces for the solo instrumentalists and the arias proper, in which the singers were prominent or the soloist and instrumentalists competed on equal terms (Simon Mayr, Paër, Rossini). The role of the orchestra increased in providing a psychological underpinning for the action or in portraying landscapes, storms, forest scenes, and the like. All these developments began around 1790 and proceeded along parallel, though not completely exclusive lines, thanks to the increasing internationalization of opera throughout the century.

The structure of opera in 1800 consisted of isolated set-numbers—arias, duets, larger ensembles—separated by recitatives or spoken dialogue. Closing each act was a highly organized finale held together by strong tonal relationships, often "tonal rondos," and recurrent thematic material. Sometimes operatic introductions were equally highly developed. The arias and ensembles followed a rather stereotyped although flexible four-part structure (not always evident from the inconsistent terminologies with which the set-numbers were entitled by composers, copyists, or publishers) which can be described as follows:

1. Scena (or *tempo d'attacco*): often an accompanied recitative with orchestral introduction and interludes to establish either a mood or a dramatic action: in *opéra comique* this section is in spoken dialogue.

2. Cantabile (called erroneously in some sources "cavatina," a term reserved for entrance arias by a principal character). This section is in a moderate to slow tempo and in symmetrical phrases, with structures that are ei-

ther ternary, ABAB, or ABAC, with an orchestral introduction (often featuring a solo instrument) and interludes. When the aria consists of a cantabile alone, with or without an opening recitative, it is often called "romanza." The B sections tend to be in a third-related tonality or a change of mode from minor to major.

    3. Tempo di mezzo: in a faster tempo, characterized by increased orchestral activity, beneath a more declamatory vocal line in a kind of musical speech *(parlante)*, and often interjections from other characters or the chorus; dramatically it signifies a shift of mood and action away from that of the cantabile.

    4. Cabaletta: usually in a brisk tempo, dramatically often depicting the protagonist's having decided on a course of action, and the location for a display of the singer's vocal prowess and range. A cabaletta can occur by itself if a preceding slow cantabile would have been dramatically inappropriate, as in the Lady's bouncy "Trionfai" in the first version of Verdi's *Macbeth*. The internal structure is generally strophic. Near the end there is often a "stretta," a coda in an even faster tempo.

From a tonal standpoint, the second and fourth of these sections are more stable than the first and third, which tend to have an established key at the beginning (especially for the instrumental introduction that sets the scene) and ending, but to modulate in between. Within a given aria or ensemble, the cantabile and cabaletta are not necessarily in the same key. Cantabile and cabaletta may be in reverse order for dramatic reasons, as in Act III of Verdi's *Rigoletto*, where the protagonist first berates, then beseeches, the hostile courtiers.

    A general structure of this sort had been established before 1800 in the "composite aria," like "Dove sono" in Act IV of Mozart's *The Marriage of Figaro* or the grand aria of Florestan with which the second act of Beethoven's *Fidelio* opens. Though the "composite aria" lasted longer in Germany, as shown in Max's aria in Act I of Weber's *Der Freischütz*, the Italian version by 1820 had been codified, with his own modifications, by Rossini (see Chapter 5), who brought this structure to France.

    Changes in this four-part structure, mostly in the interest of dramatic realism, took place during the course of the century, principally the elimination of the cabaletta by around 1875. Verdi was criticized for including a cabaletta at the end of the love duet in Act III of *Aïda* even though it was dramatically justified.

    The Romantic task was to create greater continuity between the separate vocal sections by binding the various musical set-numbers together. In the first half of the century the *scene complex* became the usual device; in this the scena and the tempo di mezzo took on greater importance and the duets became more important than the solo arias. Recurring motives provided musical coherence and became associated with certain characters,

actions, or states of mind but had not yet become a kind of symphonic texture equivalent to the fragmented themes in a development section. Other
ingredients in the construction of scene-complexes included a change to
choral *parlante* instead of the choral set number; a similar *parlante* rather
than "dry recitative" for the solo voices in the scena and especially in the
tempo di mezzo, where the orchestra would set up a rapid rhythmic-
melodic figure to accompany the vocal *parlante;* the arioso-like *scena vari-
ata,* seen at its best in Verdi's duets for two low male voices like the Spara-
fucile-Rigoletto duet in *Rigoletto* or the King-Inquisitor duet in *Don Carlo;*
and an increased role for the orchestra in providing musical connection and
coherence. The French were more inclined than the Italians or Germans
to create massive scenes in their Grand Operas which were enhanced with
full orchestral resources and elaborate sets.

The number of acts in an opera often had a certain consistency and
rationale. The two-act Italian opera of the early nineteenth century frequently had a ballet staged between the two acts; with the increased emphasis on dramatic realism and consistency after 1840, this gave way to the
opera in three acts (sometimes with a prologue) or four acts, with the ballet
either incorporated into the opera (as late as Ponchielli's *La Gioconda*) or
dropped altogether. Five acts were typical of French Grand Operas, which
included at least one grand ballet; three acts were the norm for the *opéra
comique.* The Germans adhered to a three-act format in both serious and
comic works. At the opening of the century one-act operas were comic (like
the Italian *farsa*) and a good way for a young composer to start his career;
at the end of the century came the grimly serious one-act operas associated
with the *verismo* movement.

The next step in operatic development was the creation of the continuous operatic act. This developed along parallel lines, with some regression, in various operatic media and among various composers after 1850:
Verdi in Italy, Wagner in Swiss exile, Meyerbeer in France, Dargomÿzhsky in Russia, Erkel in Hungary. The pure number opera, though given its
last lease on life in Bizet's *Carmen,* became increasingly relegated to lighter music, especially the operetta in which the spoken dialogue was still retained.

The continuous act provided more dramatic realism and more musical continuity to the opera, yet its rationale seemed to vitiate what many
regarded as the *raison d'être* of opera: the points of dramatic rest where
the emphasis could focus on the star singer. The aria and the set-number
ensemble could not entirely be eliminated because singers and the general
public wanted them retained. A compromise, used even by Wagner, was a
kind of libretto in which the isolated set-piece could still be retained as dramatic monologue, love duet, or the response to an invitation to sing a song.
For the lesser composers, one of the biggest problems became how to fill

in convincingly the musical stretches between one set-piece and the next. The set-pieces of the operas of the 1890's were much freer in structure and owed much less to the pre-existing cantabile or romanza structures established by earlier composers. By the end of the century a traditional cantabile like the tenor-baritone duet in Act IV of Puccini's *La Bohème* would seem old-fashioned. Yet, despite the attempts of composers to connect these high points into a musically coherent whole, nothing could prevent the audience's bursting into applause at the end of a favorite aria or the extraction out of the opera, for independent concert performance, of the more telling numbers, whether orchestral interludes by Wagner or arias by Puccini.

By the end of the century the continuous operatic act was the norm. The musical module at the opening of the century was the set-number, which expanded to the scene-complex and finally to the act itself at the hands of Wagner (see Figure 6–2).

Only a beginning has been made in the study of the general structure of nineteenth-century opera, and that chiefly from the standpoint of tonality. The coherence of an opera largely depends on its dramatic structure, yet purely musical factors may be tangible elements in this coherrence: not just tonality, but points of tension and repose, spacing of climactic arias and ensembles, schemas of instrumentation, and recurrences of previously heard musical material seem to be of nearly equally essential import. Some operas of the time show themselves ingeniously linked internally through tonal organization, sometimes of two or more planes that have been called "interlocking tonalities": for instance, D♭ and to a lesser extent D, in their minor or major form, have been cited as the principal tonalities of Verdi's *Rigoletto*, with E major or minor (the keys of Gilda's "Caro nome" arietta and of her solo portion "Tutte le feste al tempio" in the scene-complex in Act III) as points of intersection. Tonality was a more important factor with German composers, especially Wagner, than with the Italians or French, and given no consideration at all, because of the interruptions caused by the spoken dialogue, in *opéra comique*.

Choral Music. In both Classic and Romantic choral works many Baroque elements, chiefly contrapuntal techniques, survived. Yet whereas the Classic composer retained these elements as conventions, Romantic composers, with their strong sense of historicism, actually intensified them, particularly Protestant composers who were influenced by J. S. Bach's choral music. Haydn's last two oratorios may be regarded as the immediate precursors of the Romantic oratorio, a genre which deserves far more detailed study than it has hitherto received.

The principal features of the oratorio in the nineteenth century are (1) the development of the "continuous" rather than the "number" oratorio of Handel and Haydn, a change that is parallel, if not exactly analogous, to

the move from the "number" to the "continuous-act" opera; (2) settings of
the Catholic Mass and Requiem intended for the concert hall rather than
for the church; and (3) the immense proliferation of choral societies and
music festivals, especially in Protestant countries, that resulted in a steady
demand for oratorios and other large choral works.

A kind of ecumenicalism arose in the choices of texts. Although almost all Protestant composers based their oratorios on texts from the Bible
and Catholic composers generally wrote musically expanded settings of the
liturgy, Protestants and even unbelievers wrote Masses (Spohr, Schumann), and many Catholic composers of oratorio (Gounod, Dvořák, Elgar)
wrote some of their finest works in this genre for the music festivals of Protestant England.

For secular choral music, a number of subgenres exist, such as the
ensemble part-song for soloists that was an important part of domestic music-making during the century (Schubert, Mendelssohn, Schumann,
Brahms, and the English Victorians being main contributors to this repertoire) or the short choral piece for amateur men's, women's, or mixed
choruses. National consciousness in the course of the century evoked many
choral arrangements of folk songs, of which those by Brahms and Rimsky-
Korsakov deserve special mention for artistic merit. The dramatic cantata
or ballad beloved by nineteenth-century choral societies has virtually disappeared from the choral repertoire, perhaps because these works are not
long enough for an entire evening's concert. Mendelssohn's *The First
Walpurgis Night* is the only survivor, but there are many others deserving
revival.

Solo Song.   Three principal kinds of solo song were present in the
nineteenth century. The *Lied*, or German art-song, is one of the few genuinely new forms of the Romantic period; its Classic-era origins and early
history are treated in Chapter 3, along with a discussion of Schubert as the
one who gave the Lied its strongly Romantic cast. In the Lied the piano
and singer are at least theoretically equal partners, with the resources of
harmony and atmospheric effects in the accompaniment used to reinforce
the word-painting or the psychological import of the text. In the course of
the century the vocal part became increasingly declamatory.

A counterpart to the Lied is the French *Romance*. In contrast to the
Lied, the Romance is strongly dominated by tuneful melodies in the voice
with the piano merely providing support. Outside Germany the Romance
was dominant.

Both Lied and Romance contained problems of equilibrium. The
principal dangers faced by the Lied were overemphasis on the vocal melody with the accompaniment restricted to a mere supporting function, or,
on the other hand, overemphasis on the accompaniment to the point of creating a piano piece with words. A further danger, during the second half of

the century, was the creation of a song which would retain the partnership of voice and piano, but would focus so much attention on the music that the poem would seem to be merely a series of syllables to permit vocalization. The Romance's problems were its threat of lapsing into triviality or becoming an operatic aria with piano accompaniment. For the composer, the choice of text was a severe problem, for much poetry in itself is highly "musical" in its use of assonance, alliteration, rhyme, and broken lines, effects which are weakened or lost altogether in musical settings. Some composers, notably Brahms and Richard Strauss, have been accused by critics for often selecting poems of weak literary quality.

The Romance finally attained a musical equilibrium in the French *Mélodie*, a kind of chamber music for voice and piano that emphasized precise vocal declamation of the text with an increased importance of the piano part, chiefly for atmospheric effects. Schubert's songs in French translation, French *opéra lyrique*, and the revival of instrumental music all enriched the romance and led to the development of the *Mélodie*, which flourished in France between 1875 and 1915.

The principal developments of song in the course of the century were (1) the application of the new vistas of harmonic resources to the accompaniments; (2) a concomitant focus on musical declamation, occurring in parallel lines of achievement in the best songs of Musorgsky, Fauré, and Wolf; (3) songs with orchestral accompaniment. A kind of wrong turning took place in settings of ballads: except for a few highly concentrated examples by Schubert and Carl Loewe (1796–1869), the tendency was either to write a sprawling composition of considerable length or to create the equivalent of the operatic *scena ed aria*, until composers felt that the ballad deserved its proper setting in the dramatic cantata or reverted to strophic settings. Settings of folk songs with piano accompaniments were written in virtually every country. On the lighter level, the drawing-room song represents the popular counterpart of the Romance. Such songs, usually strophic, with mild chromatic harmonies accompanying a sentimental text, and published with an illustrative steel engraving, are multi-media presentations, literary, musical, and artistic, of nineteenth-century *kitsch*.

Between 1900 and 1914 the dividing line between the centuries became strongly evident in vocal music as well as in the instrumental sphere. The application of the aesthetic of the *Mélodie* to opera culminated in Debussy's *Pelléas et Mélisande;* the new resources of quartal harmony appear in the early songs of Schoenberg and Berg; the heightening of vocal declamation, coupled with the desire to portray the emotions of the subconscious, led to a kind of speech-song called *Sprechstimme*. One even encounters textless vocal compositions: the vocalise in the realm of solo song, or the textless choruses to create a kind of added tone color as in Ravel's *Daphnis et Chloë*.

SUMMARY

Musical form, whether in instrumental or vocal music, was the chief means of achieving equilibrium and balance during the High Classic period. The Romantics shattered this equilibrium and compelled each composer to find for himself the balance between musical shape and its individual components. The greatest composers, regarding form as a process rather than a mold, restored new vigor to the structures they had inherited from their Classic predecessors, particularly sonata form and the techniques of variation. Vocal music provided the chief areas for musical innovation, especially in the German Lied and the continuous opera, yet the Romantic use of form as a means of achieving musical equilibrium was highly individual rather than collective. Toward the very end of the century, however, one could discern that sonata, symphony, and opera were coming full circle to their origins in the early Baroque: sonata as "soundpiece" for a small group of instruments; symphony, though considerably inflated in length and resources, to a similar meaning; song, in its attention to declamation and expression of details in the text, to the ideals of the early seventeenth-century monodists; and opera, whether in the hands of Richard Strauss, Debussy, or Puccini, to resembling in structure and dramatic rationale Monteverdi's *Orfeo* rather than Mozart's "number" operas.

BIBLIOGRAPHICAL NOTES

See the bibliography for Chapter 10. Histories of various musical forms and genres, whether in English or any other language, vary drastically in both coverage and quality. Donald Grout's *A Short History of Opera* (3d ed., New York, 1987), Adam Carse's *The Orchestra from Beethoven to Berlioz* (New York, 1949), and William S. Newman's *The Sonata in the Classic Era* (3d ed., Chapel Hill, 1983) and *The Sonata Since Beethoven* (3d ed., Chapel Hill, 1983) are by far the best, with detailed bibliographies, intensive coverage of the period, and set models for investigation of all other genres. New interpretations of opera which provide fascinating possibilities for further investigations are Frits Noske, *The Signifier and the Signified* (The Hague, 1977), from a semiotic viewpoint; and Herbert Lindenberger, *Opera: The Extravagant Art* (Ithaca, 1984), from the standpoint of literary theory and social history. Scholarly journals dealing with particular genres include *Opera Journal* (1968–   ); *Opera Quarterly* (1983–   ); the *Jahrbuch für Opernforschung* (1985–   ), with articles in various languages; *Piano Quarterly* (1952–   ); *Clavier* (1962–   ); and *American Choral Review* (1962–   ).

General surveys of various genres with significant portions devoted to the nineteenth century include Homer Ulrich's *Symphonic Music* (New York, 1952) and *Chamber Music* (2d ed., New York, 1966); Robert Simpson's *The Symphony* (Baltimore, 1966, 2 vols.); F. E. Kirby's *A Short History of Keyboard Music* (New York, 1966); Walter Georgii's *Klaviermusik* (3d ed., Zürich, 1966); Fritz Egon Paner's "Das deutsche Lied im 19. Jahrhundert" in Guido Adler (ed.), *Handbuch der Musikgeschichte* (1924; reprint, Tutzing, 1961); Jack M. Stein's *Poetry and Music in the German Lied* (Cambridge, Mass., 1971); Frits Noske's *French Song from Berlioz to Duparc* (English trans., New York, 1970); Donald Ivey's *Song: Anatomy, Imagery, and Styles* (New York, 1970); the prefaces of the genre volumes in *Anthology of Music*, the English translation of *Das Musikwerk*, a multi-volume collection prepared by German scholars; and Barry Brook (ed.), *The Symphony 1720–1840* (New York, 1980–86), volumes of symphonies in score with extensive prefaces.

The standard investigations of musical form are Donald Tovey's *Essays in Musical Analysis* (London, 1935–45, 6 vols.) and *The Forms of Music* (1929; reprint, New York, 1956), and Wallace Berry's *Form in Music* (2d ed., Englewood Cliffs, N.J., 1985). Jan LaRue's *Guidelines for Style Analysis* (New York, 1970) opens new vistas for the study of musical style and structure. Newman's previously cited volumes on the sonata include considerable discussions of musical form whereas Charles Rosen in his *Sonata Forms* (New York, 1980) gives only limited coverage to the sonata form after Beethoven and Schubert.

TWELVE

NINETEENTH-CENTURY
MUSICAL ROMANTICISM
AND ITS AUDIENCE

At no time in history has music existed in a vacuum. Even during the individualistic nineteenth century, music and the relationship of composer and perfomer to their audience were affected by extra-artistic trends. We examined the historical and cultural context of musical Romanticism in Chapter 1; now we shall investigate briefly the basic questions of where and how was this music performed and heard. Since we have studied the art music of the century, we should also look briefly at the principal musical subcultures of the time—military, church, and popular music—especially as they intersected with art music. Finally, this chapter is the best place to discuss the performance practices of Romantic music; though this topic is not as knotty as those involving music of the Renaissance or Baroque, there are some salient differences between the way music was performed in Beethoven's, or even Mahler's, time and our own.

SOCIOLOGY OF MUSICAL ROMANTICISM

One of the most striking differences between the Classic and Romantic periods is the change in the social function of the musician and his music. During the eighteenth century most composers were under some form of patronage, sometimes ecclesiastical but usually that of a court, but the financial upheavals resulting from the Napoleonic wars, the growing secularization of society, and the increasing demands by the bourgeois classes for a constitutional government that would limit the arbitrary expenditure of revenues caused a sharp decline in the private patronage of music. The few composers of the nineteenth century who were under some form of courtly patronage during their careers, like Hummel, Spohr, or Wagner, bitterly resented it as demeaning. In the course of the century private patronage became more democratized and took a greater variety of forms: some examples are Paganini's lavish commission to Berlioz for *Harold in Italy*, the private support given to Saint-Saëns and Chaikovsky that enabled them to spend their time writing music, the wealthy bourgeoisie who supported musical establishments in private concerts (as Thomas Alsager did for the Beethoven Quartet Society in London), and the lavish support given to new music by eccentric royalty (Ludwig II of Bavaria) or nationalistic industrialists (Mitrofan Belyaev and Savva Mamontov in Russia). Musicians also helped themselves: consider how Beethoven, Liszt, Wagner, and Skryabin took advantage of their status as "cult figures" in order to gain support for their musical undertakings, or how astute virtuosos (or their agents) attracted audiences (who paid premium prices).

Composers and musicians became free artists, much as Handel was in eighteenth-century London. A few, like Mozart and Schubert, could not adjust to this new social arrangement. Much has been written about the exploitation of composers by unscrupulous publishers, but one must remember that copyright laws were not really enforced until the closing years of the century, that publishers had to depend for their income on exclusive relationships with composers and on rentals of performing materials, and that the less than scrupulous dealings of Beethoven or Wagner with publishers would not be tolerated today.

The musician, no longer under patronage, enjoyed a rise in social status but suffered from a corresponding drop in security. Whereas in the eighteenth century most musicians outside of Italy were trained under a system of apprenticeship, with the neophyte taken into a court orchestra under the watchful eye of his teacher, nineteenth-century musicians were generally trained in conservatories, institutions which were originally begun in Italy to teach orphans a trade but which received universal impetus after the founding of the Paris Conservatoire in 1795. These newer conservatories accepted children at an early age and their administration was characterized by frequent examinations, low tuition charges, governmental or philanthropic support, and a vocational kind of instruction. A large number of positions were available for trained instrumentalists or singers, from military bands and light music ensembles to symphony orchestras and opera companies. Rewards for leading singers and instrumentalists were great, even spectacular for star performers, although touring was extremely arduous before the development of railroads and steamships. Many opportunities (more so than at present!) existed for the humble musician, who needed an urban environment in which to prosper. Not only were there many concerts for which free-lance musicians were needed, but orchestras were required for dances at private parties in homes and in public dance halls; virtually all theaters, many restaurants, and most taverns had live music to attract patrons; brass bands were important in attracting attention at a shop opening or political rally; and at the bottom of the social scale was the shadowy world of the street musician and ballad singer. Teaching music was a genteel method of employment; although giving private lessons provided a less steady or secure income than teaching in a conservatory or other music school, a famous pianist or singer could charge premium prices for private lessons.

As in previous centuries, music was a means of achieving upward social mobility. In earlier times a musical position had often been passed down as a family trade (as in the Bach or Couperin dynasties); such a position as second oboe in the local court or theater orchestra often went to the son or nephew of the first oboist, who passed down his post as well as his skill within his family. Family connections continued to be important, but with the development of conservatories a larger pool of instrumentalists and singers was developed, and with the increase in urban population coveted operatic or orchestral positions became more widely available. If times were hard during periods of economic depression there was always the safety valve of emigration. As the century progressed and leisure became increasingly commercialized, the point was reached by 1900 where one could speak of a "market" for singers, composers, conductors, entertainers, and instrumental soloists.

Though a musician's duties were often arduous and he was more subject to exploitation than at present, his life was much better than that of a coal miner or factory hand. Though rank-and-file musicians were not lavishly paid, an instrumentalist who was willing to work at a variety of tasks—serving in the theater or opera orchestra, playing dance music, giving private lessons—could live adequately and support a family. Desire for a more stable and secure way of life led eventually to organizations of musicians similar to craft unions; whereas the musician in the eighteenth century was an artisan and in the nineteenth often aspired to the position of artist, by 1900 he was on the way to regarding himself as a skilled worker and expecting a comparable security and remuneration.

The professional musical environment, except for singers, was almost exclusively male, with strong gender-bound restrictions: examination of the lists of students at conservatories early in the century shows at first girls admitted only as voice students, then in harp and piano. Except for teachers of singing, a woman professor at a conservatory, like Louise Farrenc in Paris, was a rarity, as was a woman piano virtuoso like Clara Schumann or Teresa Carreño. Much more research is needed on the entry of women instrumentalists onto the professional musical scene, but it is probable that they followed the model of the Moravian violinist Wilma Neruda (later Lady Hallé), who studied with her father and gave her first concerts as part of a family musical group of child prodigies. The negative side of the environment for women performers should also be mentioned: by law the wife's earnings belonged to the husband, who on more than one occasion spent, drank up, or gambled these earnings away. Friedrich Wieck probably had these circumstances in mind when he opposed his daughter Clara's marriage to Schumann. We must remember too that during the nineteenth century only women of the lower classes were expected to work (and then in menial occupations, chiefly as servants), and in many circles a career in the performing arts was not considered a "respectable" one for a lady to pursue.

Frau Amann-Weinlich's "all-woman orchestra," founded in 1873, began as a string orchestra, then included well-hidden male wind players; though it was a "novelty orchestra" playing light music, it toured Europe, Russia, and even North America, and may have pioneered the idea of opening careers as orchestral musicians to women. Not until the end of the century, with the start of the "youth orchestra" movement, were women encouraged to study other orchestral instruments, and then as prospective members of amateur orchestras.

Composers were writing for a new audience. The Industrial Revolution and the improved transportation of the steamboat and railroad brought about a rapid growth of cities and distributed wealth among a wider segment of the population. Art music became an urban phenomenon, for mass audiences were needed to support resident opera companies and symphony orchestras or to attend the concerts of the virtuosos. Books on how to understand music, musical journalism and criticism, and private musical instruction to provide an "accomplishment" for the children of the bourgeoisie flourished.

More people than before participated in the making of music. Under the influence of such pedagogical reformers as Rousseau, Johann Heinrich Pestalozzi (1746–1827), and Lowell Mason (1792–1872), musical education was no longer limited to future professionals but spread through those segments of society fortunate enough to attend school. Tonic sol-fa, a form of solfège based on "movable *do*," made choral music easier to sing and, with the price of music constantly decreasing thanks to innovations in printing, brought about an efflorescence of choral societies and musical festivals. Through the improvements in technology and metallurgy brought about by the Industrial Revolution, musical instruments became both easier to make and less expensive, thus accessible to more people. The development of the concert grand and upright pianos and the addition of valves to brass instruments, more keys to woodwind instruments, and chin-rests or end-pins to stringed instruments made them easier to play although it significantly altered their timbres. Composers were not unduly hesitant to take advantage of these innovations.

The resultant growth in both orchestras and choral groups meant that by 1900 an essential manifestation of civic and national pride was the support of a resident symphony orchestra, choral society, or music festival, and even of such luxuries as an opera company or musicological investigation and publication of the works of important bygone composers, often from public funds. These replaced the princely support of music, especially in continental Europe, though it often meant that the frustrations of Wagner with courtly protocol were replaced by Berlioz's impatience with bureaucratic delay, and often such privately sponsored groups as the Société nationale de musique, École Niedermeyer, or Schola Cantorum were needed to create alternatives to officially controlled musical establishments.

Romantically or politically inclined biographers have emphasized the alienation of the artist from society during the nineteenth century. Most composers at some time felt a conflict between the demands of a Philistine public and the ideas, originally fostered by Goethe and Schiller and continued by Beethoven and Wagner, of art as a kind of religion and of the composer as a superior being. Yet the composer willing to come to terms with the lowest common tastes of his public, like Meyerbeer and Puccini, was lavishly rewarded, and some were able to enjoy both general acclaim and a large measure of artistic integrity, like Mendelssohn, Verdi, and Richard Strauss.

On the other hand, a few composers, like Schubert and Berwald, were grossly neglected during their lifetime, and one need only read Nicolas Slonimsky's *Lexicon of Musical Invective* (New York, 1953) for samples of the often venomous attacks directed against now-famous composers and their music. It was extremely difficult for a young and unestablished composer to get his music performed or published; those who were outstanding performers, had influential connections, or were affluent enough to hire musicians or pay publication costs were the most successful. Composers of the nineteenth century were not just competing against each other for performances; they were also striving to penetrate a "grand repertoire" of works written fifty or more years previously, ranging from Handel to Mendelssohn. Yet the whole concept of the general lack of public or critical appreciation for the major composers of the century has been exaggerated. The gap between composer and audience was not to become a yawning chasm until the twentieth century, and the blame for this does not rest exclusively on the musically inclined public.

DOMESTIC MUSIC MAKING

During the Classic period most performances of art music took place in private concerts, usually at a court. Such private concerts persisted throughout the nineteenth century, but the noble concert hall (such as the palace of Prince Lobkowitz in Vienna where the first performance of Beethoven's "Eroica" Symphony occurred) was replaced by the salon, the large room in a well-appointed home where musical performances took place. The salons of the aristocracy were augmented by those of the wealthier middle classes. Touring virtuosos welcomed these gatherings, where they could be heard by concert organizers and potential concert subscribers and pupils, or at least the parents of prospective students. Presiding over a salon was an excellent means of social mobility and influence. Most of Schubert's music—the piano works, chamber music, songs, and vocal ensembles—was written for these salons, as were the shorter piano pieces of Chopin or the songs of Fauré.

A typical salon evening would emphasize musical performances but sometimes include also literary and dramatic readings and, after refreshments, parlor games or dancing—which were discontinued, however, as later dinner hours became fashionable after 1830. The repertoire of salon programs varied according to the tastes of these attending and the musical proficiency of those participating. Most of the intimate art music of the nineteenth century was intended for such private concerts, and at a lower level were family concerts including small-scale chamber works, piano solos and duets (including dances and transcriptions of orchestral works), sentimental songs and ballads—the sort of works given the pejorative title of "salon music."

Household music making centered around the piano. Such an instrument indicated achievement and respectability, and it was the locus for domestic entertainment and social conviviality. A piano-owning family's daughters, and often also sons, took piano lessons; for the girls, musical ability in singing or performing on an appropriate instrument could help in making an advantageous marriage, and among the boys it facilitated social intercourse. The flute and the stringed instruments were the male amateur instruments of choice, the harp and guitar for young women, the piano (and voice) for both.

The salons have been reproached for having delayed the modernization of the public concert repertoire and competing with public concerts; nevertheless they kept a taste for art music alive, supported music publishers and instrument makers, and provided livelihoods for music teachers who taught the sons and daughters of the artistically inclined middle classes. Music played an important role in bringing together the aristocracy or nobility with the upper middle classes on the common ground of art. If snobbery was associated with the support of a salon or concert series, it was less glaringly evident than that associated with the opera, and was offset by its assistance to local musical figures in initially establishing their careers, or providing for the education and early appearances of talented youngsters from poorer families. Women with musical expertise were given the opportunity to perform in a "respectable" setting without having to abandon their familial obligations, and younger people with musical inclinations could meet potential marriage partners of similar social standing and tastes. Before the competition provided by the automobile, professional sports, the movies, and television, the private home gathering with music—whether the aristocratic salon with a professional string quartet playing Brahms or the lower middle-class "parlor" with singing around an upright piano—represented an ideal of culture.

PUBLIC CONCERTS

During the Classic period concerts open to the public were relatively infrequent and given generally in the largest cities, especially London, Paris, and Vienna. At the opening of the nineteenth century the public concert was quite different from its present-day equivalent. Often it was given by a touring instrumental virtuoso or singer, who did not perform a "solo recital" (these were invented by Liszt around 1840) but included on the program "assisting artists" and an orchestra engaged by the impresario, who also had to hire a hall or theater, get permission from the government or even the police in authoritarian cities like Naples or Vienna, and attract an audience to buy tickets. Often the virtuoso had to spend several days or weeks in a community performing in private salon concerts in order to meet members of the local musical establishment, serving as an assisting artist on the programs of others, or appearing in benefit concerts for other artists or for charities. Local musical societies, often called "Philharmonic Societies," composed of musical amateurs from the nobility and upper civil and ecclesiastical service, often put on programs given by their membership with an orchestra comprised of free-lance musicians and music students and helped by visiting artists, with expenses defrayed by subscriptions. In cities with conservatories, the prize-giving ceremonies every year included a concert by the best vocal and instrumental students, with a symphony performed by the student orchestra, which also accompanied in concertos. Sundays and religious holiday seasons like Lent were the usual concert times, since by law the theaters were closed.

At the beginning of the century concert programs were mixed and varied. Generally the first number was an overture from a popular opera, followed by one or more solo selections by the concert-giving virtuoso including a concerto or at least a movement thereof, and often a chamber work performed by the soloist with assisting artists. An orchestral work, generally a symphony or at least its first movement, concluded the first half. The second half was similar to the first. One or more numbers might be performed by the concert society's chorus; an instrumentalist would often have a singer as an assisting artist; members of the orchestra might appear as soloists in a concertino or other short display piece. Variety on such concert programs was the rule, in order to appeal to as many segments of the audience as possible. During the concert season, which began in the fall and lasted until early summer, in a large city there would be several concerts of this nature, in smaller towns two or three, the high points of the year's social activity.

What we today consider the standard concert format—an overture, a concerto, and a large-scale symphony—was basically codified by Mendelssohn around 1835 and became the norm around 1850. Not until the early twentieth century was applause between movements of a concerto or symphony felt to be disturbing to the mood of the performance. Concert audiences were divided into two basic groups, especially in the larger cities, with one faction preferring serious "art" music by "classical" composers, living or usually of the recent past, and another wanting programs with entertainment value arousing the astonishment and excitement that a charismatic performer could produce.

The growth in size of the music-loving public after 1850 resulted in increasingly specialized concerts: from dazzling virtuoso programs to "historical" piano recitals including works by Byrd, Bach, and Beethoven as well as Liszt; programs by professional string quartets; and "song evenings" (*Liederabende*). At the same time, concert artists were increasingly unwilling to go through the details of arranging concerts themselves, relying instead on local concert societies, an "advance man" who would take care of hiring the hall and selling the tickets, or, increasingly after 1870, concert promoters.

Concerts at first took place in a variety of settings. Sometimes they were held between the acts of an opera, or in the foyer of an opera house;

only the most charismatic virtuosos could sell all the seats in the theater. Piano manufacturers found their showrooms ideal locations for a recital, and some even built small concert halls after the solo recital became customary. Theaters, churches, lecture halls of the local university, even dance halls were pressed into service if a city did not have a concert hall. Some of the "monster concerts," featuring hundreds of performers, took place in industrial exhibition halls. As the century progressed, significant features of the urban landscape included a centrally located opera house, often in a bulky neo-Renaissance style, and an equally prominent concert hall, often built in the style of a Grecian temple to indicate the virtual sacredness of high art. The interiors of halls underwent many changes, from multi-purpose enclosures (which could even include dancing) at the opening of the century to structures designed exclusively for concerts, and even concert-hall complexes with a large hall for orchestral and choral concerts and smaller halls for recitals and chamber music programs. Boxes typical of opera houses were replaced with one or more balconies going three-fourths of the way around the hall. The pipes of a large organ were usually the central feature of the stage rear wall, and the interior decorations were lavish. The halls were rectangular, paneled with wood, and usually acoustically superb.

Concert life became increasingly "elevated," with members of the audience dressing and behaving as if they were at church. The privilege of concert attendance, reserved for the nobility in the Classic period, became a middle-class ritual to which music-loving members of the working class could aspire. Social stratification was reflected in the prices of tickets, and sometimes in separate entrances for the holders of the least expensive seats. The cheapest places of all in the opera house or concert hall were the standing-room places in the topmost balcony. The boxes, especially at the opera house, were often the loci of domestic intrigues, as described in the novels by Stendhal and Balzac.

As the century progressed, concert life had its more "democratic" counterparts. Opera in Italy from Donizetti through Puccini's *Madame Butterfly* was probably the only art music that was adopted by the "masses" (and that more probably through the playing of hits from these operas on street organs or by military bands than through attendance at the opera), but there was a steady democratization of nearly all art music into a more general consciousness, at least for those who wanted it.

The performances at the eighteenth-century English pleasure gardens, where one could hear music while walking around, were replaced in the Romantic period, especially after 1850, by concerts in the summer at spas, heard by strollers while "taking the waters;" at seaside resorts; and even at amusement parks like the Tivoli Gardens in Copenhagen or at zoos as in Berlin. Though dance and entertainment music was mainly featured, art music—chiefly opera overtures or arrangements of pieces from other media—was included in the orchestras' repertoires and broadened the audience for "good" music. Similar programs were included at "workmen's" or "popular" concerts, with admission at reduced prices. Children's concerts were usually song recitals or lighter chamber music. Much of the repertoire, though, belonged to the musical subcultures of the Romantic period which will be discussed in the following section.

SUBCULTURES OF MUSICAL ROMANTICISM

Throughout this volume we have been discussing the art music of the nineteenth century. More widespread, though less subject to critical or scholarly investigation, were the various musical subcultures that are often grouped under the heading of "functional music." Quite often our awareness of these musical subcultures comes when they intersect in some way with the work of a major composer, as when Beethoven wrote military marches for band as well as stylized marches in the Op. 101 piano sonata or finale of the Ninth Symphony. Similar impingements occurred when Mendelssohn, Franck, and Chaikovsky wrote church music, or when Chopin or Brahms wrote stylized waltzes.

The term "functional music" has been used in recent years to separate it from "art music." Functional music is not judged by aesthetic criteria, but by how well it does its job as an aid to marching, dancing, worshipping in or out of church, arousing political emotions, or enhancing the effect of a drama. "Popular music" is music to be heard, but not with the sophistication or intellectual involvement of art music; it is supposed to be in a familiar and recognizable vein. When either type of music becomes ingrained in popular consciousness (even though its composer has been forgotten) it is called "traditional music"; some examples are "Happy Birthday" and "Home on the Range." "Folk music" is hard to isolate as such because the early nineteenth-century collections of it were ethnologically uncritical; the line is hard to draw at that time between genuine folk music and urban popular music, some of which was in turn influenced by the songs brought to the cities by peasants. Not until the phonograph-influenced folk music researches of Bartók in Hungary, Evgeniya Linyova in Russia, and Frances Densmore with the North American Indians (the latter two influencing, in the process, Stravinsky and Busoni respectively in their art music) can we speak of a genuine ethnomusicology with which Liszt, Balakirev, and Gottschalk, for example, were unfamiliar.

Historical distance has helped to make it fashionable to listen to or study seriously as art music the functional music of bygone eras—medieval estampies, chorales of the Lutheran Reformation, street cries of London in art music settings by Jacobean composers, wind octet divertimentos to be played during garden parties of the 1780's. Although the principal musical subcultures of the Romantic period may seem too close to us to permit a similar investigation, beginnings have been made which we should explore, simply because for the majority of persons these subcultures represented their principal, if not only, contacts with music. Also, just as the furniture, crafts, interiors, design, and the other so-called "decorative" arts are now considered as much worthy of study by art historians as the "fine" arts of painting, sculpture, and architecture, so the musical subcultures equally deserve study for a rounded picture of nineteenth-century musical life. Space permits examining only the main subcultures: military music, church music, and the various types of light or entertainment music of the century.

Military Music. The main military music in general use during the Classic period was the *Harmoniemusik,* an unstandardized grouping of wind instruments with the most usual combination consisting of two oboes, two clarinets, two horns, and two bassoons. From this group the modern band was developed by adding the trumpets and timpani of the cavalry band, the percussion instruments of "Turkish" music, the fifes (replaced by piccolos) and snare drums of infantry field music, and the serpent (or later the ophicleide) to strengthen the bass line, for which the contrabassoon was too heavy and cumbersome.

In the course of the nineteenth century other instruments were added: keyed bugles, valved tenor and bass horns, saxhorns, and especially cornets. Technical innovations in building wind instruments made them easier to play, especially the brass, and more affordable. The keyed bugles were displaced after 1830 by the more flexible and less fragile cornet, serpents and ophicleides after 1850 by the tuba, and entire families of sax-horns or *flicorni,* ranging from sopranino to contrabass, provided a homogeneous sound for the brass band. At the end of the century saxophones entered the band, providing a mellifluous inner-register sound. The number of clarinets increased, strengthening the melodic line; they assumed the role of violins in transcriptions of orchestral music for band.

The march was the main staple of the band's repertoire. The pace increased as the century progressed and uniforms, arms, and equipment became lighter in weight. At the opening of the century most marches, especially German ones, were rather ponderous, consisting of two strains (rarely a trio) which usually began with dotted upbeat figures. The "classic" marches of today's bands, with a structure consisting of fanfare-like introduction, two strains, and a lyrically melodious trio in the subdominant with a contrasting agitated strain (the "break") before a fortissimo reprise of the trio, were written mostly between 1880 and 1914: J. L. Wagner's *Under the Double Eagle* for Austria, Louis Ganne's *Father of Victory* for France,

Fučik's *Entry of the Gladiators* (a circus favorite) for Bohemia, John Philip Sousa's numerous marches for the United States, and later Kenneth Alford's *Colonel Bogey* epitomizing the English spirit—all show the same national differentiations as the art music of their contemporaries Bruckner, Fauré, Dvořák, MacDowell, and Elgar.

One point of contact between band and art music may have been a negative one: the introduction of many new wind instruments into the symphony orchestra may have been delayed because the military bandmasters snatched them up as soon as they came from the factory. Though a few composers wrote for band during the nineteenth century (Beethoven's military marches, for example, superior specimens of the genre) and others, like Johann Strauss Jr. and Ponchielli, were bandmasters at early stages in their careers, the main point of intersection between band and art music, other than the stylized march from Beethoven through Mahler, Saint-Saëns, and Elgar, was the use of the band on or off the stage in operas.

From a visual standpoint, dramatic realism is heightened when an actual military band with its special instrumentation participates in a processional, and a uniformed band lends charm to the rural ambiences of such pastoral operas as Donizetti's *L'Elisir d'Amore* and Mascagni's *L'Amico Fritz*. The band enhanced spatial sound-effects in various ways: not one but two bands onstage providing antiphonal effects in the final epilogue of Glinka's *A Life for the Tsar*, or the tossing of phrases back and forth between orchestra in the pit and band on the stage in the coronation march in Act IV of Meyerbeer's *Le Prophète*. The mysterious woodwind sonorities that Verdi used to imitate the sound of the bagpipe at the apparition of the Scottish kings in Act III of *Macbeth* are heightened by having the special group of woodwind players under the stage. Perhaps culminating such offstage effects were the three different offstage groups in the march in Act I of Berlioz's *Les Troyens*, the offstage orchestra that accompanies Venus in Act III of Wagner's *Tannhäuser*, and the distant horn calls, fanfares, and martial music in the last movement of Mahler's Second Symphony.

The band concert, whether by a military regimental band or by a community municipal band, contributed markedly to the democratization of art music. Not only were marches, dance music such as polkas or two-steps (and, at the end of the century, ragtime), and cornet solos part of the repertoire, but also works of art music. These were chiefly operatic overtures and excerpts but often included concert overtures and movements of symphonies in transcriptions for band. At outdoor concerts, which the Viennese critic Eduard Hanslick called the most democratic form of all because there were no admission charges or special formalities of dress, many, especially those of humble origins, received their first exposure to art music.

Church Music.   Whereas the eighteenth century was an era of religious indifference among most educated classes, with religious enthusiasm mocked in such novels as Smollett's *Humphry Clinker* (1771), the nineteenth century was one of religious revival, with old denominations revitalized and new ones founded. This was reflected in the widespread use of church music, to which several sociological factors also contributed, such as the spread of literacy, decline in the cost of music (which made inexpensive editions of church music and printed hymnals easily accessible), and need for a large number of trained organists to direct the church music being written. For millions of people, their only regular and formal experience with music was through the church.

Music was an integral part of most religious worship but it was viewed from two contradictory standpoints. For one faction, church music was to be judged primarily on aesthetic grounds since only the artistically best music should be made an offering to God. And just as the liturgical ceremony was to be distant from everyday life (vestments for the clergy and choristers, the use of incense, Latin or the archaic English of the King James Bible or Anglican Book of Common Prayer in the Catholic or English-language Protestant service, the retention of candles after electric light was invented), so the artistic manifestations were preferably to be from a remote past, distant from the ordinary world. The Gothic or Renaissance eras provided the ideal models for church architecture, and music from the past, too, was preferred—Bach among Protestants, the Tudor church composers among Anglicans, Palestrina and Gregorian chant among Catholics, revivals of Znamenny chant in modal harmonizations in Russia. Contemporary church music was to be written in a style deliberately different from that of secular music. Standards of performance were to be raised to approach, if not equal, those of the theater or concert hall.

Diametrically opposite views were held by those for whom church music was judged on a functional basis; they were primarily concerned with how well it reached the general congregation and heightened the atmosphere of public worship and encouraged participation in it. Music was to appeal to and be used by the entire congregation, with artistic considerations secondary. This "populist" church music was scorned by the aesthetes as overly secular, consisting of subjective and sentimental texts with emotional melodies and saccharine harmonies to match (a movement that was ecumenical and international, not restricted to any particular denomination or nation); or of bouncy martial rhythms, whether by Italian bands playing for processions or by the brass bands of the Salvation Army; or (and this was a criticism chiefly of French and Italian church music) of a style almost indistinguishable from opera. The populists, on the other hand, felt that congregational worship was paramount and that the church should not be a concert hall or museum, with the congregation merely passive listeners. Compromise was difficult if not impossible between the two factions.

Four categories of church music were involved: (1) hymns, usually sung by the whole congregation; (2) settings of formal liturgies, whether Anglican, Roman Catholic, or Russian Orthodox; (3) anthems or motets, those terms implying in the nineteenth century choral works outside the liturgy or set order of worship, "anthem" being the Protestant term and "motet" the Catholic one; and (4) organ music.

There were three basic trends in the composition of church music during the century. The first is the church music written by major composers, with the primary category that written for actual worship services. Major place should be assigned the works which Mendelssohn composed specifically for the reforms of Lutheran church music decreed by King Friedrich Wilhelm IV of Prussia in 1840; the masses for limited resources that Mercadante wrote for the churches of Novara; the Austrian motets from Schubert to Bruckner; and the church music of the better French composers such as Gounod, Saint-Saëns, and Franck. Catholic church music of the century is framed by two works written by major composers specifically for church performance; Mozart's *Ave Verum Corpus* (K 618) of 1791, for a small parish church in Baden, and Fauré's *Requiem* (1887, revised 1900), written for the church of the Madeleine in Paris. The comparable Anglican peaks are the extensive anthems of Samuel Sebastian Wesley (1810–76) and the services of Charles Villiers Stanford, with their independent organ parts and avoidance of sentimental harmonies.

A subcategory consisted of works, not strictly liturgical but of religious import, which can be used in the church. Brahms's organ works and motets best exemplify this trend; but like their Catholic counterparts, the masses of Bruckner, they make immense demands on the musicianship of performers and require more rehearsals than are usually possible. The sonatas of Mendelssohn and Rheinberger, the preludes and fugues of Saint-Saëns, and the chorales of Franck require highly skilled organists and are more suitable to the recital than for the church; Franck, however, wrote several pieces that the average parish organist could perform, and individual movements of the Mendelssohn or Rheinberger sonatas could be appropriate for a Sunday morning service.

The second trend embraces strictly functional church music; perhaps it can best be identified by the fact that its composers are not to be found in the general histories of music. Judged by purely aesthetic criteria, much of their music is dull, clumsily written, saccharine, or sanctimonious; at its best, though, it is solemn, dignified, and highly suitable for its purposes. The best examples are the products of the solid training from the choir school in Regensburg or the École Niedermeyer in Paris for Catholic church music, for Protestant music the English school of hymn and anthem composers, and for Jewish synagogue music the innovations of Schubert's friend Solomon Sulzer (1804–90) in Vienna and Samuel Naumbourg (1815–80) in France.

The church composer had no lack of worthwhile models for emulation. The publication of Bach's church music and masses and motets of the Renaissance made the best models of the distant past accessible; of current examples there were contrary schools, Schubert, Spohr, and Gounod representing an "expressive" ideal and Mendelssohn, Bruckner, and Brahms a more "austere" group (Liszt had a foot in each camp). Some adaptations of secular music were, to say the least, inappropriate, such as the hymn "My Jesus, as Thou wilt" set to the horn theme of the overture to Weber's *Der Freischütz* or the Benediction hymn "Tantum ergo sacramentum" to the theme of the Act II sextet from Donizetti's *Lucia di Lammermoor*.

The third trend, a result of the religious vitality of the nineteenth century, can be strikingly seen in the proliferation of various types of demotic religious music, usually outside the main streams of "art" music and "established" churches. Examples are the sturdy hymnody of the Welsh Methodists, wordless dance songs to accompany the informal devotions of the Hasidic Jews of eastern Europe, rugged "Sacred Harp" hymns of the American frontier, "gospel hymns" of urban America that were spread around the world by the brass bands of the Salvation Army, and the blend of distantly remembered African musical elements and overheard Western music in the Negro spiritual. It remained for composers of the twentieth century, however, to transmute these popular religious musics into art music.

Russian church music was, by Imperial decree, meant to be different from its Western counterparts, with the organ and other instruments banned and only works by Russian composers to be performed. Polyphonic settings of the Russian liturgy had been made, principally under Polish influence, in the seventeenth century; Italianate styles, as seen in Bortniansky's church music, were dominant early in the nineteenth century. German influences, chiefly chorale-style settings, were then dominant in St. Petersburg under Alexei Lvov (1798–1870) and his successors; because of their control of the censorship of church music, Chaikovsky had to file a lawsuit to get his *Vespers* of 1878 published.

Balakirev's appointment as musical director of the Russian Imperial Chapel in 1883, with Rimsky-Korsakov as his assistant, resulted in a sharp change in the style of Russian church music; more emphasis was placed on the original sources, especially the old Znamenny chant and its proper harmonization, which emphasized modal rather than Western harmonies and avoided such Western contrapuntal techniques as imitative counterpoint. Characteristic of this music during its period of efflorescence, from 1883 to 1917, are full and rich sonorities arising from division of the chorus into eight to sixteen voice parts, with doublings of melodic lines or moving inner parts in octaves or thirds; contrasts of male or female voices alone; free rhythm rather than strict meters; harmonizations that emphasize secondary triads and chords with open fifths in contrast to such Western practices as pervasive dominant-tonic relationships, secondary dominants, and coloristic chords; and the exceptionally low basses who sing an octave below the customary bass register. The final stage came near the end of the century with the reforms of the Moscow Synodal choir, with emphases on modal harmonizations of the chant. Rakhmaninov and Aleksandr Dmitrievich Kastalsky (1856–1926) were its leading composers.

Political Music. The secular counterparts of populist church music were songs written for express political purposes, such as the "Marseillaise," which had been used so effectively during the French Revolution and subsequently banned by the royalist governments of the Restoration. Pierre Degeyter (1849–1932) sought to write a "Marseillaise" for the fledgling Socialist movement in 1888 with "L'Internationale," and political songs in the idiom of minstrel-show tunes or gospel hymns played important roles on both sides in the American Civil War. Parodies of pre-existing tunes were favorite vehicles: nearly every crisis brought new words to the revolutionary favorite "La Carmagnole" in Paris, whereas gospel hymns were often selected by American entertainers or politicos.

Light, Entertainment, and Popular Music. The strictly demotic "people's" music of a given period is usually the last to be critically evaluated, usually after the living remnants of the tradition have disappeared. Literacy was sufficiently widespread through the nineteenth century, however, that many records were kept about it, titles of popular songs appeared in realistic novels, and much more of the music was published than in earlier eras.

At the opening of the century composers wrote art and popular music with equal facility: the minuets of Haydn and Mozart, the German dances of Beethoven, the waltzes and écossaises of Schubert were rapidly written pieces of highly functional dance music that often possess great charm and artistic merit. Popular music was either dance music or song, much of which had been brought from the country and passed along by oral tradition, with urban crossroads cities such as Vienna, Berlin, Paris, and London repositories of mixtures and syntheses of various traditions. Much of the music was made on instruments that were less expensive and easier to learn than the piano—mandolins, zithers, hurdy-gurdy street organs; later, balalaikas, harmonicas, or accordions.

It is difficult to separate popular music of the time from the repertoires of the concert hall, the theater, or the salon. We can roughly define popular music as music that is easily understandable by most persons (some would include music that they can sing or otherwise perform) and does not require much knowledge of musical theory or techniques. Such pieces are usually short, homophonic, with prominent melodic (usually vocal) lines and simple harmonic accompaniments. We will do best by examining a few of the principal types of light music of the century, keeping in mind that light music had its masterpieces too. Among the intersections of light and art music are the stylized Ländler in such disparate works as the second trio of the minuet of Mozart's Clarinet Quintet and the second movement of Mahler's Second Symphony, the French music-hall idiom in some of Chabrier's romps, or the excursion-steamer band effect in the third movement of Mahler's First Symphony.

Dance music was rural or urban in the eighteenth century; the rustic dances in front of the village inn (stylized in dance settings by Grétry and especially Haydn) contrast markedly with the aristocratic courtly minuet so ideally exemplified by Mozart. Urban dance halls got their start in London and Vienna, with specialized dance orchestras playing dances which soon became international crazes: galops, contredanses, quadrilles, especially waltzes and (after 1840) polkas. Some composers began to specialize in writing this music and organizing dance orchestras to play it; Joseph Lanner (1801–43) and the Strauss family—Johann Sr. (1804–49) and Johann Jr. (1825–99) and the latter's brothers Josef (1827–70) and Eduard (1835–1916)—were exemplars whose musical activities in Vienna and on tours spanned nearly the entire nineteenth century and were models for others. Their main rival was the Dane Hans Christian Lumbye (1810–74); a descendant of his light-music orchestra in the Tivoli Gardens in Copenhagen, directed by a violinist-conductor, is still playing on summer evenings. Many of the popular dance rhythms of the period were stylized into art music, as in the waltzes of Chopin or Brahms, or provided high points in the ballets of Délibes and Chaikovsky. Points of comparison can be made between Smetana's stylized rural polkas and the ballroom ones of Johann Strauss, Jr.

The vocal counterparts of light music stemmed from the opera house, the Lied, the popular theater, even the church. Hymnals, for instance, were used in domestic music making in most middle-class Protestant households. At the peak were the simple, sentimental, and beloved songs of Friedrich Silcher (1789–1860) in Germany, Stephen Collins Foster (1826–64) in the United States, and F. Paolo Tosti (1846–1916) in Naples.

After 1850 art music tended to become more serious and more abstract, as is evident in the works of such composers who changed their styles after 1850 like Liszt, Verdi, and Wagner. Concurrently, many more composers began to specialize in light music, often in alliance with publishers and entertainers. A popular piece might be brought out in a variety of arrangements: for piano solo (original or simplified), piano duet, solo instrument (often violin, clarinet, flute, or cornet) and piano, flute duet, guitar, accordion, military band, or salon orchestra. Often the music itself became simplified: the danced waltz of 1900, for instance, used less musical material than one by Lanner or the Johann Strausses. Songs would often be written for popular entertainers, whose name or picture on the sheet music cover assured increased sales: one thinks of the relationship between Foster and E. P. Christy of Christy's minstrels.

At the bottom was a type of music known today as *Kitsch,* the degenerate side of light and salon music and of art music as well; a good concise definition is "triviality with pretentiousness." Among its essential ingredients are regular phrasing and rhythms, square-cut melodies, rich altered harmonies often appearing unexpectedly in diatonic contexts, delayed resolutions of non-harmonic tones, and descriptive titles intended to arouse religious, erotic, familial, or patriotic feelings—in short, the debasement of the musical idioms particularly of Weber, Schumann, and Liszt (Example 10–7c). Pictorial counterparts of kitsch are the grand battle scenes painted by German artists after the Franco-Prussian War or varnished segments of tree trunks adorned with garishly colored religious painting.

Light music became a commercial product after 1850. The role of publishers and entertainers has already been mentioned. Specialized locales for light music were developed, such as the music hall, which began as a restaurant with musical entertainers on a platform while the patrons drank and dined (the French equivalent was the *café chantant,* in Germany the beer garden); by 1900 there were chains of large music halls with variety shows usually featuring "talent" that had been sent there by centralized booking agents. Operettas became musical comedies, with plot, story line, and musical coherence secondary to the hit tunes that were their main reason for existing. Cabarets featured a more intimate and sophisticated repertoire of musical entertainments, while circuses and fairgrounds utilized popular music played by bands or steam calliopes, and American influences entered through minstrel shows with their two-steps and cakewalks and tours by Sousa's band, repaying the American tours of the European entertainment-music orchestras.

Throughout the nineteenth century the virtuoso, singer or instrumentalist, often walked a fine line between artist and entertainer, and many found a "crossover" into popular music highly lucrative, especially with the development and mass marketing of phonograph records after 1900. The segmentation of the popular repertoire, the commercial cultivation of a "youth culture," the exploitation of ragtime or dances from Latin America like the tango or maxixe, and the development of different playing and singing styles for popular and art music are twentieth-century developments, but their roots are discernible at the end of the previous century.

In summarizing these subcultures, one can see two contrary trends. First of all, they brought about the creation of a lot of poor and even bad music. This has been blamed for the neglect into which much "good" music fell. However, music was written for often quite differing audiences, and we cannot fairly say that symphonies were neglected in favor of music-hall tunes; rather, popular orchestral works from Beethoven to Chaikovsky and Richard Strauss usurped the toeholds in the repertoire of "unpopular" composers like Bruckner, d'Indy, and Mahler. In addition, a tendency toward "cultural primitivism" at the end of the century meant that much "good bad" music (e.g., ragtime) ousted much "bad good" music such as drawing-room ballads and other *Kitsch*.

Secondly, these subcultures provided employment for musicians and even those peripherally connected with music and made it possible for musicians to rise qualitatively as well. A wind player's playing in a circus band at the start of his career would do wonders for his sight reading, technique, and endurance, and would be good preparation for coping with the demands of a Richard Strauss, Mahler, or, later, Stravinsky. Next, many more people participated in the making of music than before (at least on a formal basis such as playing or singing from notes) and supported thereby music teachers, publishers, and instrument makers. Finally, a person attracted to music by Lanner's waltzes, Barnby's hymns, Offenbach's overtures, or Sousa's marches would often develop a taste for Beethoven, Wagner, or Franck. And from the perspective of the near-end of the twentieth century, can we honestly say that our musical subcultures are an improvement on those of the past?

ROMANTIC PERFORMANCE PRACTICES

The study of the performance practices of nineteenth-century music has been neglected, since priority has been given to examining the manifold problems of the correct interpretation of even earlier musics; "tradition," it has been felt, is a sufficient guide to today's performers of the "standard repertoire." Yet much is being done to obtain reasonably correct interpretation of the musical literature between Beethoven and Fauré.

One salient problem has been the existence of so many corrupt musical texts. Although almost all of the errors consist of erroneous dynamic, phrasing, and interpretative markings or inconsistent reproductions of variant versions of given passages, even wrong notes have crept in, and the policies of several publishing houses have led to the repeated re-issuing of defective scores. Also, although once-definitive complete editions are being redone, including those of Schubert and Berlioz, the eighteenth and nineteenth centuries suffer most from the absence of scholarly collected editions of the works of many major composers, from C. P. E. Bach to Fauré.

A new edition of a given work is not always the final solution to its textual problems. To begin with, for popular operas there can seldom be a "definitive" edition because the scores were so often revised and modified, new cabalettas or other passages written at the request of individual singers, and expansions or cuts made depending on the particular theater or circumstances of performance. A classic example is Verdi's *Macbeth:* does one choose the 1847 version (for Florence) or that of 1865 (for Paris)? Similar problems of choice exist among, to cite a few examples, the four versions of Donizetti's *Dom Sébastien* (two for Paris, one for Vienna, one for Italy) written between 1843 and 1845; the seven versions (1867–88) of Gounod's *Roméo et Juliette*, based on the constantly revised versions for the Théâtre-Lyrique, Opéra-Comique, and Opéra; or the three main versions of Wagner's *Tannhäuser:* the Dresden version of 1845–47, the Paris version of 1861, and the Munich-Vienna version (1867–75). Many additions or changes not authorized by the composer, such as the flute-and-soprano cadenza in the mad scene of Donizetti's *Lucia di Lammermoor*, have been hallowed as "tradition" and are expected by audiences. Piano-vocal scores of operas are probably the most laden with errors, and performances and recordings of lesser-known operas, even by composers of the status of Rossini or Verdi, have sometimes undergone such drastic cutting as to become caricatures of the original.

Scholarly editions, in the interest of regularizing inconsistencies and making decisions in ambiguous situations (such as differing dynamics or articulations between, for instance, wind and string parts), sometimes show over-editing, with the editor tending to forget that composers often left solutions up to the individual performer, singer, or conductor, depending on the circumstances of performance at a given moment. In working with a composer's autographs, one must remember that composers were often in a hurry as they sketched or wrote; that the copyists, performers, and publishers often knew what a composer meant even though he did not write it down; and that composers did not feel they needed to spell out every single detail, especially of conventions understood by every musician of the time.

As we work with scores and parts today, we must recall that we are working with guidelines for performance, not legal documents in which no jot or tittle is to be modified under any circumstances. Nevertheless, it may be helpful here to suggest some of the guidelines, specific to the nineteenth century, within which flexible approaches to performance were (and are) possible.

The changes in instrumental and orchestral sonorities between Beethoven's time and the present have seldom been considered, especially by conductors. Of the instruments that Beethoven used in his Ninth Symphony, the trombones and cymbals are the only ones whose tone colors have not undergone radical changes. Techniques of performance have undergone alterations of similar scope. The addition of chinrests to violins and violas or end-pins to cellos and basses enabled the performer to produce a wider and more constant vibrato without tiring; the addition of valves to

brass instruments and more keys to woodwind instruments made these instruments easier to play and more secure in intonation, but much of the
original tone color was lost, especially with the French horn. The modern
piano dates from 1859, the modern oboe from 1886, and all instruments
have subsequently undergone some twentieth-century modifications.

Characteristic of most nineteenth-century string playing was the use
of an audible shift of position on the string for expressive purposes (the portamento), generally to accentuate high notes within a phrase or to announce suspensions and cadences. At its most exaggerated, the portamento
became the glissandos of the gypsy fiddler; at its best (as can be heard on
early recordings), it was a tastefully and sparingly used ornament. Vibrato
on string instruments was not continuous except in expressive cantabile
passages, but was generally used on accented notes or held notes, especially at cadences. On violins and violas the upper two strings were made
of unwound gut rather than steel, the lower two of wound gut, thus producing a sweeter and less penetrating sound than today's strings.

National schools of playing woodwind and brass instruments developed as early as the eighteenth century. One can cite as illustrations the
wide vibratos of French bassoonists and hornists; the Italian technique of
clarinet performance, prevalent past 1900, with the reed above the mouthpiece, providing more facile articulation but a much shriller tone with less
dynamic shading; the opposite German technique of clarinet playing with
the reed below the mouthpiece which almost universally supplanted the
Italian school; or the veiled tone of the Viennese "Pumphorn," a single
horn with piston rather than rotary valves, and described as the original
valved *Waldhorn* of the early Romantic period. Conductors who are concerned about the proper oboe for Bach's works would do well to consider
performances of the clarinet solos in Rossini's overtures or the E♭ clarinet
solo in Berlioz's *Symphonie fantastique* to be played with the reed above
the mouthpiece, or the horn solos in the orchestral works of Wagner,
Brahms, Mahler, and Richard Strauss to be played on the *Wiener Pumphorn;* they might also consider demanding the large-bore trumpet in F with
rotary valves, so different from the piston-valved cornet with which it was
often contrasted, for late-Romantic music when it is specified. The activities of several dedicated performers show that the intonation problems associated with the older wind and brass instruments can be overcome with
diligent application. The orchestral sound would be mellower but not as
bright as is customary today, and would sound at its best with the live
acoustics of the nineteenth-century concert hall. More study of orchestral
size in the nineteenth century needs to be done, but it seems that most
orchestras, except for such special works as Beethoven's Ninth Symphony
or Berlioz's symphonies, ranged between forty-five and sixty members during the first half of the century.

The piano underwent numerous modifications during the period, and was in many respects different from the present-day instrument. The Viennese piano, to which composers from Beethoven through Schumann to Brahms were attached, generally had a lighter action and crisper sound than the English piano but less volume. Steel bracings, iron frames, heavier hammers (without the leather covers of the Viennese pianofortes of about 1800), escapements to permit the repeated strikings of a single note (one of the young Liszt's display effects), and a smooth action were typical of English and French pianos. American technology resulted in the overstrung grand piano of 1859, from which the modern piano is dated. At the end of the century the Bösendorfer Imperial concert grand, with its additional lower octave, represented the acme of piano construction. Some experiments with pianos of the last decade of the nineteenth century show a different voicing (treatment of the felt hammers) from that current today, resulting in a lighter, clearer, less massive, and less percussive sound than is usual with today's pianos. Needless to say, the songs of Schubert and Schumann take on a new character if the sonorities of the pianos of their times are produced instead of those of the modern piano.

Two extremes are possible in performing nineteenth-century piano music. One is to perform any and all piano music from the mid-eighteenth to the late twentieth centuries on a single instrument—a practice that can be defended only on the grounds of convenience. The opposite extreme is to play a recital with an entire stage full of pianos, choosing each according to the preferences of or associations with a certain composer—a Streicher for Beethoven, a Pleyel for Chopin, an Érard for Liszt, and a Chickering for Gottschalk, with a modern Steinway voiced one way for Brahms and another way for Prokofiev. No easy compromise can be envisaged between the two extremes.

Lively controversy exists about whether to use original instruments or replicas of them. Not only do strings and reeds deteriorate with age and use, so does piano wire, and 150 years or more of the polluted urban air of the Industrial Revolution and its hydrocarbon-based aftermath have adversely affected even the wood and metal of the instruments themselves. The advocates of original instruments must remember that most music lovers have grown up hearing the Romantic repertoire superbly played on modern instruments, and expecting similar standards of execution on original instruments. They do not want to hear their favorite Beethoven sonatas on a deteriorated, out-of-tune piano no matter what its historic association with the composer may be. If the instrument in question cannot be restored, a replica that duplicates as closely as possible the original construction and materials is preferable. Recordings of restored older instruments before their deterioration became total can provide some sort of standard for building reconstructed copies.

Vocal music has not received as much attention as instrumental among those seeking to recreate original conditions of performance; we have many detailed verbal descriptions of the quality of singers' voices but no reliable phonograph recordings before 1898 that can show us how the singers sounded. Yet there are a few areas where treatises on singing and phonograph recordings of the early twentieth century can provide ideas of value for further study. In Italian and much French opera, ornamentation was widespread in 1800 and persisted even after Rossini's codifications, particularly in strophic repeats and at major internal cadences. Treatises by nineteenth-century singing teachers indicate the persistence of improvised vocal ornamentation through most of the century, though trills were more commonly used in the early and middle years of the period. Phonograph records of singers associated with Verdi show that they frequently used rubato and portamenti to shape phrases as much as their instrumentalist contemporaries. Many of these recordings also display some sloppiness and exhibitionism (such as interpolating high notes) against which the newer breed of opera conductor, like Mahler and Toscanini, campaigned.

Operatic acting went to two extremes: at one end, an exaggeration of gestures, especially those of grief or dismay and during death scenes, so that the motivation would be perceptible even to viewers in the topmost balcony; and at the other, an immobile posture during an aria or ensemble on the grounds that the audience came to hear the singers sing, not to see them act. Both Verdi and Wagner must be credited with trying to get more dramatic realism onto the operatic stage, though by present-day standards the acting they wanted would seem overdone and the sets they approved overly realistic. It is most unlikely that any nineteenth-century composer would have sanctioned the policies of some present-day stage directors who, under the guise of making an artistic or political "statement," distort librettos and mutilate the music of operas. If we are going to restore nineteenth-century operas, we cannot replicate the exact quality of the voices of Malibran or Tamagno, but we can use the original instruments in the orchestra (including a contrabass valved trombone for the *cimbasso* in Verdi's operas), allow more freedom in ornamentation and use alternate cabalettas if appropriate for the singers, and keep to nineteenth-century traditions of acting (avoiding the most obvious "scenery-chewing") and set design.

Orchestral seating plans of the nineteenth century varied, especially between an orchestra on the stage in a concert hall or in the pit at an opera house, but Spontini's dictum "My left eye, first violins; my right eye, second violins" was prevalent through this period, and antiphonal writing for the two violin sections occurs as late as Bruckner and Chaikovsky; the effect is lost if, as is now customary, all the violins are grouped together. Cellos and basses should face the audience, and the brass and percussion should be grouped together, not spatially separated. It is possible to secure a reasonable approximation of the sound of a nineteenth-century orchestral performance by following these suggestions—and no one would miss the sloppy technical execution, insecure intonation, and almost hysterically subjective "interpretations" by conductors or soloists that were the negative features of much nineteenth-century playing.

The exact nature of Romantic ornamentation is still not wholly clear, yet many of the rules for eighteenth-century performance, particularly the playing of ornaments on instead of before the beat, hold true, even in the case of the compound appoggiaturas of Hummel and Chopin. Whether the trills are to begin with the main note or to follow the earlier practice of starting on the beat with the upper auxiliary is subject to dispute; Beethoven was as careless as Chopin was meticulous in indicating preparations for his trills, but it is most likely that chains of trills, such as those typical of Beethoven's last sonatas and quartets, were begun on the main note.

One problematic rhythmic question from the first part of the century is whether the pattern ♪· ♪, when it appears in a prevailingly triplet rhythm, is to be performed as ♪ 3 ♪, as it often was in gigues in late Baroque music. Though the notation of broken triplet patterns is often inconsistent until the mid-1840's, and more research is needed on this topic, there seems to be enough evidence, especially in ensemble music, to show that composers intended a rhythmic contrast and that the dotted eighth and sixteenth pattern should not be assimilated to the triplet rhythm.

Determining appropriate tempos for Romantic music also causes disputes. Chief among them is whether the metronome markings Beethoven inserted, sometimes many years after a piece was written and after he had lost most of his hearing, should be observed. Phonograph recordings and piano rolls have been used as evidence that tempos were faster (especially for andantes) than we think today (but one should remember that both recordings and piano rolls can be speeded up to create illusions of superior technique among instrumentalists and high notes among singers). Some preliminary investigations have shown that a tendency existed to have different tempos for each theme-group in a sonata-form movement, with changing tempos in tonally unstable areas like transitions, developments, and codas, and that subtle fluctuations in tempo (rubato) were often used to shape individual phrases.

In the interest of securing greater authenticity, the proposal has been made to recreate the *defects* of nineteenth-century performance. Orchestral conducting as we know it today was not introduced until the 1820's (with Spohr) and not codified until the mid-1830's (with Mendelssohn); previously, the direction of an orchestra was assigned to the concertmaster or was divided between him and a *maestro al cembalo* who supervised the performance (especially of vocal music) from the piano. Examinations of orchestral materials from the first three decades of the nineteenth century indicate that full scores were rare; the usual conductor's score was a *violino principale* part in which cues for other instruments were written; only for works after 1830 are full scores of orchestral works generally available.

Thus it has been contended that the proper direction of a Beethoven symphony should be from the concertmaster's desk, with the rhythmic movement direct and without conductorial nuances in tempo and expression. It is unfortunately true that many orchestral parts of the early nineteenth century have few rehearsal letters, or none—evidence that most performances were not carefully prepared. If we are to believe Wagner, he was a pioneer conductor in insisting on numerous rehearsals for a work, and as late as 1878 there were only two rehearsals for each concert given by the Leipzig Gewandhaus Orchestra, one of the premier orchestras of the world. However, we would not want to change the medical care, sanitation, or working hours of today for those that our great-great-grandparents endured; do we want to hear our favorite symphonies and concertos performed with few rehearsals and a minimal amount of expressive nuance? There is enough evidence, in fact, to show that solo and chamber music was expressively performed throughout the nineteenth century.

Above all, it is important to remember that there is no single correct way of performing Romantic music that can be determined by any pat formula; in fact, any such recipe would contravene the very spirit of Romanticism itself. All accounts of Romantic and post-Romantic performance testify to an ideal of experimentation and variety, not uniformity, and it was a compliment to a performer (even a composer-performer) to comment that he or she never performed a given piece exactly the same way twice. What must be avoided in interpreting nineteenth-century music is the kind of halfway authentic performances that satisfy no one, such as joining a fortepiano with modern stringed instruments in Beethoven or Schubert trios, or having under-rehearsed performances given on deteriorated and out-of-tune instruments in order to recapture the defects as well as the advantages of "historical" performance. Such activities only serve to distort the music and embarrass the musicians involved.

BIBLIOGRAPHICAL NOTES

The social history of music is an area only recently discovered by serious scholars. Alice Hanson's *Musical Life in Biedermeier Vienna* (Cambridge, England, 1985) is a model study deserving emulation for its extensive use of archival as well as musical materials, though Marcel Brion's *Daily Life in the*

Vienna of Mozart and Schubert (Eng. trans. New York, 1962) is still valuable. Ms. Hanson's discussion of concert life in Vienna can be well complemented with Jeffrey Cooper's *The Rise of Instrumental Music and Concert Series in Paris, 1828–71* (Ann Arbor, 1983), which owes many of its sociological premises to William Weber's *Music and the Middle Class* (London, 1975), a study of concert life in London, Paris, and Vienna.

England has received excellent treatment in E. D. Mackerness's *A Social History of English Music* (London, 1964) and his study of music in Sheffield, *Somewhere Further North* (Sheffield, 1974), as well as in the various essays in Nicholas Temperley's nineteenth-century volume in *The Athlone History of Music in Britain* (London, 1981). John Rosselli's *The Opera Industry in Italy from Cimarosa to Verdi* (Cambridge, Eng., 1984) is a fascinating examination of the role of the impresario in operatic life during the *primo ottocento*. The leading journal for the social history of music is the *International Review of the Aesthetics and Sociology of Music* (1970–   ).

The autobiographies and memoirs by Spohr, Glinka, Berlioz, Wagner, and others are invaluable primary sources, as are literary works with musicians as prominent characters, like Schiller's *Kabale und Liebe*, Balzac's *Le Cousin Pons*, and George Eliot's *Daniel Deronda*. George Schoolfield's *The Figure of the Musician in German Literature* (Chapel Hill, 1956) is an excellent point of departure for further studies which can contribute to a sociological history of music. The musical periodicals of the nineteenth century are the best sources for items of the social history of music, performance practice, and depictions of the musical audience. The social psychology of the nineteenth-century composer or musician is extremely difficult to reconstruct: the discussions of Vladimir Fédorov's essay "Čajkovsky, musicien-type du XIXe siècle?" *Acta Musicologica*, XLII (1970), 59–70, and XLIII (1971), 205–35, show the insufficiency of the measurements at our disposal today. Albert Lavignac's *Musical Education* (English translation, New York, 1902) is a good survey of trends in the education of the nineteenth-century professional musician, but even an elementary history of general musical education remains to be written.

I have discussed the breakdown of the patronage system in Germany in "Musical Portraits in *Sturm und Drang* Drama," *Music and Letters*, XLVI (1965), 39–49, and musical instruction as a means of achieving social mobility in "Music at the 'Hohe Karlsschule,' 1770–1794," *Journal of Research in Music Education*, XII (1964), 123–33. An excellent example of the sort of study needed on private musical patronage is David Levy's "Thomas Massa Alsager," *Nineteenth-Century Music*, IX (1985), 119–27. The world of the virtuoso is fascinatingly covered in several good studies in English, notably Henry

Pleasants' *The Great Singers* (New York, 1966), Boris Schwarz's admirable *Great Masters of the Violin* (New York, 1983), and Harold Schonberg's coverage of the performing superstars of the century in *The Glorious Ones* (New York, 1985), which also updates his earlier and more detailed *The Great Pianists* (New York, 1963) and *The Great Conductors* (New York, 1967).

Subcultures. Objectivity is rarely found in discussions of nineteenth-century church music. The main survey in English, Arthur Hutchings's *Church Music in the Nineteenth Century* (London, 1967) is as much polemic as history but does cover the entire spectrum of Christian church music. The sections in Temperley's volume on nineteenth-century English music cited in the bibliographical notes for Chapter 8 include much on church (especially cathedral) music, and his *The Music of the English Parish Church* (Cambridge, England, 1979) is a model study which could well be replicated for other nations and religious denominations. Conrad Donakowski's *A Muse for the Masses* (Chicago, 1977) explores music in both sacred and secular rituals. James Fuld's *The Book of World-Famous Music* (3d. ed., New York, 1985) contains extensive accounts of various folk and traditional musics as well as an excellent discussion on dating nineteenth-century printed music.

Performance Practices. Research continues to be done on this most fascinating and controversial topic. Articles on the various instruments in *The New Grove Dictionary of Musical Instruments* (London and New York, 1984) are usually excellent points of departure for more intensive investigations. Among the studies most helpful for instrumental performance are Jon Finson, "Performing Practice in the Late Nineteenth Century," *Musical Quarterly*, LXX (1984), 457–75, and Robert Winter, "The Emperor's New Clothes: Nineteenth-Century Instruments Revisited," *Nineteenth-Century Music*, VII (1984), 251–65; in the same journal (VII [1983], 3–54) is Will Crutchfield's thoughtful "Vocal Ornamentation in Verdi: The Phonographic Evidence," which includes mention of treatises and Verdi's own statements. Robert Garafalo and Mark Elrod, "Heritage Americana," *Journal of Band Research*, XVII (1981), 1–26, cite some of the problems of restoring brass instruments of the previous century. The *Galpin Society Journal* contains many systematic investigations of nineteenth-century instruments and performance practices. Paul and Eva Badura-Skoda, in their prefaces to the volumes of Schubert's piano music published by G. Henle Verlag, have upheld the idea of assimilating dotted eighth and sixteenth patterns to triplet rhythms in early nineteenth-century music. William S. Newman's *Performance Practices in Beethoven's Piano Sonatas* (New York, 1971) has aroused much discussion and controversy, especially on how properly to perform Beethoven's trills.

The journals of the nineteenth century and the memoirs of travelers, especially musical ones, provide much primary source information for conditions of performance; I have covered some of these in the prefaces to my editions of Italian symphonies in Garland's *The Symphony 1720–1840* (New York, 1980–83). Lively discussion of performances and recordings of nineteenth-century music on original instruments can be found in the music section of the Sunday *New York Times* and the music columns of *The New Yorker*. Excellent pictorial illustrations of Romantic music-making are contained in three volumes of the series *Musikgeschichte in Bildern*: Walter Salmen's *Haus- und Kammermusik* (Leipzig, 1969), Hellmuth Christian Wolff's *Oper* (Leipzig, 1968), and especially Heinrich Schwab's *Konzert* (Leipzig, 1971).

INDEX